Saving the Holy Sepulchre

RAYMOND COHEN

Saving the Holy Sepulchre

How Rival Christians
Came Together to Rescue
Their Holiest Shrine

OXFORD
UNIVERSITY PRESS

2008

OXFORD
UNIVERSITY PRESS

Oxford University Press, Inc., publishes works that further
Oxford University's objective of excellence
in research, scholarship, and education.

Oxford   New York
Auckland   Cape Town   Dar es Salaam   Hong Kong   Karachi
Kuala Lumpur   Madrid   Melbourne   Mexico City   Nairobi
New Delhi   Shanghai   Taipei   Toronto

With offices in
Argentina   Austria   Brazil   Chile   Czech Republic   France   Greece
Guatemala   Hungary   Italy   Japan   Poland   Portugal   Singapore
South Korea   Switzerland   Thailand   Turkey   Ukraine   Vietnam

Published by Oxford University Press, Inc.
198 Madison Avenue, New York, NY 10016

www.oup.com

Oxford is a registered trademark of Oxford University Press

Library of Congress Cataloging-in-Publication Data
Cohen, Raymond, 1947–
Saving the Holy Sepulchre : how rival Christians came together
to rescue their holiest shrine / Raymond Cohen.
p. cm.
Includes bibliographical references and index.
ISBN 978-0-19-518966-7
1. Church of the Holy Sepulchre (Jerusalem).   2. Church buildings—Jerusalem.
3. Christians—Jerusalem.   4. Christian Shrines—Jerusalem.
5. Jerusalem—Buildings, structures, etc.   6. Jerusalem—Antiquities.
7. Jerusalem—Ethnic relations.   I. Title.
DS109.4C64 2008   246'.9509569442—dc22   2007033078

9 8 7 6 5 4 3 2 1

Printed in the United States of America
on acid-free paper

For my grandchildren,
"the crown of old age,"
Omer, Maya, Uri, Ithai, Asaf, and Shira.

CHURCH OF THE
HOLY SEPULCHRE

(AFTER WILLIAM HARVEY, 1955)

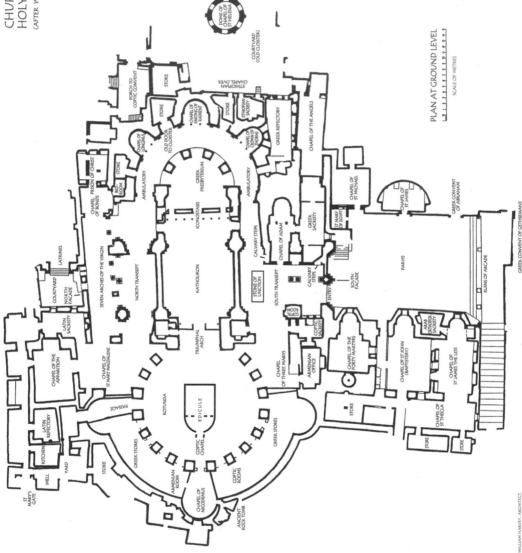

DOME OF
CHAPEL OF
ST HELENA

COURTYARD
(OLD CLOISTER)

PORCH TO
COPTIC CONVENT

STORE

CHAPEL OF
LONGINUS

OLD DOOR
TO CLOISTER

CHAPEL OF
PARTING OF
RAIMENT

STORE

ETHIOPIAN
CHAPEL OVER

ETHIOPIAN
SACRISTY

CHAPEL OF
CROWN OF
THORNS

GREEK REFECTORY

CHAPEL OF THE ANGELS

AMBULATORY

GREEK
PRESBYTERIUM

ICONOSTASIS

AMBULATORY

CHAPEL, PRISON OF CHRIST
OF BONDS

STORE

BELL
ROOM

AMBULATORY

CALVARY STEPS

CHAPEL OF
ST MICHAEL

CHAPEL OF
ST JAMES

GREEK CONVENT
OF ABRAHAM

LATRINES

SEVEN ARCHES OF THE VIRGIN

NORTH TRANSEPT

KATHOLIKON

STONE OF
UNCTION

CHAPEL OF ADAM

GREEK
SACRISTY

ST MARY
OF EGYPT

COURTYARD

NORTH
FACADE

SOUTH TRANSEPT

CALVARY
STEPS

PARVIS

RUINS OF ARCADE

LATIN
SACRISTY

TRIUMPHAL
ARCH

ENTRY

SOUTH
FACADE

COPTIC
ROOM

CHAPEL OF THE
APPARITION

CHAPEL OF
ST MARY MAGDALENE

PASSAGE

ROTUNDA

EDICULE

CHAPEL
OF THREE MARYS

ARMENIAN
OFFICE

COPTIC
SACRISTY

CHAPEL OF THE
FORTY MARTYRS

CHAPEL OF ST JOHN
(BAPTISTERY)

ARAB
ORTHODOX
SACRISTY

CHAPEL OF
ST JAMES THE LESS

LATIN
REFECTORY

KITCHEN

YARD

WELL

STORE

GREEK STORES

ARMENIAN
ROOM

COPTIC
CHAPEL

COPTIC
ROOMS

GREEK STORES

STORE

CHAPEL
OF ST THECLA

STORE

STORE

ST MARY'S
GATE

CHAPEL OF
NICODEMUS

ANCIENT
ROCK TOMB

GREEK CONVENT OF GETHSEMANE

PLAN AT GROUND LEVEL

SCALE OF METRES

WILLIAM HARVEY, ARCHITECT.

The stone-cut tomb

Is empty.

Vacated as the womb.

For, helpless as a new born babe

In Mary's arms,

The Church steals from that grave.

Leaving just swaddling clothes

Behind.

For John and Peter

(To the angels blind)

To save.

"Jerusalem," Paul wrote,

"Our Church's mother."

The blood and sweat of worlds-made-flesh

Became the birth-pangs of another.

From "Easter" by William Makin

CONTENTS

Living for almost forty years only a couple of miles from the Church of the Holy Sepulchre, it has been natural for me to take a Jerusalemite's pride in one of the great shrines of civilization. Besides the inherent interest of the place, with its religious associations and eventful history, I have always been enthralled by its human spectacle. Most of my regular walks in and around the Old City end up there.

When I decided to investigate the relations between the communities in the basilica, I assumed that the monks who live and worship there do so in the shadow of conflict. I was influenced by the numerous news stories that have appeared over the years bearing such headlines as "Monks Come to Blows over Seat at Church" and "Priests Brawl at Holy Sepulchre." My initial thought was to write about the war between the churches, a familiar tale of religious immoderation.

I discovered that this was not the most significant or even interesting story at Christianity's holiest place. It is true that after centuries of discord, the resident communities are on their guard in the defense of traditional rights. Incidents do sometimes occur between monks that are then reported around the world.

But expectations of violence have tended to reproduce a grossly distorted view of the church. One candidly tendentious article begins "There is very little as entertaining as watching monks hitching up their cassocks and laying into each other. Regrettably, when I visited Jerusalem's Church of the Holy Sepulchre, reputed site of Christ's burial and resurrection, the monks of the various sects were all tediously well behaved."[1]

Probing below the surface, I learnt that over the past fifty years something both unexpected and momentous had taken place at the Church of the Resurrection. Since it was not encapsulated in a single newsworthy event and did not cater to existing preconceptions, it seemed to have gone largely unnoticed by the outside world.

This development was the fundamental restoration and repair of the dilapidated basilica as a result of unprecedented cooperation between the churches over the course of decades. It was tortuously difficult at times, but they eventually joined forces. While competition remained, rival churches negotiated and implemented scores of agreements behind the scenes. In consequence, the edifice, which at one time was in real danger of collapse, was saved for posterity.

How they managed to do this despite their profound mutual suspicions is a question that engrossed me over what turned into a six-year pursuit of documents, witnesses, and answers.

A word of caution. This did not turn out to be a straightforward tale of enemies kissing and making up. Interchurch reconciliation is not on the agenda in Jerusalem, though relations have improved as a result of the restoration. What lends this chronicle special interest is not that all conflict was settled but that the communities were able to solve some disputes and manage others in order to cooperate for the duration of the project.

This is an account of how adversaries worked together in a common cause. Had they not succeeded, the Church of the Holy Sepulchre would today be a ruin.

ACKNOWLEDGMENTS

THE RESEARCH AND WRITING of this book has been an enormous
pleasure, not least thanks to the many interesting people who were
ready to share with me their knowledge of and enthusiasm for the Church of
the Holy Sepulchre.

Special thanks go to Father Athanasius Macora O.F.M., who first set me
thinking about the restoration of the edifice. Over the six years of this
project, he was unfailingly insightful and helpful, answering my questions
and requests beyond the call of duty.

Warm thanks, too, are due to George Hintlian, Dr. Theodossios Mitropoulos, and Dr. Paulo Pieracini, who were generous with their time and
knowledge.

I would also like to thank the following individuals for their help at
different stages of my research: Marie-Armelle Beaulieu, Gilbert Bonnan,
Clare Brown, Professor Uri Bialer, Professor Roberta Ervine, Arieh Roch-
man-Halperin, Silvia Krapiwko, Gilad Livne, Dr. Elias V. Messinas, Father
Jean-Michel de Tarragon O.P., Professor Bernard Wasserstein, and Ran
Yaron.

The Watson Institute for International Studies of Brown University
under its director, Professor Thomas J. Biersteker, and the Department of
International Relations, Boston University, under its chair, Professor Erik
Goldstein, provided space and resources for my work during a 2003–2004
sabbatical.

Photographs are reproduced courtesy of the family of Ali Zaarour, the
Custody of the Holy Land, the École Biblique photo archive, Elia Photo

Service, the Israel Antiquities Authority Archives, and the Israel Government Press Office photo archive.

The major communities in the Church of the Resurrection—Greek Orthodox, Roman Catholic, and Armenian Orthodox—decline in principle to allow outsiders access to their archives. Greek Government archives are subject to the fifty-year rule. The writing of this book would therefore have been impossible without the assistance of the following libraries and archives:

Biblioteca Custodiale and archives of the Custody of the Holy Land, Jerusalem; Centre des Archives Diplomatiques, Nantes; the library of the École Biblique, Jerusalem; the Israel Antiquities Authority Archives, Jerusalem; the Israel State Archives, Jerusalem; the Lambeth Palace Archives, London; the Middle East Centre Archives, St. Antony's College, Oxford; National Archives (formerly Public Records Office), London; the Truman Institute library, Hebrew University of Jerusalem; National Archives, College Park, Maryland.

If there were an award for preserving an historical resource, it would have to go to Father Jean-Baptiste Humbert O.P. of the École Biblique, who saved the papers of Father Charles Coüasnon O.P. from the rain.

Terry Ball kindly allowed me access to some of his private papers. Masha Halevi put me on to the papers of Antonio Barluzzi and generously placed copies she had made at my disposal.

I am very grateful to all those who granted me interviews: Brother Fabian Adkins O.F.M., Archbishop Aristarchos, Terry Ball, Ambassador Avi Binyamin, Yves Boiret, Dr. Magen Broshi, Archbishop Christodoulos, Father Dimitrios, Professor Roberta Ervine, Canon Edward Every, Shmuel Evyatar, Stuart Goodchild, Reverend Guido Gockel, Yossi Hershler, Metropolitan Isichios, Father David Jaeger O.F.M., Father Norayr Kazazian, Rafi Levi, Israel Lippel, Uri Mor, Daniel Rossing, John Seligman, Haim Shapiro, Ambassador Yitzhak Shelef, Archbishop Shirvanian, Father Thomas Stransky C.S.P., Archbishop Timotheos, Dr. John Tleel, and Ambassador Yael Vered.

Theo Calderara of Oxford University Press was a superb editor. I greatly appreciate his encouragement and advice during the writing of the book. Thanks, too, to Joellyn Ausanka, the production editor, for her exemplary professionalism.

My major debt is owed as ever to my loving wife and fellow author, Rivka, without whose support and tolerance this book would never have been written. Working side by side on our separate projects was fun. She was always there with sound advice and also very helpful with the choice of photographs.

Saving the Holy Sepulchre

CHAPTER ONE | The Earthquake

B Y T H E C L O C K T O W E R of St. Savior's Franciscan monastery, a prominent Jerusalem landmark, it was just after three o'clock in the afternoon of July 11, 1927.

Suddenly there was a rumble and roar, followed by a crash. Doors and windows began to shake and clatter, crockery shattered, books fell off shelves, locked cupboards swung open, meter-thick walls split apart, roofs collapsed, stone blocks smashed to the ground.[1]

Mired in the torpor of a hot summer's day, Jerusalem's eighty-thousand-odd inhabitants were taken totally unawares by the shift of the earth's crust beneath their feet. For ten seconds, solid ground shook and shuddered. People were hurled to the ground. Passersby were hit by falling debris. Scores were trapped under rubble as walls and ceilings fell in. It was as if a gigantic sledgehammer swinging up from the bowels of the earth had struck at the foundations of the city.

A German eyewitness described

a sudden subterranean clap of thunder shaking the entire city, like a whirlwind suddenly blowing up out of nowhere to rip off the roofs. As the house tottered and the floor lurched underfoot, tiles rattled, doors banged, and objects crashed down. Without a shadow of doubt it was an earthquake—an earthquake the likes of which I have never experienced in Jerusalem. The whole commotion, together with the thunderous din, scarcely lasted ten seconds, but it seemed to me like ten whole minutes.[2]

Inside St. Savior's, one of the Franciscan friars charged with protecting the holy places for the Catholic Church was seized by a sense of foreboding. Running up to the terrace, with its panoramic view, he saw plumes of dust rising up from the Damascus Gate and the Church of the Ascension on the Mount of Olives. But from where he was standing, nothing seemed to have happened to the nearby Church of the Holy Sepulchre in the heart of the Old City. The familiar gray domes over the edifice nestled safely amid the surrounding roofs and towers.[3]

When the din of the earthquake had subsided, wailing and shouting rose from the crowds of panic-stricken people who had poured into the streets.[4] In the narrow alleys of old Jerusalem, the limestone-faced houses were wedged together, one on top of the other, like cells in a honeycomb. If one building collapsed, all the surrounding buildings might be dragged down with it. As the houses settled back into the bedrock following the first tremor, a shroud of dust covered the town, blocking out the fierce July sun.

In the Parvis, the paved forecourt of the Holy Sepulchre, sweating Greek Orthodox monks were joined by fellow priests from other ancient Christian communities. Caught inside the cavernous Holy Sepulchre complex by the first startling convulsion, their common instinct had been to flee into the open air. The open courtyard, though hemmed in on all sides by monasteries and chapels, offered more protection than the interior of an old building.

Archbishop Pantelemon Athanassiades, splendid in his heavy vestments, had been conducting the Greek Orthodox first vespers service for the eve of the feast day of Saints Peter and Paul. As the monks rushed for the exit, Archbishop Pantelemon was left standing alone at the altar.[5]

Within a couple of minutes, the ground shuddered again. Dislodged stones plummeted down from buildings adjacent to the basilica. Now the monks, knots of men distinctive in the somber robes of their religious orders, were gripped by terror. For 1600 years, monks had served here. Their world was now threatened with collapse.

To St. John of Damascus, writing in the eighth century, the Church of the Holy Sepulchre (also known as the Anastasis or Church of the Resurrection) was the "mother of all the churches."[6] Tradition locates the *omphalos*, the "navel of the world," only a few yards from the tomb. This is the place where Christians believe it all began, where Jesus Christ was crucified and rose from the dead and "where every Christian was born."[7]

From the fourth century onward, there are records of Christian pilgrims coming to Jerusalem. In 313 Constantine, ruler of the Roman Empire in the West, issued the Edict of Milan, which granted Christianity legal status. In

324, Constantine became sole Roman emperor and the following year convened the first ecumenical Council of Nicaea. It is believed that the question of restoring the Tomb of Christ to Christian possession was raised at the council, possibly in the form of a petition presented to the emperor.[8]

The location of the tomb may have been preserved in the collective memory of local followers of Jesus from earliest times. To St. John of Damascus, "tradition handed down from father to son" was sufficient grounds for belief.[9] In his *Life of Constantine*, Eusebius, who was bishop of Caesarea at the time, tells us that the emperor's mother, Helena, arrived in Jerusalem and located the sites of the Crucifixion and Resurrection under a Roman temple of Venus. A less convenient site for Christ's tomb could not be imagined. When the temple and landfill were cleared away, the cave containing Christ's tomb was revealed, "against all expectation." The emperor then ordered "a place of worship worthy of God to be built with rich and imperial munificence" to testify to the Resurrection.

The burial cave, "which looked towards the rising sun," was cut away from the surrounding rock and enclosed within an Edicule, "little house." A sumptuous rotunda, known as the Anastasis (Resurrection), was raised over it. Constantine's massive foundations and lower walls still support the present-day rotunda, which basically follows the original ground plan. In 638, Muslim armies captured Jerusalem, and in 1009, an Egyptian caliph finally destroyed Constantine's battered church and razed the burial cave.

Constantine's Anastasis was entered through an open court with porches on three sides (hence *triportico*). The rock of Golgotha—Calvary—stood in one corner, open to the sky, surmounted by a platform. Later, a cross was erected there. At the east end of this court, Constantine built a splendid basilica, the Martyrion, divided by four colonnades. Stairs led down to a crypt named (by the Crusaders) the Chapel of St. Helena. More steps descended to another chapel deep underground commemorating the spot where Helena found the True Cross. The entire compound was entered off the Cardo, Jerusalem's north–south thoroughfare, through a porticoed atrium fronted by three doors facing east.[10]

The medieval edifice that survives incorporates two structures from different periods joined at the seam by a Triumphal Arch. One is a rotunda with a great dome, essentially a late Byzantine reconstruction of Constantine's round church. It replaces, in effect, the nave in a conventional cathedral.[11] The present neo-Byzantine Edicule, which it contains, was built in 1810.

The later adjacent building is a Romanesque cathedral, entered via a courtyard to the south. It was built over the open court before Calvary by Crusader masons during the twelfth-century Latin Kingdom of Jerusalem.

Though consecrated in 1149, it was likely only completed in the 1160s.[12] Vaulted transepts, with a dome towering over the crossing, flank a high central choir, today known as the Katholikon or Greek Choir. An ambulatory or processional corridor surrounds the choir, which ends in an apse.

The medieval construction brought the rotunda and tomb, Calvary, and various shrines, such as the Prison of Christ and the Chapel of St. Helena, under one roof. Detached from the chapels and convents (as monastic communities for both men and for women are known in Jerusalem) that press in on all sides, the layout of the edifice can be likened to a royal orb, a globe surmounted by a cross missing its lower foot. It is the product of an unplanned collaboration between Byzantine and Frankish architects living in different centuries.

The Holy Sepulchre is a building dedicated to a single great belief shared by all Christians, that humanity was saved through the sacrifice of Jesus Christ. At the same time, it is marked by extraordinary cultural, liturgical, and aesthetic diversity. Many Western visitors are repelled by the mixture of styles, the mediocrity of much of the art, the cacophony of sights and sounds within a confined space, and the line to get into the tomb. Of course, the Holy Sepulchre would be more decorous if it were simply a museum. But this is a living place of worship, charged with faith and passion.

On any given day, vigilant Greek monks, their long hair tied back in ponytails, can be seen at their posts, only a few yards from Calvary or the tomb, while Franciscan friars walk past deep in contemplation. An Armenian priest may come by swinging his censer, on his round of altars. Groups of monks and pilgrims process from one shrine to another. At peak times the church bustles with life. Sometimes services in different keys and languages are conducted simultaneously in and around the rotunda, one drowning out the other.

While the rounded Romanesque style of the twelfth century, with its soaring vaults, semicircular windows and arches, and curved apses, is the prevailing theme, archaeology and architecture from the seven ages of the Holy Sepulchre blend together. This is the only church in the world where first-century Herodian, second-century Hadrianic, fourth-century Constantinian, eleventh-century Byzantine, twelfth-century Crusader, nineteenth-century neo-Byzantine, and twentieth-century modern masonry are visible in one place. The church is not only a monument to the culminating events of the Gospels but also a record in stone of the Christian saga.

Other great temples, such as the Parthenon in Athens, the Pantheon in Rome, Hagia Sophia in Constantinople, and the nearby Dome of the Rock in Jerusalem may be more beautiful. Long decay and neglect have certainly left their traces on the timeworn face of the mother church. Some of its finest ornamentation—the exquisitely carved decorative panels over the main entrance, its mosaics, and many of its original capitals—is gone.

In material terms, its faded air and relatively modest dimensions invite comparison to a provincial cathedral rather than to the vast Renaissance splendor of St. Peter's Basilica, Rome.

After the fall of the Crusader kingdom, parts of the Constantinian compound were destroyed or expropriated for adjacent mosques. All but one door was walled up; only a single portal was left in the south façade next to the bell tower and the keys entrusted to Muslim doorkeepers whose job was to levy an entrance fee on Christian pilgrims.[13]

There is no unfolding vista as one approaches, just a jumble of buildings hemmed in on all sides by the crowded markets, shops, and homes of a medieval town. You turn a corner past some souvenir stores and there it is. But few holy places can match its record of virtually continuous veneration since the time of Constantine.

It is also the only church in the world where six of the most ancient Christian denominations worship side by side. The Greek Orthodox, Roman Catholic, and Armenian Orthodox churches are known as *major* communities, with rights of possession and usage at the holy places. The Coptic, Ethiopian, and Syrian Orthodox churches are deemed *minor* communities, with rights of usage but not rights of possession at the holy places.

The Greek Orthodox community is headed by a patriarch elected from among the monks of the Confraternity of the Holy Sepulchre. Leadership of the Roman Catholic community in the Holy Land is shared by a Latin patriarch and a *custos*. Both are appointed by Rome, but whereas the patriarch has largely parochial responsibilities for local Catholics, the custos, who heads the Franciscan Custody of the Holy Land, is traditionally responsible for the holy places.[14] The monastic Armenian Orthodox Brotherhood of St. James elects its own patriarch.

Once these separate churches were in full communion. For all their differences, they remain in accord on the fundamentals of Christian belief and the sanctity of the holy places, of which the Holy Sepulchre is paramount. If they did not agree on the essentials, they would not all be here. A tradition of shared celebration (*sylleitourgia*) existed in early centuries. Egeria, a nun who visited Jerusalem in the early fifth century, paints a picture of harmonious communal worship. She describes the bishop always speaking Greek in the church and his words being translated into Aramaic and Latin "that all may understand what is being explained."[15]

Over the years, the communities grew apart. The Armenian Orthodox Church, dating back to 301, was absent from the fourth church council, that of Chalcedon in 451, and declined to accept its pronouncements on the union of the divine and the human in the person of Christ. To this day, like the Coptic, Ethiopian, and Syrian Orthodox churches, it accepts only the decisions of the first three church councils.

Theological and liturgical controversies, exacerbated by cultural, philosophical, and political differences, gradually divided the Latin West under the authority of the pope, the bishop of Rome, from the Byzantine Greek East, with its tradition of autocephalous patriarchates, that is, churches electing their own heads. There was disagreement over the nature of the Trinity. The Eastern Church rejected the addition of the term *filioque*, meaning "and from the Son" to the Latin creed, the statement of Christian faith. The Holy Spirit, it insisted, proceeded solely from the Father. While recognizing the pope's primacy of honor, it rejected his supreme jurisdiction. Differences also emerged over rules for fasting, the doctrine of purgatory, priestly celibacy, the use of unleavened bread for the sacrament, the date of Easter, and so on.[16]

Schism between the churches led to each claiming for itself the mantle of the True Church, the legitimate successor of the Church of Peter and Paul, the repository of doctrinal truth and authority. Since the Crusades, Greeks and Latins (as Greek Orthodox and Roman Catholics are known in Jerusalem) have been locked in a fierce struggle over the family home—the Church of the Holy Sepulchre.

During the four centuries that the Turks ruled Palestine (1516–1917), the contest between the churches for the holy places was stubbornly waged on three fronts: on the ground in Jerusalem, with stones and staves; through the courts, with ancient decrees and documents, sometimes forged and usually contradictory; and in the corridors of power in Constantinople, where the different Christian denominations mobilized bribes and influence in a competition for imperial decrees bestowing rights of possession and usage.

What the churches were fighting for was *praedominium* or preeminence. At the Holy Sepulchre, this meant in concrete terms possession of as much as possible of the edifice, with the Edicule and Calvary assigned supreme value. The ground rules regulating this contest were derived from *shari'a* or Muslim sacred law (which had applied at the holy places since the original Islamic conquests in the seventh century) and Ottoman property law. It is hard to decipher events at the Holy Sepulchre without realizing that it is neither church law nor common law categories that count here but those of Islam.

Under shari'a law, a holy place of whatever religion is *waqf*, an inalienable religious endowment, not *mulk*, private property. Ownership of a shrine, such as the Church of the Resurrection, is not absolute. Those who reside in it have rights of *possession*, in the sense that they can hold and use it, but they do not have title and cannot dispose of the property either by sale or gift. Once a mosque, always a mosque.

As sovereign, the sultan had custody of the Holy Sepulchre and the right to repair or restore it. He certainly could not transfer ownership of any part of it to a private institution. However, he could grant that institution certain privileges by means of a firman or edict. But that firman was not a title deed of ownership, just the record of the grant of a privilege that could always be retracted. Indeed, throughout the Ottoman period the authorities time and again transferred rights of possession and usage at the holy places from one community to another.

This basic principle of Turkish rule at the holy places was strikingly (if somewhat simplistically) expressed in 1757 by the grand vizier, Rajib Pasha, to the French ambassador, the Comte de Vergennes, following the Latin loss of preeminence to the Greeks: "These places, My Lord," he explained, "belong to the Sultan and he gives them to whomsoever he pleases. It may well be that they were always in the hands of the Franks, but today his Highness wants them to belong to the Greeks."[17]

Greek primacy was confirmed in a series of imperial edicts issued at this time. Broadly speaking, this is the situation that has prevailed ever since. In the Holy Sepulchre, the Greeks retained the Katholikon with its apostolic thrones and acquired the Chapel of Adam under Calvary and the Seven Arches of the Virgin. Crucially, they obtained guardianship of the tomb. Their possession of the northern half of Calvary was recognized. The lion's share of the Church of the Resurrection was theirs.

The Latins were left with the two southern altars on Calvary, namely, the Stabat Mater (Our Lady of Sorrows) and the Nailing to the Cross. They retained the diminutive Latin Choir between the Edicule and the Arch of Triumph, the Chapel of the Apparition of Christ, the Chapel of Mary Magdalene, and the Chapel of the Invention (Finding) of the Cross deep underground. The Stone of Unction was to be held in common, as was the courtyard around the Edicule.

The 1757 status quo was consolidated by extensive rebuilding work carried out in the church by the Greek architect Nikolaos Komnenos of Mytilene, following a devastating fire in 1808. When he completed the restoration in 1810, he had transformed a Latin Crusader church into a neo-Byzantine edifice, acquired Greek space at the expense of common areas, and replaced Latin markers and decorations with Greek ones.

———

Since the mid-nineteenth century, the term Status Quo (henceforth capitalized) has had the special technical meaning of the normative regime or set of binding arrangements covering possession, usage, and ceremony at the holy places. On the eve of the Crimean War, Sultan Abdul Mejid, ruling over a gravely weakened Ottoman Empire, the "sick man of Europe," found himself pulled in opposite directions by France and Russia. Whereas Louis Napoleon urgently pressed for the restoration of Latin preeminence, Tsar Nicolas absolutely insisted that the 1757 status quo be maintained.

At first the sultan sought to maneuver between the parties but, faced by the threat of Russian invasion, capitulated to pressure and agreed to freeze the situation indefinitely. In a first firman of February 1852, he solemnly confirmed and consolidated Greek rights. In a second firman of May 1853, he definitively affirmed the status quo: "The actual status quo will be maintained and the Jerusalem shrines, whether owned in common or exclusively by the Greek, Latin, and Armenian communities, will all remain forever in their present state."[18]

This constituted a defeat for France and by extension the Holy See. Thereafter, the Status Quo resembled a cease-fire imposed on local belligerents by great powers to prevent a wider conflagration. It was most decidedly not, as is often misleadingly said, an "agreement," signed and sealed by the communities themselves. Only the Greeks were reasonably satisfied with its provisions. The Latins deeply resented it. No one had asked for their consent but a third party had imposed a standstill on them, locking in place the situation on the ground.

The sultan's purpose at the time was not even to prevent local conflict between Latins and Greeks, simply to defuse the situation between the great powers by removing the question of the holy places from the realm of international politics. Nevertheless, strict enforcement of the Status Quo by the authorities became thereafter the primary tool for preserving order between the communities. In 1878, the 1852 Status Quo was incorporated into public international law by the Treaty of Berlin, which confirmed "that no alterations can be made in the status quo in the Holy Places."

The Status Quo functioned as an informal, if controversial, system for coexistence between rivals. In the main its provisions were understood, if not explicitly agreed on, by all the parties. But it was contested, and no single version enjoyed general acceptance. Each community had its own exhaustive compilation of usages and customs. Because of substantial discrepancies between versions and numerous unresolved disputes, friction was common and serious discord always possible. Nevertheless, the Status Quo mostly permitted the communities to worship and bear witness at the sanctuaries without being embroiled in perpetual conflict. Issues under contention were said "to fall under the Status Quo," and no change was permitted. Only the last community to have repaired a certain wall, hung a certain picture, or swept a certain step could continue to do so in the future. If it had held a particular ceremony on a particular date and at a particular place in the past, it could continue to do so in the same circumstances next time.

Historically, disputes about the holy places had been brought before shari'a courts. After 1853, disputes were removed from the purview of the local courts and handled administratively by a government official who determined what had been customary practice.[19]

Change could be introduced if an amicable arrangement was reached between communities. Within their own chapels, the communities had substantial freedom of action, though other communities might have censing rights at specific times, indicating that possession was not "exclusive." Repairs to property in the sole possession of a major community required the notification but not permission of the others. Minor repairs to common property required a consensus of all three communities and the equal sharing of expenses.[20]

The minor communities—Copts, Ethiopians, and Syrians—were not involved in this property arrangement but deemed to be *yamaklik*, assistants or apprentices of the Armenians, who represented them before the sovereign.

The main achievement of the Status Quo was to remove the holy places from the scope of international conflict and so prevent a repetition of the diplomatic crisis that preceded the Crimean War. At the local level, it was a cease-fire with frequent violations. Relations between the communities became a byword for immoderation.

Quarrels over unresolved issues, attempts to gain minor advantage, and friction between monks living cheek by jowl produced recurrent flare-ups. Among many disputes, that over precedence at the ceremony of the Holy Fire on Easter Saturday was the most notorious. The British consul recorded the events of 1856:

> Immediately on the appearance of the flame a disturbance broke out between the Greeks and Armenians but both sides had evidently been prepared beforehand for a conflict. Pilgrims were provided with stones and cudgels, which had been previously concealed (it was believed by the Armenians) behind the columns and in dark corners, and our

Vice-Consul, who had accompanied some English travellers into the gallery to witness the ceremony, saw a further supply of this sort of ammunition being thrown down into the body of the church from a window in the circular gallery which communicated with the Greek convent. A dreadful conflict ensued.

The Pasha left his seat in the nether gallery and ran down to direct his attendants, civil and military, in separating the combatants, and only succeeded in dividing them after he had himself received several severe blows on the head, and his secretary got a cut on the hand from a knife. The colonel in command of the troops and many of his soldiers got wounded and bruised. Some twenty-five Greeks and Armenians were severely wounded, and great numbers received heavy blows.[21]

Similar incidents of greater or lesser severity have occurred repeatedly over the years. How could men of peace be so prone to violence? One reason is institutional: the monastic orders present in the Holy Sepulchre have borne responsibility since time immemorial for defending the sacrosanct rights of their parent churches in the sanctuary. They are prepared to resort to extreme, premeditated measures to do so. A second reason is individual: the perception that rights are threatened arouses the monks to fury. In a righteous rage, otherwise pious men are capable of violent acts.

The British assistant district commissioner in the 1920s observed a typical assault:

In the scrimmage round the Holy Sepulchre after the Holy Fire had been distributed, while guarding his bishop, [a Syrian Orthodox monk] saw a young Coptic priest trying to prevent his Grace's traditional chair being carried to its rightful place in the procession. Priest Yacub, as he then was, stepped back a pace and, with one blow on the chin, knocked the offending Copt completely out.[22]

To keep the peace, the Ottoman governor was obliged to provide a force of six hundred soldiers on Easter Saturday. At other times, a government official had to be on hand to ensure that the Status Quo was scrupulously observed. If a community felt that there had been a nontrivial violation of the Status Quo, it would submit a protest. If it was upheld, then the state of affairs before the violation was restored. In one instance in the 1880s, the Latins protested when the Greeks unilaterally set up a cross and other emblems outside the Prison of Christ. The governor visited the site, accompanied by the French consul, and ordered the symbols removed at once.[23]

The most blatant loophole in the Status Quo regime was that it did not provide a satisfactory mechanism for enabling major repairs to be carried out to contested areas of the Holy Sepulchre. The reason for this lay in two features of Turkish property law: first, payment for the repair of a structure indicated possession, and second, the owner of the covering of a building owned the building. As much as one community might want to pay for a certain repair as an assertion of ownership, the other two communities would be eager to block it.

For half a century the Greeks, who viewed themselves as the householders of the mother church, vetoed both Armenian replacement of the paving in the Chapel of St. Helena and Latin repairs to the steps leading down to the Chapel of the Invention of the Cross. True, the authorities could always step in if a situation became insufferable from the point of view of safety or security or if urgent repairs were required. In 1853, the sultan placed a new silver star in the Manger Grotto in Bethlehem at his expense. When the Greeks tried to appropriate the two gateways leading from the street into the Parvis of the Holy Sepulchre in the 1880s, the governor installed gates at government expense and placed them at the disposal of all three major communities.[24]

Even so, long before the 1927 earthquake, the dead hand of the Status Quo ensured the habitual neglect of the edifice. A visitor to the Holy Sepulchre before World War I described the melancholy sight "of the half-ruined, half-rebuilt remains of one of the grandest monuments of the Middle Ages."[25]

Within hours of the earthquake, local correspondents telegraphed news to the outside world from the crowded booths of the damaged but still functioning main post office on Jaffa Road. In all quarters of the Old City, they informed their editors, people had been killed and injured, houses made uninhabitable, places of worship destroyed, historical monuments endangered.

In the shock of these general reports of devastation and human suffering, the thoughts of Christians everywhere were directed to the fate of the Church of the Resurrection. For hundreds of millions of believers, this collection of shrines, each associated with the climax of Christ's ministry, was witness of the truth of the Gospels. The prospect of its destruction was too distressing to contemplate.

The reports, fed by rumor and confusion, were alarming. Then more reassuring news stories emerged. The famous Romanesque façade with its twin, arched portals was said to be unscathed. The Edicule housing Christ's tomb was in one piece. Calvary, the site of the Crucifixion, had escaped harm. Only the cupola over the Greek Choir had suffered supposedly minor damage.

To the untrained eyes of journalists and foreign consuls, the edifice appeared indestructible. The time-worn stones remained in place; no wall or column toppled. The location of the church, at the heart of the Christian Quarter, implied massive permanence. A message of reassurance went out to the world.

The *New York Times* asserted: "Slight damage was done to the Citadel of the Holy Sepulchre, but the façade is intact."[26] Complacently, the London *Church Times* reported the edifice to be "entirely safe." Indeed, the damage to Jerusalem had been "greatly exaggerated."

> The great Greek chapel in the Holy Sepulchre, commonly known as the Catholikon, has suffered damage to its roof, and therefore is closed for the time being, and many small houses in the poorer parts of the city have been wholly destroyed. Fortunately, the loss of life was not great, and funds have now been raised for those that are homeless. Where it is not a question of loss of life, such clearance of ancient slums is a cause for thankfulness.[27]

The acting British high commissioner's dispatch to the colonial office of July 22 listing historical buildings damaged by the earthquake had only a single word on the Holy Sepulchre: "intact."[28] A few days later, a government minister responding to a question in the House of Commons could officially set the public's mind at rest about the extent of the damage.[29]

The Christian world breathed a collective sigh of relief. A place that had survived countless previous natural and human-made disasters was not going to surrender to just another earthquake. So in the gloomy, neglected interior of the mother church, the bowed walls, cracked vaults, and traces of powdering rock in dusty corners went unnoticed.

| Mr. Cust's Immobile Machine

DECEMBER 11, 1917, was a gloriously clear and sunny Jerusalem winter day after recent heavy rain. At noon, General Sir Edmund Allenby, the British commander of the Allied Expeditionary Force, entered Jerusalem on foot through the Jaffa Gate. Outside the gate, modest contingents of British and Commonwealth troops had formed up; inside, small detachments of allied French and Italian forces stood to attention. The hands of the Swiss clock over the gate had stopped at half past seven.[1]

The Ottoman Empire had chosen the German side in the war, and a large German military staff had been in Jerusalem since December 1914, using the Augusta Victoria hospice as its military headquarters. After capturing Gaza on November 7, 1917, British and Commonwealth troops had plodded up through the Judean Hills to take Jerusalem. On December 8, Sir Philip Chetwode's XX Corps, poised in a great arc, launched attacks on the Holy City, from Bethlehem in the south to Nebi Samwel in the north.

Panic swept through Turkish ranks, and bootless, half-clothed troops began to flee the city. At midnight the district governor, Izzat Pasha, smashed the telegraph machines. He then deposited a letter of surrender with the mayor and abandoned the city in a borrowed cart, the last Turkish official to leave.[2]

In this way, Britain took over from Turkey responsibility for the Christian holy places.

Accompanying General Allenby on his entry into Jerusalem was a party of British officers that included T. E. Lawrence, the legendary Lawrence of Arabia, who later called the occasion "the supreme moment of the war."[3]

Also present was M. François Georges-Picot, former French consul-general in Beirut, there to assert France's traditional role of protector of Catholic interests. He bore the title French high commissioner but noted bitterly that General Allenby presented neither him nor the French and Italian military commanders to local dignitaries.[4] This hardly accorded with the spirit of a 1916 agreement providing for an international regime for the Christian holy places.

On the steps of the Citadel, before a select crowd of Muslims, Jews, and Christians of all denominations, General Allenby declared martial law and solemnly pledged to maintain existing rights at the holy places:

> I make known to you that every sacred building, monument, holy spot, shrine, traditional spot, endowment, pious bequest, or customary place of prayer, of whatever forms of the three religions, will be maintained according to the existing forms and customs and beliefs of those to whose faiths they are sacred.[5]

The logistical and administrative problems facing the British military government were daunting. The Ottoman Empire had abandoned Jerusalem after four centuries like a departing swarm of locusts, leaving its buildings and souks half derelict, the streets filthy, the moats around the Citadel overflowing with rubbish. Forced to forage for food, Turkish soldiers had looted houses and farms, cutting down olive groves and fruit orchards for fuel, commandeering beasts and vehicles. That did not leave much for the civilian population in what would prove to be a harsh winter.[6]

At the time of the Turkish retreat, the Christian religious establishments in Jerusalem labored under varying degrees of hardship. After the outbreak of war in August 1914, the consuls representing Turkey's enemies had left the city one by one. By the end, only the consulates of Catholic Spain and Austria-Hungary remained open.

The Armenians and Greeks were without consular protection. The small Armenian community, which had taken in several hundred survivors of the Anatolian massacres, was reasonably safe as long as there was a German military presence in Jerusalem, and no breakdown of law and order. However, its resources were desperately overstretched.

The Greek Orthodox Patriarchate, which had enjoyed immense wealth before the war, was almost ruined by its end. Patriarch Damianos, well over six feet tall with a long snow-white beard and commanding presence, presided over a divided community. In 1908, he had been temporarily deposed by his synod for supposedly being soft on the demands of his Arabic-speaking parishioners for greater participation in the administration of the ethnic

Greek-controlled church. (The conflict between Greek and Arab Orthodox was to dog the patriarchate throughout the twentieth century.)

After the outbreak of war, the patriarchate was cut off from its main sources of income in the form of pilgrim revenues and rents on vast properties in mainland Greece, the Aegean Islands, Moscow, Bessarabia, and elsewhere. Forced to borrow in hard currency at ruinous rates of up to 40 percent while its earnings were in depreciating Turkish currency, by December 1919 it owed the astronomical sum for those days of 500,000 Egyptian pounds.[7]

Despite his financial (and diplomatic) dependence on Russia, Archbishop Damianos had no affection for the tsar. After the fall of Constantinople in 1453, the rulers of Muscovy claimed to have succeeded the Byzantine Empire as guardians of Orthodox Christianity. Russian representatives in Jerusalem had lately supported local Arabs in their struggle with the patriarchate. In 1914, Damianos repelled a Russian Orthodox bid to acquire altars for the exclusive use of Russian priests and pilgrims in the Holy Sepulchre.[8]

From Damianos's Hellenic perspective, a tsarist victory over Turkey would have been a disaster. It would have brought Russian Slavs to Constantinople and Jerusalem, replacing Greek control of the holy places with Russian. For the Brotherhood of the Holy Sepulchre, guardianship of the holy places was the sacred heritage of the Greek race. This put Patriarch Damianos in the pro-German camp of King Constantine of Greece (and his enemies into the camp of the Allies). During 1917, a year of turmoil in Russia culminating in the Bolshevik revolution, threat of a Russian victory receded. But having thrown in his lot with Turkey and Germany, Damianos dreaded the prospect of an Allied victory.

When the Turks retreated, they took along with them the heads of communities and their moveable wealth. Monsignor Filippo Camassei, the sixty-nine-year-old Latin patriarch, was taken to Nazareth; Father Luigi Piccardo, the acting custos, who headed the Custody of the Holy Land, was forced to travel in shocking conditions at the age of seventy-two to Damascus, where he died two days after his arrival. Archbishop Ormanian Surpazan, the Armenian patriarch, left behind an impoverished community £80,000 in debt; but he enterprisingly substituted charcoal for valuables in his treasure chests.[9]

Archbishop Damianos, too, traveled with the Turkish army to Damascus, bringing with him his synod, the governing body of the church, so that they would not get up to mischief in his absence. The belief that Damianos was a willing guest of the retreating Turkish army was never entirely disposed of because of his known pro-Turkish views and virulently anti-British statements. "A sly, suspicious, ignorant, crafty old peasant" is how one British official described him.[10] After the war, General Allenby chose to accept Damianos's claim that he had remained in Damascus under duress and let him return in time to celebrate Greek Orthodox Christmas in Bethlehem on January 6, 1919.[11]

Of the major Christian communities, the Latins were in the best shape and had much to hope for from an eventual Allied victory, though they also had some concerns. With growing optimism, they followed the steady British advance across the Sinai in the late summer and fall of 1916. There were some Catholics among British staff officers, but the Church tended to typecast Britain as diehard Protestant and to suspect the Anglican Church of designs on the holy places.

Nevertheless, given Damianos's pro-Turkish orientation, Allied victory in the Middle East, they felt, would be to Latin benefit and Greek detriment. At a great peace conference at which the map of the world was redrawn, the victorious Catholic powers of France and Italy would surely support Latin demands for a revision of the Status Quo at the holy places. If justice were served, could not the Custody of the Holy Land hope to restore its golden age of predominance in Jerusalem?

First, though, they had to overcome the immovable objections of the Greeks, who had absolutely no intention of agreeing to change a state of affairs under which they had enjoyed supremacy for the last 160 years. An opportunity for the two churches to advance their respective claims came up at the Paris peace conference of 1919.

The new custos of the Holy Land, Father Ferdinando Diotallevi, submitted a sweeping historical memorandum to the great powers condemning past usurpations of Latin rights at the holy places and demanding a "return to the status quo legally established in the course of the fourteenth century, after the final fall of the Latin kingdom of Jerusalem."[12]

Father Diotallevi's 1919 memorandum drew a furious rejoinder from the chief secretary of the Greek Orthodox Patriarchate, Archbishop Timotheos, who dismissed the Latin memorandum as "a most insulting and indecent pamphlet" reflecting a Franciscan desire to expel the Greeks from the holy places. Since the sixteenth century, there had been "almost continual war" there, and only the firm maintenance of the Status Quo had kept the peace.[13]

The problem facing Britain was how to administer a set of arrangements that at first they neither knew nor fully understood. Beneath the surface appearance of calm continuity, an imperceptible if far-reaching transformation was under way in the working of the Status Quo, stemming from the change of sovereign. After 1878, foreign consuls could keep a watchful eye on the

Status Quo and their clients' rights, but Ottoman Turkey remained the linchpin of the system. Only the governor had the local knowledge and authority to deal with disputes between the communities and issue administrative rulings. He also benefited from the combination of respect and fear due an autocratic power that had ruled Jerusalem, sometimes in a brutal and arbitrary way, for centuries.

With the installation of a British military governor, Lieutenant Colonel Ronald Storrs, on December 28, 1917, one conception of law and governance replaced another. The Status Quo was a cloak cut to fit Muslim Turkey and only with difficulty accommodated Christian Britain. British officials found themselves facing intricate problems in both principle and practice.

"Who owns the Holy Sepulchre?" they wondered—a meaningful inquiry under common law but not under the Muslim law of waqf applying to charitable foundations. As noted, during the Ottoman period neither the sultan nor the churches had title to the property, which belonged in an absolute sense only to God and was to be administered for the good of the community.[14] The communities, however, did have rights of possession or usage granted by grace of the sovereign. Since the sultan transferred these rights from one community to another from time to time, all possessed "proofs of ownership" in the form of contradictory firmans, which they misleadingly inferred were title-deeds.

With the departure of the Turks, the Greeks insisted that they owned the entire building on behalf of the Hellenic nation and, as successor to Byzantium, always had. Other communities were there only by their permission. This was a far-reaching claim that would have overturned the Status Quo.[15]

To counter the Greek claim, some Catholics argued that the Turks had had theoretical title, since the Muslim doorkeeper held the keys to the great door on their behalf.[16] Presumably, this title then passed to Britain. Another Catholic view, put forward by Monsignor Luigi Barlassina, who became Latin patriarch in 1920, was that the major communities were the true proprietors, not the government.[17]

Then there was the critical practical issue of financing conservation. Throughout the entire Mandate period (1922–48), little money was ever available. At first, Colonel Storrs sought to raise funds from private sources through a charitable trust, the Pro-Jerusalem Society. Private donations were matched dollar for dollar by the civil administration, but even so the society had raised only $30,000 by 1925.[18]

After Storrs left Jerusalem for the governorship of Cyprus, the next year the society was wound up. Sir Herbert Samuel, the high commissioner, had already turned down the proposal of a tourist tax because of opposition from the shipping companies.[19] The idea of a "traveler's tax" came up again later, when it fared no better. A solution was never found, and conservation was always paid for on a hand-to-mouth basis.

———

Matters were not helped by the financial and administrative disarray of the Greek Orthodox patriarchate—"the most venerable and dignified historic institution for which the new Government of Palestine has become responsible," as a 1921 report put it—which enjoyed enormous power and influence. The Russian Revolution turned out to be no less a disaster than the tsarist victory Patriarch Damianos had feared.

Before World War I, the revenue of the patriarchate sometimes amounted to £120,000 a year, a great sum at the time. After the war, it dwindled to 30 percent of this figure.[20] Russian Orthodox pilgrims no longer poured into the country to shower gifts on the church. Russia lost Bessarabia to Romania, and the government confiscated church lands. Five hundred sacks of flour were presented to Damianos in compensation for the loss of property worth £500,000.[21]

But there was also gross mismanagement by the autocratic Damianos, who wielded absolute power. According to the 1897 *berat*—official warrant—confirming him in office, he "held and governed" without hindrance "the vineyards, gardens, farms, mills, fields, pastures, houses, work-shops, trees, whether fruit-bearing or not, shrines, monasteries, flocks and all similar properties which are dedicated to the Churches."

In 1919, the Greek consul general accused him of squandering the revenues of the patriarchate for personal ends. So despite its vast properties in Palestine and abroad, the patriarchate could not pay its debts and had to be protected from its creditors by a special moratorium.[22]

In 1921, Patriarch Damianos was able to beat off a revolt by his synod thanks to a favorable British commission of inquiry. Harry Luke, who was one of the commissioners, privately admitted: "the Bishops who tried to depose him were not altogether wrong in principle, though the methods they chose were uncanonical and illegal in form." By 1923, the patriarch had become very senile and increasingly violent.[23]

In 1926, a second commission of inquiry, the Bertram-Young commission, reported on the bitter, longstanding dispute between the Greek-controlled patriarchate and its Arab laity, who were treated like second-class citizens. To alleviate Arab grievances the commission recommended a revision of the patriarchate's 1875 constitution so as to permit the admission of Arabs to the Confraternity of the Holy Sepulchre, the participation of

Arab parish priests in the election of the patriarch, and the establishment of a mixed council permitting Arabs to share in the administration and revenues of the patriarchate.

The report also touched on the demoralizing effect on the community of the irregular behavior of some members of the Confraternity, the brotherhood of monks that controlled the patriarchate and bore responsibility for protecting the holy places. Illicit commissions from land transactions, the embezzlement of pilgrim donations, and the "unofficial" relationships of supposedly celibate monks were all cited as sources of local resentment.[24]

In the confidential supplement to the report, the commissioners noted that "unofficial women" were openly included in a list of Confraternity dependents eligible for financial support. Two of the seven monks mentioned in this connection were of the rank of archbishop. One of these, Meliton, Archbishop of Madeba, who had been obliged to leave Athens after World War I because of a scandal involving "an Athenian lady," ran in the 1935 patriarchal elections. The chief secretary of the synod, Archimandrite Epiphanios, was caught submitting false receipts to the commission of inquiry.[25]

The Bertram-Young findings rankled deeply, adding to Greek suspicion of British intentions. The British report made fund raising abroad difficult and was seen as a deliberate attempt to undermine the patriarchate. As the commissioners foresaw in the confidential supplement, no reform was likely to be implemented in Patriarch Damianos's lifetime. The old prelate's final years were marked by inaction, and the indiscipline of the brotherhood went unchecked. Epiphanios remained chief secretary of the synod and was let off with a rebuke. A new set of regulations was issued, one that forbade the brothers to divulge their secrets to nonmembers or publicize the deficiencies of other brothers. "They should rather conceal them."[26]

Meanwhile, lack of detailed knowledge of the Status Quo gravely hindered the work of British officials. After the Turkish governor's flight from Jerusalem, his archive was never recovered.[27] As a result, the indispensable records of Ottoman administration of the holy places disappeared without trace. Without a definitive version of past decisions, the British authorities found themselves seriously handicapped.

Some former Ottoman officials, such as Abdullah Effendi Kardus in Bethlehem, continued in British employment and could give valuable advice drawn from long experience. But this was no substitute for the official archive. Without it, British officials had to rely on documents selected by the communities from their own archives and on the contradictory evidence of witnesses, not all of whom were equally reliable.[28]

All was not quite lost in the absence of records. Minor violations of the Status Quo were quickly resolved, such as the decoration of the Edicule with a cross bearing Franciscan insignia before the feast of St. Francis, 1919, and the introduction of small side tables around the Edicule before a Greek Orthodox pontifical mass in 1920.

Calendrical differences between the communities meant that liturgical complications were less common than might have been expected. Since the Latins went by the Gregorian and the Greeks by the Julian calendar, Easter Day only coincided in the two rites once every three or four years. Patriarch Damianos, indeed, vigorously opposed a proposal in 1923 to adopt the Gregorian calendar, arguing: "A change in the Church Calendar is of no use and will not be accepted by our Patriarchate because it would place us in an unfavorable position in relation to the holy places of pilgrimage and to the Latins."[29] He meant that Catholic pilgrims would far outnumber Orthodox ones, exposing his diminished relative standing.

When feasts fell on the same day, the superiors of the major communities in the Church of the Resurrection readily cooperated "to ensure good order and avoid misunderstanding."[30]

Greeks and Latins also negotiated a bilateral convention in October 1923 settling disputes arising from the building of the Roman Catholic Basilica of the Agony (now known as the Church of All Nations) in the Garden of Gethsemane.[31] So, even though relations were dogged by mutual suspicion, productive discussions did take place.

Friction tended to recur over certain perennial issues of principle. In 1920 Storrs's deputy, Harry Luke, was called in to sort out an old dispute on Calvary over a Greek altar cloth that the Latins wished to replace for their own devotions. The Greeks thought replacement of their cloth would imply that the Latins had a right of possession to which they were not entitled. Plied by Greeks and Latins with contradictory firmans, Luke was unable to discover who was in the right. He decided to prevent an incident by packing the chapel with police, only to discover that the Greeks had glued their altar cloth to the altar. Faced with this *fait accompli* he decided to leave the cloth in place "until the matter had been cleared up."[32]

If an administrative approach to handling disputes at the holy places was hindered by an absence of proper records, the obvious solution was to put a judicial procedure in place so that claims could be adjudicated objectively. An idea the British Foreign Office first raised in 1919 was to establish a British commission to settle once and for all disputed questions of ownership at the holy places and thereby arrive at a definitive version of the Status Quo.

The Holy See, wishing to regain lost historical rights, took up the idea in the modified form of an international commission.

At the San Remo conference in April 1920, the Allies formally decided to grant Britain the Mandate for Palestine, and France reluctantly agreed to end its protectorate over Catholics in the Levant. Protracted negotiations between Britain, Catholic states, and the Vatican then followed over the composition and powers of a commission. France soon regretted conceding its protectorate and claimed the presidency of the commission. Italy vigorously rejected this. Spain, too, wanted a role.

No agreement had been reached, therefore, when the Council of the League of Nations approved the British Mandate for Palestine on July 24, 1922. Article 13 placed all responsibility for the holy places on Britain, which was accountable to the League. Article 14 called for a special commission to determine the rights and claims of the religious communities in Palestine, the details to be filled in later.

Talks on the scope of the commission fell through when the Vatican insisted that only Latin claims be considered and that voting rights be restricted to Catholic nations. Britain could not agree to this. Besides, the Greek government had begun to play an increasingly active role in Jerusalem, filling the vacuum left by the fall of the tsar. The Vatican now reversed its position and informed the British government that it would prefer to maintain the Ottoman Status Quo, bringing disputes for adjudication before the local British courts.[33] Father Paschal Robinson, an official of the Holy See, quietly acknowledged the impracticability of the Franciscan claims.[34]

The colonial office was inclined to go along with the Vatican's suggestion, only to have it refuted by Sir Herbert Samuel, the high commissioner for Palestine (1920–25), who argued that the local courts were not equipped for the task and would find it very difficult to deal with the holy places on a strictly legal basis. Experience showed that the rivalries between religious bodies, arousing international interest, should be dealt with by a higher authority than a local court.[35]

Samuel had in mind a complicated lawsuit brought by the Spanish government against the Custody of the Holy Land over the ownership of some houses in Jaffa. Under Ottoman law, the Catholic Church, as a foreign entity, had not been allowed to own private property in its own right. The houses, purchased with Spanish charitable donations for the use of the Franciscan Order, had therefore been registered in the name of a Spanish friar. If Madrid won its case, the Custody could potentially forfeit most of its real estate holdings.[36]

Samuel's analysis provided the basis for an order-in-council of July 25, 1924, regulating the handling of disputes among the different religious communities at the holy places, a key document to this day. No court in Palestine was to have jurisdiction over these issues. In the event of doubt, the high commissioner would decide whether a particular case involved the Status Quo and therefore fell outside the purview of the local courts. The intention—left unclear by ambiguous drafting—was that the high commissioner would refer any such case to the Council of the League of Nations.[37]

The intention was most decidedly not, as subsequently turned out, that disputes would never be resolved and would remain sources of conflict forever. Rather, they were to be referred to a special international body—a commission or court—that would settle them once and for all. But the communities have awaited such an authority in vain ever since.

Given the failure either to establish a special commission or to settle jurisdiction on the local courts, for the rest of the Mandate period, disputes were settled by local officials, effectively the system adopted by the Ottoman authorities after 1852. To make a provisional decision on the state of actual practice, the Jerusalem authorities clearly needed, in the absence of the archives, a detailed manual on the Status Quo. A young British district officer, Archer Cust, possessing a good knowledge of Greek and the confidence of the Greek Orthodox patriarchate, was chosen to draw it up.

Lionel George Archer Cust had played cricket with the royal princes and sung the chorus "The Heavens Are Telling the Glory of God" from Haydn's oratorio *The Creation* at Windsor Castle for King Edward VII. His father, Sir Lionel Cust, was an eminent art historian, surveyor of the king's pictures, and knight of the Order of St. John of Jerusalem. In 1910, father and son had come to Jerusalem for St. John's Day and attended Anglican Holy Communion, conducted with the permission of Patriarch Damianos in the subterranean Greek Orthodox Church of St. John Prodromos. At the age of twenty, in 1915, Archer Cust went from Eton, an elite private school, into the Royal Field Artillery; he was decorated for gallantry on the Western Front.[38]

After the war, his cousin Ronald Storrs put in a good word for him with Sir Herbert Samuel, and he joined the Palestine civil service. With his poise, language skills, and complete discretion, Cust soon became Samuel's aide-de-camp. He then did an excellent job as secretary to the commissions of inquiry on the Greek Orthodox patriarchate.

Cust's classic report on *The Status Quo in the Holy Places* was drafted not long after the earthquake and went through various revisions before achieving its final version in September 1929. The report is part history; part description of places, furnishings, and liturgy; part summary of government rulings; part account of contemporary practice. The Holy Sepulchre is dealt with in twenty pages. Such subjects as the right to open the great door, the ownership of lamps at the Stone of Unction and the Edicule, liturgy on Calvary, and rights of usage and cleaning in the rotunda are discussed.

Harry Luke, by then chief secretary to the Palestine government, who personally edited and amended *The Status Quo*, described it as a vade mecum or handbook of practical value to officials obliged to administer the Status Quo. However, he thought that many details were of so debatable a nature that distributing the report to the heads of the religious communities would simply lead to endless argument.[39]

The Cust memorandum is neither a comprehensive nor authoritative code. There are errors and contradictions. In one place Cust argues that it is a fixed principle that the right to hang a picture indicates "exclusive posses- sion" of the wall or pillar on which it is hung. Later he himself notes that there are Coptic pictures hanging on two Armenian columns in the rotunda. Cust did not realize that there is no such thing as "exclusive possession" under the laws of religious endowments. One church can "own" a shrine while another church has traditional rights of usage at the same place.[40] Be- sides, it is very difficult for a text to capture precisely process, choreography, or decor.[41]

Nevertheless, in the absence of any other objective historical document not assembled for purposes of special pleading, the Cust memorandum has demonstrated its usefulness over the years. Though incomplete, it is an in- formative introduction to the subject and touches on some of the major issues. Over the years, it has contributed to the peaceful accommodation of differences. The churches accept without question only their own records but cite Cust when he is on their side.

An unsure style of administration at the holy places was inevitable in the early years, while British officials found their feet. However, the situation was exacerbated by the erratic decision-making of Ronald Storrs, the mili- tary and then the civilian governor of Jerusalem from 1917 to 1926.

Caught up in the excitement of running Jerusalem, Storrs brought his own romantic personal agenda to administering the holy places. An aesthete and art collector, Storrs took enormous pride in the preservation and beau- tification of the Holy City and its surroundings. Through his Pro-Jerusalem Society, he encouraged the development of arts and crafts, maintained the architectural style of the Old City, prohibited development in certain areas south of the walls, regulated billboards, designed ceramic street signs, banned asbestos or corrugated iron roofing, insisted on building in local stone only, and enacted a town planning scheme for Jerusalem's development. His aim was to protect the Old City "from industrial desecration."

Sometimes Storrs could not resist imposing his own idiosyncratic views on the improvement of the Holy City. Contemporary conservationists recognized that ancient buildings had often been altered over the ages in response to changing needs without compromising their beauty or value. Attempts to recreate some lost ideal of authenticity might result in a pious fake. Storrs insisted that later additions should be stripped away and the pristine past recovered. Among his various projects were the demolition of the amusing Turkish clock tower at the Jaffa Gate, built in 1909 on the thirty-third anniversary of the coronation of Sultan Abdul Hamid, and—more justifiably—the removal of shops and houses built up against the exterior of the Old City walls.[42]

Given Storrs's dedication to restoration, the holy places posed an irresistible challenge. But his enthusiastic commitment and his inability to leave well enough alone were not consistent with the impartial administration of the Status Quo. Furthermore, he tended to overestimate his own freedom to maneuver vis-à-vis the major communities. They were more powerful and influential than at first appeared. As a result, he made a series of misjudgments that undermined British authority and prestige.

His first intervention came in 1918, when he pulled down a gray protective wall built by the Greeks across the chancel of the Church of the Nativity in 1842.[43] The impoverished Greeks, without their supportive Turkish masters or tsarist patrons, were terrified of where the slightest change in the Status Quo might lead, and were determined to defend it uncompromisingly. With the utmost reluctance, they agreed to the demolition of the wall, provided they did it themselves, at their own expense. The Latins submitted a formal protest, meaning that they reserved their rights under the Status Quo. The government mistakenly paid for the work and took possession of the rubble. A Greek priest wielded the first pickaxe to symbolize his community's right of possession.

Storrs knew from his inquiries that the demolition was in contravention of the Status Quo. Nor was it any of his business. Nevertheless, he carried it out, to his lasting satisfaction, because he thought the wall "hideous" and it blocked the view of the iconostasis. "If it fell not under the edict of a military despot, it would stand for ever."

Storrs's architectural taste may have been impeccable, but his political sense was not. The sovereign could act unilaterally at the holy places for safety reasons or in an emergency. But an act of demolition on purely aesthetic grounds was unprecedented and fomented suspicion of his real motives. For years afterward the Greek patriarchate nursed a grudge about this episode. It was the first issue the patriarchate referred to in an embittered memorandum it submitted to the government twenty years later in which it set out a long litany of grievances.[44]

The issue for the Greeks was not so much the wall, as such, as the principle of the inviolability of the Status Quo. Viewing the Status Quo as of one piece, to be preserved in its entirety, they considered a violation of a part to threaten the overturning of the whole. After all, if the wall, which was protected by the Status Quo, could be destroyed at the whim of the governor, how safe could their other rights and possessions be? Fear that a minor infringement may be the thin end of the wedge is a consistent theme in the psychology of the communities.

Another of Storrs's projects was in the Parvis of the Holy Sepulchre. To the right of the main entrance lay the tomb of a Crusader knight, Philip d'Aubigny, who was tutor to King Henry III of England. Until 1867, the tomb was protected by a stone bench used as a seat by the Muslim doorkeepers.[45] Once the bench was removed, people entering the church trod on the uncovered tombstone, wearing away the inscription. This so bothered Storrs that in 1925 he petitioned the Greek patriarch to have the tomb moved to one side and the face of the tombstone protected.[46]

In financial straits and under pressure from his Arab parishioners, Patriarch Damianos felt obliged to humor the governor. As a compromise, he therefore reluctantly agreed that the Pro-Jerusalem Society should arrange for the tombstone to be recessed below the level of the paving and covered with an iron grille. Funds were provided by the Daubney family, the lineal descendants of Sir Philip, and the Island of Guernsey.[47]

The affair used up political capital and unnecessarily agitated the Greeks, who could only wonder at the significance of the British governor's odd behavior. If Storrs was so anxious to preserve the tombstone of an Anglo-French Crusader knight, did he want to turn the clock back to the time of the Latin Kingdom of Jerusalem? As British officials opened D'Aubigny's tomb, sullen crowds of Greek monks observed them from the terraces.[48]

Archbishop Timotheos, the patriarch's right-hand man, was afraid that the British government would sell out the Greeks in return for concessions from the Catholic powers, just as he believed it had sold out the Arabs to the Zionists.

Storrs now turned his attention to the Garden of Gethsemane at the foot of the Mount of Olives. The Greek Orthodox Church owned the upper part of the garden. In 1887 Czar Alexander III built the Church of St. Mary Magdalene further up the hill in the Muscovite style, onion domes and all. The

Franciscan Order owned the lower part of the garden, revered by Catholics as the place of the Agony, where Jesus prayed on the night before the Crucifixion. A late-fourth-century basilica was known to have once stood there. In 1891, the foundations of a later twelfth-century structure were found, but the site remained as it had been for centuries, a pleasant hillside dotted with ancient olive trees.

At the end of World War I, a movement to rebuild a basilica on the site gained momentum, and a fund-raising drive was launched in the Catholic archdiocese of Tolosa in northern Spain. Father Diotallevi enthusiastically adopted the construction as a way of adding to the luster of the Custody after the bleak war years. He gained the support of Monsignor Barlassina, the Latin patriarch, though the men disagreed over the division of responsibility for the holy places. While the Custody was the historical guardian of the sanctuaries and bore all the costs, it was the duty of the patriarch to submit an official protest in the event of a violation of the Status Quo. Occasionally Barlassina acted behind Father Diotallevi's back, even after the Vatican had worked out a truce between them.[49]

At all stages of the project—from laying the foundation stone to excavating the foundations, to building the church—the British authorities were approached for their help and approval. This was vital not only for technical planning reasons but also because of the opposition of the Greeks, who owned adjacent land and claimed that the construction was in violation of the Status Quo. On several occasions there were disturbances at the site, provoked by disgruntled Greek and Armenian monks, when the police had to be called.

Storrs was very attached to the Garden of Gethsemane at moonlight and felt antipathy toward the project from the start. "My prayer was that it should be allowed to remain as it was in the time of Christ." He thought that there were already too many churches in the Holy Land and temporized for as long as he could.[50] But he could not make a good case against the request. After centuries of Muslim restrictions on construction, the Catholic Church wanted to restore a church to a site where there had been two separate basilicas in antiquity. The Latins owned most of the land (except for one corner, which the cash-strapped Greek patriarch eventually agreed to sell). Besides, the Turks had permitted the Greeks to build their own basilica just up the hill.

The Franciscans, forcing Storrs, who fought a futile rearguard action, to cave in at each stage, ran an effective lobbying campaign.[51] The lessons to be drawn were obvious: here was a weak governor, vulnerable to pressure. Storrs's civic adviser, Charles Ashbee, thought that Barlassina had played Storrs "like a mouse, and held him softly but firmly, first mouthed to be last swallowed."[52] Storrs found himself having the worst of both worlds for a colonial governor: to be neither loved nor feared.

Storrs's final misjudgment was at the Edicule itself. The marble veneer covering the kiosk-like mausoleum bulged outward above the plinth, giving cause for concern, so Storrs decided to have the municipal architect, Cliff Holliday, examine it. Patriarchs of the major communities were notified that an inspection would take place on June 2, 1925. They were assured that the government would pay for any repairs and that the Status Quo would not be affected in any way whatsoever.[53]

Under the Status Quo, however, the Edicule was the shared possession of the major communities, and the cost of repairs was supposed to be equally divided among them. Only if the communities refused to pay did the government bear the cost. All three patriarchs pointed this out, while expressing their willingness for the survey to go ahead, provided their rights were protected. Barlassina insisted, in addition, that his own architect be present and that nothing be decided without his consent. Catholic consuls should also be allowed to attend.[54]

For some years, the Latin patriarch had been a thorn in the side of the Palestine government, deploring British rule and the terms of the Mandate. Britain, he believed, had no business at the holy places and was guilty of pro-Greek bias. On a trip to Rome in 1922, he scurrilously attacked the government's alleged moral turpitude in a lecture. Back in Jerusalem, he insisted that he was owed precedence over the Greek Orthodox patriarch on public occasions, such as the celebration of King George V's birthday, and boycotted them when his primacy was not recognized.[55]

Barlassina's Armenian and Greek colleagues did not support his demand that his architect take part in the survey, and Storrs ran out of patience. On June 2, Holliday went ahead with the inspection; the Catholic consuls were conspicuously present in full dress uniform. Barlassina submitted an official protest, and the Holy See complained through diplomatic channels.[56]

In its official response, the British government backed up Storrs, who had recently been knighted. In private, they acknowledged that Storrs's lack of judgment had alarmed the churches and he should not have offered to pay for repairs. Lessons should be drawn, and foreign consuls would not be welcome in the future.[57]

By the time Storrs departed for the governorship of Cyprus a few months later, both Greeks and Latins were equally disenchanted with what they felt to be his unsure and sometimes arbitrary handling of the Status Quo. The steadier Edward Keith-Roach then took over responsibility for maintaining order at the holy places. Known affectionately as Keith-Roach Pasha, his shrewd, broad face was set off by a nose broken while playing rugby football. An exemplary public servant, he was passionately attached to Jerusalem and served the city until shortly before his death in 1943.

The rule of thumb adopted from now on was to maintain every jot and tittle of the law. To this end, the district commissioner would take immediate, on-the-spot action against any infringement of the rules, even at the most sacred services. If he did not, he risked creating a precedent that would transform an infraction into an integral portion of the Status Quo. He was well aware that he was not in a position to give an authoritative ruling on what the existing rights were in the cases in dispute. Still, if only to ensure public order, he was bound to make a provisional decision and make sure it was enforced.[58]

As a result of the 1925 controversy, a more complete survey of the Edicule was delayed until the summer of 1926. During the inspection, Cliff Holliday removed a stone from the plinth and probed behind the paneling. He discovered that the marble outer casing, which was unsightly but not dangerously decrepit, was detached from the rubble inner walls of the tomb. This internal structure was safe, but he recommended that the marble paneling should be taken down and replaced.[59] The district commissioner overruled him.[60]

Sadly surveying the church, Archer Cust observed: "The fetters of the Status Quo account for the state of dirt and dilapidation which is characteristic of many parts of the building." Rights of possession were arcane and contested. Repairs could be carried out in uncontested areas or, if urgent, by the government. Otherwise, "in the parts in dispute nothing is allowed to be done in the way of innovation or repair by any party."[61]

Under the Status Quo, there was simply no provision for a situation in which the entire edifice was imperiled. Luigi Marangoni, a distinguished Italian architect, in a 1934 report on the state of the basilica, rightly observed that alongside the rights of the communities under the Status Quo, there was no explicit duty of care and responsibility toward the church. Indeed, to preserve their rights at all costs, the communities tended to ignore the needs of the edifice.[62] If they continued with this irresponsible line of conduct, the Holy Sepulchre would be left to fall into ruin.

After the 1927 earthquake, this was the conundrum to which the British authorities were obliged to find a solution. First, though, someone had to wake up to the calamitous condition of the mother church.

CHAPTER THREE | Ready to Fall

A MID THE GENERAL MISERY caused by the earthquake of July
11, 1927, few people were concerned about the state of the Holy Sepulchre. The only visible damage was to the small dome over the Katholikon,
which from the adjacent terraces looked like a cracked boiled egg. But it did
not seem likely to collapse, and no one considered the possibility of extensive
structural harm. Besides, decay and neglect were nothing new in the church.
Cracks and disintegration were the rule, good repair the exception.

A British pilgrim from Wycliffe Hall, Oxford, has left us a graphic
description of Christianity's mother church in the summer of 1927:

> The condition of the Church of the Holy Sepulchre is deplorable.
> Probably there is no church or cathedral of any importance in the
> whole world that is so hopelessly shabby. It contains the most pre-
> cious relics of the Christian religion: and yet because the three chief
> Churches connected—Greek, Latin and Armenian—cannot agree, its
> walls are left to rot. The Chapel of Calvary and the Holy Sepulchre are
> kept fairly well; for the rest, the less said the better. The most beautiful
> chapel of all, St. Helena, with its amazing fourth-century capitals, has
> a broken floor, and the altars are in desolation; the same applies to the
> Chapel of the Finding of the Cross, and many other chapels besides.[1]

Immediately after the earthquake, Colonel Symes, the chief secretary,
committed the Palestine government to undertaking repairs. The Greek
patriarchate, which claimed exclusive ownership of the Katholikon, had
no objection to this, as long as Greeks paid. The Latins and Armenians,

however, insisted that the costs be split three ways, on the grounds that the fabric of the church was common property.

In the past, the Greeks had repaired the Katholikon dome on their own, subject to Latin and Armenian protests. In order to avoid the opposition of the other two communities, they had (allegedly) acted surreptitiously. They were said to have erected a stone cross over the dome in 1888 in the middle of the night in a torrential downpour.[2] So disagreement over the right of repair emerged very soon after the earthquake.

Because of an enormous backlog of work throughout the Jerusalem area, it was not until September 20 that the Department of Public Works (DPW) engineers got around to the church. They could only survey the damage from the outside, as an internal examination would have required the erection of scaffolding. This meant that they were restricted to inspecting the drum and dome. That they overlooked the underlying structure was to prove unfortunate. But nobody in the DPW was an expert in the conservation of ancient buildings.

The cupola was made of horizontal courses of dressed Malaki stone—a fine local limestone—with very thin lime joints. It weighed approximately 230 tons, and had a vertical radius of 6.5 meters (21.3 feet). It stood on a drum 5 meters (16.4 feet) high and 13 meters (42.6 feet) in diameter, with windows and columns. Some previous earthquake—there were jolts in 1834, 1837, 1846, and 1847[3]—or perhaps the 1808 fire had long ago destroyed the cohesion of the joints in the lower part of the dome. To contain the outward movement of the voussoirs (the curved, interlocking stones of the dome), iron and lead clamps and hoops had been inserted. But these metal stays were ineffective, and the earthquake had further shaken the joints so that they no longer offered any resistance to the pressure. Stones lower down were therefore splintering, and the vertical joints opening up.

The DPW report's conclusion was unambiguous: at any time, the stones might collapse or overturn. Some were already hanging out two inches below the others. If they went, those above would also fall in. Any further tremor would immediately bring down the cupola. It had to be demolished at once.[4]

This was bad news for the Greek Orthodox Patriarchate. A good deal of its property in Palestine, including Justinian's Tower in Bethlehem, had been seriously damaged in the earthquake. The patriarchate was only just emerging from a financial crisis, but it had no choice but to undertake repairs.

Late in 1927, the DPW carefully dismantled the stone masonry of the dome. In its place, a temporary conical roof covered with galvanized iron sheets was installed to keep out the winter rains. The stones were numbered and stored away for reuse. After the rainy season ended, the DPW proposed to erect a new dome.[5]

Important issues of principle soon arose. The Katholikon dome was the first really major conservation project at the Christian holy places since the end of World War I. Colonial office and Palestine government files bulge with discussions of legal responsibility, ultimate ownership of the Church of the Holy Sepulchre, and liability for funding any work carried out.

Following a legal review, the colonial secretary, Leopold Amery, concluded that article 13 of the Mandate for Palestine did not confer on His Majesty's Government "any responsibility for, or rights to carry out, repairs of non-Muslim religious buildings." It would not, therefore, be reasonable to expect the Treasury to bear the cost of the upkeep of such buildings from British funds. This key ruling was to limit the activities of the Palestine government at the Church of the Resurrection for the rest of the Mandate.[6]

On receipt of the DPW report, the Greek Orthodox Patriarchate made known its intention to pay for repairs, drawing Latin and Armenian protests. In order to explain the situation, the French consul general convened a meeting of all the Catholic consular representatives in the country—those of Austria, Belgium, Czechoslovakia, Hungary, Italy, Poland, and Spain. The Italian consul general accused the British authorities of "interfering in the affairs of the Holy Sepulchre in order to bring the Protestants into the church." This was a widely held view among Catholics in Jerusalem in the interwar period.

The consuls decided only to keep their governments informed.[7] Nevertheless, it was an impressive display of Catholic diplomatic solidarity and concern that the government could not help noting.

Meanwhile, Edward Keith-Roach, the deputy district commissioner of Jerusalem, was shuttling between the patriarchs in an attempt to work out a solution to the disagreement over payment of repairs. This is the first recorded instance of the secular power acting not as adjudicator or supervisor but as mediator, shepherding the parties toward an understanding. Because of tension and mistrust between the communities in the 1920s, direct negotiations were infrequent. Keith-Roach's approach was to talk to the disputants separately to elicit their views and identify common ground and possible trade-offs.

By the beginning of November 1927, a tentative package deal had been worked out. The Armenians were interested in making repairs and improvements to their own Chapel of St. Helena; the Catholics had long wanted to install an iron grille staircase over the old steps down to the Chapel of the

Invention of the Cross and to restore the mosaic flooring in their southern section of Calvary. These would be the quid pro quo for their agreeing to the Greeks' covering the entire cost of repairing the cupola over the Katholikon.[8]

Until the last minute, Greeks and Latins withheld their blessing. Archbishop Damianos, the infirm Greek Orthodox patriarch, held out for a share in the cost of the new stairs. Monsignor Barlassina, the Latin patriarch, rejected both this demand and the Greek claim to sole ownership of the dome. Indeed, he bitterly resented British "interference" altogether, rejected a proposal to divide up the costs at a later date, and accused the government of trampling on Catholic rights.[9]

Colonel Symes now concluded that the government had to throw its weight behind a common-sense decision. He therefore instructed Keith-Roach to ignore Greek and Latin objections, proposing a grand compromise that allocated each patriarch his own pet project. He also suggested securing the good will of Father Paschal Robinson, an austere Irish Franciscan, as a counterbalance to the Latin patriarch. Robinson was well thought of by the British and had been sent to Jerusalem by the Vatican as a moderating influence.[10]

As Symes anticipated, the package deal ultimately proved acceptable to all three major communities, not least because it was in the form of a government decision rather than an explicit agreement relying on consent. Parallel letters to the patriarchs set out the arrangement, stating that it was without prejudice to any future investigation of the communities' claims, thereby reassuring them that no formal loss of rights was involved.

The episode showed that the religious leaders were tough but pragmatic negotiators, open to persuasion, who benefited from the assistance of a skillful and firm moderator. At the final stage, the government had become an arbiter, presenting a fair solution involving a balanced allocation of benefits as an authoritative ruling.

———

Just after the earthquake, Ernest T. Richmond took up the post of director of antiquities. Fifty-three years old and independent-minded, Richmond brought to the job vast skill and experience. Trained as an architect, he was also an Arabist and administrator with a thorough knowledge of the workings of colonial government. During a fifteen-year stint in Cairo at the turn of the century he had worked on the conservation of ancient buildings and rose to become the top town planner for the Egyptian government.

Back in 1920, Richmond had been appointed assistant secretary for political affairs in the Palestine government. He strongly supported Arab political aspirations in Palestine. Among other things, he encouraged restoration of al-Haram al-Sharif, the site of the Dome of the Rock and al-Aksa mosque. Violently anti-Semitic, he resigned in 1924 in disgust at Britain's continuing support for Zionism and returned to England.[11]

When the post of director of antiquities in the Palestine government came up in 1926, Richmond applied. His credentials were excellent. A top official noted: "It is true that he is not a professional archaeologist, but I do not think you would get a first class man for this pay which Palestine can afford to give." The only problem was his fierce opposition to government policy. Over lunch with the high commissioner, Lord Plumer, however, he promised that he would refrain from all political activities and confine his work to furthering archaeological interests.[12]

Richmond was deeply attached to the Holy Sepulchre, both as a Christian and as an architect. In February 1926, he had converted to Roman Catholicism. He was convinced of the authenticity of the traditional places of the Crucifixion and the Resurrection and saw the church as enabling Christians to give "architectural expression to their natural veneration for these sites." His dream was to restore the Crusader church to its former glory. It was still possible, he later wrote,

> by careful examination to gain some appreciation of the architectural ingenuity, of the constructional skill, and of the perfection of workmanship in matters of detail, that were shown by the original builders. So much of this is, in point of fact, still recoverable, that, were it possible to remove the plaster botching which conceals much admirable detail, carefully to repair all that is left and now concealed of the original work, and to reopen windows for the most part blocked up, a considerable measure of its former beauty and character could be given back to the church.[13]

Given his idealism, a number of unpleasant surprises were in store for Richmond on his arrival in Jerusalem. The Holy Sepulchre was losing its most priceless assets. The tympanum over the entrance, consisting of a carved pair of panels, was crumbling away. During a snowfall early in 1927, a section had fallen off the left-hand frieze, a twelfth-century Crusader masterpiece of unique importance depicting three scenes: the resurrection of Lazarus, the entry of Jesus into Jerusalem, and the Last Supper. The Muslim doorkeeper had considered this so unremarkable that he had not even bothered to report it.[14] All efforts at conservation over the next three years—using the latest laboratory techniques—failed, sadly, and the panels had to be removed for storage to the Palestine Archaeological Museum (now the Rockefeller Museum), where they remain.

Notwithstanding this lamentable state of affairs, Richmond found the communities reluctant to cooperate with the authorities in the conservation of their own archaeological heritage. Even before the earthquake, he had initiated contacts with religious leaders to persuade them to undertake long-delayed repairs, only to find them devoid of all urgency.[15] Nor did they have any compunction about replacing ancient features of the edifice with new ones.

They were particularly reluctant to accept professional supervision of their building activities. Under the Palestine antiquities ordinance, any work at the holy places had to be approved by the board of antiquities on the advice of the archaeological advisory board. On repeated occasions during the Mandate (and, indeed, ever since) this obligation was ignored and irreplaceable historical features of the edifice lost. In March 1928, Richmond discovered that unauthorized repairs were being carried out to the belfry of the Holy Sepulchre.[16] Again in 1932, he found that the mosaic flooring of the Latin Chapel of the Apparition, dating to the second half of the twelfth century and in perfect condition, had been destroyed.[17]

By then, it was clear that the Palestine government was simply not organized for the specialized task of conservation. Conservation requires historical buildings to be preserved in conformity with principles already well known and accepted in the 1920s. As much as possible of the original has to be spared, without addition or subtraction. Skilled craftsmen using appropriate materials should carry out repairs. Above all, conservation requires the supervision of an architect trained in the special structural problems of ancient monuments.

Richmond soon found that he had responsibility without power. His situation, in fact, mirrored the wider frailty of the government in the affair. The antiquities ordinance granted the director of antiquities the authority to inspect and order repairs to ancient monuments, but not the means to implement them. Having already surveyed the Katholikon dome, the DPW proposed to go ahead on its own. However, though it had the manpower and the resources, it lacked the expertise. It soon discovered that it was saddled with a job it did not know how to carry out. Mending a twelfth-century cathedral presents utterly different problems from building a road or bridge. Richmond tried very hard but ultimately failed to obtain for his department its own construction capability.

Despite all these obstacles in his path, Richmond enjoyed one major asset, the good will of the acting high commissioner, Harry Luke, an old colleague from the early days of the Mandate. Luke was highly knowledgeable about the holy places and the Christian communities, and had written widely on the subject.[18] He had been one of the commissioners appointed to look into the affairs of the Greek Orthodox Patriarchate in 1920 and was an adviser on the eastern churches to the archbishop of Canterbury.

In July 1928, Luke was brought back to Palestine from Sierra Leone as chief secretary, number two in the government. When Lord Plumer left Palestine shortly afterward, Luke became acting high commissioner and set his mind to reorganizing the machinery for conservation of the holy places. He prepared an administrative blueprint for the colonial secretary, Leopold Amery.

All the holy places, Luke wrote, were deplorably neglected, and a works program was urgently required. The main façade of the Holy Sepulchre was steadily deteriorating, the vaults were saturated, the roof and windows needed repair, and the belfry was in an unsatisfactory condition. Unless the maintenance of the holy places was placed on a proper footing the process of decay would result in the collapse of the edifice.

Luke acknowledged that the failure in 1922 to set up a special commission of the League of Nations on the holy places had left the disputes between the Christian communities in limbo. Until questions of ownership were settled, it was hard to decide who had the right to repair what. Since it was unthinkable in the meantime to allow the Christian sanctuaries to go to rack and ruin, Britain had no choice but to take over maintenance. Allowing the different communities to go ahead separately risked the destruction of much that ought to be preserved.

Three steps had to be taken. First, to set up a historical monuments section within either the DPW or the department of antiquities. Second, to pay for conservation with a tax on travelers payable on entry into Palestine. Third, to settle the question of conservation in consultation with interested governments, over the heads of the local communities.[19]

Amery, the colonial secretary, began a process of consultation with other government agencies. At the same time, he suggested that Luke convince local religious leaders to entrust the government with responsibility for repair and conservation of the holy places. He did not believe they could be bypassed, since they resented British interference and could always lobby foreign governments on their behalf. The Vatican was to be kept fully informed.[20]

At this critical point, with the DPW wondering how to proceed with repair of the dome, Luke's plans for conservation were totally disrupted by a convulsion in Arab–Jewish relations. Major Arab rioting against Jews, resulting in death and injury to hundreds of people, broke out in August 1929, against the background of a dispute over the Western or Wailing Wall, the Jews' holy place below al-Haram al-Sharif. These disturbances shockingly demonstrated to the British authorities the potential for violence at the holy places and the vital need to maintain the Status Quo at all costs.

During the riots, Luke was again acting high commissioner in the absence of Sir John Chancellor. A subsequent parliamentary commission exonerated Luke of all blame, but he was held to account by the Jewish community for the government's loss of control over events. Until he was transferred to Malta as lieutenant governor in the summer of 1930, he spent the rest of his stay in Palestine under the shadow of these accusations.

No other Palestine official at the highest level was to match Luke's expert knowledge of the Holy Sepulchre. Nor were the relatively quiet days of the 1920s ever to return, as the Arab–Jewish conflict spiraled in the 1930s into open revolt by the Arabs against Jewish immigration. After Mussolini's invasion of Abyssinia in 1935 and Hitler's remilitarization of the Rhineland in 1936, there were always more pressing problems on the British government's agenda.

<hr />

At the end of June 1929, the Greek patriarchate approved building plans for the Katholikon dome prepared by Austen St. Barbe Harrison, the young chief architect of the DPW. The patriarchate then deposited with the authorities £5,900, provided by the Greek government, which saw the Christian holy places as part of the Hellenic national heritage. Unlike its Latin counterpart, the Greek patriarchate did not object to a British government role. The episode demonstrated that conservation was politically uncontroversial, as long there was no dispute over ownership.

Work was supposed to begin in the spring of 1930, to be completed by the end of the summer, before the onset of the rains. Plans called first for the strengthening of the drum at the base of the dome. The dome itself would strictly maintain the form of the original, using old stones as far as possible, and would be reinforced by steel bands.[21]

Richmond was unhappy about proceeding without a fundamental survey of the entire edifice, an axiom of conservation. If the DPW lacked the expertise, the project should be postponed before irreversible damage was done. Concretely, the Department of Antiquities proposed that the current piecemeal approach to conservation should be abandoned and a specialist unit established. There were, it emphasized, serious risks involved in rebuilding the cupola before determining whether the underlying arches and piers could support the extra weight. At the very least, repairs to adjoining vaults should be completed first.[22]

On July 30, 1929, a debate took place in Luke's office between the DPW, represented by its director, Fawcett Pudsey, and the antiquities department, represented by its assistant director, the archaeologist Charles Lambert, in the absence of Richmond, who was on leave. Rejecting the call for a postponement, Pudsey insisted that the stability of the drum could be relied on and that no damage would be caused to the church by erecting the dome. This misjudgment was to have far-reaching consequences.

Harry Luke was highly conscious of the government's commitment to the Greek patriarchate and international scrutiny of its stewardship of the holy places by the Permanent Mandates Commission of the League of Nations in Geneva. He saw insufficient grounds for a postponement and decided that the DPW should rebuild the dome without delay. The Latins and Armenians could also go ahead with their own repairs to Calvary, the Chapel of the Invention of the Cross, and St. Helena's Chapel, under proper supervision.[23]

Once the work got under way, the DPW soon found itself out of its depth. According to the overall plan, the drum had first to be strengthened. It was built in the Romanesque style, with an arcade of pointed arches resting on sixteen triple columns with carved capitals and bases, the alternate spaces being occupied by windows. A balcony ran around the inside of the drum.

A number of unfamiliar problems soon arose. What should be retained of the original drum, with its fine carving? How were cracks in the stonework to be treated? When did a stone need to be discarded? What materials should be used in reconstructing the window frames? Was a balustrade needed for the balcony and if so of what material? No one in the DPW could answer these routine conservation questions.

There was no choice but to bring in an outside expert in conservation. The architect chosen, William Harvey, was a recognized British authority on historical buildings and was surveyor of structure of St. Paul's Cathedral, London. Earlier in his career, Harvey had acquired considerable experience on the staff of the historic buildings branch of the British office of works.

Harvey had achieved professional recognition in 1925 when he published a textbook on the new science of conservation, written in rebuttal of the report of a commission of experts set up to investigate the structural condition of the dome of St. Paul's.[24]

Vaulted, arched buildings, such as medieval churches, were built without the use of reinforced concrete. For such a construction to stand firmly in place without its masses falling apart, Harvey argued, the thrust—pressure exerted by gravity—of its heavy upper sections must be apportioned in such a way that it is safely transmitted downward to the lower supporting structures, to be finally opposed by solid earth. Whenever thrust in a building is unevenly distributed and the supports are inadequate to take the load imposed on them, these supports—arches, pillars, walls, buttresses—will be gradually but inevitably overturned, with the eventual sudden collapse of the building.

Ancient buildings, Harvey continued, are subject to certain recurrent causes of decay. By the systematic study of such structures, general principles can be derived that can be used to ascertain the causes of decay of other buildings in distress. In particular, the scientific conservationist seeks to distinguish between structural movement (known as drift) caused by ordinary, ascertainable causes (such as traffic vibration or the settling of earth) and that resulting from fundamental structural defects requiring radical reinforcement.

In Harvey's view, a historical building in danger of collapse expresses its appeal for help in an intelligible language of decay and movement. Such signs are symptoms of deeper structural defects and tell a story about the balance of parts and the whole structural circumstances of the building. Drift in a building resulting from destructive forces can be estimated by carefully observing the positions of cracks and the deflection of walls from their regular alignment. Without a proper survey of this kind, the causes of movement in old buildings risk being wrongly diagnosed.

The director of the DPW first contacted Harvey for advice in July 1929. Besides his impeccable qualifications and long experience, Harvey had spent 1909 in Jerusalem and Bethlehem studying the Churches of the Holy Sepulchre and the Nativity, as well as the area of al-Haram al-Sharif.[25]

While the British government was sorting out the terms of Harvey's contract, a large piece fell out of a ridged rib in one of the high vaults in the transept. But it was not until October 1930 that Harvey got down to the report. He had to work in his London office using photographs, plans, and sections of the old dome and drum provided by the Jerusalem authorities. He was expressly not called on to advise on work below the level of the dome and was not informed of the broken rib.

Harvey finally submitted his report and plans for reconstruction of the dome in March 1931. Most of this report is as sensible a set of observations and recommendations as could be expected from someone not on the spot. He pointed out the difficulty of arriving at a "true estimate of the state of the old stones from photographs." Nevertheless, he did notice a couple of disquieting features of the building.

One was the appearance of cracks over all the windows of the drum and one of the windows of the south transept. A two-ton chandelier had been suspended from the dome on a long chain. During an earthquake, every vibration would create stress, shaking the stability of the drum and the pendentives on which the drum rested. The other was "a serious bowing out" of the south façade above the main entrance. Given the unusual height (for Palestine) of the tower at the crossing, 31 meters (101.7 feet), and the materials used in its construction—stone-faced masonry supposedly held together by a lime mortar core—Harvey had cause for concern.

His advice was that "all parts of the substructure and the foundations should be examined in detail for any signs of failure." This was "important because apart from the dome structure having been damaged by earthquakes the great age and the continual vibration by wind pressure may have strained the building." Harvey then went on to provide detailed instructions for the rebuilding of the dome and drum.[26]

Unfortunately, a detailed examination of the substructure was not carried out. The Greek patriarchate did agree to let the DPW carry out soundings of the piers' foundations but then objected to their extent and depth. In order to keep to its pressing schedule, the DPW contented itself with a cursory investigation, though it did factor the unknowns into its stress calculations.

In June 1931, the director of the DPW decided to go ahead with the restoration of the cupola on the basis of Harvey's report. From the first, this was a remarkable project, involving the use of dressed stones, without benefit of reinforced concrete, in the construction of a dome.

To build the cupola required transporting rough-hewn blocks of Malaki limestone from a quarry near Ramallah to the roof of the Holy Sepulchre. This stone is easy to work with but on weathering hardens into a creamy gold stone of great resilience. Thirty skilled masons, working for twelve months, dressed thousands of voussoirs—wedge-shaped stones that had to slot together with absolute precision, course after course, in a smooth convergent curve. Construction of the dome began in April 1932, and installation of the voussoirs proceeded very quickly. Meanwhile, the inner mortar core of the drum, which consisted of little more than dry rubbish—powder and loose stones—was cleaned out and refilled with lean concrete. Cracked stones were cut out and replaced with new ones. The forty-eight marble columns, bases, and capitals were mostly replaced.[27]

At this point Austen Harrison, architect for the project, began to have serious doubts. Measurements at the north and south façades showed significant movement, and further investigation of the arches and vaults strongly suggested that the entire structure of the edifice required an indeterminate, but considerable, amount of repair. In the summer of 1932, Harrison advised suspending operations to avoid causing irreparable harm.

In a strongly worded memorandum, he declined "to repair ancient buildings otherwise than in accordance with the generally accepted principles of conservation" and questioned the competence of the DPW to carry out conservation work on the Holy Sepulchre. Despite his best efforts, "only the most reckless of optimists could suppose that these buildings are now sound."[28]

Work on the cupola was now temporarily suspended by the acting director of the DPW, J. F. Rowlands, who was unwilling to risk loading tons of stone onto a structure that might be unsound. Noting that the discovery of various unforeseen deficiencies had made reconstruction "much more complicated than was contemplated," he recommended a survey throughout by a competent person.[29]

———

The future of the project now came before Sir Arthur Wauchope, the new high commissioner. "Little Arthur," as he was known to his subordinates, was not a man to suffer fools gladly. Of slight build, he wore his silvery hair long and had the habit of staring into space with his mouth open. He was a career army officer of indomitable will who had been severely wounded twice and commanded a battalion in the trenches in World War I. Eccentric and self-important, he struck his own war medal, which he awarded to soldiers who distinguished themselves. He was promoted to the rank of major general in 1923.

Appointed high commissioner of Palestine in 1931, Wauchope had great ambitions for the success of his administration, drove his staff hard, and totally identified himself with the task of developing the country. Indeed, he spent a great deal of his own private fortune on pet projects for which no government funding was available, such as experimental agriculture and training young Arabs. At the same time, he was an aesthete, a lover of music, art, and fine china, and the perfect host—he kept a beautiful table at Government House decorated with mess silver on loan from his old regiment.[30]

After the 1929 riots, the budgetary situation in Palestine steadily deteriorated, and very limited funds were available from the British Treasury. Wauchope, who loved the small details of administration, immersed himself in micromanaging government finances, intervening in local tax collection and querying the treasurer's figures.

Back in Jerusalem from home leave, Richmond came to see Wauchope about the Katholikon dome and the wider problem of the instability of the Church of the Resurrection. Wauchope was fascinated and told Richmond to put his concerns into writing. From this point on, Wauchope became increasingly involved in the restoration of the Holy Sepulchre and did what he could, in difficult circumstances, to support the project.

Richmond wrote a seminal analysis of the situation based on a survey by his department. The influence of Harvey's textbook on conservation, with its advice to look beyond the symptoms of decay to the underlying structural defects, is evident in this survey. An attached portfolio of photographs illustrated the damage. It did not take much imagination to connect the dots. Even the original captions are an ominous catalogue of disintegration: "crack...crack...open joints in the masonry...dislocation of stones...dislocation of stones of the cornice...cracks between cross-vaults...bulging of wall...bulging and opened joints...outward lean and bulging cornice...cracks over the arches...ribs badly calcined...perished dry rubble."[31]

Richmond began by demonstrating that the Crusader edifice had to be considered a unit consisting of various structurally interdependent parts, so that the instability of any one part must affect the whole. The Katholikon dome, covering the towering middle bay of the transept, was carried on four pendentives—triangular segments of vault—supported by four arches at the crossing. For the latter arches to stand, they in turn had to be abutted by the arches and vaults that supported the rest of the building, north, south, east, and west.

In an arresting sentence, he described the mother church as an arched and vaulted structure that was "alive with pressures and counter-pressures so disposed by its designers as to ensure a balance that would not be easily upset." That balance, however, had been disturbed by eight centuries of progressive deterioration and the 1808 fire, not to mention twenty-three recorded earthquakes. No real consolidation or conservation had ever been carried out. Apart from the visual evidence, common sense dictated that the stability of the building was likely to be seriously compromised.

A number of disturbing facts that had recently come to light reinforced his foreboding. Layer on layer of waterproofing material had been added to the roofs of the church over the years, placing an enormous, unplanned extra load on the vaults. This only added to the pressures transmitted through the arched and vaulted system to the abutting southern and northern walls of the transept. The vaults were visibly cracking in places. When plumbed, the southern façade was found to be bulging outward seventeen centimeters (about six inches). Other evidence indicated that both outer walls, buttressing the entire church, were moving outward.

It was true, Richmond observed, that buildings like the Holy Sepulchre had a remarkable ability to readjust to shifting stresses. But there was a point where decay overtook the capacity for adaptation. "When that stage is reached the building collapses." It might occur suddenly, but it was "merely the spectacular conclusion of a long process of unobserved deterioration."

Richmond's recommendations were clear. An expert technical survey had to take place without further delay to provide the data essential to assessing the building's overall structural condition, diagnosing the causes of that condition, and recommending remedies. Since there was no one with the necessary qualifications in the country, a specialist would have to be brought in from outside. In the meantime, the reconstruction of the dome should be postponed.[32]

Shortly after Richmond submitted his report, he received a letter from the great archaeologist Father Hugues Vincent, reinforcing his case. Pointing to ominous signs of decay, Father Vincent expressed surprise that a new dome was being built over the Katholikon before the rest of the building had been strengthened to take up the new pressures. He strongly urged that the structure be consolidated before it was too late.[33]

While deliberations were under way, work on the dome continued. On October 10, 1932, Rowlands again recommended that the work should be stopped, this time entirely, leaving the dome unfinished. Faced with government indecision, however, Rowlands changed his mind. With winter and the original November target date approaching, he argued that it would be best to finish the job, since the whole could then set homogeneously and the added weight would not be great. Moreover, a complete dome could be waterproofed, and no temporary roof would be required before the onset of the rains.[34]

General Wauchope accepted this argument. He agreed that the cupola should be finished, but without the heavy outer lead sheathing. At the same time, he also accepted Richmond's recommendation of an immediate survey. This compromise decision involved an internal contradiction: what if the survey indicated retrospectively that the underlying structure at the crossing could not bear the weight of the new dome?[35]

Richmond's report came as a surprise to the colonial office, which was aggrieved that it had not been consulted earlier. It therefore approved with alacrity Wauchope's proposal of a survey.[36] Its officials were only too aware of the political implications of a disaster at the Holy Sepulchre. The 1929 Wailing Wall riots had already been a major setback for the Palestine Mandate.

William Harvey was therefore again approached, this time to investigate the condition of the Church of the Holy Sepulchre firsthand, together with his architect son, John. He was to spend eighty-four days in Palestine and was also to conduct a survey of the Church of the Nativity.[37]

The major Christian communities in the Holy Sepulchre did not conceal their lack of enthusiasm for a survey. They disliked government involvement and had little faith in the government's competence in conservation matters in the light of its mismanagement of the dome's reconstruction. The Greek patriarchate was particularly exasperated to discover that, having been asked to pay cash in advance, the estimated cost of repairs had now gone up from £5,900 to £9,500.[38]

When first approached, the communities made a plea for postponement on the grounds of financial stringency. After months of negotiation, they finally agreed to surveys being carried out at both the Holy Sepulchre and Nativity. Any reports would have to be submitted to their own experts. They would not oppose temporary measures if they were shown to be essential to the safety of the edifice, but preferred to postpone them until permanent works of conservation were undertaken at some (indeterminate) later date. They insisted that they were unable to contribute to the cost of a survey. Not until the end of October 1933, five weeks after Harvey arrived in Jerusalem, did the communities agree to the erection of light scaffolding in the Holy Sepulchre to enable the inspection of the crossing of the Greek Choir and transepts.[39]

The churches' refusal to pay for a survey left the British government in a quandary. It did not believe it was liable for repairs at the Christian holy places but could hardly wash its hands of the matter. Rather than face the "obloquy" that would follow if the Holy Sepulchre were allowed to fall into hopeless disrepair, it decided that it had no choice but to fund a three-month trip by Harvey at the expense of the Palestine taxpayer. The Treasury approved expenditure of about £750 for the purpose. This was to prove a serious underestimate, as Harvey stayed for a year and a half.[40]

Even so, the decision was to prove a source of political embarrassment to the government in London. Members of Parliament intensely resented the churches' refusal to pay and the imposition of the cost, in effect, on non-Christians, who were a large majority in Palestine.[41] Having recently built new churches on Mount Tabor, in the Garden of Gethsemane, and elsewhere, the Roman Catholic Church in Palestine did not appear to lack funds. The Greek Orthodox Patriarchate's notorious record of financial irregularity and "the moral scandals which prevail in its midst," paraded in two government reports in the 1920s, did not help the government's case much either.[42]

Within days of his arrival on September 19, 1933, Harvey confirmed Richmond's worst fears in almost every detail. After his very first, brief examination of the Holy Sepulchre, he issued an urgent alert, warning that the church was "structurally in imminent danger." Moreover, visitors risked being hit by falling stones from the decayed stonework over the main door.

He judged that the greatest danger of collapse was at the end wall of the north transept. Due to outward thrust from the Katholikon dome and the vaults at the crossing, there was a severe overhang—in other words, the north wall was bulging outward.

> While collapse might occur at any moment, due to special vibration such as that caused by an earthquake shock or a violent storm, it cannot be too strongly emphasized that collapse within a comparatively short term of years may be regarded as inevitable if the wall is left in its present state, even without such special motive cause for failure.

Urgent steps, he continued, had to be taken to prevent further movement. Considerable time had elapsed since the 1927 earthquake. Further delay risked a fate similar to that of the famous campanile of St. Mark's, Venice, early in the century, which had collapsed after the repeated warnings of the architect in charge had been disregarded.[43]

After years of delay, the authorities quickly issued instructions to shore up the church. It was to take eighteen months, from the moment of decision to completion of the task, before the imminent danger was removed. These measures of consolidation were supposed to be temporary, until it could be decided what permanent restoration was required.[44]

Harvey's initial recommendation was for shoring to the southern façade and northern outer wall, protective casing to avert the danger of falling masses of stone, internal scaffolding at the eastern apse and crossing supporting the piers and arches, and an external steel girdle encircling the upper central mass, that is, the high vaults, tower, and apse of the Crusader basilica.[45]

As Harvey continued his investigation of the entire Holy Sepulchre complex, yet more temporary shoring was found to be essential. The rotunda over the tomb, the southern chapels adjacent to the Parvis, and all the other buildings clustered around and effectively buttressing the Crusader basilica needed to be supported by scaffolding or shored up by stanchions and beams to prevent their collapse. Following Harvey's fourth interim report, Wauchope was in a position at the beginning of December 1933 to alert London to the gravity of the situation: "I am advised that the processes which he describes are well known as those which immediately precede final collapse."[46]

In January 1934, as Harvey was working on his final report, a slight earthquake tremor was felt. There was no doubt in his mind that movement was continuing. He judged from other medieval abbeys such as Rievaulx and Tintern that the disintegration he observed in Jerusalem had reached a critical point, beyond which further decay would inevitably lead to downfall.

In his final report, Harvey showed that the principal danger to the Holy Sepulchre arose from the weight and thrusts of the Katholikon dome, the rotunda dome, and surrounding vaults on their spheres of influence—in effect, the rest of the church. All the exterior walls leaned outward, a tendency that earthquake shocks, culminating in the violent tremor of 1927, had exacerbated. The process of disintegration Harvey described was exactly as Richmond had depicted it. Like a ship sinking to great depths, the church was being forced apart at the seams, its sides splaying out uncontrollably.

An alarming picture emerged of gaping joints, pervasive cracks, overhangs, vaults detached from shifting walls, and split columns. Every part of the church was affected—the south transept, Katholikon, rotunda, Calvary, adjacent chapels, and monasteries. The most dangerous evidence of movement was confirmed to be at the end wall of the north transept. A great overhang at the top of the wall and the poor state of the mortar joints meant that facing stones might fall off at any time, the high vaults behind soon following. Though decay was rampant throughout, the grave state of the bell tower and the Chapel of St. James on the Parvis (with an overhang of twenty-two centimeters—about eight inches—over the adjoining alley) received special mention.

Besides requiring measures of immediate consolidation—which could only be temporary and palliative—Harvey also presented an outline scheme of permanent restoration. As Richmond had feared, the mortar that kept the masonry of the church together had perished from top to bottom. Harvey called for this useless debris to be sluiced out of walls and piers and replaced by new cement inserted in the form of liquid grout. Where necessary, the piers underpinning the structure could be provided with a new core of reinforced concrete, surrounded by a sheath of the original stonework. Steel bands would be inserted in the walls at different levels to provide reinforcement and counteract the thrust of the arches and vaults above.

In addition to these essential measures, Harvey also suggested a list of optional alternatives intended to restore as much as possible of the pristine dignity of the church. It included opening long-blocked doors and windows to let light into this gloomiest of all cathedrals and the removal of the dingy nineteenth-century plastering to reveal the fine medieval detail beneath.[47]

By the end of 1933, all parties with any stake in the survival of the Holy Sepulchre had been alerted. The major communities were kept fully informed throughout the investigation, receiving all Harvey's reports. It was clear to the Palestine government "that further work of some magnitude will be necessary to restore the church to a state of permanent security."[48] Yet implementation of the measures of conservation envisaged by Harvey did not even begin until 1963, thirty years after he first sounded the alarm.

CHAPTER FOUR | # William Harvey's Temporary Repairs

A LARMED BY WILLIAM HARVEY'S prognostications of impending catastrophe and consequent huge expenses, Greeks and Latins
sought second opinions on the state of the Church of the Resurrection. Their
own experts refuted Harvey's diagnosis, and the two communities submitted
written objections to the government's plans for restoration, making cooperation appear unlikely.

The Greek Orthodox report was written by Anastasios K. Orlandos and
Periclis Paraskévopoulos. Orlandos was an historian of classical Greek and
Byzantine architecture who had studied architecture and philosophy in
Athens and gone on to attend universities in England, France, and Italy. He
was appointed professor of architecture at Athens Polytechnic in 1920 and
excavated the ruins of ancient Stymphalos from 1924–30. Paraskévopoulos
was professor of engineering at Athens Polytechnic.

Relying for their information on Harvey's preliminary reports and their
own cursory survey, the two men were not at all convinced of continuing
movement, let alone imminent collapse. They did observe long-term, cu-
mulative damage from earthquakes but somehow simply did not see the
cracks that Harvey saw. Much of the deterioration they put down to the effect
of metal wedges and nails inserted in the walls and vaults in 1810 to hold the
stones and plaster in place. As a result of rusting, they argued, the iron had
expanded and splintered the masonry. Their observation was true but insufficient to explain the overall state of the building.

So, on balance, they did not believe the condition of the church justified the extensive system of supports Harvey urgently proposed. They were particularly skeptical about the need for scaffolding at the crossing, which would require the closure of the Katholikon and needlessly disrupt services. However, they were concerned about the state of the rotunda pillars and did concur that strong supports were required there. In their conclusion, and assuming that money was no object, they suggested a plan for the thorough consolidation of the building.[1]

Luigi Marangoni, the consultant architect brought in by the Custody of the Holy Land and one of the most eminent conservationists of his generation, wrote a particularly critical counter-report. Born in 1872, Marangoni had been appointed *proto,* or custodian, of St. Mark's Basilica, Venice, in 1910 and gained international renown. Among other commissions, he was called in as consultant by the Ottoman authorities in Istanbul to advise on the conservation of Hagia Sophia, which had been damaged in the 1894 earthquake that leveled the grand bazaar. Between 1924 and 1940, he worked on Rome's Palazzo Venezia, which was the office of the Italian dictator Benito Mussolini, beginning in 1929. Marangoni also worked on various town planning schemes, a passion of Mussolini's regime. Official patronage, therefore, put Marangoni at the heart of the Fascist establishment.[2]

Harvey had already spent five months investigating the state of the church by the time of Marangoni's arrival in Jerusalem at the end of February 1934. When the two met to discuss the situation, Harvey told his Italian colleague that he was absolutely certain that the edifice might collapse at any moment. Marangoni asked how he could be so certain and Harvey replied in two words: "the cracks." This failed to impress Marangoni, because Harvey had not put any telltales in place. Telltales are strips of glass or chalk fixed over a fracture that snap if there is continuing movement. The sound of their giving way became an ominous indicator of the progressive deterioration of the Holy Sepulchre in subsequent years.

As a result of this conversation, Harvey installed 265 telltales throughout the church over the next three weeks. On March 19, 1934, the day he was to file his own report, Marangoni examined the telltales and discovered that only one, on the wall between the eastern apse and the Katholikon dome, had actually fractured. On the basis of this evidence, he felt "tranquil" that no part of the church was in imminent danger and that there was no urgent need for emergency scaffolding.[3]

Marangoni's report was a rebuttal of the five interim reports Harvey prepared between September 1933 and March 1934. Marangoni did not dispute the evident signs of decay but noted that these were nothing new. He explicitly rejected Harvey's central thesis that the structure of the church was fundamentally unsound. In his view, only the short outer lengths of wall were unsupported and vulnerable; the rest was buttressed by surrounding buildings.

Marangoni thought the decay was largely the result of seismic activity over the centuries and localized causes. The southern façade had been damaged by the 1808 fire and rainwater; the cement composition of the northern wall was defective; the bell tower, lacking its upper stories, had long been at the mercy of the weather and the vibration from its bells. He also criticized the weight of the new Katholikon dome, which he thought should have been built of light metal arches rather than stone voussoirs.

Marangoni's view, therefore, was that most of Harvey's proposals for reinforcement were either hasty or premature, and would anyway prove ineffective. He advised delay until all the facts were in. Writing of the northern wall, for instance, he argued that there was "a case for leaving things as they are for some time yet," while keeping an eye on the telltales. Supporting materials could be kept ready nearby but should not be erected straightaway, as this would prejudice research into the movement of the structure. Harvey's interim reports, he believed, provided insufficient information to resolve the problem.[4]

Of course, the authorities did not have the luxury of waiting for certainty. If there was even a suspicion—let alone reasonable probability—of imminent collapse, emergency action had to be taken swiftly and decisively. As the chief secretary wrote to church leaders in March 1934, thanking them for their opinions, in case of doubt it was far better to take emergency measures "than to neglect a precaution which may conceivably save hundreds of lives."[5]

The critical reports written by the Greek and Latin experts soon hardened into received truth and shaped the communities' later reluctance to cooperate with the authorities' plans for consolidation and restoration. It is true that the two reports were based on insufficient evidence and snap judgments, but the government also mishandled the situation.

Harvey's analysis of the condition of the Holy Sepulchre was grounded in his integrated theory of the decay of ancient buildings set out in his 1925 textbook. The cracks told him of the existence of underlying structural defects and destructive forces. None of the communities' experts read the edifice in this way. However, they should have been given the opportunity to hear Harvey's views and ask questions in an appropriate professional setting prior to the publication of his final report.

It would have been difficult to convince the Latins. Even before Marangoni submitted his written report the French consul reported that they had already made up their minds. They were skeptical about any immediate danger and disputed the need for urgent repairs that would merely arouse disagreements over the Status Quo. They suspected the British authorities of having an ulterior motive in proposing permanent restoration of the Holy Sepulchre, namely, a desire to obtain a foothold for the Anglican Church. They alleged that the government had persuaded Harvey to give his report a more pessimistic tone than was really warranted in order to supply the colonial office with ammunition to put pressure on the three major communities.[6]

The Greeks might have been more open to persuasion. Their locum tenens, or acting patriarch, Archbishop Timotheos, was a pragmatic and reasonable individual. Ernest Richmond, however, turned down a request from the Greek patriarchate for a meeting in the presence of their experts. In his view, the communities had no right to be consulted, and the government had to maintain undivided control.[7] His assumption that the communities could be ignored in this way and that they would meekly fall into line was—one can see, albeit with the benefit of hindsight—a serious error.

Even though fresh evidence was coming in all the time to corroborate Harvey's diagnosis, it was not shared with Marangoni, Orlandos, or Paraskévopoulos until it appeared in Harvey's final report, which was published in book form in late 1935 by Oxford University Press. New cracks were reported on March 20, 1934, in the Arch of Triumph between the rotunda and the Katholikon, in two columns in the north transept, and in a vault over the south transept. Telltales placed on the south front, on the high vault of the south transept, and on the high vault abutting the apse had all fractured.

After new scaffolding was erected in April 1934, Harvey found fresh evidence of progressive movement, and vaulting stones were found to be about to fall on both transepts, including one weighing about twelve kilos (about twenty-six pounds). Most would have been sufficient to kill a person had they fallen. All this tended to confirm the diagnosis of uncontrolled thrusts at the crossing and convinced Harvey that the building was moving.[8]

Admittedly, the communities' experts had gone home by then, but there was no attempt to keep them informed. In the end, only the municipal architect, Cliff Holliday, hired in his private capacity by the Armenian patriarchate, corroborated Harvey's findings.

Among the Latins, the first to realize the true state of affairs was Father Hugues Vincent. In an internal report submitted to the Custody in May 1936, he warned that the Holy Sepulchre was in "a dangerous state" and, without wishing to sow panic, noted that immediate repairs were needed in order to prevent a "catastrophe."[9] When this had no effect, he went public in 1938, deploring the "superficial examination of otherwise highly distinguished architects" and criticizing the recriminations the communities had leveled at Harvey for his emergency measures.[10] But by now it was too late, with the Palestinian Arabs in full-scale revolt against British rule.

In a final note of March 15, 1935, Harvey reported the completion of the temporary consolidation of the church after fifteen months' hard work. Telltales showed that movement throughout the building had been checked. The Holy Sepulchre, he concluded, might now be considered safe from immediate danger of collapse. But he repeatedly warned that temporary shoring weakened over time, so it would be wise to insert permanent reinforcement within the next two years.[11]

The entire edifice was now held in a tight embrace of wood and steel. A steel band ran around the inside of the rotunda, and a tension ring encircled the upper parts of the Katholikon, including the unfinished dome. Shoring supported the exposed southern and northern outer walls of the edifice. Four massive steel tubes bolted together and embedded in concrete blocks propped up the front of the basilica on the Parvis.[12] They almost totally obscured the façade for years to come.

<hr />

Harvey's stay had been much more expensive than budgeted. His original commission was for a visit of eighty-four days at a cost of about £750. In the end he stayed for eighteen months, at a cost of more than £5,000. Besides salaries and wages, the work of temporary consolidation proved expensive. When the original appropriation ran out in August 1934, work had to be suspended for some weeks.[13]

If it had proved so difficult to fund emergency repairs, how was the permanent restoration of the Holy Sepulchre to be paid for? At the time, Harvey put the cost of essential repairs at £92,400. This estimate increased to £150,000 by 1937, then £200,000 in 1938. For purposes of comparison, this was exactly the cost of building and equipping Ringway Airport, opened to serve the Manchester area of northern England in June 1938.

Several basic funding options were open to the British government. The first was international funding. A historical precedent existed in the 1862 international treaty between Turkey, France, and Russia that had enabled the repair of the great dome of the rotunda, with costs divided equally. Leopold Amery, the colonial secretary, rejected this idea in 1929, ostensibly because of rival French, Italian, and Spanish claims to represent the Catholic Church, and the lack of acceptable candidates to represent Greek Orthodox and Armenian interests. Greece was not considered, and the Soviet Union was out of the question. Besides, he did not want to give foreign governments a say at the holy places.

Amery's conclusion at the time was that the local religious authorities could not be bypassed but should somehow be induced to entrust the Palestine government with the conservation of the holy places.[14] The problem with this suggestion was that the major communities, while appealing to the inviolability of the Status Quo, in reality did not want to see Britain filling the central role Turkey had played earlier because it limited their freedom to act.

The second funding option was the public purse. Parliament's lack of enthusiasm for this plan, however, was made very clear at parliamentary question time on no fewer than four occasions in the spring of 1934. For example, on April 25 the colonial secretary, Sir Philip Cunliffe-Lister, was questioned in the House of Commons about the steps being taken to prevent the Church of the Holy Sepulchre falling into ruin. After assuring the House that measures were in hand to protect the church, he was cross-examined by Colonel Josiah Wedgwood, a famous parliamentary gadfly and great-grandson of the nonconformist pottery manufacturer.

> COL. WEDGWOOD: Is British money, or Palestinian money, being used
>   for this purpose?
> SIR P. CUNLIFFE-LISTER: Certainly there is no charge upon the British
>   tax-payer . . .
> COL. WEDGWOOD: Does the right hon. Gentleman realise that it is
>   not fair to take the money of Jews and Muslims in order to rebuild
>   a Christian Church?
> SIR P. CUNLIFFE-LISTER: I must greatly deprecate statements of that
>   kind. This is a great world memorial, and it is obviously in the
>   interests of the country in which it is situated that it should be
>   maintained.[15]

Cunliffe-Lister's revelation to Parliament on May 7, 1934, "that the ecclesiastical bodies concerned were unable at present to provide the necessary funds" and that the Palestine authorities were provisionally meeting the cost of emergency works was unwelcome news and embarrassing to the government. The solution of a Treasury grant was publicly ruled out, and denial of financial liability remained a central plank of government policy.[16] One possible way out of the conundrum was a dedicated tax on travelers. But this was again examined by a committee in 1933 and found to be impracticable.

The third and seemingly most obvious option was for the major communities themselves to raise the money and bear the cost. Throughout history, the churches had always avidly sought to undertake repairs at the holy places in order to assert their rights of ownership. But now, ironically, when the government was persuaded of the pressing need for repairs and only too eager for the churches to pay, the Greeks and Latins lost all their enthusiasm.

They had various reasons for dragging their feet. With counter-reports to hand, they were skeptical of Harvey's findings and mistrusted Britain's motives. They were also convinced that their mother church, like a beloved parent, was indestructible. When approached by the district commissioner to contribute £250 to help pay for Harvey's visit, they refused to do so.

They agreed in principle that an expert survey should be undertaken but claimed that they were "unable to contribute to its cost on the ground of the present financial stringency throughout the world, which, in their opinion, renders it unlikely that adequate funds could be raised for the purpose by voluntary subscription."[17] This is like refusing to go to the doctor because you fear she may recommend expensive treatment.

In the past, the Latins had succeeded in raising funds for construction projects in the Holy Land, and the Greeks had only recently invested in a number of new buildings in the Christian Quarter. Besides, they could also expect help from the government in Athens. In general, both the Greek and Armenian patriarchates were substantial property owners in Palestine, and from 1933 onward, land values and rents shot up with the arrival of Jewish refugees from Hitler's Germany.

When the major communities proved obdurate, the Palestine government gave up on them and covered the costs resulting from Harvey's survey and works of temporary consolidation.[18] This set a precedent and established a pattern of ecclesiastical noncooperation at an early stage in the repairs. While the government could not compel the communities to pay for repairs, it was certainly entitled to expect them to be more cooperative. Both sides had things they wanted from each other, so there were obvious deals to be made.

The communities had their own individual requests for renovations at the Holy Sepulchre awaiting government approval. The Latins, for instance, had had an application for permission to redecorate their Chapel of the Nailing to the Cross on Calvary pending since 1930. Father Nazzareno Jacopozzi, the custos, had even written to Richmond in April 1933 complaining of a long delay. The government finally issued a ruling on the permissible subjects for the new mosaics in June 1933, at the very time that the Custody professed itself unable to contribute to the cost of repairs to the Holy Sepulchre.[19]

All the churches ran considerable establishments in Palestine and depended for the ease of their existence on British good will in the form of exemptions, permits, and benefits. They enjoyed exemption from customs duties, produced wine on which no excise duty was levied, and owned property on which no land tax was paid. The Notre Dame de France hospice provided hotel facilities for pilgrim-tourists without paying taxes and profitably sold wines and spirits without paying duty. A conservative estimate put the loss to revenue on all these exemptions at more than £50,000 a year, money that could have gone toward the cost of restoring the edifice.[20]

These were privileges within the discretion of the authorities and not rights under the Status Quo. New churches and facilities were built all the time, requiring planning permission, building permits, and import licenses for building materials. Obviously, crude pressure would have been ineffective and would probably have led to an outcry. Indeed, the withholding of government approval for the newly elected Greek Orthodox patriarch after the 1935 election proved totally counterproductive. But each side was entitled to expect the other to respect its genuine needs and concerns.

Two factors prevented the Palestine government from adopting a realistic policy of reciprocity toward the communities. One was a high-minded distaste for give and take as reflecting the mentality of the bazaar. The other was a reluctance in Government House to consider the resident churches as anything other than unruly subordinates. Wauchope was used to his orders being obeyed, not discussed. Richmond, the influential director of antiquities, was also loath to admit the claims or criticisms of the communities.[21] But a relationship in which the parties seek to accommodate their mutual needs is one of equality of status. It was also wholly sensible in the affair of the restoration, since both sides possessed a veto.

In November 1934, the colonial secretary, Sir Philip Cunliffe-Lister, wrote to Wauchope suggesting that he open negotiations with the ecclesiastical authorities in order to secure their friendly cooperation in the permanent restoration of the Church of the Holy Sepulchre (and at the same time the Church of the Nativity). During the course of these talks, he might propose the appointment of a special commission to deal with funding and administration, on which the government and communities would be represented.[22]

In his belated reply, Wauchope rejected the idea of a special commission because it "would tend to impede the full Government control of the works which is essential to their rapid and effective execution." Neither questions of funding nor administration nor planning should be referred to the communities. Harvey's proposals for essential repairs (though not optional improvements) should be presented to them on a take-it-or-leave-it basis. Indeed, it was essential that the government should avoid giving the impression that it entertained any doubts regarding the necessity of these works, since these were a matter of public safety. However, the communities might be invited to launch a worldwide appeal.[23]

The soldierly fallacy at the heart of Wauchope's argument was the assumption that once Harvey had defined the objective of the operation, the problem reduced itself to one of efficient and expeditious implementation. For this, unified command was vital. But in politics and diplomacy, where different communities have legitimately different values and wishes, consensus must precede implementation. What use is unified command without an agreed plan and with divided forces?

The colonial office pointed out the serious flaws in Wauchope's approach, realizing that it would lead the communities to conclude that he was not giving them an opportunity for adequate discussion. They would be unlikely to cooperate in launching an appeal for funds for work they thought unnecessary. The possibility of intervention by the Greek government and the Vatican, and attacks by "Catholic propagandists" alleging that Catholic rights in Palestine were endangered, was also of concern. The advice of the colonial office was to place no restriction on the points open for discussion.[24]

Following this exchange, John Hathorn Hall, the chief secretary of the Palestine government, wrote to church leaders on May 2, 1936, in an attempt to gain their support for the permanent restoration of the Holy Sepulchre. He asked for their views on Harvey's recommendations. Repairs deemed structurally indispensable were not open to discussion, only nonessential work desirable on aesthetic grounds. All work would have to be entrusted to a single authority charged with full control, without prejudice to the rights and claims of the communities under the Status Quo. This authority could be the government or a suitable and competent expert acceptable to all the parties concerned.

Harvey had estimated the cost of essential repairs at approximately £92,400 and of desirable but nonessential improvements at £25,400. Hall explained that the Palestine government could not make any contribution out of revenue, nor could it promote a public appeal. He therefore encouraged the communities to cooperate in drafting a worldwide appeal or come up with a better idea for raising funds. If they failed to do this and repairs were unduly delayed, he warned, the government might have to limit access to the Holy Sepulchre or close it altogether in the interest of public safety.[25]

Notwithstanding skepticism toward the Harvey report and government plans for restoration, there was room for an exchange of views to determine whether common ground existed between the government and the major communities. Harvey could have been brought in to explain his conclusions.

A satisfactory joint mechanism for managing repairs and agreement on a schedule of work to be carried out were not unattainable. What is certain is that the consent of all the principal parties was a precondition for restoration of the Holy Sepulchre, and this could only be obtained through negotiation. Compromise would at any rate have been better than deadlock.

Instead of a discussion or negotiation, as the colonial office suggested, Hathorn Hall proposed a mere expression of views. The letter was sent to all church leaders except the Ethiopian bishop—tactlessly placing Greeks, Latins, and Armenians on a par with the minor communities. Under the Status Quo, the Syrians and Copts were not recognized to have rights of possession, and the major communities would never accept their sharing in the restoration.

Antonio Barluzzi, the Franciscans' resident architect, reflecting Latin opinion, reacted to Hathorn Hall's proposals just as the colonial office had predicted. He wondered about the "strangeness of English intentions," rejecting as totally unacceptable a scheme that subordinated the communities to the government, leaving them to fund and implement projects with which they disagreed.[26]

Monsignor Testa, the apostolic delegate, was the only church dignitary ever to reply to Hathorn Hall's letter, the most crucial initiative on the Holy Sepulchre of the entire Mandate period.[27] He offered a constructive counterproposal. In order to avoid difficulty in the course of the work, he suggested that the government investigate in depth the extent and cost of the restorations required. Inquiring about the views of the other major communities, he wondered whether it might be possible to take the opportunity to conclude an overall arrangement removing all causes of dispute. He also suggested that the custom of a Muslim doorkeeper be abolished.

For the first time, Testa floated the radical idea of a new church. Deeming the present building "unworthy of the precious memories which it enshrines," he suggested that a reconstruction of the entire basilica be considered, freeing it "from the wretched dwelling places" that had become attached to it over the centuries. He concluded by hinting that the immense cost of the project merited an amicable solution to these questions.[28]

Testa's reply was a reasonable invitation to dialogue. He was saying that he needed to be convinced about the need for the repairs proposed and the price tag put on them. He directed the government's attention to those with rights in the building, that is, the major communities, and intimated that restoration presupposed an arrangement between them. His remark about removing the Muslim doorkeeper was a way of suggesting that the church was owned by the major communities and not the sovereign (whom the doorkeeper represented). The scheme for a new basilica was at this point simply a vision. Several of these ideas were more or less impractical within the framework of the Status Quo, but the evident wish to be consulted as a partner and the implicit advice that the others be considered in the same light were valid points.

The government rebutted the apostolic delegate's letter in its entirety, as if putting an inconsequential underling in his place.[29] So much for an expression of views—there was to be no dialogue; it was take it or leave it.

Later, Archbishop Testa was to interpret the British position as an attempt, unworthy of a civilized power, to restore the sovereign's claims to the Holy Sepulchre. The Holy Sepulchre, he insisted, was the common property of the three major communities.[30]

Ironically, the government's position was exactly the opposite of the one imputed to it; it had renounced any pretension to ownership in 1928. But it had clearly failed to communicate this to the communities or to draw the logical conclusion from its refusal to accept financial responsibility. If the churches were to share in the cost, they had to share in the decision-making.

At least the Latins had responded to Hathorn Hall. No reply was received from any of the other communities. The government had completely failed to engage them. The worst gap was left by the silence of the Greek Orthodox patriarchate, since no work of restoration could be envisaged in its absence. Government misjudgment was directly responsible for this.

Patriarch Damianos had died in August 1931, plunging the convent—the local shorthand term for the Greek Orthodox Patriarchate—into another crisis over relations between the Greek church establishment and their Arab parishioners. Disagreement over electoral reform delayed elections until 1935. The result was a victory for Archbishop Timotheos, the former chief secretary of the patriarchate.

Like his patron Damianos, Timotheos Themlis was a native of the island of Samos in the Aegean Sea. A charming, intelligent, and dignified figure who had studied at Magdalen College, Oxford, Timotheos spoke excellent English. As chief secretary, he had taken pains to cultivate good relations with the British authorities and the Anglican Church. At the beginning, he was popular with the clergy of St. George's Cathedral, the seat of the Anglican bishop in Jerusalem. One cleric described him as "a thoroughly presentable person, interesting to meet, and knows how to hold his knife and fork; smokes if he feels thoroughly at home."[31]

His election placed an experienced and energetic administrator on the patriarchal throne. The authorities would never find a better man to work with. He was pragmatic and moderate in tone in his dealings with the authorities. He could get a grip on the patriarchate's finances and enforce discipline on the monks. If anybody could get the restoration of the Holy Sepulchre moving, he was the one.

But General Wauchope now clumsily chose to try to impose reforms on the patriarchate by effectively suspending the result of the election. His motives were well-meaning; the discrimination against the Arab clergy, who could not vote in patriarchal elections, was widely seen to be unjust. Apparently, here was an opportunity to correct an anomaly once and for all. Unfortunately, Wauchope misjudged the importance of the issue to the confraternity, which would fight tenaciously to defend its Hellenic character.

In the face of Greek clerical opposition, Wauchope stubbornly continued to withhold Timotheos's berat, or warrant of appointment, for the remainder of his term of office. The outcome of his two-front war was that he failed in both campaigns, achieving neither a restoration of the Holy Sepulchre nor the enfranchisement of the Arab Orthodox community. With his own hands, he undermined the standing of the single most influential ecclesiastic at the holy places. The effect of his maneuver was to paralyze the Greek patriarchate at the very moment its cooperation was most indispensable.

Without official recognition, Timotheos was hamstrung. Internally, he could not act with authority, because his subordinates refused to obey orders. The morale and discipline of the confraternity reached a low point. Externally, the affairs of the patriarchate remained in a state of deadlock throughout the 1930s.[32]

In the circumstances, the patriarchate, under its acting patriarch, Archbishop Keladion, took the position that since it was an interim authority it was unable to make any decisions on the restoration of the Holy Sepulchre or the Church of the Nativity. Only an officially confirmed patriarch in synod had the constitutional authority "to confront the questions which unavoidably would emerge from the restoration and repairs under consideration of the two most important Holy Shrines in the Holy Land."[33]

In the meantime, the two-year deadline set by William Harvey in 1935 for the initiation of permanent works of reinforcement passed without action. In September 1937, the DPW carried out a regular inspection of the church. Since it still had no qualified conservationist on its staff, it sent its report to Harvey in England. Broken telltales and new cracks were visible to all, but the government needed an authoritative opinion if, as seemed increasingly likely, it was going to have to close the church to visitors. To add urgency, yet another slight earthquake shook the Holy Sepulchre in October 1937.

Harvey read the latest report with great anxiety and advised that the church was in "grave and imminent danger of collapse in whole or in part." Even a partial collapse would cause grave damage to the fabric. He worried that the vault of the south transept in its present precarious state might collapse telescopically as a result of another tremor or the vibrations set up by the large crowds who noisily celebrated the Holy Fire ceremony during Easter week. If the south transept came down, the only exit from the church would be blocked. Artistic and religious considerations aside, hundreds of people might be killed or injured.[34]

To alert the major communities to the danger, their leaders were invited to a meeting with Edward Keith-Roach, back as Jerusalem district commissioner. Despite his warning that unless effective action was taken the government might be obliged to close the church before Easter 1938, they all refused to attend. So Keith-Roach wrote again before Christmas 1937, drawing attention to the serious condition of the edifice and asking them to work together to raise the minimum sum of £150,000 required to cover indispensable repairs. He repeated the warning of closure.[35]

This time the communities were stirred to reply, but only the Armenians accepted the need for immediate action. The rain damage in their section of the church was worse than ever before. They suggested a constructive compromise proposal: that repairs should be carried out according to Harvey's report and plans, under the supervision and control of government architects, provided that they were implemented by a commission appointed by the three major communities.[36]

The Greeks made it clear that before they could come to a decision concerning any works of restoration, three conditions had to be fulfilled: the grant of the berat, a just solution of various points in dispute, and assurances about the Status Quo.[37]

Testa, on behalf of the Roman Catholic Church, basically reiterated an argument he had put forward in 1936: that those who contributed large sums to the cost of the restoration should be entitled to the right of legitimate control by their own technical representatives.[38]

These replies ruled out a program of permanent restoration for the time being. There was no prospect of funding, and there was no Greek Orthodox interlocutor. But the government was boxed into a concept of all or nothing and found it difficult to think of the communities as partners. The high commissioner would not concede any measure of control, since he thought it "obvious that for the sake of artistic unity, as well as for other considerations, the whole of the repairs should be executed by one centralised authority." Representatives of the communities would be able to make representations on points of detail to the archaeological advisory board.[39]

The government now decided to publicize the problem in order to prepare public opinion for a possible closure while shaming the communities into a more compliant attitude. The *Times* of London was asked to approach Harvey for an article on the state of the Holy Sepulchre and the Church of the Nativity.[40] Under the heading "Two Great Shrines in Danger," Harvey described at length the unfolding of the situation at the Holy Sepulchre since 1927. "Now," he wrote, "it is in grave peril of collapse, and the communities responsible for its safety seem blind to the danger." He proposed an international appeal, a call that was repeated by the *Times* in a lead article.[41]

As Easter loomed, the colonial office sent Harvey back to Jerusalem to determine what should be done. In a visit on March 23–29, 1938, he discovered further deterioration. In the Katholikon, there were many new cracks throughout the structure supporting the dome—piers, arches, vaults, and drum. The story repeated itself in the rotunda.

The north and south transepts showed extensive cracking. One wall was in such a fragmentary state for want of mortar that it was hard to distinguish cracks from open joints. Cracks had now appeared in the piers of the Triumphal Arch, which linked the Katholikon to the rotunda. In the rotunda itself, the steel band installed in 1934 seemed to be bearing its load, but horizontal cracks had spread from the Katholikon to the wall of the upper gallery. Several of the rotunda piers were badly fractured at ground level.

The roof of the eastern apse was damaged and letting in a great quantity of water. Rain was also leaking through the lower flat roofs of the building. The Armenian galleries, chapel, and rooms were particularly badly affected. Depressions where rainwater gathered showed the sinking of the underlying arches. Telltales were snapping a few hours after they were installed.

Harvey's somber conclusion was that the earthquake tremor of October 1937 had shaken the church in every part.

> It is impossible to say whether the Catholikon dome, with its high vault and heavy masonry, will fall first or the many piers of the Rotunda or of the Apse. There is also a danger of the vault of the South Transept sliding telescopically to the ground or the iron gallery giving way and allowing the stone staircase to fall. The defects in the building are so pronounced that the structure is not safe for the people who live and work in it.[42]

Harvey immediately recommended an entirely new round of repairs and reinforcements. The existing steel and wooden supports had helped, but now even the steelwork showed signs of buckling. Additional shoring was required at the transepts and Triumphal Arch, and steel bands would further strengthen the Katholikon dome. Steel stanchions, a girder, and additional bands were called for in the rotunda.

Sir Harold MacMichael, the new high commissioner, announced that the Church of the Holy Sepulchre would be closed to pilgrims for Easter Week 1938. The communities responded with indignant protests and appeals for a reprieve. Monks from the resident churches would be allowed to carry out their usual ceremonies in private at their own risk.[43]

MacMichael had arrived at Government House only a few weeks earlier to replace Sir Arthur Wauchope. He was a very different character from his predecessor. After a classical education, he had entered the colonial service in West Africa. Shrewd and cynical, he had spent years of lonely service in the Sudan and gone on to become governor of Tanganyika. He discontinued Wauchope's elegant dinner parties, with their accompaniment of harpsichord and violin, and ornaments of china and glass gave way to the carved heads of African deities.

MacMichael inherited a serious security problem. Law and order had broken down in the countryside. Wauchope's schemes of training young Arabs and improving local agriculture had to be abandoned, as experimental farms were attacked and looted. The police withdrew from isolated posts and traveled around in armored cars. District officers went in danger of their lives. In the circumstances, the prospect of a permanent restoration of the Church of the Resurrection receded into the future.

Nevertheless, the closure of the Holy Sepulchre did create a new situation. Harvey's published report had failed to generate sufficient public interest for a worldwide appeal as hoped. Dry and technical, it did not even impress the resident communities. But there is a difference between an architect's survey and facts on the ground. To have the mother church placed out of bounds to pilgrims at Easter Week shocked the churches out of their complacency as had no other event since the 1927 earthquake.

At last, the heads of the three major communities accepted Keith-Roach's invitation to meet to discuss repairs. Their overriding concern was to see the church reopened as soon as possible. At the meeting, the district commissioner sought their consent to the immediate undertaking of the urgent repairs, at a cost of no more than £10,000, to be shared equally. All three agreed in principle, while postponing consideration of a general restoration to a later date. However, there was to be no quick agreement on a division of costs, and work would not begin any time soon.

Although the Latins and Armenians agreed with alacrity to Keith-Roach's suggestion that they pay one-third of the cost, the Greeks rejected this blanket payments formula. True, it worked in the rotunda and south transept, which were jointly owned by the three major communities. In the Katholikon, they pointed out, they were sole proprietors, so should bear the entire cost, while at the Triumphal Arch and north transept they were joint owners with the Latins but not the Armenians.[44]

Within the framework of its interpretation of the Status Quo, the Greek patriarchate had actually decided to go ahead. An article that was believed to reflect its policy appeared in the Athens newspaper *Proia* for May 6, 1938, pointing to the urgent need for radical repair to the Anastasis and appealing to the generosity of the Greek people. The archbishop of Athens and the patriarch of Jerusalem were said to be making joint cause in the matter.[45]

The Custody of the Holy Land was also now ready to discuss Harvey's 1935 recommendations in their entirety, provided that the costs were divided equally among the three major communities. Father Eugene Hoade, an Irish friar representing the custos, told a colonial office official in London that early action and a firm line were required on the part of the government. It should tell the communities what work was to be carried out and allocate the cost among them. In response, the official explained that it could hardly do this unless it was prepared to fund much of the project, a suggestion Father Hoade rejected out of hand.[46]

A drawn-out and complicated negotiation over the division of costs now ensued. For a time, the Palestine government waited on the outcome of the negotiations before beginning repairs, in line with the colonial office's longstanding policy that it bore no financial liability for the holy places. Further delay was ruled out when the Permanent Mandates Commission in Geneva brought up the Holy Sepulchre at its June 1938 session. What steps were being taken, it asked, to repair the basilica and reopen it for public worship? What action had been taken to ensure against the collapse of the building? Was the world not in danger of losing through delay over procedure a unique and historical religious monument?

Sensitive as always to League of Nations opinion, the Palestine government decided it could not wait on the Greeks any longer and authorized £10,000 under special warrant for the DPW to install temporary bracing to avert the immediate danger of the building's fall.[47] Urgent work to the exterior could now go ahead, but it was only in September 1938, after substantial concessions to the Greeks, that DPW workmen were allowed into the Katholikon.

The funding issue was never definitively resolved. Keith-Roach labored under a heavy burden of work as district commissioner. A global payments formula proved elusive because, among other reasons, the Armenians would not budge from their claim to a share of the north transept. Once the British Treasury turned down MacMichael's request for funding, the financially strained Palestine government was left to cover the costs from its own resources in the hope that it could reclaim them from the communities at a later date. It never did.

By the time work started in September 1938, the government's hands were full with the Arab Revolt. The DPW was kept busy repairing blown-up roads and bridges. That month, Arab rebels burned down government offices in Bethlehem and Jericho, telephone lines were destroyed, and the Jerusalem–Lydda railway line was sabotaged. Terrorists carried out nine murders and sixteen attempted murders in the Old City of Jerusalem alone.

As if this was not enough, Keith-Roach also needed to prepare for the safety of the city's population in the event of a general European war, which was looking increasingly likely. Overshadowing the concerns of the Christian communities to preserve their rights at the Holy Sepulchre was the daunting task of planning for the wartime needs of 125,000 people on a remote hilltop.[48]

| Monsignor Testa's Temple

T HE FATE OF THE Holy Sepulchre has been repeatedly determined
by war. On Italy's entry into World War II on June 10, 1940, Palestine
found itself a target for hostile action. It was within range of Italian bombers
flying out of the island of Rhodes. It was also under threat of invasion should
Egypt, lightly defended by British troops under a 1936 treaty, fall to the
Italian tenth army, based in Libya, on the North African coast.

With Britain's position in the Middle East in jeopardy, and Jerusalem
and the holy places under contention, finishing touches were being put on a
radical Catholic plan for the reconstruction of the Church of the Resurrection. Commissioned in July 1938 by Archbishop Gustavo Testa, the apostolic delegate to Egypt and Palestine, the plan was completed in Venice in
November 1940 after Italian forces invaded Egypt.

The plan called for demolishing the entire Holy Sepulchre complex. In
its place a grandiose edifice was to rise, surrounded by a broad piazza. The
plan embodied a startlingly revisionist architectural vision that was diametrically opposed to the conservative outlook on Jerusalem town planning
that had been firmly established in the 1920s. If implemented, it would
require the clearance of about half the Christian Quarter. The Status Quo
would be superseded and the Catholic Church elevated to a position of
preeminence.

The plan is reminiscent of other modernist schemes of urban redevelopment that were in vogue in Italy at the time, such as the Via della Con-
ciliazione, which leads from the Tiber into St. Peter's Square in Rome. Begun
in 1936 by the architects Marcello Piancentini and Attilio Spaccarelli, this

avenue was intended as a symbolic link between the capital of the Italian state and the Vatican state in commemoration of the historic 1929 concordat of reconciliation between Mussolini and Pope Pius XI. It entailed the controversial destruction of most of a medieval quarter, the Borgo Vecchia, and excites controversy to this day.

An American friar later put his finger on the most puzzling feature of the plan for the total reconstruction of the Holy Sepulchre—its apparent detachment from reality—when he remarked: "It should have been done by Constantine the Great, but he is dead."[1] Was the Testa plan, then, intended simply as a thought-provoking academic exercise?

The concept of a new Church of the Holy Sepulchre was first linked to the name of Monsignor Luigi Barlassina, the Latin patriarch of Jerusalem, shortly after his return from a visit to Rome in September 1934, on the eve of Monsignor Testa's arrival as apostolic delegate.[2] But what gave the idea momentum was the letter of May 2, 1936, from Hathorn Hall, the chief secretary, proposing the restoration of the edifice. Catholic leaders were outraged by the demand that they accept Harvey's plan without appeal.

On May 24, Archbishop Testa wrote to Antonio Barluzzi asking for his views. The Italian architect wrote back reviewing developments at the edifice since 1934 and expressing serious reservations about the British handling of the question of the restoration to date.

Harvey's report, he charged, was "a poor job" that covered up the fact that the pressing and likely reason for the urgency of the main restorations at the Holy Sepulchre was the government's own botched-up reconstruction of the Katholikon dome. The cracks and subsequent alarm, he suggested, were the result of the work having been initiated without a prior study of the static conditions of the old walls.[3]

Shortly after this, the custos, Father Nazzareno Jacopozzi, began talking of a radical plan for the complete reconstruction of the church as a preferable option to carrying out repairs.[4] Archbishop Testa put forward this radical solution frankly to Hathorn Hall in December 1936, describing the old church as "unworthy of the precious memories it enshrines."[5]

It is not hard to understand Testa's feelings. True, the present edifice was a cherished shrine of great sentimental and historical value, a cultural treasure. But from an ecclesiastical point of view, its continued existence could not be considered an end in itself if it had outlived its usefulness. The Holy Sepulchre had first and foremost to provide a fitting setting for Calvary and the Tomb of Christ, and a safe and accessible venue for the many thousands of Christians from all over the world who came to Jerusalem on pilgrimage in order to strengthen their faith.

As things stood, the edifice was an unsatisfactory place of worship. It was too small to accommodate the pilgrimage groups that were being brought by train and boat and plane to Palestine in growing numbers. It was cluttered with scaffolding and, alarmingly, had only one entry and no emergency exit. For every pilgrim inspired by the sanctuary, another left disappointed by its dilapidation and clutter. Finally, the dead hand of the Status Quo complicated every attempt at restoration. In the circumstances, might it not be preferable to replace the old lady with a fitting modern monument, along the lines of Antonio Barluzzi's splendid new Holy Land churches?

In their belated reply to Testa of July 1937, the authorities—who had other things on their minds in the light of the Arab revolt—responded evasively to his extraordinary proposition. In private, they thought it was outside the realm of probability, contrary to the Status Quo, and open to grave objection on political grounds.[6] Officially, they diplomatically noted the suggestion made by the Holy See but pointed out that it could only be put into effect with the full consent of the other religious communities concerned. Should the Holy See wish to pursue the suggestion, it should initiate negotiations with those other communities.[7]

Vehement objections to Testa's ideas were also raised in Catholic circles. Roberto Paribeni of the Italian Academy utterly deprecated the scheme. Describing himself as one who loved and venerated the ancient monument, he wrote of his "pained surprise that persons albeit of a deep religious sense, possessed of historical learning and artistic sensibility, should have proposed without more ado to level everything to the ground and to start from scratch an absolutely new construction of the Sanctuary of the Holy Sepulchre."[8]

Another troubled critique of the idea came from the pen of Father Hugues Vincent, the respected Dominican archaeologist of Jerusalem. While praising the nobility of intention and elevated religious inspiration of those who envisaged "an exceptionally grandiose edifice," he warned about ignoring completely the archaeological dimension. "Whatever the solution adopted, it is out of the question to erase everything, putting in its place a new monument thought up by masters of contemporary architecture. Instead of saving a timeworn edifice that has survived the centuries, so as to prolong its living witness, they would bring about its ruin."[9]

Despite these powerful objections, it became clear by mid-1938 that a thoroughgoing program of restoration was unlikely to be implemented any time soon. The church itself was in a more dismal state than ever, closed to the public and further disfigured by another round of emergency supports. Yet the British government showed itself either unwilling or unable to deliver a comprehensive scheme acceptable to and paid for by the three major communities.

The reason for this lethargy seemed apparent: the days of the Mandate in its existing form were numbered, one way or another. A British royal commission headed by Lord Peel had presented a report on the Arab revolt in 1937 recommending the partition of Palestine into Jewish and Arab states, with a separate enclave carved out for the holy places under a fresh international mandate.

Two additional documents on the future of an independent Palestine issued before the outbreak of war, the Woodhead Commission Report (1938) and the MacDonald White Paper (1939) envisaged the creation of a special regime for Jerusalem and surroundings. None of these documents called for the perpetuation of the status quo. What would replace it was of the most profound concern to the Holy See.

At a meeting in Whitehall in May 1938 with Sir John Shuckburgh, the deputy undersecretary of state at the colonial office, Father Eugene Hoade, representing the Custody of the Holy Land, explicitly referred to the consequences of the Peel partition scheme for Palestine's Christians. With the edifice closed to the public as a result of Harvey's follow-up survey, Father Hoade declared for the first time that the Custody was prepared to accept Harvey's recommendations for restoration in whole, contributing one-third of the cost. But there was no breakthrough in the talks; the British official said nothing new, and the Franciscan envoy repeated a proposal for a panel of architects, one appointed by the government and the others by the three major communities.[10] The British government had already rejected this model as a recipe for paralysis.

In this vacuum of immobility, Archbishop Testa officially approached Antonio Barluzzi on behalf of the Vatican secretariat of state to draw up a plan for the demolition of the existing Church of the Resurrection and the construction of a new one. The plan would rebuff the charge, to which Testa was acutely sensitive, that the Holy See was ignoring the danger threatening the Holy Sepulchre.[11] It would demonstrate to the world the depth of Catholic commitment to the sanctuary and provide a valid Catholic alternative to counter the "English plan."

Antonio Barluzzi was a natural choice for the task. He was born in Rome in 1884 to a family that had been in the service of the Holy See for generations. After studying architecture at the University of Rome, he traveled to Jerusalem in 1911 to build a hospital for the Italian Missionary Society. He served in the Italian army in World War I as an officer, returning to Palestine in 1917 as part of the Italian contingent that accompanied General Edmund Allenby's Allied Expeditionary Force.[12]

A devout Catholic and an Italian patriot, Barluzzi was strongly attached to the Holy Land. At the end of the war, he was approached by the new custos, Father Ferdinando Diotallevi, and asked to work on a program of church construction and rebuilding throughout the country. Barluzzi determined to devote his life to this mission, living with the Franciscans as an informal lay brother. By 1938, he had already made a remarkable impact on the landscape, building churches at Gethsemane, Mount Tabor, and Jericho. He helped to restore the Chapel of the Flagellation on the Via Dolorosa and to redecorate the Catholic chapel on Calvary.[13]

Barluzzi was also the architect of the black and white Church of the Beatitudes overlooking the Sea of Galilee, with its octagonal shape that evoked the eight beatitudes. He built it in 1937 for the Italian Missionary Society, with funding from Benito Mussolini. This mixture of religion and politics is not as surprising as at first appears, for Barluzzi was secretary of the Jerusalem branch of the Fascist Party in the years 1927–37, while Mussolini was a knight of the Equestrian Order of the Holy Sepulchre.[14]

Barluzzi wrote at once to his friend and colleague Luigi Marangoni inviting him informally to take part. Marangoni was an equally obvious choice, with an international reputation gained as custodian of St. Mark's and already trusted and respected by virtue of his 1934 report on the state of the edifice. The two architects also saw eye to eye on political issues, sharing ultranationalist views of Italy's imperial mission.

Following the Italian invasion of Ethiopia in October 1935, Marangoni wrote proudly of the spirit of the Italian people in the face of the iniquitous economic sanctions that the League of Nations, under British and French leadership, imposed on Italy.[15] The decisive Italian victory at Amba Aradam and the performance of "our admirable soldiers" left him "vibrant with enthusiasm."[16]

He also shared with Barluzzi a mystical sense of Italy's destiny in the Holy Land, which he linked with their personal work and dreams. Palestine, he was convinced, had some surprises in store. If Palestine became Jewish, no human force would be able to mitigate the enactment of "the greatest human and divine drama that has ever occurred under the sun." At the same time, he wrote, "I nurture in my heart the hope that a good gust of new Italian life will blow over the peaks of those sacred mountains."[17]

In the face of Testa's extraordinary vision, however, both men were left equally perplexed. Marangoni admitted that he was horrified and was unable to ignore "the complex consequences of an artistic, historical, and religious nature that would follow from razing the church to the ground and reconstructing it." He loved the existing Holy Sepulchre, with all its defects and memories, and had difficulty calmly considering the replacement of the "holy and glorious edifice." Still, there was no choice but to follow the instructions of religious authority.[18]

On November 2, 1938, Archbishop Testa raised the plan at an audience with Pope Pius XI—who was dying of heart disease—later reporting that his holiness showed a "lively interest" in the subject. "For that reason," he wrote Barluzzi, "you will not fail to reveal to the world as soon as possible just how much Catholics want to do in the sanctuary, close as it is to their hearts."[19]

A golden opportunity now arose to provide Christians everywhere with a sense of what a new basilica might look like. In the summer of 1938, the Italian government had announced plans for a world's fair in Rome, L'Esposizione Universale di Roma (F. 42), to be held at the beginning of 1942. New roads, parks, and facilities were planned for the fair, which would have a green field site on the road to the old Roman seaport of Ostia.[20]

At the end of November 1938, the custos suggested to Barluzzi that he might like to prepare a replica of the Holy Sepulchre to be displayed at an exhibition of oriental missionary art the cardinal prefect of the Sacred Congregation for Oriental Churches was planning for E. 42. Both men agreed that the survey of the edifice that Testa's project called for would serve to build the scale model.[21]

As Barluzzi pointed out to Archbishop Testa, the plan for a model had a clear benefit. It would "provide an opportunity to obtain with a minimum of difficulty permission to circulate freely in the Holy Sepulchre without causing undue alarm."[22] From now on, work on the model, which was a secondary, spinoff job, was used to account for all the planning being carried out for the reconstruction project.

Testa impressed on Barluzzi the need to move ahead without delay, though Barluzzi had recently broken his arm and was hard at work on the Church of the Visitation in Ain Karim. At Barluzzi's request, Testa agreed to bringing in Marangoni to direct the project.

On December 1, 1938, the apostolic delegate asked Barluzzi to use the following words in his invitation to Marangoni:

The Holy See wishes to overcome delays in dealing with the deplorable condition of the Holy Sepulchre by involving itself directly and offering the moral, scientific, artistic, and material contribution of Catholics to restore to the revered Temple the dignity due to the memory and worship of the sublime and glorious mysteries of our religion.[23]

Over the course of 1939, Barluzzi and Marangoni struggled to reconcile their natural preference as architects and conservationists for a conventional plan of restoration with Testa's insistence on a "vast plan of reconstruction" involving redevelopment of the Christian Quarter of the Old City. In Barluzzi's view, demolition of the edifice at this time was out of the question, or as he put it, "spitting into the wind." The British and Greeks were against it, and the French sought an outcome that would be to their advantage, not the Italians'.[24]

In April 1939 Barluzzi visited Marangoni in Venice, and the two architects worked together for several days on the Holy Sepulchre plan, preparing a concrete proposal for Testa. The document that emerged acknowledged that a grand plan for a new basilica offered the most to the "artist's creative fantasies" and would do away once and for all with the ancient disputes between the communities. But they noted that it would also expunge all record of centuries of Christian worship. In its stead, therefore, they proposed a less radical plan, taking major account of existing reality, for a reconstituted Crusader church within its contemporary surroundings.

Such a program would leave the church substantially intact. Besides necessary repairs, a number of alterations would restore the appearance of the original Latin masterpiece. In the rotunda, the 1869 dome would revert to the conical form given it by Michael Paphlagon in the eleventh century, and the old columns, plastered over by Komnenos in 1809–10, restored to view. A new Edicule on Crusader lines would replace the neo-Byzantine Edicule, which was not worth conserving artistically and was anyway unstable. Walls added by Komnenos would be removed, including those separating the north and south transepts from the nave. A gallery believed to have been originally envisaged for the choir (now known as the Katholikon) would be built. The top of the bell tower, demolished in 1719, would be restored.

Marangoni recommended the establishment of a small bureau made up of technical and artistic representatives of the communities. Imbued with a local team spirit, it would keep track of the situation, taking any action required with the full accord of the proprietors of the Holy Sepulchre. At any event, he stressed, agreement between the communities would always be necessary.[25]

This more modest scheme, though still likely to face formidable obstacles, was favored by Father Alberto Gori, Father Jacopozzi's successor as custos. Gori was convinced that the solo plan Testa envisaged would be impossible to implement. Monsignor Domenico Tardini, the deputy of Luigi Cardinal Maglione, the new cardinal secretary of state, also wrote approving the text of the Marangoni-Barluzzi report in May 1939.

Meanwhile, the planning for a scale model of the Holy Sepulchre began to gather momentum. On March 31, 1939, Monsignor Celso Constantini, the secretary of the Sacred Congregation for the Propagation of the Faith, officially announced that the Catholic Church intended to participate in E. 42. Constantini had favored a Catholic pavilion since visiting the 1937 Paris world's fair. Originally a local French church initiative, the Catholic pavilion in Paris, consisting of exhibition halls, a church, and a cloister, had proved a great success. Attracting an estimated thirty thousand visitors a day, it had impressed the cardinal secretary of state at the time, Eugenio Cardinal Pacelli, who was now Pope Pius XII.[26]

For E. 42 a similar setup was planned. There would be a Catholic exhibition, into which a great deal of thought was invested. The scale model of a new basilica of the Holy Sepulchre would exemplify the commitment of the modern Catholic Church to exalting the Holy Land sites associated with Jesus Christ. A new Church of Saints Peter and Paul would be built at the fair for the Catholic visitors who were expected from all over the world, and it was hinted that Pius XII himself would consecrate it.[27]

The timing and substance of the Vatican announcement was significant in a diplomatic sense. On February 10, 1939, Pope Pius XI had died. His outspoken 1937 encyclical *Mit brennender Sorge*, with its attack on the idolization of "the idea of race or people or state or form of government," had placed the Holy See in the forefront of opposition to totalitarianism and anti-Semitism. As a result, relations with Fascist Italy, regularized by the 1929 Lateran Treaties establishing the Vatican state, had seriously deteriorated.[28]

A few days after the coronation of Pius XII on March 10, 1939, the German army marched into Prague and dismantled the rump of Czechoslovakia, in violation of the 1938 Munich accords. In Rome, all possible means of Fascist propaganda were mobilized to prepare the Italian people for the eventuality of war in the near future. The Fascist press denounced the "policy of encirclement of the totalitarian states on the part of the democracies."[29] The Holy See, changing its tune virtually overnight, avoided all critical comment.[30]

The Vatican announcement on March 31 of its participation in E. 42 was a signal of a sea change in Vatican policy—away from confrontation with Fascist Italy to conciliation and cooperation, with the hope of strengthening forces for peace. Before very long, the Fascist press was singing the praises of the pope's understanding of the regime and the "new times."[31]

Cooperation between church and state may have been an innovation in Italy but was nothing new in Palestine. For many years, Italian consuls had worked with Catholic institutions, often dominated by Italian clergy and functioning in Italian, with the aim of spreading Italian culture and influence, and providing protection for local Catholics.[32]

Since 1920, Archbishop Barlassina, the Latin patriarch, with an ambitious program of development and limited resources, had been receiving an annual subsidy of 25,000 Lire and first-class travel privileges from the Italian government. In addition, extraordinary payments were sometimes made to the patriarchate, for example, in October 1937 to fund enlargement of the seminary.[33]

King Vittorio Emanuele III of the Royal House of Savoy, who reigned in Rome from 1900 to 1946, had inherited the traditional family title of "king of Jerusalem." At its seizure of power in 1922, the Fascist regime sought to foster the historical association between the monarchy and the holy places, and Fascist consuls assiduously cultivated Italian prestige in the Holy City.

In February 1927, a Fascist Party official wrote to the Equestrian Order of the Holy Sepulchre, to which Barlassina as Latin patriarch had the right to nominate knights, observing "how greatly H. E. Mussolini has at heart the prestige of Catholicism and Italy in Palestine; and how it is always the wish of the Duce to acquire greater influence through our joint institutions which have such historical and political importance."[34] Following the signature of the Lateran Treaties in 1929, Mussolini was decorated with the insignia of a knight first class.[35] By accepting the decoration, he symbolically associated himself with the protection of the Church of the Resurrection.

Barlassina certainly considered himself a loyal servant of the church and was very independent-minded. But he had Fascist sympathies at a time of nationalist fervor and fell under the suspicion of the British authorities during the war. Among his friends he was known as L'Italianissimo. The verifiable charges against him were never more serious, though, than a tendency to appoint and give preference to clergy of Italian origin.[36]

Luigi Marangoni joined Antonio Barluzzi in Jerusalem at the end of January 1940, staying at the Casa Nova, the Franciscan guest house in Jerusalem. His party included his wife and two technical experts from Venice, a building engineer, Ferdinando Vienna, and a draftsman, Emilio Sartorio.[37]

Marangoni's explanation for his visit was carefully coordinated in advance with Testa. Testa instructed Barluzzi to have the *Palestine Post* publish an item noting that Marangoni was coming to Jerusalem to prepare a grand model of the Holy Sepulchre for the next missionary exhibition in Rome. He added, "News of the plan must be kept, as far as possible, 'secret.' "[38] Presumably, "the plan" referred to the scheme for a new basilica.

In his application for permission to carry out the survey, Theophilus Bellorini, the secretary of the Custody, wrote to the authorities that Marangoni was "to prepare 'a scholar's plan' of a future Basilica which will be offered to the scholars for consideration" and would be displayed at the 1942 world's fair. The phase of actual reconstruction, when it was obvious that the full consent of all religious communities would be required, had not been reached, "nor do I know or foresee when such period will be due to blossom." He added: "What the Holy See wants to do now is to be in a condition to say to all who might have an interest in the Church of the Holy Sepulchre: Look here: We propose to reconstruct the Holy Sepulchre on these lines. Do you agree? And the Holy See is fully aware that the project will, when ready, require an exhaustive study of all concerned."[39]

Edward Keith-Roach, the veteran Jerusalem district commissioner, agreed without enthusiasm, provided that Marangoni kept off Muslim property, and the Armenian and Greek patriarchates did not object.

At any rate, he thought the Vatican idea for a new building was not feasible, since it would involve expropriating surrounding property, most of which belonged to the waqf, the Muslim religious trust.[40]

In London, the colonial office saw no great harm in exhibiting an ideal model at the 1942 world's fair, so long as it was clear that the authorities had not approved the scheme. Better not to give needless offense to the Holy See, when much might have happened before then. At the same time, it was felt that the Catholics were inspired less by considerations of

> public safety in the building or of architectural excellence than by a desire to establish a basis for enlarged claims of control over the reconstructed building. They are the only community who have sufficient funds to contemplate a scheme of this sort, and, by literally destroying the status quo brick by brick and rebuilding it at their own expense, they would, of course, be in a very strong position.[41]

The official communiqué issued by the Palestine government in response to a request by the Holy See accordingly granted Marangoni "permission to take measurements of the Basilica of the Holy Sepulchre for the purpose of preparing 'a scholar's ideal model' for exhibition at the 1942 world fair in Rome."[42] Clearly, this was a narrow characterization of the purpose of his trip.

Marangoni spent about a month in Jerusalem, working with Barluzzi. To Testa's pleasure, during this period of intensive collaboration, the two architects were won over to the thesis of a radical reconstruction.[43] Later, Marangoni told a friend of the agonies they had gone through before finally accepting the job.[44]

Returning home via Cairo in March, Marangoni gave several newspaper interviews, carefully sticking to the agreed account. In an interview with the Egyptian *Giornale d'Oriente*, he emphasized that his stay in Jerusalem had been for the purpose of carrying out "a survey necessary to prepare the ideal plan" of a model to be exhibited at E. 42. All preparatory work on this "ideal model" had been scrupulously carried out, and the plan kept in mind the need "to leave intact the rights of the three major communities acquired over the centuries."[45] Archbishop Testa, he later wrote to Barluzzi, had been especially satisfied with this report.[46]

Back in Venice, Marangoni was interviewed in a lengthy article in the national newspaper *Corriere Della Sera*. Here, too, he repeatedly stressed that this was "an ideal plan." The Holy See intended that the model to be constructed would facilitate the study of a solution and would demonstrate the Catholic world's interest in the future of the Tomb of Christ. The heritage of the present basilica would be scrupulously preserved for future generations.[47]

Marangoni and Barluzzi set to work separately in Venice and Jerusalem. For the dispatch of material, Marangoni used the diplomatic bag.[48] It is unclear whether this indicated the involvement of the Italian consul in Jerusalem in the scheme or was a privilege granted him because of his elevated status as a member of the Italian Academy.

Testa's instructions called for a monumental construction. They were to think in terms of a "vast space," on which would "arise a new Temple, sufficiently grandiose to hold the sacred memories of the Tomb and Calvary." It would evoke and renew Constantine's ancient basilica, and would consist of three principal churches, for the separate worship of the major communities, leading off the central sanctuary. There might be chapels for the minor communities. Convents for monks and nuns and residence halls would be constructed nearby, apart from the sanctuary. Aside from these general guidelines, the architects were encouraged to give their creative imaginations free play.[49]

Beyond the walls of Marangoni's palatial home, where he had a room set aside for the reconstruction project, Europe was in turmoil. On April 9, 1940, Hitler attacked Denmark and Norway. In Rome, rumors spread that Mussolini was about to launch military operations. On Sunday, May 5, Pope

Pius XII, in a sermon at the Church of Santa Maria sopra Minerva, made an impassioned plea for peace. But Hitler's stunning victories proved an irresistible temptation to Mussolini, and with France about to fall, Mussolini declared war.

Mussolini's decision cast Testa's planning for the future of the Holy Sepulchre in a new light. If Hitler and Mussolini won the war, the holy places would change hands. Barely a week after Mussolini entered the war, on June 19, two Italian archbishops and forty-seven bishops petitioned Mussolini to take the Holy Sepulchre out of Britain's hands and entrust it to the Royal House of Savoy. The bishop of Terracina told his flock "that only when the Flag of Fascist and Catholic Italy is unfurled over Christ's Sepulchre will the Holy Land have received the veneration it deserves."[50] D'Arcy Osborne, the British minister to the Holy See, had no illusions about the *Italianità* (Italian character and identity) of most members of the Curia.[51]

The Middle East was the place where British and Italian interests most obviously clashed. After a meeting between Hitler and the Italian foreign minister in Berlin on July 7, 1940, Germany recognized an Italian sphere of influence over the Mediterranean and the lands bordering it.[52] Italy's aim, the German ambassador to Italy reported on July 17, was to obtain bilateral treaties with Egypt, Palestine, and Syria to secure its influence and interests.[53]

Britain and Italy were at war almost at once. Palestine was not a major theater of combat compared with North Africa and the Horn of Africa but was quickly drawn into hostilities. Italian warplanes flying out of Rhodes repeatedly bombed Haifa, the major Palestinian port and oil terminal. In an air raid on July 24, forty-six people were killed and eighty wounded.[54] British Somaliland on the Red Sea was conquered in August. Tel Aviv, only 40 miles from Jerusalem, was bombed on September 10, with 119 people killed and 151 wounded.[55]

In these circumstances, there was clearly going to be no E. 42. Yet what had been presented to the Palestine government a few months before as a "scholar's plan" might soon become a builder's blueprint. If Egypt fell to Marshal Graziani in 1940 or to Field Marshal Rommel in 1941 or 1942, Palestine would follow shortly. Then the Italian bishops would have their wish, the Holy Sepulchre would be entrusted to King Vittorio Emanuele, and what had looked like an impossibility—a grandiose new edifice—would enter the realm of possibility.

The detailed plans, drawn up mostly on Marangoni's drawing board over the period April–November 1940, faithfully followed the letter and spirit of

Testa's instructions. Cardinal Maglione, the secretary of state, was consulted on issues of principle.[56]

By the end of August the scale model was ready, but another two months were needed to complete work on the architect's drawings. A disagreement between Marangoni and Ferdinando Vienna over technical calculations for the conical dome planned for the rotunda developed into an open break. An outside engineer, Professor Zanaboni, was consulted on the stability of the monument.

With the involvement of a growing number of people, Marangoni became concerned that the real purpose of the project might leak out. Marcello Piancentini, the modernist town planner and one of the architects brought in to design E. 42, showed an interest. Marangoni admired Piancentini's work and was flattered but wary. He was relieved, he wrote Barluzzi on September 11, that they had provided "explanations for our well-known interest in the Holy Sepulchre."[57]

Marangoni might have feared premature disclosure because of potential ecclesiastical or political opposition to a new basilica in Rome. Alternatively, it may be that he feared that the practical rather than the academic dimension of the scheme would come to the attention of British intelligence and be interpreted as evidence of plans for an impending attack on Britain in the Middle East.

The very next day, September 12, Italian and Libyan troops invaded Egypt. Marangoni wrote Barluzzi: "Let us hope that the Arabs remain loyal to us and that our armies' certain victory brings forward the solution that we want."[58]

On October 30, 1940, Marangoni could declare that their work was finished. All that remained was to plan the interior of the Latin basilica. "Unfortunately," he wrote Barluzzi, "there is nothing else to be done for now concerning the Holy Sepulchre. We shall await final victory with the hope that it will bring us the solution that we also await for the Holy Sepulchre of Our Lord." [59] These two notes suggest that in Marangoni's mind, at least, there was a clear connection between the invasion of Egypt, military victory, the plan the architects had been working on, and a solution to the problem of the Church of the Resurrection.

The central theme of Marangoni and Barluzzi's great cruciform basilica was to be a dramatic progression from a splendid entry to the east, through a central nave to Calvary and the Holy Sepulchre. In style they chose an intriguing pastiche of the neoclassical and oriental; the main building was to be entirely surrounded by loggias or arcaded galleries on two levels, with numerous domes and four minaret-like *campanili* towering over the skyline.

Constantinian in spirit, the plan evokes both the original Church of the Resurrection and the trefoil Basilica of the Nativity in Bethlehem.

The medieval warren so familiar to countless generations of pilgrims—the crumbling Romanesque church with its twenty-two chapels, sacristies, and monasteries crammed between mosques, shops, and crowded dwellings— would be swept away. In its place would arise a new edifice on an elevated platform surrounded by a vast paved area dotted with fountains and trees. Convents, halls of residence, and pilgrims' hostels would enclose the piazza. Where visitors in the past could only approach on foot down narrow alleyways, there would be access to the new complex by transport from the Jaffa Gate to an adjacent square.

The dimensions were immense, for what is not a large city within the walls. Where the entire Constantinian compound (roughly the area enclosed by today's surrounding streets) consisted of a rectangle about 160 meters east-west and about 120 meters north-south (524 feet by 393 feet), the Marangoni-Barluzzi design called for a massive basilica 180 meters long and 140 meters wide (591 feet by 459 feet). Not taking into account the surrounding piazza and communal buildings, it would be twice the size of the existing Church of the Holy Sepulchre.

Pride of place would be given to a Catholic martyrium—a church commemorating the martyrdom of Jesus Christ—constituting the foot of the cruciform complex and the largest of three churches. It would be entered through an elegant triple-arched façade and atrium, leading on to a sacred garden containing St. Helena's Chapel and the Hill of Calvary, to be ascended up four convergent flights of steps in the shape of a cross. The Tomb of Christ, in the form of a circular temple, would stand on a plinth at the center of a new rotunda of the Anastasis.

Greeks and Armenians were to be allotted churches at the arms of the crucifix, roughly over the existing north and south transepts. Four chapels off the rotunda were to be devoted to the worship of the minor communities. Instead of the cacophony of contending services and the constant friction of the old Status Quo, new, decorous arrangements would finally lead to peace among the communities.

The vast new structure would utterly dominate the Old City of Jerusalem. Its monumental size would overshadow the Dome of the Rock on nearby (and lower) al-Haram al-Sharif. The design envisaged not just a reconstruction of the Holy Sepulchre but a comprehensive redevelopment of much of the Christian Quarter and some of the Muslim Quarter. Only a small proportion of the total site that was earmarked for the project was Latinowned.

Apart from shared property, most of the existing church was Greek and Armenian. In addition, the Greeks owned a large part of the former Constantinian compound outside the church complex, including the nearby Greek Orthodox patriarchate, the Church and Convent of St. Charalampos on al-Khanka Street, and the shops on Dabbagha Road next to the Lutheran Church of the Redeemer. The Armenians owned adjacent monasteries and chapels, and the Copts had their patriarchate next door. The Russian Orthodox Church owned the Church of Alexander Nevski on the corner of Dabbagha Road and Khan al-Zeit Street. The majority of the surrounding property, however, including the mosques of al-Khanka and Omar, belonged to Muslim religious trusts.

Only a government with the resources and powers of a totalitarian state could expropriate the patchwork of Muslim and Christian (non-Catholic) property that was earmarked for demolition. Any form of League of Nations mandate for Palestine under the rule of law guaranteeing religious and property rights would have disqualified such a project at the drawing board stage.

The project improbably counted on the non-Catholic churches in and around the Church of the Resurrection voluntarily conceding cherished rights enshrined in the Status Quo in exchange for a minority stake in a Roman Catholic cathedral. The new edifice would triumphantly mark Latin preeminence in Jerusalem. Since all other interested parties were most unlikely to give their consent freely, the implication was that they would be faced with no alternative but to agree. This could happen only if the Axis Powers won the war, replacing the British Mandate with Italian colonial rule.

No doubt, Testa's idea for a new Holy Sepulchre started out before the outbreak of war as contingency planning in preparation for an international debate on the future of Jerusalem. Yet a number of factors suggest that the "scholar's plan" for an ideal new edifice changed, with the outbreak of war, into the blueprint for a real building to be built on the capture of the Holy City.

The persuasive evidence includes the misleading account of "the ideal model" that was methodically propagated to explain Marangoni's activities; the secretiveness; the persistence with the project even after E. 42 ceased to be relevant; the preparation of detailed architect's drawings of the new building inside and out incorporating technical calculations; Marangoni's agonized deliberations over whether or not to accept the commission, hardly justified by a mere academic exercise; the fear of premature disclosure; and then, most tellingly, his hope that Marshal Graziani's invasion of Egypt would bring about the desired solution to the problem of the Holy Sepulchre. All this implies that it was not just discussion but action on the ground that was to promulgate the great new basilica.

———

Finally, there is the enigmatic figure of Archbishop Testa, the motor driving the project forward. Like other protagonists in this story, he was a staunch adherent of Fascism. So, too, were Barlassina, L'Italianissimo, who received a modest stipend from government funds; Barluzzi, the Jerusalem Fascist Party secretary; Marangoni, the pillar of the Fascist establishment who was able to use the diplomatic bag. All would have echoed the conviction of the Bishop of Terracina "that only when the Flag of Fascist and Catholic Italy is unfurled over Christ's Sepulchre will the Holy Land have received the veneration it deserves."

During the course of 1941, British counterintelligence investigated Archbishop Testa and a number of other Catholic prelates in the area, including Archbishop Barlassina. On February 12, 1942, the British government asked for Testa's replacement, together with three other Italian ecclesiastics, on the general grounds of the "Fascist and pro-Axis attitude and activities of the Catholic Church in the Middle East and East Africa."[60]

The investigation had started in April 1941, when the British army, after occupying the Ethiopian capital, Addis Ababa, searched the papal legation and found a quantity of small arms and an Italian army–type radio transmitter. Nine Italian ex-soldiers on the premises had passes signed by Castellani, the apostolic delegate, identifying them as legation employees.[61]

Lieutenant Colonel Count John de Salis, who was chief of counterintelligence in the Middle East, put together the file on Testa. Colonel de Salis was a practicing Catholic, the son of a former British minister to the Holy See, and fluent in Italian. He brought several allegations against Testa, including his bypassing of restrictions on the transmission of information and of censorship regulations.

Testa's pro-Fascist views were evident. In November 1941, he had written to Cardinal Maglione a letter (which counterintelligence had opened) revealing his hostility toward the anti-Fascist, "so-called" Free Italian movement. On another occasion, at dinner at the Jerusalem Custody of the Holy Land, he had reassured a group of Italian prisoners of war on pilgrimage to Jerusalem that they need have no scruples about signing a declaration not to engage in sabotage. On a third occasion, while visiting prisoners of war, he allegedly encouraged them "to take courage, because our people are coming."[62]

Between September 1940, when Italian forces crossed into Egypt, and February 1942, when Testa returned to Italy, the expectation that "our people are coming" was a not unreasonable inference. This was the only conceivable circumstance in which the new basilica could have been built.

But by Christmas 1942, this prospect had largely evaporated. With the defeat of General Erwin Rommel at El Alamein in November 1942 by the British Eighth Army under General Bernard Montgomery, and the German retreat from Egypt with heavy casualties, it became clear that Jerusalem and the Holy Sepulchre were now beyond the reach of the Axis powers.

Still, Testa did not give up what he called his "longed-for plan for the reconstruction of the Holy Sepulchre," and he visited Marangoni in Venice at the beginning of January 1943. Now the talk was largely of an article Marangoni would publish on the project with an explanatory preface, the overall plan, and an engraving of the model. Testa eventually concluded that the time was not ripe to go public.[63] There was silence on the issue for the next four years.

In April 1947, shortly after the United Nations set up a special commission to consider the future of Palestine, Testa submitted a memorandum to Pope Pius XII. In it he reviewed the plan of a new basilica in broad-brush terms and requested permission to present it to a wider audience in the form of an attractively produced book. This was the origin of an album that eventually appeared in 1950.[64]

Testa leaves his reader in no doubt that the plan was the result of his individual efforts in bringing Marangoni to Jerusalem and overcoming "various not inconsiderable difficulties." All this concluded "at the end of 1942 in a magnificent and painstaking design for the complete reconstruction of the sanctuary that took fairly into account the rights of the Latins and those vaunted by the schismatics (Greeks and Armenians)."

"The main idea," he explained,

> was to publish this plan, not so much to foster belief in the possibility of its immediate implementation (given the immense difficulty of reconciling the rights of owners, rights obtained in extensive adjacent areas, cost of construction etc.), as to demonstrate . . . the interest of the Holy See and of Catholics everywhere in the sanctuary closest to their hearts.

But in context, the Testa plan looks uncannily like the blueprint for a triumphalist monument to Italian victory in World War II.

Holy Sepulchre from air. Photo by Ya'acov Sa'ar. Courtesy of Israel government press office.

Edicule. Artist: Thomas Allom, 1838.

Exterior of Holy Sepulchre. Artist: David Roberts, 1839.

Stone of Unction.
Artist: Thomas
Allom, 1838.

Fathers Abel
(bespectacled) and
Vincent on south
façade about 1905.
Courtesy
of École Biblique.

Scaffolding
in rotunda,
mid-1930s.
Courtesy
of Custody
of the
Holy Land.

Façade of Holy Sepulchre, 1925. Courtesy of École Biblique.

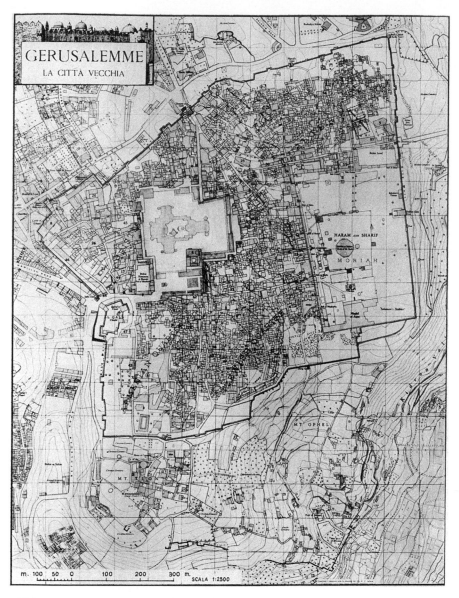

Old City with planned basilica. Courtesy of Custody of the Holy Land.

Marangoni's
1940 plan for
new basilica.

Courtesy of
Custody of
the Holy
Land.

War damage to rotunda dome, 1948. Courtesy of Elia Photo Service.

Fire at dawn, November 24, 1949. Courtesy of Elia Photo Service.

CHAPTER SIX | The Fire

AT ABOUT EIGHT O'CLOCK in the evening of November 23, 1949, a Greek Orthodox priest, standing on the flat roof next to the rotunda, suddenly noticed flames shooting out of a hole in the great dome. He ran back through the Greek convent, past the Chapel of St. Constantine, to the patriarchate next door to raise the alarm.[1]

The fire had started earlier that afternoon. The Jordanian DPW had been at work on the dome, repairing damage caused by a mortar shell during the 1948 battle for Jerusalem between Jews and Arabs. A welder mending the hole in the lead with an oxyacetylene blowtorch was thought to have accidentally set fire to slow-burning insulation material inside the cupola's cavity.

The patriarchate immediately contacted the Jordanian authorities and sent for the Muslim doorkeeper of the church. All the resident monks were already locked inside for the night, and only the doorkeeper, by ancient tradition, had the giant key to the great wooden doors.

Was there a risk that the monks might have burnt to death had the doorkeeper not been found? Probably not. Although there is no official emergency exit to the Holy Sepulchre to this day, the Greeks do have a private passage from their convent to the Church. This was placed at the disposal of the Franciscans when one of their friars had a heart attack inside the locked church in June 1967.[2]

The first that Franciscan friars in St. Savior's heard of the fire was the sound of indistinct shouting down the hill. From the terrace of the monastery, they were able to make out a red glow in the darkness in the direction of the Holy Sepulchre. Within a few minutes, the church bells began to toll.

Monks and local Christians quickly gathered in the Parvis to try and save whatever liturgical objects they could from the basilica. Most precious among these was a Madonna from the altar of Our Lady of Sorrows on Calvary, which had been given as a gift by Queen Maria I Braganza of Portugal in 1778.

The situation erupted into chaos. At first it looked as though there would be a horrible repeat of the 1808 conflagration. The church was full of combustible material—thickets of wooden scaffolding, paraffin for heating, and oil and candles for services. Unaccountably, there was no firefighting equipment in the church, and indeed virtually no organized firefighting service in Arab East Jerusalem—let alone the West Bank—at all, apart from a useless old pump at al-Haram al-Sharif, which was manned by a few untrained people.

All the Jordanian governor of Jerusalem could do that November night was to phone through to Amman, 40 miles away, where at least there was a fire brigade. An offer of assistance later came from Jewish West Jerusalem—literally, over the road—which had a modern fire brigade, including chemical equipment, but this was turned down. (Afterward, a rumor went around that Jewish spies had actually set the fire.[3])

An SOS then went out from the royal palace to the British ambassador, Sir Alec Kirkbride, asking for the firefighting squad of the Royal Air Force station in Amman to be sent to Jerusalem. Britain had granted Transjordan under Emir Abdullah full independence in 1946 but maintained a military presence there in return for financial aid and support for the Arab Legion. British service personnel were not supposed to cross the Jordan River into Arab Palestine (which Abdullah had annexed in December 1948, to international disapproval). Kirkbride got around the restriction by sending a party of sixty airmen dressed in civilian clothes.

At 8:30, the "fire brigade" from al-Haram al-Sharif arrived. Unfortunately, the rickety pump could not produce enough water pressure to carry water up to the dome. There was a futile attempt to set up a bucket chain. A mechanic from St. Savior's managed shortly after midnight to connect an electrical pump with a benzene pump. This produced a modest flow, but the outer lead casing of the cupola effectively kept the water away from the flames.

During this episode, the limited water supply of the Old City, compounded by the lateness of the rains, severely hampered the firefighters. Ironically, the Holy Sepulchre is located over numerous ancient cisterns containing water that would have been more than sufficient for fighting fires, given the right equipment. But contingency planning for mundane disaster has never been the communities' strong point. Firefighting equipment installed during the Mandate had not been replenished after the 1948 war.

Finally, at about one o'clock in the morning, the Royal Air Force squad, enthusiastic but untrained for this kind of fire, turned up under a group captain. The nearest they could get to the fire with their truck was Christian Street, just west of the church. After considerable effort, they succeeded in reaching the cupola with a single hose. However, they had no hydrant, and their water supply was limited to the contents of the water tank of their truck. This proved sufficient for only half an hour, with some of the water simply drenching bystanders the local police had failed to disperse. At four o'clock in the morning, out of water, the airmen went home.

By this time it was clear that the fire was localized within the dome itself and was not spreading through the rest of the church. Priests were already back at their posts, chanting before stripped altars, while outside others knelt in prayer, as showers of sparks rained down.

The fire had slowly eaten through the pine and felt insulation, starting high up in the timber beams that formed the dome's frame and melting the outer lead sheathing. Flames occasionally flared out into the open air but did not spread to the rest of the church.

Father Hugues Vincent spent an anxious night expecting the entire edifice to go up in flames at any moment. In hindsight, he concluded that it was only thanks to the foresight of Charles Mauss, the French architect who supervised the construction of the 1869 cupola, that a cataclysm had been averted. Mauss had covered the inner face of the dome with fire-resistant concrete plates, sealing off the cracks between the stones. This had ensured that the inside of the dome was completely blocked off from the highly flammable insulation material.[4]

Once it was realized that the fire was contained within the dome cavity, it was left to take its course. Now the main effort went into extinguishing burning debris as it rained down onto the roof of the Edicule and the surrounding flagstones inside the rotunda. After thirty-one hours, at about three o'clock in the morning on November 25, the fire finally burnt itself out. Two-thirds of the woodwork was destroyed, and the cupola had lost almost all its lead covering. A rough estimate put the damage at £10,000. But the iron and stone frame of the cupola was left standing, and the interior of the church had been spared.

From the outset, King Abdullah was kept fully informed, and early in the morning of November 24 he arrived at the Holy Sepulchre, together with

Brigadier General John Bagot Glubb, chief of staff of the Arab Legion. As water dripped down, the two short, plump figures surveyed the scene. Abdullah was dressed in a turban and flowing white robes. He had ruled Transjordan since 1921, first as emir under the British Mandate, and since 1946 as king. With a grizzled, grandfatherly beard, shrewd, hooded eyes, and fine features in a kindly but careworn face, he looked all of his sixty-seven years.

Hashemite historians have the king taking personal charge of firefighting operations on the spot. He must have been on the phone all night, but by the time he got to the Holy Sepulchre, there was not much to be done. Nevertheless, Abdullah's appearance at the church together with his Christian chief of staff was an important political act. It signified his personal concern for what had occurred and his commitment to put things right.

Later that morning, King Abdullah received a visit from the heads of the Christian communities. He told them that he had taken the matter in hand and thought that the fire had been an accident. He wanted to repair the damage and proposed to set up a commission of architects to study the issue. In his opinion, wood and electricity should be excluded from any future reconstruction so as to avoid a new conflagration.

That midmorning meeting was a historic turning point. A summit of church leaders with the ruling monarch was without precedent. No previous sovereign had ever expressed his personal concern for the upkeep of the church. Local prelates had never before gathered together to consider their common problem—the care of the edifice. Admittedly, there was hardly an exchange of views at this meeting. Nevertheless, this was the day when the custodians of the Holy Sepulchre were confronted with a new reality: that the sanctuary was not indestructible and that a Muslim king wanted to repair the great dome.

The government commission convened in a few days to inspect the site of the fire, inviting Antonio Barluzzi to take part. Its conclusion was that the dome had been solidly built and that it could be restored to use. In the meantime, temporary steps had to be taken right away to keep out the rain.[5] No one yet thought to connect the feasibility of repairing the cupola to the overall deplorable state of the rotunda, with its unsound piers and arches braced by wood and steel supports.

For King Abdullah—running the government in the highly traditional, personalized style of a Bedouin chieftain—the relatively limited scope of the damage and the reassuring findings of the commission must have come as a great relief. The last thing he needed at this time was for Christendom's holiest shrine to burn down on his watch. Such a disaster might even have undermined the legitimacy of his rule.

Abdullah was the son of Sherif Hussein, the last Hashemite guardian of the Muslim holy cities of Mecca and Medina. His family traced its descent from the Prophet Mohammed and acquired its peculiar distinction from a heritage of protecting the Muslim holy places. After World War I, the British installed him as the client ruler of Transjordan, a territory lying east of the Jordan River between Palestine and Iraq. Like other post–World War I Arab states, it was carved by Britain and France out of the lands of the defeated Ottoman Empire.

Emir Abdullah was devoted to the Holy City of Jerusalem for religious and personal reasons. Al-Aksa Mosque there is the first *qibla*—direction of prayer—of Islam, commemorating the spot whence the Prophet Mohammed ascended to heaven. Nearby was Sherif Hussein's grave.[6]

Four days after the low-key departure from Jerusalem of the last British high commissioner, Sir Alan Cunningham, on May 14, 1948, Abdullah ordered Glubb Pasha and his Arab Legion to capture the Old City. In a bloody battle, they took the Jewish Quarter and withstood fierce counterattacks by Israel.[7] While the fighting was still in progress, Abdullah insisted on going to al-Aksa Mosque to pray.[8]

After the war, he decided to annex the West Bank—including Jerusalem—to his kingdom. Jerusalem would be for him what Mecca and Medina had been for his father. On November 15, 1948, on a visit to Jerusalem, he was crowned king of Palestine in the Coptic cathedral next to the Holy Sepulchre by a Coptic priest—though not the bishop.[9] Conducted, it is believed, at Abdullah's request, the ceremony strikingly exemplified the importance he attached to two cardinal principles: the legitimacy bestowed by protection of the holy places; and Christian, not just Muslim, validation of his kingship.

The trouble was that Abdullah's plans for a Hashemite Jerusalem flew in the face of United Nations plans for an internationalized Jerusalem. In a resolution of November 29, 1947, the UN General Assembly proposed the partition of Palestine into Jewish and Arab states, and the creation of a separate enclave, a *corpus separatum*, for Jerusalem and surroundings. This would be administered by a UN commissioner under a special international regime. On the eve of the outbreak of war, the UN Trusteeship Council submitted a draft statute for the city—but this was to prove a dead letter when Transjordan and Israel divided Jerusalem roughly along east–west lines into Arab and Jewish halves during the fighting of May–June 1948.

Regardless of the reality of a partitioned Jerusalem on the ground, support for internationalization came from the international community and emphatically from the Holy See and the Catholic nations. In his encyclical *In Multiplicibus Curis* of October 1948, Pope Pius XII expressed his indignation that the Holy Land had been devastated by war: "It seems to us utterly incredible that the Christian world will allow the Holy Places to be ravaged and the Tomb of Christ destroyed." He then went on to call for an international regime, and this became the central plank of Vatican policy for many years to come.[10]

On September 13, 1949, the United Nations published a draft instrument for an international regime, including provision for a force of guards, employed by the UN commissioner, to ensure protection of and free access to the holy places. The issue was to be discussed in the ad hoc political committee of the General Assembly at the end of November.

Thus the fire in the Holy Sepulchre occurred at the worst possible moment for Abdullah. When the representative of Jordan told the UN committee that internationalization of Jerusalem would serve no useful purpose, since the holy places under the control of his government had never been safer, his claim rang embarrassingly hollow. On December 9, 1949, the General Assembly restated its call for the internationalization of Jerusalem.

Since Abdullah had absolutely no intention of relinquishing control over Jerusalem and the West Bank, he was determined to rehabilitate himself as a worthy guardian of its holy places. Thus it was essential to undo, in a timely and effective fashion, the damage caused by the fire that had so nearly discredited his rule—in short, to repair the great dome.

At the beginning of 1950, Abdullah could have no idea where this commitment would lead his dynasty—nor that it would prove impossible to repair the cupola over the rotunda, as Britain had discovered in the early 1930s with the Katholikon dome, without restoring the entire Church of the Resurrection. Still, the task had fallen to a man imbued with an unshakeable sense of honor. He would not evade the responsibility.

Abdullah inherited a thankless situation at the Holy Sepulchre that had confounded the greatest of imperial powers: righteously intransigent local religious communities, uncooperative parent churches, and meddling Great Power patrons. Most perplexing, he assumed responsibility for an infirm sanctuary, the mother church of Christianity, that the communities revered but in which they were afraid to make the smallest political concession.

The point of departure for Abdullah's stewardship, like that of Britain, was the Status Quo. One of his first moves on capturing the Old City on

May 28, 1948, was to cable the pope, assuring him that the Christian holy places would be protected.[11] His government also adopted all the mandatory orders-in-council that had applied to Jerusalem's religious and international institutions.[12]

But, uncannily recalling the British experience in 1917, many of the district commissioner's files relating to the administration of the holy places were missing. Not a single copy of the 1929 Cust memorandum, the Mandate handbook on the Status Quo, was to be found.

Najib Bey Bawarshi, an Anglican Arab who had been an official under the Mandate, remembered seeing the records being placed in two cases for dispatch to London. When the British colonial office was asked to look into the matter, they responded: "no records relating to the Ottoman firmans and the Status Quo were sent home to us by the Palestine Secretariat," so they must have been left behind. They could, however, offer a copy of Cust.[13]

In the absence of up-to-date archives, Jordanian officials, like the British before them, found it difficult at first to administer the disputes inevitably arising between the communities. Dr. Hussein al-Khalidi, the high custodian of the holy places for a brief period, was forced to rely on such copies of official correspondence as the communities saw fit to show him, and on the memory of Bawarshi. Obviously, the communities would not let him see copies of decisions that had gone against them.[14]

From the beginning, there was no shortage of disagreements to deal with. As Khalidi remarked, "he had something like one minor dispute to settle each day, involving perhaps only a matter of centimetres or millimetres in the placing of a picture or a carpet but representing none the less an important issue for one or other of the religious communities."[15]

On its departure from Palestine, Britain had left behind a tangle of chronic disputes at the holy places, including several at the Holy Sepulchre. Latin renovations on Calvary, begun by Antonio Barluzzi in the 1930s, proved a source of friction. One typical territorial dispute arose over the Latin repaving of the mosaic floor of their Calvary chapel. Another concerned the Latin claim to the exclusive right to wash a marble slab in front of the altar of our Lady of Sorrows on Calvary.

A third involved the route to be taken by Latin priests on their way to that altar and the adjacent altar of the Nailing to the Cross. The Greeks objected to the Latins ascending the northern stairs up to Calvary, pausing before the Greek altar of the Exaltation of the Cross to genuflect. Pushing and shoving took place between monks from the two communities. The district commissioner issued administrative rulings on the state of current practice, but the losing community would not accept them.[16]

With the Jordanian takeover, new disagreements arose. There were several incidents involving groups of Catholic pilgrims to the Holy Sepulchre. In one case, Greek monks objected to a banner carried by visiting Italians, claiming that it was a national flag, prohibited under the Status Quo. Latins argued that this did not apply to pilgrimage standards, and the Greek superior eventually accepted this. In another case, Greek monks prevented French pilgrims from taking benches out of the church for a group photograph on the porch. The Greek monks produced cudgels, and there was a brief scuffle. The police upheld the Greek position.[17]

For Catholics, such incidents were proof that they had "to be always on the alert in Jerusalem, opposing with all their means and energy the continuing Greek invasion." Greek actions provided evidence "of a state of mind that had to be kept under close observation since it might be turned tomorrow against our most important rights." Greeks felt the same way about Latins. Ancient animosities flourished.[18]

From the beginning, the *mutassarif*, or governor, of Jerusalem dealt strongly with religious communities' breaches of the peace. Lapses into violence by the Copts in early 1949—trying to improve their position in the rotunda—were firmly suppressed. A police contingent was on hand during services, and policemen posted at the door searched the congregation for concealed weapons.[19] At Easter, serious bloodshed was only averted by the Arab Legion, who employed quarter staves on the skulls of unruly Copts.[20]

King Abdullah was determined to assert Jordanian sovereignty at the holy places and did so by successfully withstanding a series of challenges. He could do this because the Hashemite kingdom enjoyed several advantages Britain lacked. First and foremost, Jordan could assign the sanctuaries, Christian and Muslim, a priority that Britain never could. Under British rule, the holy places were a distant imperial responsibility, chronically underfunded and always of secondary importance. Under Jordanian rule, East Jerusalem was admittedly a quiet provincial town, but the holy places were a prime source of revenue and prestige, and received royal attention.

At home with shari'a law and the concept of waqf, Jordanian officials were more comfortable with the logic of Ottoman decrees and legal decisions than were British officials. Moreover, they had access to a documentary resource that the Mandate government had overlooked, namely, the pre-1853 records of the Jerusalem shari'a court containing the original rulings underpinning the Status Quo.

Again, as Muslims, they had no sentimental feelings about the Christian communities or sanctuaries. Unlike Ronald Storrs, they were indifferent to the Garden of Gethsemane at moonlight. This meant that they could be more objective. It also meant that the Christian communities themselves had less reason to question Jordanian objectivity. Where the Jordanian authorities compared most unfavorably to the British was their susceptibility to bribery and intrigue.

Surprisingly, they were less vulnerable to external pressure than the authorities had been during the Mandate. Britain, because it had to submit a yearly report to the Council of the League of Nations, had been extremely attentive to international opinion, whether in the shape of the Holy See or various European governments. Theoretically, the four Catholic consuls general in Jerusalem, representing France, Italy, Spain, and Belgium, should have constituted a powerful lobby. But the Jordanian government deeply resented, and fiercely rebuffed, all attempts at interference in its sovereign administration of the holy places.

A final considerable advantage was that Jordan used methods of persuasion, gentle and not so gentle, that Britain could not contemplate. Jordan was not a democracy, did not have a free press, would not tolerate dissent, and would not hesitate to withhold ecclesiastical privileges or confirmation of church appointments to get its way. This did not mean that the government could arbitrarily impose solutions. But it could ensure that the communities took its wishes seriously, something not always the case under the Mandate.

The major strategic challenge in the early years to King Abdullah's authority at the holy places was the abortive UN plan for internationalization of Jerusalem (already mentioned). The king handled the affair deftly, and was even able to derive benefit from it. Conversely, the Vatican mishandled it, rigidly sticking to its line long after it had ceased to be politically practical.

Given resolute Jordanian and Israeli opposition, and the waning interest of the United States, Britain, and the British Commonwealth countries, the UN plan ran out of steam during 1950. In the meantime, the Vatican ran a vigorous campaign to promote it that had an unsettling effect at the local level.

At Easter 1949, the pope followed *In Multiplicibus Curis* with a new encyclical, *Redemptoris Nostri*, promoting an international regime as the best guarantee for the Christian sanctuaries. He also reaffirmed "all rights to the Holy Places which the Catholics acquired many centuries ago." Vatican Radio made it clear that this meant regaining lost rights, in a broadcast on September 1, 1949, stating that Catholic rights "have priority before those acquired by other Christian denominations."[21]

Just after Christmas 1949, the *New York Times*, in a scoop that received international attention, published two detailed articles on the Testa plan for a grandiose new basilica under the headings "New Plan for Holy Sepulcher" and "Plans for Restoration of Holy Sepulcher."[22]

This blueprint, said to have the backing of the Vatican, was leaked at the very moment the proposal for an international regime, supported by the Catholic world, was under discussion at the UN. The Greek and Armenian patriarchates surely asked themselves if this could be mere coincidence. Against the backdrop of *Redemptoris Nostri,* the plans must have seemed ominously like a concerted diplomatic offensive to restore Latin primacy at the holy places.

The Greek and Armenian patriarchates' considered reaction, given in testimony to the UN Trusteeship Council, was to reaffirm the inviolability of the Status Quo. Any new and radical disposition at the holy places, Bishop Tiran Nersoyan stated, on behalf of the Armenian patriarchate, would reignite dissensions and disputes among the Christian communities. The Status Quo had to be the sole legal basis for any new dispensation.[23]

The Greek Orthodox Patriarchate, represented by Archbishop Germanos, the Greek cleric dealing with Status Quo issues, concurred in almost identical terms. In obvious reference to the wholesale clearances called for by the Testa plan, he added "that the Holy Places, the shrines and attached property should be exempt from all taxation and should on no account be subject to expropriation."[24]

The effect of the episode was to throw the Greeks and Armenians into the arms of King Abdullah. On a visit to the Church of the Nativity in Bethlehem in April 1950, the Greek bishop welcomed the king. In a fulsome address evoking the Muslim conquest of Jerusalem in 638 (which magnanimously left the Church in charge of its holy places), the bishop said: "Every time we stand in front of the altar, we remember Caliph Omar Ben Khattab. He was the first to create good relations between Muslims and Christians. We consider Your Majesty the inheritor of the great Caliph and the bearer of his message. Whenever we go to pray, we ask God to lengthen your years and support you forever."[25]

The difficulties and contradictions inherent in Vatican support for internationalization soon became apparent. Later that summer, Archbishop Testa was received in audience by King Abdullah to discuss the Marangoni-Barluzzi plan for a new basilica, recently published in book form.

Testa had returned to Jerusalem as apostolic delegate and regent of the Latin patriarchate in June 1948, toward the end of the battle for Jerusalem. With strong features and twinkling eyes, he was now sixty-two years old and suffered from gout. Shelled out of his residence on Mount Zion by the Haganah, he was criticized for moving to the Franciscan convent in Bethlehem, at a safe distance from hostilities—only returning to his post at Easter 1949.

The endorsement of the project by the king, as effective sovereign of East Jerusalem, was essential if the new basilica was ever to be built. This hardly squared with a parallel campaign calculated to undermine Jordanian legitimacy. Testa found himself in the untenable position of appealing for the benevolent exercise of Jordanian sovereignty in Jerusalem while at one and the same time rejecting that selfsame sovereignty.[26]

King Abdullah's reply was subtle. He promised Testa that he would lend his support on the condition that all the communities were in agreement. However, as he well knew, this was virtually inconceivable: the waqf could never transfer its property, which was inviolable, or accept the demolition of mosques; the Greek patriarchate, possessing a major share of the rights in the present Holy Sepulchre complex, was not going to abandon its privileged position; non-Catholics could not agree to Catholics getting the biggest church.[27]

Predictably, within a short time articles began to appear in the local Arabic press attacking the proposed demolition of mosques adjacent to the Holy Sepulchre. The Greek patriarchate rejected the plan on the grounds that it was contrary to their traditions and that they would lose three of their monasteries. A Catholic Institute of Press bulletin then reported on September 20 that the plan's implementation had been postponed indefinitely.

With the Vatican archives closed, it remains unclear why Testa's temple scheme was ever revived. There was no great enthusiasm for it either in the Custody of the Holy Land or the Latin patriarchate.[28] The new patriarch, Monsignor Alberto Gori, later acknowledged that he had only supported the "tiresome project" for "political reasons." Since it envisaged an Anglican foothold in the new Holy Sepulchre, it may indeed have been intended, as the British Foreign Office suspected, as a device to muster Anglo-American support for internationalization of Jerusalem.[29] Monsignor Giovanni Battista Montini, a senior official in the Holy See at the time, later Pope Paul VI, summed up with the remark that "the whole plan was . . . little more than a dream."[30]

To underline his attachment to Jerusalem and rebut the threat of internationalization, King Abdullah now took an unprecedented step. On January 5, 1951, he appointed Ragheb Pasha Nashashibi to the new post of guardian of al-Haram al-Sharif and high custodian of the holy places. Nashashibi was a former mayor of Jerusalem (1921–35), a member of a prominent Jerusalem family, and currently minister without portfolio with special responsibility for Jerusalem.

In his royal warrant of appointment, Ragheb Pasha was instructed to protect "all communities and pilgrims of all nations" and "preserve their liberties, shrines, rites and places of worship." This would be "in accordance with the established status quo governing the rights of all communities, mosques, churches and monasteries." He was also instructed to "uphold the Imperial Firmans and Orders in force held by their Beatitudes the Patriarchs, recording all rights in a special register to be consulted whenever necessary and enforced at all times."[31]

Ragheb Pasha would be the king's deputy, embodying royal dignity and authority. He would bear personal responsibility for the safekeeping of the Muslim and Christian sanctuaries and outrank the heads of communities. Creation of a special register would, it was hoped, solve the problem of the missing British and Ottoman records, facilitating the work of handling disputes at the holy places.[32]

Abdullah's creation of a special post should have given a tremendous boost to the administration of the Christian sanctuaries. Specifically, it should have finally unlocked the door to the much-needed and long-awaited restoration of the Holy Sepulchre. For Abdullah's project of repairing the burnt dome was stuck. The governor, Ihsan Hashem, lacked resources and a clear idea of what to do. Certainly, the DPW lacked the specialist skills to address the problems of an ancient structure. Perhaps a high custodian, enjoying the backing of the king, could focus on the job and get things moving.

All that had been done to date was to remove the debris of the fire, patch up the stonework of the cupola with a large quantity of cement, and apply a copious layer of tar. Over the winter of 1950–51, this had completely failed to stop rainwater leaking into the rotunda.[33] There was serious concern among Franciscans, moreover, that the repairs had been bungled and that the additional weight had increased the risk of disintegration and collapse that all now understood menaced the Holy Sepulchre. The Jerusalem engineer seemed oblivious to this danger.[34]

Unfortunately, Ragheb Pasha's appointment was immediately enmeshed in controversy. No one was enthusiastic; quite a few interested parties, domestic and foreign, were hostile. The Holy See and the French government were dismayed at what they perceived as a serious threat to their interests. As far as the Vatican was concerned, the appointment was a further obstacle to internationalization. The high custodian's powers would be a usurpation of those earmarked for a future UN commissioner.

Nor did the Vatican like the idea of a codification of the Status Quo, which they claimed would lead to its eventual modification.[35] Their unstated objection was that it might rule out the redressing of grievances and the restoration of the Latin predominance lost in 1757.

France had its own particular reasons for deploring the appointment. In 1924, it had relinquished its historical role as protector of Latin Christianity in Jerusalem and Bethlehem. The end of the Mandate and the return of Muslim rule recreated precisely those conditions that had justified French intervention in the past. Put another way, they presented an opportunity for France to claw back some of its prestige in the Levant at a time of postwar, colonial decline in Indo-China and North Africa. A Jordanian high custodian would not only preclude internationalization, he would also reduce the scope of French influence.

René Neuville, the veteran French consul general and dean of the consular corps, was therefore instructed by his government not to attend Ragheb Pasha's installation and to organize a diplomatic boycott. He argued to his colleagues that the appointment was an infringement of the Status Quo, on the ground that only the governor, as successor to the district commissioner, could administer the holy places. In fact, the 1924 order-in-council had made clear that the high commissioner was the ultimate authority at the holy places. As his successor, King Abdullah was entitled to delegate his functions to any official he chose.[36]

At the ceremony on January 15, 1951, the Catholic consuls general of France, Belgium, Italy, and Spain were all absent. The Latin patriarch was represented by his secretary. Given the enormous importance King Abdullah attached to his role of guardian of the holy places, this was certainly taken as a personal insult. Monsignor Domenico Tardini, the senior Vatican official dealing with the issue, seemed surprised when told that this had damaged relations between the patriarchate and the royal court.[37]

To complicate matters, on April 9, Ragheb Pasha died at the age of seventy-eight. In his place, the king appointed another Jerusalem notable, Dr. Hussein Khalidi. From the beginning, he faced an uphill task. His budget was inadequate, he had a single clerk, and Najib Bey Bawarshi, the only person who knew anything about the Status Quo, resigned when his salary was cut to that of a typist. Policing of services in the Churches of the Holy Sepulchre and Nativity was arranged directly by the police, who also sorted out squabbles on an ad hoc basis.[38]

During his abbreviated eighteen-month tenure, Khalidi was engaged in turf wars with two successive governors. The first, Ihsan Hashem, muttered darkly that "the Custodian had no function and was never likely to have any."[39] His successor, the formidable Hassan al-Katib, who took over toward the end of 1951, dealt in person with the consular corps and had to be continually reminded by his superior, the minister of the interior, to forward correspondence on the holy places to the high custodian.[40]

The final straw for Khalidi came when his own government undercut him. A Greek attempt to illuminate the cross above the Church of the Nativity in Bethlehem, the centerpiece of Christmas celebrations, using electric light rather than, as in the past, oil lamps, was contested by the Latins, who maintained that this affected the main fabric of the basilica and so was the concern of all the major communities. Khalidi found in their favor.[41]

The Greeks then went over his head, appealing the decision in Amman. The governor of Jerusalem supported them. In August 1952, the Jordanian cabinet upheld the appeal. A light was a light, whether electricity or oil. Significantly, they argued that the royal decree defining the high custodian's duties was constitutionally flawed. His position now untenable, Khalidi resigned.[42]

Remarkably, it was in such seemingly inauspicious circumstances of diplomatic squabbling, communal disputation, and bureaucratic infighting that, away from the limelight, the first hesitant steps toward repair of the Holy Sepulchre were taken.

| Hassan Bey Takes Charge

B Y THE EARLY 1950S, many sympathetic observers, on the assumption that the Christian communions would never agree among themselves, had concluded that the mother church was doomed. Hence they expected that the unsightly supports would remain in place until another fire or earthquake came along to topple the church for good.[1]

News of progress in talks to save the Holy Sepulchre was therefore received with astonishment. On September 30, 1955, the *Times* of London described "a remarkable degree of agreement as to the practical steps to be taken" and "an atmosphere favourable as never before to the restoration of this most venerable shrine of Christendom."[2]

How, after years of denial and procrastination, did the three principal communities finally manage to agree to cooperate in the restoration of the Holy Sepulchre?

Two events, one on top of the other, stirred the communities out of their complacency. The first was the November 1949 fire, a sobering experience that caught them woefully unprepared in a church packed with fuel. It could easily have burnt to the ground.

Next, while the fire was still smoldering, came King Abdullah's unprecedented visit to meet church leaders. The effect of this gesture was not to gratify the ecclesiastics but to shock them. They greeted his promise to undertake repairs with alarm. In conjunction with the Nashashibi appointment, the royal initiative suggested to them that the Hashemite kingdom intended to assume direct responsibility for the church. Under Ottoman law, he who repaired the roof of a house owned the house. They concluded that if the king paid for the dome, then he would own the dome; and if he owned the dome, the rotunda was his.

For all the Greek Orthodox talk of a golden age of Muslim custodianship, this was a most unwelcome prospect. During the British Mandate, Christian title to the holy places had never been questioned, and the communities had enjoyed substantial freedom from government interference. Jordanian activism threatened their relative independence and the return to a system based on the allocation of church assets by fiat. The shrunken dimensions of the Anastasis complex, surrounded by two mosques and other waqf property standing on Constantinian foundations, were a reminder of past Muslim encroachment.

What brought the communities together initially, in other words, was a shared threat. In order to face that threat, they had no choice but to cooperate. It was this, not an ethic of ecumenical reconciliation, that brought about the change of heart.

They were then drawn along by the logic of events, as one step led to another. It proved impossible to escape King Abdullah's emergency repairs, but these soon turned out to have been faulty. The harsh winter of 1950–51 was one of the worst Jerusalem had seen in years. Heavy snowfalls led to overburdened walls collapsing and roofs caving in throughout the Old City. Everyone in the church was thoroughly miserable from the cold and damp; the steady trickle of water onto altars—soaking plaster, spoiling pictures, altar cloths, and carpets—posed the practical problem: how was one to stop leaks in the great dome and further dilapidation without invoking further Jordanian interference?

The final stage in the education of the major communities came when it dawned on them that a sound dome could not sit on an unsound rotunda. Harvey's supports had bought time, but now it was clear that inaction was no longer a viable option. Since the major communities possessed a veto on repairs to common areas, a permanent solution to the problem of the dome required decision-making by negotiation and consensus.

A protracted diplomatic process of frustrating complexity ensued in which representatives of the churches, with the assistance of the Jordanian government, struggled to adjust their incompatible expectations and claims to reality. Some of their goals, they discovered, simply could not be achieved. All the rest depended on their rivals' compliance. After years of dreams and rhetoric, they realized that to save the church they had to compromise.

But before they could piece together the agreements needed to go ahead with the restoration, many crises and disappointments had to be surmounted.

Some of the most formidable resistance to agreement emanated from within the communities themselves.

When the spring of 1951 arrived, and the barren surrounding hills came alive with wild cyclamen, anemones, irises, hyacinths, rock roses, and fragrant broom, the heads of the three major communities took a highly unusual step. In the contentious world of the Holy Sepulchre, it was the sort of action reserved only for the direst of emergencies. The temporary repairs carried out by the Jordanian DPW had failed to keep out the water. Something had to be done, and if the churches did not act, the authorities would. They decided, therefore, on a joint initiative.

The novelty of this move may be hard for an outsider to grasp, but at the time there was still controversy over rights of possession to the great dome. In the 1860s, it had been reconstructed at the joint expense of Russia, France, and Turkey, representing the Greeks, Latins, and Armenians, respectively. Even so, the Greeks continued to maintain their exclusive claim, while the Armenians' acquisition of rights was still contested.

On March 19, 1951, the mutassarif of Jerusalem wrote a routine letter to the heads of each of the three major communities asking what they wanted him to do with the melted lead salvaged from the fire. That disposed of any lingering doubts about copossession. It also presented an opportunity to act. In a joint letter of April 5, the three principals wrote back pointing out the deplorable state of the dome and suggesting that it be re-covered with lead. They wondered whether the recovered metal could be reused, and tactfully undertook to divide the cost of repairs among themselves on an equal basis in order to preempt an undesirable Jordanian offer of payment.[3]

A tragic event now intervened to delay matters and remove the unwelcome prospect of royal philanthropy. On July 20, 1951, King Abdullah was assassinated at the entrance to al-Aksa Mosque on his way to prayer. The murder plunged the country into uncertainty.

After the grief-stricken Arab Legion had run amok through the streets of the Old City, there was a wave of arrests, including that of a priest belonging to the Latin patriarchate: Father Ibrahim Ayad, the head of the Jerusalem ecclesiastical court. He was put on trial for associating with Palestinians hostile to the monarchy. The military court acquitted him, but he was expelled from the country. This was less than an exoneration, and the episode triggered an anti-Christian campaign.[4]

Prince Tallal, the heir to the throne, was proclaimed king on September 5, 1951. He had been declared fit to reign by five Swiss psychiatrists, but Archbishop Testa could personally testify to his mental instability. Testa had been in Amman's Italian Hospital on the very night that the prince tried to murder his wife, the Amira Zein, who was convalescing after giving birth to a daughter. An Italian ward sister saved the princess by seizing the dagger and running into the apostolic delegate's private room. Testa later quipped: "We priests see some funny things but I would never have believed that I would be awakened in the middle of the night by a nun running into my bedroom waving a bare knife in her hand."[5]

The situation remained fragile throughout Tallal's reign. Security was tight, to guard against further terrorist acts by followers of the mufti of Jerusalem, Haj Amin al-Husayni. Shared fears also drew Christians closer together. Their enemies did not make fine denominational distinctions. At one point, the Italian legation reported: "The position of Christians in Jordan, and of Catholics in particular, is far from good," expressing anxiety that at any time there might be "some massacre of Catholics on the part of Muslims."[6]

In September 1951, the Jordanian government decided to go ahead with repair of the dome, and a committee of five DPW engineers serving under the Jerusalem district engineer was appointed.[7] After an on-the-spot inspection, they reported that temporary repairs had proved ineffective and that a permanent covering of reinforced concrete capped with lead or copper had to be installed as soon as possible.

They were confident that, correctly positioned and balanced, the weight of the covering would "neither affect the strength of the structure nor of the pilasters supporting the Church." They anticipated no difficulty about dividing the cost of the lead or copper sheathing, whichever was preferred, among the communities.[8]

Unfortunately, like its predecessor during the Mandate, the Jordanian DPW had no specialized knowledge of ancient structures and failed to draw the obvious conclusion from the steel beams, scaffolding, and tension bands supporting it: that the church was structurally weak throughout. Nor had they troubled to look up past British reports.

Representatives of the major communities met in the high custodian's *divan,* or reception room, on February 21, 1952. They attended on behalf of their principals, each of whom was eager for agreement on the dome. There were three key church leaders:

The veteran Greek Orthodox patriarch, Timotheos Themlis, was sick with Parkinson's disease and unable to participate in public ceremonies. However, he dominated his synod and decided personally on major policy matters, particularly concerning the holy places, his special expertise. For years he had observed the progressive decay of the Anastasis. After being elected patriarch in 1935, his capacity to act was frustrated, first by Britain's withholding of his berat of appointment, then by war, and finally by debilitating illness. Now he had little time left to leave his mark. He would not abandon his beloved Anastasis to dereliction.

Father Giacinto Faccio, the Franciscan custos, had succeeded Father Alberto Gori in 1950 at the age of thirty-eight. Originally from Venice, Father Faccio came to Palestine to study in 1939. When Italy entered the war, he was interned at Emmaus as an enemy national. Imaginative and energetic, but somewhat disorganized, he liked to keep a personal eye on custodial affairs by traveling around his vast province, which included Cyprus, Egypt, Israel, Jordan, and Syria.[9]

He mostly delegated responsibility for the work of restoration to Father Albert Rock, a local Palestinian who traced his family back to the Crusades. In an early open letter to the Custody of the Holy Land, Father Faccio had surveyed the history of the Franciscan presence in a scholarly way. He was well aware of the obstructive role played by the Catholic powers in the 1920s, when they had blocked the establishment of a special commission to settle disputes at the holy places.[10]

For his part, he was determined that the Custody vigorously assert its historical role of guardian of the holy places and contribute to repairing the rotunda dome without outside interference. By the end of his incumbency in 1955, his activism and independent-mindedness had made him thoroughly unpopular with all the other Catholic leaders in Jerusalem—the Latin patriarch, the apostolic delegate, and the French consul general.

Archbishop Yeghishe Derderian had become locum tenens, or placeholder, of the Armenian Orthodox Patriarchate following the death of Patriarch Kevork Israelian in 1949. Born in Van in eastern Anatolia, Derderian had lost his entire family—parents, brother, and sister—in the Ottoman massacres of 1915 and had arrived in Jerusalem as an orphan in 1922. A supreme survivor, he was worldly and politically astute, and was ambitious to become patriarch. The affair of the dome provided him with an opportunity to demonstrate strong leadership and consolidate the standing of his community in the Holy Sepulchre. But Derderian did not lack enemies within St. James, the Armenian convent and fraternity.

In the aftermath of the 1949 fire, Patriarch Timotheos, Father Faccio, and Archbishop Derderian concluded that they must make their own decisions and reach agreement directly among themselves in order to present the Jordanian authorities with a united front. Working at cross-purposes, they would be vulnerable to tactics of divide and conquer. Furthermore, they could allow no one else to speak in their place. Diplomatic interventions in the past had often led to deadlock, one power canceling out the other. The logic of the Status Quo, as they saw it, was precisely to insulate local relationships between the communities from international power politics.

In the presence of the high custodian of the holy places, Hussein al-Khalidi, their delegates finalized agreement on re-covering the dome, opting for the cheaper and heavier lead option. The expeditiousness of the negotiation and the absence of quibbling are striking evidence of a prior meeting of minds at the highest ecclesiastical level in Jerusalem.

In essential respects, the February 1952 agreement foreshadowed many features of subsequent accords. All agreed to divide the cost of work on the dome, which was common property, into three equal parts. The cost of repairs to privately owned property would be met by the community concerned. The government, with the consent of the three communities, could carry out minor repairs. A request the Copts submitted to participate in the restoration was rejected, as they were deemed *yamaklik*—a minor, dependent community. The scrap lead would be sold and the receipts distributed to the major communities equally. At a second meeting a few days later, it was further agreed that the leading of the cupola would be carried out by the authorities, with the assistance of three engineers, one representing each of the communities.[11]

Altogether, the February 1952 agreement focused narrowly on a specific point, repair of the cupola. Nevertheless, it was a milestone. The importance of direct negotiations cannot be overstated. Jordan's provision of good offices, meaning technical support and hospitality, is also noteworthy.

But the agreement was never implemented. The communities' engineers warned that a concrete and lead outer covering for the dome would constitute a grave danger. A simple calculation indicated that it would weigh significantly more than the old wooden one and exceed the strength not only of the lower supports, which were in a pitiful condition, but probably even of the temporary struts installed as reinforcements.[12]

Reports of the landmark February agreement were greeted with indignation by France and Italy: They felt that they should have been consulted and that they, not the Custody of the Holy Land, should pay the Latins' share of repairs.

Since King Abdullah's death, they had become increasingly agitated by Jordan's "interference" in the matter of the repair of the dome, which they saw as a ruse to obtain proprietorial rights and consolidate sovereignty over Jerusalem. Over the winter of 1951–52, they became thoroughly alarmed at what they perceived to be a consistent pattern of flagrant Jordanian violations of the Status Quo, including appointment of the high custodian and preferential treatment of the Greek Orthodox Patriarchate.

The February 1952 agreement, made behind the backs of the French and Italian consuls general, was the last straw. The local communities had allegedly unlawfully seized rights that had traditionally belonged to states. French diplomats based their case on the precedent of the 1862 international agreement between Turkey, Russia, and France for the last repair of the rotunda dome.

Not only did the letter on the cupola, signed by the custos and his colleagues, imply recognition of Jordanian authority and disenfranchisement of the Catholic powers; it would also, they argued, leave the Latins helpless in the face of future Jordanian violations of the Status Quo in favor of the other communities.

What was to be done? For months, France and Italy pondered the pros and cons of various diplomatic initiatives. Appeal to the 1862 treaty was problematic, because it would invoke Russian rights alongside those of France. No one wanted a Soviet foothold in Jerusalem. France did want to involve Britain, both on principle and because of its influence over Jordan, but Britain sympathized with Jordan's practical problems and questioned the contemporary relevance of the 1862 accord. A united Catholic front also seemed desirable, but Spain was reluctant to get involved, and the Holy See had lost its enthusiasm for a confrontation with Jordan— indeed, they defended the arrangement.[13]

Unwilling to be more Catholic than the pope, the Italians pulled out of any joint move with France. This left René Neuville, the French consul general, who was seriously ill at this time and had not long to live, to fight alone. He met twice with the Jordanian governor, Hassan Bey al-Katib, to press France's case. The French foreign ministry had decided against a formal protest, so Neuville insisted on France's prerogatives at the Christian holy places in general, and its right to be consulted on repair of the dome in particular.[14]

Neuville had long experience of the holy places. He had first served as vice-consul in Jerusalem in 1926–37, returning as consul general in 1946. A distinguished palaeontologist, he had worked on many digs throughout Palestine and knew the country intimately. He was inspired by a deep feeling for France's historical role in the Holy Land. Nevertheless, regardless of Neuville's personal standing, by the early 1950s France played only a minor role in Jordan and was unpopular because of its colonial role in North Africa.

The French thought of the Status Quo primarily as an international regime under international law involving states, rather than a local arrangement involving communities, as the British tended to see it. International treaties concluded between France and the Ottoman Empire and centuries of protectorate had given France inviolable legal rights at the holy places, it was maintained, expressly reserved in the 1878 Treaty of Berlin. The 1862 treaty confirmed France's standing in the repair of the dome. Nothing that had occurred since, certainly not under the inherently transient British Mandate, could alter this.[15]

Politely but firmly, Hassan Bey dismissed Neuville's case, pointing out that the mandatory government had undertaken repairs to the Katholikon dome after the 1927 earthquake without consulting foreign powers, so that any French claim had lapsed.[16] Moreover, after the affair of the Edicule in 1925, the Palestine government had excluded the Catholic consuls altogether from involvement in the administration of the Christian sanctuaries.[17]

The affair of the cupola was Neuville's last effort, and he deserves admiration for his devotion to duty in the face of terminal illness. Still, France's attempt to revive traditional French rights in Jerusalem, decades after the departure of the Turks, was an exercise in futility. With its evocation of the Crusades and the capitulations—legal immunities and exemptions enjoyed by European powers in the Ottoman Empire—it was a romantic and anachronistic gesture.

For the governor, Hassan Bey, a judge by profession, it was a question of the supremacy of Jordanian sovereignty over outdated French privileges. Whereas Neuville saw France's capitulatory treaties with Turkey as continuing sources of obligation, the Jordanian mutassarif saw them as unequal and now defunct treaties extorted during a period of Western hegemony. They were now neither just nor relevant.[18]

Hassan Bey (*bey* was used as a term of respect in the Ottoman empire) spoke from deep conviction. His family were of Bedouin origin from the Hijaz—now part of Saudi Arabia—and had come to Transjordan with the Emir Abdullah after World War I. He was a classic Ottoman-style civil servant, who had trained as a jurist under the old regime.

Men of his generation had lived until they were in their twenties or thirties as subjects of the mighty Ottoman Empire and were a product of its educational system. Steeped in a deep sense of duty, they had an enormous pride in Turkish civilization and its tradition of service. Even King Abdullah preferred to speak in Turkish, as the language of culture, rather than Arabic, to a Turkish-speaking interlocutor.[19]

Deeply loyal to the Hashemite dynasty, Hassan Bey had served King Abdullah as governor of Nablus before being appointed to the position of mutassarif of Jerusalem by King Hussein. For the next seven years, this tall, dignified "Ottoman official" (as the communities tended to see him) was to play a key role in the life of the Holy Sepulchre.

At first he did not know a great deal about the Status Quo, though he had the experienced Bawarshi to advise him, and asked the British for advice on occasion. But with his judicial background, he soon grasped the essentials of a case and had the advantage of a thorough knowledge of Turkish law. He could not be bamboozled by Ottoman firmans, which he could read in the original, and would not be intimidated. He was also incorruptible—as a former official of the Armenian patriarchate confided: "We knew, because we tried."[20]

A courtly host, with the immense courtesy and soft-spoken tone of the Bedouin, he could be ruthless if need be. "He was in the tradition of receiving someone graciously for dinner, the next day sentencing him to hang."[21] Dealing with the Christian communities, he used every means at his disposal to bring them into line. He became totally committed to the restoration project and would not be diverted by consular pressure. His persistence, flexibility, and rejection of foreign interference from the start, with the full support of Amman, created the necessary conditions for Jordan's ultimate achievement in brokering the restoration of the basilica.

Had Jordan admitted a French right to be consulted, there would have been no end to it. Egypt, Ethiopia, Greece, the Vatican, Italy, Belgium, and Spain would all have demanded that they be consulted, too. Italy and France would have revived their old quarrel over the right to represent Catholicism. If the 1862 precedent were reinstated, the Soviet Union might also claim a share in the cost of restoration. As the successor state to czarist Russia and ruler of Armenia, it could demand to speak on behalf of both the Greek Orthodox and Armenian Orthodox patriarchates. The upshot would have been unending diplomatic conflict and paralysis, while rain continued to pour through the roof.

***

Following the conclusion of the February 1952 agreement between the communities to repair the rotunda dome, and with the Catholic consuls general held at bay for the moment, Hassan Bey's instinct was to get on with the job. Waterproofing a dome should surely not present insuperable difficulties. At first, talk was of beginning work after Easter 1952. This was delayed when technical calculations indicated the impracticality of a heavy concrete and lead outer dome. A permanent solution would also require settlement of a number of political and administrative problems.

First among these was the supervision of the project. The DPW could not undertake responsibility because it lacked the expertise, so the governor proposed to entrust the task to an intercommunal committee appointed by church leaders. Dr. al-Khalidi, the high custodian, opposed this proposal, fearing serious disagreement with international repercussions.

In response, the minister of transport suggested bringing in an Egyptian or Syrian expert, as had been done at the Dome of the Rock, which was currently being repaired.[22] Unfortunately, there were few specialists in the Arab world in the conservation of Romanesque churches. Eventually, the solution that emerged was an intercommunal committee of foreign experts.

The question of overall administrative responsibility was settled when the post of high custodian of the holy places was allowed to drop, following Dr. al-Khalidi's resignation in August 1952. Hassan Bey took over the Holy Sepulchre file and was soon busy fixing the paved lane next to the edifice, meeting foreign consuls, corresponding with church leaders, and pondering the crucial issue of paying for the restoration of the cupola.[23]

A shortage of funds troubled everyone. As yet, Hassan Bey had no budget to administer the Holy Sepulchre, let alone repair it. Jordan, after all, was a small country with limited resources and an onerous refugee problem stemming from the 1948 war. At the same time, with Amman as capital, Palestinian Jerusalem was relegated to provincial status. Not for the first or last time, operations in the Old City were run on a shoestring.

The obvious answer was to solicit contributions from abroad, which is how repairs to the Dome of the Rock were being funded. Hassan Bey was troubled that financial assistance might have strings attached.[24] The problem was not Greek or French government aid but communist influence bought with Russian Orthodox gold. Given the opportunity, the Moscow patriarchate was said to be ready to pay for the entire cost of reconstruction.[25]

The Greek Orthodox Patriarchate's lack of ready funds might leave it open to temptation. As a result of the 1948 war, the most valuable Greek rental property had been left on the Israeli side of the armistice line in West Jerusalem. However, lucrative leasing arrangements finalized with Israeli bodies in early 1954 helped to ease the situation. Once restoration became a real prospect, the Greek government promised £500,000, an enormous sum, considering that Greece was itself receiving economic assistance of £20 million per annum. The Greek patriarchate did its best to resist the attachment of conditions.

If need be, the Anglican Church in England and its sister Episcopal Church in the United States would have been happy to launch an appeal.[26] By mid-1954, this was felt to be no longer necessary.

The Armenian patriarchate was also in trouble following the 1948 partition of Jerusalem and had been inundated with Armenian refugees. Archbishop Derderian, the locum tenens, had managed to raise some funds for displaced persons from the Armenian diaspora. Rumors that began to circulate about irregularities in the administration of these funds put a strain on this tightly knit but fractious community.[27] Later, funding for restoration came from the Gulbenkian Foundation of Lisbon and wealthy Americans of Armenian extraction.

The Franciscan Custody of the Holy Land was in a fundamentally sound position financially. Since the thirteenth century, popes had decreed that an annual collection be taken up on Good Friday for the care and maintenance of the holy places. In the twentieth century, an international network of Commissariats of the Holy Land had been established to help the work of the Custody.[28] There was a lack of ready funds in the short term, however, and a fund-raising drive was planned.

The balanced multinational character of the Custody, governed by a nine-member Discretorium, and regular audits ensured the sound management of its financial affairs. The custos, a simple friar, was appointed from the ranks for a fixed term and might be reappointed but was an overburdened administrator rather than an absolute ruler.[29] This contrasted with the Greek and Armenian patriarchs, who were elected for life and exercised the power of the purse—a system prone to abuse.

Within the precincts of the Holy Sepulchre, life went on as usual. Contacts between the communities over repairs had the positive effect of reducing day-to-day friction. The American ambassador, Joseph C. Green, visited the Holy Sepulchre in September 1952 and marveled that it was still standing. "If it were not of extraordinary strong construction it would now be a mass of ruins. As it is it is shored up with steel beams and scaffoldings and bands. Evidently someone will have to put a good many thousands of dollars into its restoration."[30]

While the governor of Jerusalem wrestled with the thorny issue of the rotunda dome, there was much else on his mind. There was widespread local support for the exiled mufti of Jerusalem, the personification of Palestinian nationalism. A cultural gap separated the Palestinian West Bank from the Bedouin East Bank. Each population despised the other. There was occasional firing across the armistice lines between Israelis and Jordanians.

The winter and spring of 1952–53 was a period of wait and see as Jordan prepared for the crowning of the seventeen-year-old Emir Hussein the following May. The new king's youth and inexperience would be less important than the message of legitimacy and continuity his coronation would send. Meanwhile, there was no progress on the dome, and disagreements were multiplying. As during the Mandate, the authorities, in this case Muslim, sometimes seemed more concerned with the state of the basilica than were the communities themselves.

On the one hand, the chief justice of Jordan, Ruhi Pasha Abd al-Hadi, who as a member of the Muslim religious board had a consultative role in the conservation of the holy places, was disturbed by the precarious condition of the Holy Sepulchre and the danger that it might come "tumbling down at any moment." He was struck by the failure of the three major communities to agree with the Copts on a plan for the repair of the church and told Ambassador Green that Jordan had been attempting to coerce them into agreement.[31]

On the other hand, the Latin patriarch, Alberto Gori, a former custos, felt that there was "no immediate danger," thanks to the basic solidity of the cupola and the sturdy scaffolding throughout the edifice, and wanted a settlement postponed. He criticized the custos's direct talks with the Jordanian authorities, whom he called "both Muslim and incompetent."[32]

Once Hussein was crowned king on May 2, 1953, the Jordanian government could resume normal business. Among other things, the Holy Sepulchre returned to the agenda. Hassan Bey was in for a shock about the grave overall state of the church.

For some time, the British Foreign Office had followed the affair of the rotunda dome, careful to avoid taking a lead. Any initiative was felt to be inadvisable, given Jordan's direct responsibility and the strong feelings of Catholic powers, especially France. Officials had, however, done their homework, searching through the archives for relevant documents on the Holy Sepulchre.

In colonial office files from 1947, they came across a report prepared by C. T. Wolley of a London firm of civil engineers. Wolley had not carried out a complete inspection of the Holy Sepulchre but only a general survey to ascertain fundamental weaknesses.

He confirmed Harvey's findings about the urgent need for restoration and preservation. Specifically, he found extensive parts of the fabric to be unreliable and calculated that the loads on the northeast pier under the Katholikon dome (about 10 tons per square foot) and on the piers in the rotunda (about 8 tons per square foot) were extremely high, in view of the character of the construction. Many walls and piers had either to be reconstructed or consolidated. Wolley found the masonry facing of the Edicule to be in an unsafe condition and liable to be disturbed by some unusual event, in which case the entire structure would almost certainly collapse. He also warned that the foundations of the church were in an unsound state, weakened by cisterns and drains in the rock below. This had serious implications, he argued, for the viability of the rotunda piers and pilasters. In conclusion, he recommended a thorough investigation of the entire building.[33]

In the twilight of British rule, nothing could be done except to install steel bands around the Edicule to prevent its complete collapse in the event of a seismic disturbance.[34] Copies of the Wolley report had been given to representatives of each of the major communities by the Jerusalem district commissioner. It was then filed and forgotten.

In the very changed circumstances of 1952–53, the report made its way back from London to Jerusalem to be examined by the British consul general. It concluded that a restoration would require a special team of experts under a resident engineer and would be unlikely to cost less than £1,000,000—a huge sum at the time and far beyond Jordan's means.[35]

The report placed Britain in a conundrum, for it could not draw attention to the problem without suggesting a solution. Nevertheless, it felt an obvious obligation to help. The report would have to be given to Hassan Bey the moment he was in a position to make use of it. That moment came when the Jordanian government made proper budgetary provision for supervision of the holy places toward the end of 1953.

Wolley's warnings about the state of the foundations and the piers in the rotunda put a new face on things. If he was right, it would be clearly out of the question to repair the great dome separately. At the very least, the Holy Sepulchre would have to be thoroughly examined, as Wolley recommended.

At the beginning of December 1953, Hassan Bey wrote to the three major communities informing them of Wolley's conclusions and asking for their views on the eventual restoration of the entire monument. He proposed that each undertake repairs to its own part of the church. However, he reserved for the government the restoration of common areas, such as the great dome, with costs to be shared by the communities.[36] On the basis of precedents from the Ottoman and Mandate periods, he hoped to bypass anticipated deadlock between the churches. But church leaders were appalled by the prospect of a leading Jordanian role.

Between December 1953 and May 1954, church leaders and the governor engaged in a series of talks that were unprecedented in the annals of the Church of the Resurrection. Issues on the table included the respective roles of sovereign and communities, whether a new survey was needed, and if so, who was to conduct it, and whether reconstruction or repair was envisaged.

Despite the auspicious February 1952 understanding, considerable mistrust remained among the communities and hostility at the level of the rank and file. Deep theological and cultural differences separated the three ancient churches. All had radically opposing interpretations of the Status Quo, generating a plethora of rival claims, so any negotiation was sure to arouse dormant disputes over possession and usage.

Nevertheless, the communities had a strong incentive to coordinate their positions before meeting the mutassarif. If they did not come up with a proposal, he surely would. The communities quickly decided not to rely on the government's technical adviser but that each would appoint its own expert. Father Faccio, conscious of the need to conciliate the critical French government, approached its consul general, Bernard Rochereau de la Sablière, to request the services of a French architect.[37] With the finest examples of Romanesque churches in Europe, France had acquired considerable expertise in conservation over the past century.

The French government accepted this approach with alacrity. The appointment of a French architect not only was consistent with France's traditional role of protector of the Christian holy places but also would allow it to follow events from the inside, "foil intrigue," and support the policy it favored—repair rather than radical reconstruction.[38]

Within a few weeks, the communities named their architects: Professor Anastasios Orlandos, director general of Greek antiquities, would represent the Greek Orthodox Patriarchate. Since writing his 1934 report on the Anastasis, he had been given responsibility for restoration of the Parthenon. Pierre Coupel of the French government department of historical monuments, who was an expert on Crusader architecture in the Levant, would be the architect for the Custody. Mardiros Altounian, who had graduated from the Paris École des Beaux-Arts in 1918 and was architect of the 1931 Beirut parliament building, would be the representative of the Armenian Patriarchate.

Church leaders now wrote to the governor recommending a thorough, updated survey of the structure, but they could not agree on who would carry it out. The Greeks wanted it done by Wolley, since they approved of his conservative view that the basilica should be "reinforced and put in good repair." This would best preserve their predominant position under the existing Status Quo. For the same reason, the Latins preferred that someone else do it. If it could be shown that the present church would have to be pulled down and replaced, then the Status Quo became moot. The Armenians were anxious to preserve their existing position in the Holy Sepulchre and wanted the Jordanian authorities to decide.[39]

Rival Greek and Latin conceptions, repair versus reconstruction, were debated at several meetings with Hassan Bey. Realizing that agreement at the level of principle was unattainable, Hassan Bey made a practical suggestion to break the impasse on May 26, 1954. A tripartite commission of experts representing the major communities, together with the Jerusalem assistant engineer, should make an on-the-spot investigation of the condition of the

Holy Sepulchre. They would then report back to the mutassarif and church representatives.

This suggestion was accepted. Why argue about hypothetical plans for rebuilding the church before conducting a thorough survey of the problem? Admittedly, Hassan Bey's proposal left him in the key role of arbiter, but the communities were not being bypassed. Whatever the experts recommended, church leaders would retain the final say.

By consenting to Hassan Bey's proposal, in effect the Latins gave up their longstanding dream of a new basilica. It was unlikely that a group of conservation experts would recommend the demolition of a unique historical monument. The Custody was isolated on the issue, and the Testa scheme was clearly unfeasible. Thus, early on in the negotiations the Latins had already made a significant concession.

Hassan Bey, whose political skills were evident in this entire exercise, now shrewdly brought in the international press. His aim was to exert pressure on the churches and their architects to produce results. All the churches were sensitive to public opinion and would need to call on the generosity of coreligionists, particularly in the United States, for financial help.

A *New York Times* article of May 27, 1954, reported on a new attempt to save the Holy Sepulchre from "shoddy ruin." It cautioned that an inspection by experts was only a small first step toward the goal of renovation. There was no guarantee that the experts would present a unified report, and to date church leaders had been unable to agree on a plan of action. But at last there was hope.[40]

The commission, a team of three architects and two engineers, was able to survey the rotunda in an intrusive way that had not been open to any previous investigator.[41] For the first time, they broke through the plaster of the pilasters at several points. They found the original pillars in no state to be reconstituted with a reinforced concrete core (as Wolley had suggested). They would have to be demolished and entirely rebuilt.

In addition, the commission proposed that horizontal ties of reinforced concrete should lock the pillars into the floors of the surrounding galleries, forming a monolithic cage able to withstand earthquakes. The Katholikon cupola and drum would also have to be rebuilt with reinforced concrete, as the cut stone used in 1932 was far too heavy. The upper part of the south façade should be dismantled and rebuilt with the Crusader stones where possible. Weak masonry should be consolidated throughout by grouting, and, following Wolley, the cisterns should be examined.

Each community would have its own technical bureau. Proposals for private areas would be communicated to the other bureaus and would have to conform to the Status Quo. Special studies of common areas would be drawn up by the three technical bureaus working together at joint expense. If a dispute arose, a meeting would be convened, presided over by a Jordanian official. Acting as arbiter, he would give a definitive ruling. Labor would be directly employed, and subcontractors hired by tender only for projects requiring special expertise.

The commission's consensus report, dated July 11, 1954, was the first time since 1927 that representatives of the three major communities had reached a common architectural conception of a solution, albeit in very general terms. Some of the commission's recommendations were unacceptable to the clerics; others were subsequently superseded. Obviously, it was not comprehensive and had not addressed a number of contentious issues. (The communities even contested ownership of individual pillars, not to mention the Seven Arches of the Virgin.) The churches remained suspicious rivals. The Greeks would not agree to any modification of the Edicule. None of the communities really wanted Jordan involved, certainly not as an arbiter.

Nevertheless, it was an encouraging, businesslike document. The architects had worked well together. Sharing the same professional assumptions, they did not hesitate to speak truth to power. For instance, they concurred that "the architectural aspects of the actual Aedicule no longer correspond to the exigency of the time." They acknowledged, though, that "a more religious and more rational" structure depended on unanimous agreement between the communities. They proved that technical experts could drive the project forward by cutting through theories to practical realities. Though it was a technical and not a political breakthrough, it provided an agreed reference point for all future negotiations.

Hassan Bey was ebullient. He concluded that the Latins were now reconciled to keeping the present church and saw "no real difficulty between the communities except about the Edicule." Eager to get down to business, he looked forward to recommending implementation of the report to his government. It seemed that at long last a solution was at hand.[42] But the way ahead would be strewn with more obstacles than he realized.

CHAPTER EIGHT | Terrors in the Way

H ASSAN BEY, ELATED at the 1954 tripartite commission report, had underestimated the difficulties still to be overcome. The prospect of change at the Holy Sepulchre stirred up all those who stood to lose or gain from the restoration. The French government made a last stand in defense of its historical role of protector of the holy places. Crises of succession in the Greek and Armenian patriarchates paralyzed both communities. And in the middle of it all, the Suez War erupted.

Throughout, Hassan Bey remained a steadying influence and worked hard to get the project started. But for a long time, he overestimated the capacity of the government to impose its will on the churches, a problem that was compounded by conflicting interpretations of the tripartite commission report. Whereas Hassan Bey saw the government as directing the project with the communities providing advice, the commission envisaged the government playing the part of arbiter only in the event of disagreement between the communities. Ideally, the ecclesiastics would have liked to keep the government out of the project altogether.

An early critic of the report was the French consul general in Jerusalem, Bernard Rochereau de la Sablière. Worried that a Jordanian-led project would dispose of France's traditional role at the holy places, he insisted that he be informed and consulted. He also wanted the Holy See to act in place of the Custody of the Holy Land, which he criticized as "too weak, timid, and prone to intrigue to discuss things effectively with the Jordanian Government."[1] This charge was aimed at the custos, Father Faccio, and his expert on the Status Quo, Father Rock, who had declined to involve de la Sablière in the process.[2]

The Coptic Church presented another problem for Hassan Bey. Its bishop demanded to pay a share of the expenses of any restoration in order to win full-fledged rights of possession in the church. The Egyptian consul tried to bring pressure to bear on the authorities, but the small Coptic community was weak on the ground in Jerusalem, with only seven monks serving in its tiny chapel behind the Tomb of Christ. Hassan Bey dismissed Egyptian interference, which was both politically unwelcome to his government and unacceptable to the major communities. It would also have encouraged the demands of the other minor communities who claimed a share in repairs, too.[3]

Following publication of the July 1954 commission report, the Jordanian government decided to bring in Wolley, the author of the 1947 report, as a consultant.[4] The prospect of Wolley's visit upset the communities, partly because they questioned its technical rationale, given that they had competent experts of their own. More fundamentally, they deplored any kind of Jordanian involvement implying proprietorship. In the meantime, they began their technical preparations.

The Greek government of Field Marshal Alexander Papagos quickly offered aid of £500,000 to the Greek patriarchate, fearing that if it did not, then the Soviet Union, through the Russian Orthodox Church, would. This was a substantial sum for Greece at the time, with the country destitute after occupation and civil war, and it would insist throughout on getting its money's worth in terms of influence. With the welcome funds, the patriarchate set up a technical bureau of engineers, draftsmen, and ancillary staff.

Given their short-term financial shortfall, the Latins contented themselves with establishing a modest technical bureau under the experienced Dominican architect Father Charles Coüasnon. Coüasnon, working on a voluntary basis, set up office at the Franciscans' Casa Nova hostel and was joined in the new year by draftsmen the French government sent.

Father Coüasnon was a most appropriate choice for the position. Besides language, he shared with Pierre Coupel, the Custody's principal architect, who was based in Beirut, membership in France's architectural elite. Born in Rennes in 1904, Coüasnon followed in his father's footsteps to study architecture at the prestigious École des Beaux-Arts in Paris. After passing the competitive examination for entry into the French government's department of historical monuments, at age twenty-one he became director of historical monuments for Brittany, responsible for conserving the region's architectural heritage.

His future seemed bright when he was put in charge of designing the Brittany pavilion at the 1937 Paris World's Fair. He revised the black and white Breton flag for the occasion and made known his extreme Breton nationalist views. As a result, he was excluded from the exhibition, with serious damage to his career prospects.

Coüasnon entered holy orders in his forties. Called up to fight for his country in 1940, he was evacuated from Dunkirk under machine-gun fire with a group of French soldiers who rowed across the Channel to England. He immediately returned to Brittany, where he was taken prisoner by the German army, and spent three years in a prisoner-of-war camp.[5] After the war, he was one of a group of older men who elected to join the Dominican Order. In July 1954, he was sent by his province to St. Stephen's monastery, Jerusalem, to work with the archeologist Father Roland de Vaux of the École Biblique. He was soon dividing his time between Father de Vaux's excavations at Qumran and the Church of the Resurrection.

Coüasnon saw the edifice as a unified whole that could not be segmented into separate compartments. Following French practice, there should be a single architect in chief in charge of the project, answerable to an association formed by the three communities. He would be represented in Jerusalem by a resident architect running a unified technical bureau, which would prepare one set of plans and one set of drawings. The Greeks, haunted by their fear that they might lose their preeminence in the basilica, completely disagreed. They insisted on a tripartite model from top to bottom, and they tried to impose their agenda at meetings of the coordinating committee.[6]

Before Christmas 1954, the Greek and Latin technical bureaus embarked on a detailed survey of the Holy Sepulchre in order to prepare scale drawings of the entire edifice. This would enable the foreign-based principal architects to prepare their plans. Each community was supposed to survey its own property, cooperating on common areas, such as the south façade and rotunda. But the old spirit of suspicion remained, and Coüasnon grumbled that he was followed around everywhere by a Greek monk who stuck to him like a leech, hindering his work.[7]

Dissension continued between the communities over arcane details of the Status Quo. In February 1955, Greek and Latin clergy came to blows over the replacement of old chairs in the Church of the Nativity in Bethlehem. The Greek Orthodox Father Artemius struck the Franciscan Father Augustinus in the face. Father Artemius then allegedly attacked the Jordanian police with a chair. A few days later, a scuffle broke out between groups of Latin and Greek monks at the southern door to the Grotto of the Nativity over rights of entry. In another incident shortly thereafter, fourteen friars, led by Father Augustinus, reportedly beat up two Greek monks next to the Grotto.[8]

Hassan Bey acted firmly to preserve the peace and determine existing rights in these cases, and the heads of both communities promised to prevent further outbreaks of violence. His fairness in holding the balance between squabbling Christian sects exempted him from local consuls' criticism of the Jordanian government. Amman was accused of ignoring the interests of Christian institutions in Jerusalem and extending legislation to the Holy City that was discriminatory toward Christians in order to appease Muslim nationalist sentiment.

Anti-Western excitement was rampant throughout the Arab world at this time, as the result of the signing on October 19, 1954, of a treaty between Britain and Egypt under which Britain agreed to cede its Suez Canal military bases within two years. Britain had originally intervened in Egypt in 1882 to protect its interests in the vital waterway linking the Mediterranean to the Red Sea and ended up running the country. Opposed by a mounting tide of Egyptian nationalism and guerrilla attacks on the bases, Sir Winston Churchill's government decided to cut its losses and quit Egypt.

Colonel Nasser's victory was achieved against a background of antimonarchist and anticolonialist propaganda, and support for revolutionary forces throughout the region. Among various targets of abuse was the Hashemite Kingdom of Jordan. The churches, too, which were identified with the West, were placed in an uncomfortable position. The slogan "Keep Jerusalem a Muslim City" began to appear in the local press.[9]

The tense climate did not affect the Jordanian government's friendliness to the West, however, and its support for the restoration of the Holy Sepulchre remained firm. But Hassan Bey was strengthened in his resolve to retain a leading role, free of foreign pressure.

Before the British engineer's February 1955 visit, Hassan Bey explained to the French consul that Wolley was being brought in to draw up a report on the state of the basilica as the basis for a restoration project to be carried out by Jordan. It had never been his intention to place responsibility on the Christian communities, because differences of opinion would prevent them from working together harmoniously. The tripartite commission was solely an advisory body. Taken aback, the French consul registered an immediate protest.[10] In his view, it was France, not Jordan, that should be directing operations.

Wolley arrived in Jerusalem on February 7, 1955, for an initial week-long visit.[11] Hassan Bey instructed him to make a general inspection of the structure of the Holy Sepulchre and prepare drawings. Jordan would be responsible for carrying out repairs, he added. Wolley was to study the tripartite commission report and listen to the views of the communities' experts but need not accept their suggestions.

During his stay, Wolley met with key figures involved in the project, including government officials, clerical representatives, and architects for the tripartite commission. At a two-day conference, the British engineer asked probing questions of his colleagues and challenged their ideas. He emphasized the need for thorough analysis of the materials to be used in the concrete mixture, since it would have to have a "life" of many centuries. He pointed out the disadvantages of top-heavy construction in earthquake-prone buildings and urged an early study of the drains and cisterns before arrangements were made for the foundations.

Absent from the official report of the proceedings is a sense of the tension between the government and the communities over ultimate responsibility for the project. However, a hint of the disputes that were to delay the onset of restoration for years can be read between the lines of a seemingly innocuous discussion about the Edicule.

At one point in the conference, Wolley remarked that replacing the cracked marble facing of the Edicule could begin, if necessary, soon after Easter. The mausoleum was marred by its temporary steel frame, and work on it would be independent of other repairs to the church. Wolley was unaware of the supreme sensitivity of this question and of the Greeks' displeasure with uncomplimentary comments about the Edicule made in the tripartite commission report.

While the architects remained silent, Archimandrite Kyriakos, the Greek Orthodox superior of the Holy Sepulchre and guardian of its treasury (and soon to be a leading contender for the post of patriarch), objected that the tomb should await completion of the repairs to the rotunda and the Katholikon, that is, the very end of the entire project. In rejoinder, the Jordanian chairman commented that the issue was a technical one best left to the architects—implying that Wolley should have the last word.[12]

In reality, the question of who would have the final say in the repair was highly political. Wolley represented the Jordanian government and Kyriakos the Greek patriarchate. The Greek monk's fear was that repair of the Edicule, which had a Greek plaque over the entrance honoring Komnenos, the hero of the 1810 restoration, and was embellished with Greek verses from the Gospels, would erase the Greek Orthodox character of the centerpiece of the entire basilica. The Greeks could never agree to any change that implied the impermanence of the 1757 Status Quo.

The stubborn, defensive approach of the Greek Orthodox Patriarchate throughout the entire negotiation stemmed from a deep sense of vulnerability to the might and wealth of Rome. This had national and ecclesiastical roots. As a nation, Greece was small, was poor, and had suffered greatly. Historically, it possessed a strong sense of having been an outpost of Christendom frequently under siege. Mussolini's Italy had only recently attacked it without provocation. In the Holy Land, Greek Orthodoxy had felt itself besieged since the nineteenth century, with the establishment of the Latin patriarchate, and the loss of local Arab parishioners to Catholicism.

At the Holy Sepulchre, the Greeks feared that any sign of weakness would lead to an erosion of their cherished rights. Nor could they overlook the Testa plan for a new basilica, which they saw as evidence of a Latin ambition to overturn the Status Quo. As late as March 1957, the Greek Orthodox newspaper *Aegyptos* warned of the Latin intention "to destroy the church, no more and no less, because it was about to fall into ruin."[13]

At the beginning of June 1955, Wolley returned to Jerusalem to complete his survey.[14] His final report contained some radical recommendations, including that the rotunda columns be rebuilt in reinforced concrete and the heavy stone Katholikon dome replaced with a light aluminum structure. He also suggested clearing away the storerooms and lower gallery built in the rotunda ambulatory by Komnenos. This would extend the floor space and restore the original harmonious internal proportions of the Byzantine Anastasis, while opening to view three seventh-century apses of great historical interest.

Wolley concurred with Coüasnon's view that the parallel existence of three separate technical bureaus would prove a cumbersome and unworkable procedure. In their stead, he proposed that a high official of the Jordanian government, assisted by a self-standing technical organization, take charge of the reconstruction, thereby assuring unity of purpose. This was exactly what Hassan Bey wanted to hear—and exactly what the communities feared.

Wolley was accompanied on his June trip by the Scottish architect Basil Spence, who was asked to advise on the aesthetic and religious dimensions of the project. Spence had recently gained celebrity with his plan for a new cathedral at Coventry, adopted from among two hundred competing designs.

His report is a wise document. His premise was that the twin goals of the restoration should be unity and dignity. To achieve this, as much of the stonework dating to 1048 as possible should be revealed. Simplicity was the key, and elaborate, patterned ornamentation should be avoided, for instance in the interior of the dome. In the Katholikon, "the greatest contribution to architectural grace will be the removal of shores and scaffolding." In second place came the repair of plaster, cleaning, and painting. Dirt and darkness were the enemy. Light-colored paint was recommended, and light should be let in to make its "magical contribution." Ornaments and fittings not in ceremonial use should be removed. Had Spence's advice been followed, it would have made for a more beautiful church.

While Wolley was working on his report, yet another diplomatic row erupted between France and Jordan over French rights at the holy places. A dispute over Jerusalem had been brewing since the end of 1950. Whereas France supported the territorial internationalization of Jerusalem as a separate entity under a UN governor, Jordan saw it as sovereign Jordanian territory, an integral part of the kingdom.

After UN debates in 1950–51 on the future of Jerusalem proved inconclusive, Britain went ahead on its own and recognized de facto Jordanian authority over East Jerusalem and the Old City. Jordan had been bound to Britain by a treaty of alliance since 1948. Throughout the 1955 diplomatic crisis, the British Foreign Office was loath to make common cause with its old rival, France. British officials thought that France was taking advantage of the legal vacuum in Jerusalem in order to restore its former role of protector of Latin Christians and the Christian holy places.[15]

The dispute started after remarks Hassan Bey made at a farewell reception for Wolley on February 13, 1955. In the presence of representatives of all the churches, he said "that his government intended to play the role of 'sovereign' and 'protector of the Holy Places.' " This blunt assertion was followed up the next day by a report in the semiofficial Jerusalem newspaper *Jihad* that Hassan Bey was to be appointed to the new post of *mohafez* of the city of Jerusalem and the holy places. A separate official of the ministry of the interior would be appointed mutassarif of the Jerusalem district. The French consul, de Beauvais, understood this as an assault on the envisaged international status of Jerusalem.

In fact, the practical difference between the titles was not entirely clear, though *mohafez* was thought to be slightly more honorific. In the Ottoman system, a mutassarif was the governor in charge of a district (*mutassarifiyya*) and a mohafez was the governor in charge of a region (*mohafaza*). But in Egypt, a mohafez could also be the governor of a city. The governor of Jerusalem was traditionally a mutassarif.

The Jordanian minister of the interior explained reassuringly that the post of mohafez had simply been created to show the importance his government attached to Jerusalem and the maintenance of the Status Quo. Its incumbent would deal with the holy places and settle disputes between the communities. Hassan Bey confided that the new post had been created in order to give a relative of a government minister a job. The British consul general glumly wondered: "What can be expected of such an appointment except corruption and intrigue?"[16]

The French government saw the promotion as a revival of the post of high custodian of the holy places—strongly opposed by France in 1951—that was aimed at preempting an international regime.[17] It also reflected, they argued, a Jordanian wish to act alone at the Holy Sepulchre.[18] The French concluded that they could not remain silent without forfeiting France's historical role at the holy places. A diplomatic offensive was launched on two tracks: rejection of the new post and insistence on France's rights, which had allegedly never been forfeited, even under the British Mandate.

On the first track, France tried to persuade Britain that the new appointment implied a shift in legal responsibility and a Jordanian wish to assume complete sovereignty over the Holy City. The British Foreign Office, however, was not going to join a French diplomatic initiative against its longtime ally Jordan because of an honorific change of title when no substantive change of function could be detected.[19]

Having failed to persuade Britain to intervene in Amman, there was not much France could do, so it let the matter drop. But when it came to France's right to be involved in the restoration of the Holy Sepulchre, the French were determined to make a fight of it.

The French government reminded Hassan Bey of their rights under international treaties and UN resolutions. In a diplomatic note of March 16, 1955, they insisted that works of repair or modifications to the Holy Sepulchre could not be carried out without the prior consent or participation of France.[20] Hassan Bey, who denied that any government other than Jordan had any rights whatsoever in the church, vigorously rebuffed this claim.[21] After further attempts at friendly persuasion over the next couple of months fell on deaf ears, the French government decided to put together a coalition of interested governments to assert the international status of the Holy City.

The initiative aimed to set up a "Committee for the Repair of the Holy Sepulchre in Jerusalem," to be made up of the consuls of Catholic France, Italy, Belgium, and Spain, together with Orthodox Greece. Britain and the United States would be associated in some way. The body would promote agreement between the communities on a plan of restoration and a division of the costs, if necessary by direct intervention. Were Jordan to decline to cooperate, the Jerusalem question would be brought before the UN General Assembly.[22]

Reaction to this initiative was generally lukewarm and evasive. The British Foreign Office saw the creation of such a committee as a delaying tactic, prejudicing future UN arrangements and skewed in favor of the

Latins. It argued that some progress, albeit slow, was being made at the Holy Sepulchre through the tripartite commission. Rather than start again on a different basis, as the French scheme required, it surely made more sense to speed up existing plans.[23]

Catholic governments disliked what they saw as a blatant attempt by the French to restore their guardianship of the holy places. An Italian diplomat commented that his government would not help France to restore a position "lost centuries ago."[24] Greece particularly feared Russian interference and condemned any departure from the Status Quo.[25] The State Department in Washington, like the Foreign Office, disliked Catholic overrepresentation on the committee. It also doubted whether the U.S. Congress would approve government funding for a foreign church. And even if it did, the State Department did not relish the prospect of Protestant communities vying for rights in the edifice, further complicating matters.[26]

Even the Holy See was opposed. They thought it unwise to seek out a confrontation with Jordan. Direct agreement between the communities was the best option, since it held out the hope of rapid implementation. The custos had invited an international team of architects to visit Jerusalem in August, and in its conclusions might lie the basis of an accord.[27]

In June 1955, the wily Armenian locum tenens, Archbishop Yeghishe Derderian, was in London raising sorely needed funds for the Jerusalem patriarchate. In the making of foreign policy, influence tends to be exercised by those who happen to be in town, and Derderian's views were sought out eagerly. The last thing he thought he needed was an international body running the restoration, so he seized the opportunity to arm British officials with some convincing counterarguments.

One of his London contacts was Herbert Waddams, the general secretary of the Church of England Council for Foreign Relations, who handled ties between the archbishop of Canterbury and his counterparts in the Eastern churches. Waddams was a frequent caller at the Foreign Office. After a briefing from Derderian, he launched a devastating critique of the French plan at a meeting with Michael Rose, the responsible Levant department official.

Reverend Waddams warned that the envisaged committee's balance of four to one in favor of Roman Catholics was intolerable. The Armenians were not represented at all, and the committee would be a "centre of intrigue, probably to the great disadvantage of the Orthodox and Armenians." It would be impossible to resist an application by the Soviet Union to be represented on the committee. He thought that the probable reason for the French initiative was not a lack of progress at the Holy Sepulchre but rather the reverse.

It was nothing but a retrograde attempt by the French to get back into the Middle East.[28]

A few days later, Derderian had the chance to speak to Rose directly. He made two compelling arguments. First, he refuted the French claim that the religious communities were irreconcilable and would not be able to overcome their differences. Second, he adeptly invoked the red menace—not for the last time. The center of Armenian Orthodoxy was the great monastery of Etchmiadzin, in Soviet Armenia, the seat of the Supreme Catholikos, or senior primate of the church. Derderian suggested that the Soviet government might decide to offer, through the Armenian Church, a contribution toward the rebuilding of the Church of the Holy Sepulchre.[29]

From here it was a short step to the possibility of the Soviet Union claiming a seat on the committee and reviving imperial Russia's traditional interest in the Holy Land. In fact, there was no Soviet consul in Jerusalem, because the anticommunist Hashemite Kingdom of Jordan had no relations with the Soviet Union at this time. Nevertheless, the claim that the French proposal would provide the Soviet Union with an opening in Jerusalem was widely repeated and convinced a lot of people.[30]

For some months France battled on. An American diplomat commented that France was apparently unaware that "Europe lost the Crusades or that the Crimean War is over."[31] Hassan Bey again rejected the right of any foreign government to have a say in the question of the Church of the Holy Sepulchre or, indeed, to intervene in any religious matter at all.[32]

The British government finally killed off the proposal of a consular committee in November 1955, warning the French that it would provide an opening to the Soviets. Jordanian responsibility for the safeguarding and upkeep of the holy places was undeniable. With barely concealed glee, the Foreign Office argued that the churches had reached a considerable measure of agreement on the repairs, thanks in no small part to the British Wolley report.[33]

News of agreement between the communities was premature, though they had made significant progress. Yet there was still a long way to go in practical and political terms. A psychological barrier stood between them and the execution of a rescue plan.

Publication of the Wolley and Spence reports, together with the progress of the Greek and Latin draftsmen, brought the contrasting architectural conceptions of the two communities to the fore. The Greek patriarchate, under its ailing patriarch, Timotheos, tended to think in terms of essential repairs only, with no alteration of any kind to the Status Quo. The Latin custos, Father Faccio, envisaged a restitution of the twelfth-century Holy Sepulchre that would clear away Komnenos's "profane" accretions of 1810, requiring modification of the Status Quo. He thought that Wolley's ideas for a complete refurbishment of the church were on the right track but rejected his administrative recommendations for overall Jordanian control.[34]

To advance the Custody's vision of a restored Crusader edifice, Father Faccio had invited an international commission of Catholic architects to Jerusalem. He hoped that its authority would help overcome any opposition from the other communities. Among its members was Jean Trouvelot, an eminent Paris conservationist, since 1942 assistant inspector general of the French department of historical monuments, who had worked on the Château of Vincennes and the rotunda of La Villette. Thanks to Trouvelot's architectural and diplomatic skills, the team unanimously endorsed "the principle of resuscitating the church the Crusaders used."[35] Concretely, this meant a return to the situation existing before the great fire of 1808.

The architects' religious reverence and excitement are reflected in the preamble. It evokes the "wounds inflicted over the centuries on the unity" of the mother church; the danger of losing the "spiritual sense of this masterpiece of Christian art"; and the need to keep in mind the ultimate goal of the project: "the exaltation of the Holy Sepulchre, the centre on which the gaze of all Christianity converges."[36] It is clear that for all their squabbling, those involved in the restoration never thought that they were working on just another old building.

Freed from the need to take Greek Orthodox objections into account, the group of Catholic architects proposed the removal of the 1810 additions and a restoration of the twelfth-century basilica. They particularly stressed the danger of fire and the absence of an emergency exit, and therefore also recommended reopening three of the Crusader entrances walled up by Saladin at the end of the twelfth century.[37] From a strictly conservationist point of view, their recommendations were incontrovertible. But they were politically anathema to the Greeks and not calculated to advance an actual restoration.

Despite the proliferation of commissions and reports, the sad reality was that the project was stuck. More stones had fallen. Desperately anxious at the state of the south transept and the Katholikon dome, the principal architects for all three major communities decided on a joint appeal. They, at least, had a common conception of the problem. On August 24, 1955, they wrote to their patrons pressing for urgent measures of consolidation.[38] Jean Trouvelot, who had taken over as expert for the Custody of the Holy Land, energetically set to work on a plan of action.

The Greek experts Orlandos and Paraskévopoulos, veterans of the Holy Sepulchre and of the politics of conservation, hoped that the joint appeal would be a wakeup call but had no illusions that the actual work of refurbishment would begin any time soon.[39] This was because the Greek Orthodox Patriarchate rejected central features of the Wolley report commissioned by Jordan. No modification to the internal layout of the church could be considered. Conservatives denied that there was any danger to the church at all, claiming that warnings of collapse were simply aimed at depriving the Greek Orthodox Church of its rights and privileges in the Holy Sepulchre. Moderates thought strictly in terms of repairs to existing installations, what the Latins decried as patching up. All were ferociously hostile to any change in the Status Quo.[40]

At the beginning of October 1955, the Greeks issued a rebuttal of the Jordanian insistence on full control. They argued that the Wolley report had only envisaged Jordanian intervention in the event that the communities failed to reach agreement. Orlandos, not Wolley, was the only authority they recognized.[41]

Greek Orthodox dismissal of Wolley's recommendations coincided with the views of Father Faccio, one of whose last decisive acts as custos was to turn the British engineer's report down flat. Thus Greeks and Latins concurred that the communities and not the authorities should have the determining role, though they remained far apart on substance. It was unclear how the gap between limited repairs and a general restoration might be bridged.

In the meantime, the architects' call to arms of August 24, 1955, pleading for immediate consolidation at the south transept, was being ignored by the ecclesiastical authorities, just like all the other warnings. On September 12, an earthquake off the Egyptian coast, registering 6.7 on the Richter scale, destroyed three hundred buildings in Alexandria, driving home the urgency of the situation.

The Jordanian prime minister, Sai'id al-Mufti, was concerned that a further tremor might shake Jerusalem, finally bringing down the Holy Sepulchre. He worried that he would "be blamed by the civilized world for failing to intervene to secure the preservation of what was after all one of the most sacred of places as well as an ancient monument of unique interest." But he was perplexed about how to overcome the communities' recalcitrance.[42]

The French and Greek consuls general, Marcel Laforge and Angelos Vlachos, were alarmed, too, by the communities' passivity in the face of impending disaster and were convinced that if the communities did not act then the authorities would have no choice but to impose the deplorable "Anglo-Jordanian" scheme. Laforge was particularly frustrated by the behavior of Father Albert Rock, the Custody's expert on the holy places. Rock was not being particularly cooperative with either Father Coüasnon or Jean Trouvelot, the Custody's architects. Since Rock had been educated under the British, Laforge suspected him of being a Francophobe. He also accused him of being pernickety, a master of specious argument, prone to Byzantine intrigue, manipulative, and dishonest.[43]

It was true that Father Rock was born in London and spoke perfect English. A Palestinian Arab from the village of Ain Karim, he grew up under the British Mandate for Palestine and attended English-speaking schools. He joined the Franciscans after leaving school and studied in Rome before coming back to Jerusalem to serve in the Custody of the Holy Land. He was fiercely loyal to his order, and his fluency in Arabic and English had made him an obvious choice as the Custody's expert on the holy places. But he had been interned by the British under the Mandate, had lost his family home to Israel, and was no blind Anglophile.

Laforge and Vlachos concluded that the best way forward was to build on the agreed note of August 24, 1955, which had been signed by architects from all three major communities, appealing for urgent repairs at the crossing. Erection of a temporary roof to protect against stones falling from the southern transept would buy time and signal to the Jordanians (at minimal cost) the willingness of the communities to work together, if only in a safety matter.

While the Greek consul intervened at the Greek patriarchate, the French consul, supported by the apostolic delegate, approached the custos. Father Faccio was unenthusiastic and objected that the installation would mostly benefit the Greeks, since adjacent property belonged to them. Once the roof was in place and the danger from falling stones removed "they would immediately lose interest in the rest of the project." The French diplomat wondered in despair whether Greeks and Latins would ever get over their mutual mistrust.[44]

At this point Hassan Bey intervened to break the deadlock. At a meeting in the Holy Sepulchre at the beginning of November 1955, he gave church representatives forty-eight hours to reach agreement on consolidation measures—otherwise he would step in. Jolted by this ultimatum, the communities swore to carry out the work without delay.[45]

There was an element of bluff in Hassan Bey's threat. True, the communities feared Jordanian intervention, since this would call their cherished independence into question. But it would have been hard for the government to implement repairs without the consent of the interested parties, for diplomatic and practical reasons.[46] Jordan also lacked the means to pay for substantial repairs. On a trip to London in September 1955, the mohafez failed to obtain British support (or financial help) for a project, to be led by Jordan, that would cut through the tangle of disputes. The Foreign Office advised him to give the churches a last chance. Only if they declined to cooperate should the Jordanian government take responsibility. Funds might be raised by an appeal to the Christian world.[47]

The drawback to this idea was that there were only two realistic sources of funding besides the major communities and their supporters, namely, the Moscow-based Russian Orthodox Church and Protestant churches in the United States. Both were politically unacceptable, since their involvement might undermine the local churches' position in the Holy Sepulchre. Red gold and Communist infiltration were anathema to the Greeks, Protestant involvement to the Latins. Relations between Anglicans and Latins in Jerusalem were no more than proper. Without an independent source of funding, such as Her Majesty's Treasury, Hassan Bey could not go it alone.

For the time being, though, Hassan Bey's ultimatum worked, and Father Coüasnon immediately traveled to Paris to consult his principal, Jean Trouvelot. Together, the two French architects completed a study of the south transept. Their plan called for the immediate consolidation of the cross vault. Before the work could begin, elaborate scaffolding would have to be installed, the masonry cleaned and thoroughly examined, and probings made. In the circumstances, Trouvelot posed the telling question: Did it not make more sense to move straight to a definitive restoration rather than spend time and money on yet another temporary repair?[48]

Trouvelot's next step was to secure the approval of his Greek and Armenian colleagues. After celebrating Christmas 1955 in Jerusalem and Bethlehem, he and Paraskévopoulos drafted a work program for the south transept. Father Coüasnon prepared a plan for the scaffolding. By the beginning of April 1956, both Altounian and Orlandos had agreed to both sets of plans, though the Greek architect withheld his signature. All seemed set to go, when the whole project ground to a halt.

The basic reason for this hiatus, which was to last for two years, was that the parties were distracted by leadership changes. In particular, the Greeks and Armenians were in disarray because of prospective patriarchal elections. In the absence of stable, established leadership, they could neither make decisions nor raise funds. Until new patriarchs were installed, no real progress could be made.

In addition, 1956 was a year marked by growing unrest in the Middle East that spread to Jerusalem. It began with an attack on the U.S. consulate in East Jerusalem and ended with the burning of the French consulate. Infiltration and reprisal on the Israeli–Jordanian border, procommunist and Nasserist ferment, and revolutionary rhetoric over Cairo's Voice of the Arabs radio station made life increasingly uncomfortable for the Hashemite monarchy.

The first transfer of ecclesiastical authority took place smoothly enough in the Custody of the Holy Land. Father Angelico Lazzeri replaced as custos Father Giacinto Faccio, whose relations with the apostolic delegate had become increasingly strained. On December 8, 1955, the new custos made a splendid solemn entry into the Holy Sepulchre to the strains of a *Te Deum*, the traditional hymn of joy and thanksgiving. In the presence of the consular corps, other dignitaries, and congregants, Father Lazzeri walked in procession around the church. After the Tomb of Christ, he visited Calvary and other shrines, then celebrated mass in the Chapel of the Apparition, where the friars renewed their pledge of obedience.[49]

Father Lazzeri had never visited Jerusalem before his appointment and admitted to knowing nothing of the problems that awaited him in his new post. Many of the friars were concerned that the new custos, on the instructions of the Holy See, intended to curtail the autonomy of their independent-minded institution. In the past, reforms had been abandoned because of the friars' refusal to cooperate with a new superior imposed by Rome. Lazzeri would need all his skill to assert his authority without too many clashes.[50]

He made a good start on the restoration and agreed to draw up a contract regularizing Trouvelot's terms of employment. Father Faccio, the previous custos, had been unhappy about the engagement of a French government architect—rather than an Italian, such as Ferdinando Forlati, the custodian of St. Mark's, Venice—and had dragged his feet on the issue for a year and a half.[51]

Meanwhile, the Greek Orthodox Patriarchate was again in crisis. With the death of Patriarch Timotheos on December 31, 1955, Arab parishioners and Greek monks resumed their long dispute over the patriarchate's basic law. At issue was the laity's demand for greater participation in the governance of the patriarchate, allowing them a share in its funds and the right to vote.[52] Over the course of 1956, the elections were repeatedly postponed as the contest swayed back and forth in the law courts and Amman's corridors of power.

The candidate of the Arab Orthodox was Archbishop Isidoros of Nazareth, but he was smeared as a communist sympathizer. The favorite of the Greek government, as a barrier against Soviet infiltration and loss of Hellenic control, was the titular archbishop of Tiberias, Benedictos. His main opponent was the superior of the Holy Sepulchre, Archimandrite Kyriakos.[53]

While these events were unfolding, the Armenian Orthodox Brotherhood of St. James was also divided by bitter feuding. At the end of 1955, Archbishop Tiran Nersoyan returned to Jerusalem from the United States to challenge Archbishop Yeghishe Derderian for the patriarchal throne. Charging Derderian with embezzlement, Nersoyan's supporters called for a probe into the patriarchate's finances.

Lawsuits, elections and reelections, accusations of communism, bribery, and forgery, expulsions and deportations, intrigue at the royal court, and violent demonstrations raged for the next five years. In the midst of negotiations over the restoration, Archbishop Derderian therefore had to fight for his ecclesiastical life. In September 1956, he was forced to leave Jerusalem, though he continued the battle from abroad.[54]

Throughout this period of uncertainty, Hassan Bey waited for the communities to come up with a solution to the disintegrating south transept. On March 27, 1956, almost five months after the communities had promised to reinforce it without delay, he invited their representatives to his office to settle the issue. Paraskévopoulos and Trouvelot had drawn up an acceptable plan. Who would be in charge of its implementation? He gave them until April 10 to designate an architect-in-chief to direct work in common areas. This architect would have a determining voice but might be chosen from among the principal communal architects. If they failed to come up with an agreed name, the government would put its own man forward.[55]

At stake were many of the key issues and rivalries in the microcosmic world of the Holy Sepulchre. The conflict between Byzantium and Rome was reflected in the question of the character of the work—neo-Byzantine versus Romanesque; piecemeal repair versus overall restoration; punctilious preservation of the Status Quo versus change. Subconflicts included historical rivalries between the churches and the sovereign, Britain and France, France and Italy, Russia and Greece. With little mutual confidence, a leadership vacuum, and a preoccupied sovereign, deadlock descended.

When the communities arrived at the office of the mohafez on April 10, 1956, they seemed to have a solution within their grasp. The experts and architects had agreed that the architect-in-chief would be chosen by the architects themselves and that Orlandos, with his great prestige, was generally acceptable. He and Trouvelot got on well. As far as the Custody was concerned, he was certainly better than the English Protestant that the Jordanian government seemed to have in mind. Orlandos had not been able to come to Jerusalem, but a letter offering him the position had already been sent.

Unfortunately, on April 12, Vlachos received a disappointing reply from Orlandos declining the post, pleading old age and the burden of work.

(Orlandos was a fit sixty-seven-year-old and lived till the age of ninety-one.) Trouvelot determined to fly to Athens to persuade him to change his mind. If he persisted in his refusal, everything would unravel. In Athens Orlandos was adamant, but the two men agreed on another simple and sensible solution: to have each architect serve in turn as chief architect. If it was up to them, work could begin very shortly.[56]

The Latin and Armenians were ready to accept the idea of rotating responsibility, as was Hassan Bey. The Greek patriarchate, wracked at this time by profound divisions, was not. Nor would they go along with the Latin-Armenian proposal to undertake a complete restoration of the south transept and façade once work got under way.[57] With the entire Status Quo at stake, they would only proceed with the utmost circumspection and were determined to protect their position with ironclad guarantees.

An unexpected reversal now occurred. Hassan Bey had favored all along the idea of a neutral, independent architect not beholden to the communities. At a meeting in June 1956, Orlandos first proposed his old friend Trouvelot, which suited Father Rock. Then, unaccountably, the Greek and Armenian representatives suddenly argued for a neutral architect. Orlandos inquired whether they had a Buddhist in mind. Following the meeting, he left for home in disgust.[58]

What had happened was that the two patriarchates had buckled under government pressure. With the Armenian archbishops Nersoyan and Derderian locked in litigation, the authorities could withdraw the residence permit of either at will. The list of candidates and the holding of elections were subject to government approval. As for the Greek Orthodox Patriarchate, the very identity of the Confraternity of the Holy Sepulchre, whether it would retain its Hellenic character or become an Arab institution, as the Greeks dreaded, was in the hands of the Jordanian government, which if it so wished could impose a new basic law and enfranchise the Arab Orthodox parishioners. Hassan Bey now held strong cards.

Temporarily outmaneuvered, Father Rock accepted the new Greek-Armenian line in principle, while fighting stubbornly over the actual appointment. Over the summer, the field was narrowed down to two independent architects. The Latin candidate was a thirty-six-year-old Lebanese Muslim, Amin Bizri, the inspector general of historical monuments for Lebanon, who had studied in France. Father Rock hoped that his Muslim background would appeal to the Jordanian government. However, Bizri's experience was undeniably limited, and he would find it hard to direct senior architects.[59]

The Armenians and Greeks preferred Austen St. Barbe Harrison, the former chief architect of the Palestine DPW under the Mandate, who had designed several important buildings in Jerusalem, including Government House, the central post office, and his masterpiece, the Rockefeller Museum. Harrison, now sixty-four, lived in a picturesque old house on the north coast of Cyprus.[60] Hassan Bey thoroughly approved of the candidacy of this distinguished British architect, who had spent most of his career in the Middle East.

But Harrison's candidacy was torpedoed on political grounds. The French consul deplored his British nationality, and Rock cast doubt on his qualification to work on churches.[61] In reality, it was Harrison's supposed Anglican and pro-Greek bias that Rock disliked. Ironically, the blackball was cast by the Greek government.[62] With Greek Cypriots fighting on Cyprus against British colonial rule, a British architect was unacceptable to Athens.

Cyprus was not the only place in the Middle East where nationalist, anti-British feeling was running high at this time. On July 26, 1956, Colonel Nasser nationalized the Anglo-French Suez Canal Company. Pro-Nasserist, anti-Western euphoria swept Jordan. In the elections for the Jordanian parliament held on October 21, pro-Egyptian parties won an overwhelming majority, and Suleiman al-Nabulsi, the leader of the left-wing National Socialist Party, was asked to form a government. Within days Britain, France, and Israel attacked Egypt, and Jordan's relations with Britain and France took a striking turn for the worse.

At the Holy Sepulchre, the talks over an architect-in-chief were suspended. Hassan Bey, a stalwart royalist, was replaced by his deputy, Adnan al-Husayni. Father Eugene Hoade, the Custody's English-speaking discreet (member of the governing Discretorium), had to leave the country as a precautionary measure.[63] Altogether, the prospect of a British chief architect now looked dim.

On the centennial of the 1856 Treaty of Paris, which followed the Crimean War with Russia over the future of the Ottoman Empire, both Britain and France found themselves unable to influence events at the Holy Sepulchre. This was good news for the mother church. Without great power meddling, the communities would be in a better position to make the accommodations needed to get down to the work of restoration.

| A Patriarch Open to Reason

T HE ENTHRONEMENT OF HIS BEATITUDE, Patriarch Kyr Benedictos I, took place on a spring day at the beginning of March 1957 at the Church of the Resurrection. In the presence of the sumptuously robed monks of the brotherhood, many Arab village priests, and an invited audience of 350 dignitaries, the patriarch of Holy Jerusalem and all Palestine, Syria, Jordan, Cana of Galilee, and Holy Sion was installed in splendor on the canopied marble and gilt patriarchal throne in the Katholikon, the Greek church within a church.

Patriarch Benedictos had waited a long time for this moment. Born Basil Papadopoulos in 1892 in Turkey, he was brought to Jerusalem as a fourteen-year-old boy by his uncle, a bishop in the Confraternity of the Holy Sepulchre. He entered the seminary attached to the patriarchate and was ordained dean in 1914. After spending the war as a secretary in the patriarchate, Benedictos was sent to study law and theology at the University of Athens. During 1929–46 he served as the patriarchate's exarch (deputy) in Athens. On his return, he became legal counselor to the patriarchate, a member of the holy synod, and the president of its economic commission. In 1951, he was made titular archbishop of Tiberias.[1]

With his connections in Athens and pivotal financial role as principal treasurer of the patriarchate, Benedictos had steadily acquired influence over the ailing Patriarch Timotheos. At the same time, his love of pleasure drew criticism. "Although he is reportedly unpopular for his indifference towards the Arabs and loose morals," the U.S. embassy in Amman reported before the patriarchal elections, "he may win because of his shrewd character and having at his disposal the unaudited patriarchate funds to finance his electoral campaign."[2]

In the second round of the elections—restricted to Jordanian citizens who were members of the holy synod—Archbishop Benedictos received ten votes to eight for Archimandrite Kyriakos. Kyriakos was the candidate of the powerful clique of monks born on Samos and the nephew of the former patriarch, Damianos. Benedictos, as the first patriarch in 115 years not from the island, emerged indebted to the Greek and Jordanian governments. In particular, the authorities' removal of one name from the approved list of candidates, and their willingness to issue Jordanian passports to four bishops, giving them the right to vote, proved decisive.[3]

At his enthronement, the royal berat recognizing his election as canonical was read out, and the new patriarch was acclaimed. Benedictos then preached his inaugural sermon, taking as his text the words of the apostle James (3:17–18): "But the wisdom from above is in the first place pure; and then peace-loving, considerate, and open to reason; it is straightforward and sincere, rich in mercy and in the kindly deeds that are its fruit. True justice is the harvest reaped by peacemakers from seeds sown in a spirit of peace."

Never very interested either in theology or ecumenism, Benedictos was a businesslike person who was fully prepared to cooperate with Latins and Armenians if need be. Appropriately, the substance of his address was practical. He thanked the king for the berat and undertook to preserve the faith and traditions of the Brotherhood of the Holy Sepulchre. He reaffirmed his predecessors' resolve to maintain their full rights at the holy places. Finally, he promised to care for the brotherhood's resources, investing them wisely and avoiding waste.[4]

Benedictos entered office determined to restore the Church of the Ana-stasis, whose steady deterioration he had witnessed. He certainly did not plan to preside over the collapse of this most cherished sanctuary, "the sacred heritage of the Hellenic race." He believed that the brotherhood had existed for eighteen hundred years to protect the holy places and the right of pilgrimage, and that Greece was a religious Great Power by virtue of its role in Jerusalem. Golgotha and the Acropolis were twin beacons of civilization.[5]

Another less obvious but very powerful motive was a sense that Greek Orthodoxy was under siege in the Middle East. This was a perception that had deep roots in the historical experience of Byzantium, which had fallen to the Ottoman Turks in 1453. But it was reawakened by two contemporary developments, as follows.

First, Turkish riots against the Greek community had taken place in Istanbul on September 6, 1955. During the disturbances, thousands of people carrying Turkish flags and portraits of the late president Atatürk attacked Greek property with stones and iron bars, shouting "Cyprus is Turkish." Of the eighty Greek Orthodox churches in the Turkish capital, twenty-nine were completely destroyed by fire, and thirty-four were badly damaged.[6] After these events, thousands of Greeks fled Turkey, and the ecumenical patriarch Athenagoras was left with a rump community. Mob violence against the Armenian community at the same time created a common bond between the two churches.

Second, in Jerusalem, Western institutions were the target of communist and Nasserist mobs from the Old City. Coming after the Suez War, Christmas 1956 was a gloomy time in Jerusalem. Pictures of President Nasser and Egyptian flags were everywhere, and pilgrims nowhere to be seen.[7] To the Greek patriarchate, the Hashemite monarchy was like a dam holding back a deluge of enmity.

It was therefore imperative to improve relations with the other churches. Armenians and Greeks faced a common plight in the Muslim world. Latins and Greeks were rivals, but both Athenagoras in Istanbul and Benedictos in Jerusalem could see that conflict in the face of common threats made no sense. A high-level conference between Greek Orthodox and Roman Catholic delegations to discuss church unity was held in Jerusalem in November 1959. In a press interview, Patriarch Athenagoras called on all Jerusalem's clergy to work for the realization of the union of Orthodox and Catholic churches.[8]

Preliminary contacts to restore interchurch relations took place more or less at the same time that negotiations were under way to restore the Holy Sepulchre. Church leaders understood restoration of the mother church as a metaphor for reconciliation of the Mother Church.

If Benedictos began his patriarchate committed to saving the Church of the Resurrection, the Jordanian and Greek governments were independently dedicated to the same goal. For Greece, it was a question of national-religious vocation; for Jordan, responsibility and reputation. Both were determined to avoid a disaster at the Holy Sepulchre that the Soviet Union could exploit to their equal detriment. They resolved to use the leverage at their disposal to hold Benedictos to his duty.

The Greek government's leverage over Benedictos derived from its commitment to funding the restoration. By special act, it guaranteed to meet the full cost of Greek work, and an appropriation for the Anastasis first appeared as a line item in the national budget for 1957. This gave Benedictos a powerful incentive to find independent sources of funding, but for years the Greek government exerted a dominating influence on the reconstruction program.

The Jordanian government also possessed an effective lever of influence in the form of the new basic law of the Greek Orthodox patriarchate. The Jordanian Parliament approved the ordinance, which was intended to redress Arab Orthodox grievances, on the very day of the patriarchal election. A key clause admitting Arabs to the brotherhood was withdrawn for further consideration because of opposition in the senate. If passed, it would spell the end of Greek control in Jerusalem, since Arab Orthodox outnumbered Greek Orthodox by one hundred to one. This prospect hung like a sword of Damocles over the brotherhood, but it helped Benedictos whip his synod into line.[9]

For all these reinforcing reasons, Benedictos accepted from the first moment the need for early progress on the restoration and proceeded in a conciliatory manner, within the framework of the Status Quo. He was not going to jeopardize that, nor would his synod have allowed him. After the death of the moderate chief secretary of the patriarchate, the Archimandrite Palladios, Benedictos had to tread carefully. He was ready to confront reactionary elements in the synod, but he could not appear to be conceding Greek rights at the Anastasis.[10]

———

Within days of Benedictos's enthronement, Hassan Bey's replacement, Adnan Husayni, resolved to get negotiations back on track and invited representatives of the communities to meet him on March 7, 1957. Plans for the south transept and the scaffolding to protect worshipers and support the south vault had already been agreed on the year before.

Two big issues had not been settled. The first was control over the project. While the Jordanian government wished to supervise it directly through its own chief architect, doubting that the communities would be able to work together, the communities, as the householders, wanted to manage it on their own. The second issue was the link between repairs at the south transept and the overall restoration of the church. Here the Greeks' insistence on "consolidation" arose from fear that an overall restoration would jeopardize the Status Quo by uncovering original Latin features (such as mosaics, tombs, and carvings) of the twelfth-century church. To avoid the possibility of repartition, one faction in the Greek Orthodox synod wanted the patriarchate to go it alone, carrying out repairs by itself.

Latin insistence on "restoration" derived from an uneasy feeling that the Greeks had no intention of proceeding beyond the reinforcement of the south transept, especially the visibly disintegrating overhead cross vault. Once the supporting scaffolding was in place, they feared, the Greeks would call a halt to further work.

Before their meeting with the mohafez, the communities broadly agreed that their architects should prepare detailed blueprints of the parts of the edifice to be restored. Any chief architect should be their appointee, not the government's. Failing that, he should be bound by the unanimous decisions of the communities' architects.

With hindsight, their most important understanding was on the need for a common technical bureau (CTB), to be jointly funded by the three major communities and housed within a single suite of offices. Here technical experts could work together on the common dimension of the restoration, directing operations and coordinating individual projects.

The CTB was an excellent idea that might, if it worked, end the call for a separate government architect. It could permit, through the cooperation of professionals sharing a common technical language, unity to emerge out of diversity. Father Rock liked it because it embodied an integrated approach to restoration. Coüasnon and Trouvelot's work on the south transept had made the need for it apparent.

A piecemeal approach to the south transept was ruled out, because all three denominations owned the structure. On the ground floor, the Stone of Unction and surrounding floor space were common, while the adjacent Chapel of Adam and superior's office were Greek. On the first floor, Calvary was divided into Greek and Latin chapels. And on the second floor, the Armenians had a chapel and rooms, the Greeks their treasury. The south transept could only be restored as a single entity. For this, there had to be a unified mechanism of management.

At the meeting of March 7, 1957, Adnan Husayni signaled his intention to jolt the project into action. Flanked by the Jordanian ministers of public works and development and construction, he informed the communities that a high-level ministerial committee on the restoration had been set up. Since the communities had not been able to agree on a candidate, the government now intended to appoint its own chief architect.[11]

The communities did not like this at all. They could live with a friendly government architect checking to see that plans their own architects agreed on were being implemented. But they ruled out government supervision, let alone a chief architect with the power to impose his own views. Orlandos, Trouvelot, and Altounian were all eminent international architects who had proved that they could work well together. They were surely best qualified to come up with technical solutions to differences of opinion between the communities.

While the Jordanian government scouted around for a chief architect, the communities decided to press forward. On May 31, 1957, they agreed on arrangements for the CTB. Their principal architects would be invited to Jerusalem in July for preparatory work. A joint architectural report on the restoration would then be submitted to the governor. The question of government supervision would be left pending. They hoped it would go away.[12]

And so it did. Austen Harrison dropped out of the running because of ill health. Freeman, Fox Partners in London were approached and in October 1957 proposed an architect with a substantial salary of 2,000 dinars a month, two months' annual leave, and all living expenses paid. This was beyond the means of the Jordanian government and spelled the effective end of the search for an architect-in-chief.[13] When Hassan Bey returned as mohafez, he quietly let the matter drop.

Just when all seemed to be going smoothly, fresh problems arose. Orlandos and Altounian declined to attend the July 1957 meeting, pleading illness but more likely because of continuing difficulties within their own communities. Trouvelot, doing most of the work, flew in alone to present his plans for the south transept.

He emphasized that to complete his work he needed drawings of the Greek treasury. In addition, scaffolding should go up and soundings be made in the walls to investigate their condition. Apart from scraps of plans drawn up by their architect, the Greeks had not done much. Now it was their turn. This request was to be the first test of the CTB.[14]

On his visit, Trouvelot was well received at both the Greek and Armenian patriarchates, confirming the support of their leaderships for the project. Benedictos greeted the French architect with demonstrative warmth and affirmed his wish to arrive at an agreement. Trouvelot, ever the diplomat, took the opportunity to put any fears to rest by showing that his plans would not modify the Status Quo in any way. "We architects," he reassured Benedictos, "are working together with all the communities at the same time to save the Holy Sepulchre."

He put forward some concrete suggestions for uncontroversial repairs at the crossing that could go ahead right away, since they had no implications for possession. Only at a later stage would more far-reaching questions arise.[15]

Benedictos approved Trouvelot's plans "by and large," implying that he had political problems. Antellos Mallios, a Greek government engineer, more concerned by a new fall of plaster from the south cross vault, disagreed with Trouvelot's insistence on the need for soundings in the walls of the south transept. In a report that bypassed Coüasnon, he recommended the removal of 160 tons of excess weight from the exterior of the vault and the adjacent terrace.[16] Even if his advice was sound, his refusal to work within the framework of the CTB was unhelpful.

Mallios was a civil engineer, an expert in reinforced concrete—his specialty was airplane hangars and runways—who took his marching orders from the department of antiquities of the Greek ministry of education and cults. They, and not the Greek Patriarchate, paid his wages. His instructions were to carry out only the most urgent work at this point and not to proceed with any overall restoration of the edifice.

Father Rock was depressed by the lack of progress. At meetings in September, Mallios proposed to erect the scaffolding at the south transept, at long last, in order to proceed with "consolidation" of the vault. Rock reacted angrily that it was not just a question of consolidation but of wider restoration. Mallios retorted that the synod had only authorized him to carry out a consolidation. Rock shot back that it was inconceivable that the vault be repaired and not the foundations and walls of the south transept. If features of architectural value were uncovered, they should be preserved for all to see.

So the meetings ended inconclusively. Rock, more suspicious than ever of Greek intentions, insisted that the program of work to be carried out at the south transept should be put into writing and approved by the three principal architects before the scaffolding went up. In effect, this meant another postponement. Once again, the communities were at an impasse. They knew what had to be done but disagreed on how to do it.[17]

Nevertheless, Benedictos's warm reception of Trouvelot had indicated an encouraging shift in Greek attitudes. And Mallios was eager to get started before the roof fell in. Before a breakthrough could occur, though, several pieces of the jigsaw puzzle had to fit into place. They were as much political as architectural.

The first piece involved the Custody of the Holy Land, which was going through a crisis. Father Angelico Lazzeri had not established his leadership. The basic problem was the arrangement, only altered in 1968, whereby a custos was appointed by Rome and not elected by the friars. In August 1957, Father Alfredo Polidori was sent out to replace Lazzeri. Meanwhile, discord surfaced in various ways that interfered with the restoration.

France had lost prestige as a result of the Suez debacle. After the burning of its consulate in East Jerusalem, and its obvious failure to protect itself, it hardly inspired confidence as protector of Catholic interests. Italian friars, who formed the largest single national grouping at St. Savior's, had never liked Trouvelot's appointment and, given France's discomfiture, sought to have him replaced with an Italian architect.[18]

Relations between Father Rock and Father Coüasnon had also taken a turn for the worse. "It is difficult for a Dominican from Brittany," the French consul general wrote, "to work with a Franciscan Arab without the sparks flying."[19] To replace Coüasnon, Rock brought in a Franciscan architect from New York, Brother Cajetan Baumann. Unfortunately, Rock did this without consulting Trouvelot, who had the warmest regard for Coüasnon. Moreover, Baumann spoke no French and Trouvelot no English.

Trouvelot did his utmost to have Father Coüasnon reinstated. He considered the Dominican, with his thirty-plus years experience with medieval church architecture, indispensable. The CTB, which Baumann had tried and failed to set up, could only be organized by Coüasnon. In the meantime, work in the Latins' own technical office ground to a standstill.[20]

The second distraction was at the Armenian patriarchate. On March 20, 1957, the general synod of the Brotherhood of St. James elected Archbishop Tiran Nersoyan Armenian patriarch of Jerusalem. King Hussein, however, declined to confirm the election. Archbishop Yeghishe Derderian, the ambitious former locum tenens, greatly strengthened his own position by obtaining the Golden Hand of Antalias, a venerated reliquary believed to contain the bones of the right hand of St. Gregory, who converted the Armenian nation to Christianity at the beginning of the fourth century. Possession of this reliquary had come to be regarded as a validation of the owner's fitness for office.[21]

An extraordinary series of legal and political developments and reversals now followed over the winter of 1957–58. First, the courts found that Derderian had been illegally deposed as locum tenens, and then that they had no jurisdiction in the case and that Nersoyan's election was after all canonical. Vast bribes were paid to the Jordanian judges. "It was unfortunate," the American vice-consul wrote, "but in Jordan you had to pay money whether you were in the right or not." The chief judge was reported to have prepared two verdicts to be shown to supporters of the two archbishops in turn, extracting bribes from both.[22]

With powerful friends at court, Derderian was able to trump the courts' verdict. A deportation notice against Nersoyan on the orders of the king was to be served on January 30, 1958—but it was withdrawn at the last moment. A few days later, Jordanian officials entered Derderian's sealed chambers, where their search reportedly revealed numerous pictures of Derderian and his lady friends, pornographic literature, and ladies' lingerie. A communist symbol was also supposedly found.

No one could know, the U.S. consul wrote, whether these items "were planted there or not, but the discrediting of the ex-Locum Tenens, poet and one-time brilliant student of theology, seems to be final and irrevocable."[23]

Yet within the year, Nersoyan had been forcibly deported and Derderian restored to power.

The third piece of the puzzle was the governorship of Jerusalem. On April 10, 1957, Suleiman Nabulsi resigned as prime minister after a test of strength with King Hussein over the establishment of diplomatic relations with the Soviet Union. Then followed two attempts at military coups, organized by "free officers," that were only put down thanks to the king's personal courage and ability to rally loyal Bedouin troops to his cause.

The failure of the conspiracy brought to power an outspokenly monarchist, pro-American government under the respected elder statesman Sayed Ibrahim Hashem.[24] With his installation in office, supporters of the king, like Hassan Bey, were restored to key positions in the administration. Communist leaders in the Jerusalem area were arrested, and the Egyptian-sponsored Middle East News Agency was shut down. Stability returned to Jordan, and its financial situation greatly improved as American Cold War aid began to flow into the kingdom.

By Christmas 1957, the picture in Jerusalem in general and at the Holy Sepulchre in particular looked much rosier than a year earlier. Benedictos proved a strong leader. Under Polidori, calm prevailed at St. Savior's. Baumann had gone home, and thanks to Trouvelot's intercession, Coüasnon had returned to his old job. Nersoyan had beaten off Derderian's challenge for the time being. Finally, Hassan Bey was back at the governor's residence.

Since the September 1957 standoff, the communities had been trying to settle their differences. Convinced of Benedictos's good faith, the Latins were aware that the new patriarch had to be helped against reactionary members of his synod who feared the consequences of a restoration. They were therefore ready to provide ironclad guarantees that the restoration would not affect Greek rights.[25] All that was lacking was a way to bridge the consolidation-restoration gap. This was provided by Hassan Bey, who intervened to propose a solution. If they rejected his compromise, he warned, he would implement the restoration himself.[26]

The result of his intervention was a landmark agreement that was ceremonially signed on March 4, 1958, in the Greek Orthodox Patriarchate by the communities' experts on the CTB, Mallios, Coüasnon, and the newly hired Musallam for the Armenian patriarchate. Patriarch Benedictos, Father Polidori, and Archbishop Nersoyan also attached their signatures as having read and approved the agreement.[27]

In the official photograph, dark-clad monks are clustered fittingly around Father Coüasnon in his white Dominican habit. It was a harmonious gathering that was unprecedented in the history of the Church of the Resurrection.[28]

The master plan was contained in a carefully crafted document that met the essential psychological needs of the Greeks and Latins. Under the heading "Restoration of the Basilica of the Holy Sepulchre at Jerusalem," the plan was described as a program for the "consolidation and restoration" of the south transept and façade of the basilica. So the word "restoration" was there, as Rock had demanded. Moreover, the plan called for overall reconstruction and not just piecemeal consolidation. It did not, however, envisage a return to the original Crusader basilica.

A set of complementary notes, longer than the accord itself, provided the Greeks with safeguards that the Status Quo would be strictly respected. The walls separating the transepts from the nave would remain, preserving the Katholikon as a walled-off Greek enclave. The sealed-off second portal into the basilica and the adjacent staircase to Calvary would be left undisturbed, leaving the Greek superior's offices behind the entrance intact. Restoration of any antiquities revealed by repairs would require the explicit approval of all the communities, implying that lost Crusader features would not be recovered.

Architectonically, all this was a great pity, for these provisions preserved the worst features of the 1809–10 restoration. They also represented a major set of concessions by the Latins, who gave up their dream of a reconstitution of the medieval masterpiece. However, there was no chance of restoration without them. The agreement of March 4, 1958, set the Latins' seal on the 1757 Status Quo.

On April 14, 1958, Hassan Bey conveyed to the three communities the prime minister of Jordan's written approval of the accord. He expressed his own satisfaction. Nothing more was ever said about the need for a chief architect or formal dispute settlement by the government. Nevertheless, informally, the governor still had a major conciliatory role to play.

———————

The rest of 1958 was taken up with the scaffolding. Timber would be made fireproof by immersion in the waters of the Dead Sea. The respective virtues of Japanese and Swedish steel were discussed. Tenders had to be published and contractors located. Every detail had to be agreed on by all three communities. Restoration by committee was clearly going to be a laborious business. "At this rate," the French consul general joked, "one can foresee that the final contract may just about be signed in 1976."[29]

The scaffolding was erected before Christmas 1958. This brought the practical issue of organizing building work to the fore. Negotiations were protracted and difficult. Coüasnon wanted the CTB to run the entire operation, using a small local subcontractor familiar with conditions in Jerusalem. Mallios thought the work would be too complex for a small firm, favoring a certain large Greek concern specializing in public works projects, employing hundreds of engineers. "Exactly what we need," Coüasnon remarked sarcastically.[30] He and Trouvelot feared that an international company of civil engineers, with its own design office, would impose soulless technical solutions, ignoring the requirements of art and architecture.

While the irascible Dominican architect grumbled about Mallios, whom he found an uncooperative partner, Rock complained about his counterpart, Kyriakos, whom he accused of being obstructive. Trouvelot, a force throughout for reason and moderation, advised that the essential thing was not to get upset. "Our work methods, Greeks and Latins, are difficult to reconcile, I know, but we have to reach agreement."[31]

A breakthrough required a meeting of the communities' principal architects. Patriach Benedictos appealed to the Greek government for Orlandos to be allowed to come to Jerusalem so that work could go ahead.[32] On April 23, 1959, Trouvelot and Orlandos met at the Holy Sepulchre. It was the first visit by the Greek architect in more than two years. Sadly, Altounian had died before Christmas, and his successor had not yet been appointed.

Trouvelot proposed a sensible way out of the impasse in the shape of a French master foreman whom the communities would engage to set up and run the construction site. This man, Henri Deschamps, a native of Tournus, Burgundy, had spent twenty-five years working on some of France's great cathedrals. Described as a man "who loved his work passionately and knew it perfectly," Deschamps was in the mold of the master masons of the Middle Ages, the builders of the great cathedrals of Europe. He was, at one and the same time, a skilled carpenter, stonecutter, sculptor, and draughtsman.

Now fifty-six years old, Deschamps had recently lost his wife. As a soldier, he had spent time in Lebanon and had always wanted to return to the Levant. With no children, he was now free to do so. Deeply religious, he would view the task of restoring the mother church as the culmination of his life's work. His employers were ready to assign him to Jerusalem without asking any fee or compensation for lost services. Deschamps asked only his modest Paris salary, his food and lodging, and an annual return trip to France for a three-week summer holiday.[33]

As a result of their discussions, Trouvelot and Orlandos were able to suggest solutions to the problems at hand. With Orlandos playing a conciliatory role at the Greek patriarchate, their proposals, albeit in a watered-down version, were broadly accepted. The heads of the communities signed a further milestone agreement, with all due ceremony, on May 27, 1959.

It was formally agreed that the restoration of the north transept and Katholikon would follow that of the south transept and south façade. Deschamps, who would come under the jurisdiction of the CTB, was accepted as foreman of work in both transepts. A local firm would be entrusted with its execution. All work, common or separate, had to be authorized by the three communities and their principal architects. Supervision of work in private areas was the responsibility of the relevant expert architect, but the CTB could later check implementation.[34]

The Jordanian authorities were delighted with the agreement. On August 20, 1959, King Hussein arrived in Jerusalem for a three-day visit to give greater recognition to the Holy City as the second capital of Jordan. He visited the Holy Sepulchre to view progress and savor success. The Jordanian cabinet, meeting in special session in Jerusalem, expressed its satisfaction.[35]

But Benedictos's critics were not happy with what they saw as one-sided concessions. The agreement made clear that work on the Greek Choir, the Katholikon, would be a continuation of the restoration of the transepts. If the CTB were allowed to encroach on Greek areas, what would become of the Status Quo? In the end, hardliners feared, a Crusader cathedral would be reconstituted and with it Latin primacy. In Athens the reaction of the Greek press was mixed.[36]

Benedictos's finances further limited his freedom to maneuver vis-à-vis his critics. The reconstruction of the Katholikon, the heart of the entire project as far as the Greeks were concerned, would cost a fortune. An Anastasis appeal ordered in all the churches of Greece at Easter 1959 had produced disappointing results. To raise funds and strengthen his position, he visited Athens in October 1959.[37]

Benedictos's problems directly translated into a protracted hiatus at the Holy Sepulchre that lasted through the summer of 1960. On August 1, 1959, Coüasnon, who was working on an overall study of the structure, was refused entry into the Greek treasury and the adjacent Chapel of Melchizedek. Kyriakos told him: "It is too late to undertake work this year."[38] The Greeks were uncooperative on all the main issues and hindered the operation of the common technical bureau.

In particular, the crucial next step, examination of the foundations, which raised far-reaching Status Quo issues, failed to materialize. At a meeting of principal architects on August 31, 1959, a dispute arose over who was to carry out the soundings. The Latins and Armenians asserted that the foundations were owned in common, while the Greeks argued that ownership underground followed possession above ground. They alone should excavate the foundations of the Katholikon.

Over the winter of 1959–60, Mallios was particularly uncooperative and wanted the Greeks to go ahead by themselves. He declined to share the studies he was making, dragged his feet over the employment of Deschamps, and gave orders without consulting Coüasnon. Relations between the two men became testy: "Why do you not follow M. Trouvelot's instructions?" Coüasnon asked him on March 7, 1960. "Who is M. Trouvelot here?" was the rejoinder.[39]

A few days later, Archimandrite Kyriakos died. Morton Smith, the New Testament scholar, remembered him as "a pleasant old gentleman who drove a hard bargain." Trouvelot also recalled him with affection, "although he did not usually completely agree with us." Coüasnon thought that there would now be a hardening of the Greek position.[40]

In an attempt to break the deadlock, Trouvelot forwarded for Orlandos's approval the grand plan for the restoration and reinforcement of the north and south transepts in their entirety. Coüasnon, with no help from Mallios, had single-handedly completed the structural analysis on which the plan was based. Trouvelot also pointed out the importance of completing the arrangements for Deschamps's employment before work began. Finally, he urged Orlandos to communicate to him and to Edouard Utudjian, the new Armenian architect following Altounian's death, Greek plans for the restoration of the Katholikon.[41]

Utudjian, a French Armenian whose family had lived in Constantinople for centuries, had moved to France at the age of fifteen and studied architecture at the École des Beaux Arts. A naturalized French citizen, he had served in the French army in World War II. Although his expertise was in town planning, he had taken courses in historical monuments and understood the problems of restoration.[42] He was a convenient colleague, and he and Trouvelot got on well, but he would not be a particularly active partner.

Despite Trouvelot's appeal, Orlandos withheld his signature from the plans for the transepts. He called for further calculations and evaded the question of Deschamps's contract. He did promise to transmit Greek plans.[43] On July 3, 1960, he wrote to Trouvelot suggesting a meeting of the three experts at the end of the month, when it would be possible to settle "certain questions concerning the Status Quo" and sign the contract. It seemed to Trouvelot that Orlandos was not a free agent but was subordinate to the Greek patriarchate, which was riven by intrigue and jealousy of the Latins.[44]

Father Polidori, the custos, thought that the Greek objections were simply intended to gain time. He refused to agree to a meeting in Jerusalem before Orlandos gave his opinion on the contract and signed the plans. The Greek consul general thought "only minor difficulties had to be overcome."[45]

The Jordanian government grew increasingly frustrated. The international publicity was awful. *Time* magazine published an embarrassing article in June 1960 expressing what diplomats and visitors were all thinking—that the present situation was a disgrace.

> The thousands of pilgrims who seek it out every year find the church little more than a musty ruin. The southern façade is some 6 in. out of plumb, held up by a cat's cradle of iron shorings erected by the British in 1935. Under the crumbling vaulting of the south transept, a scaffold has been put up to protect tourists from falling masonry. The façade of Christ's tomb itself is crumbling; large stones fall from the cornice of the cupola ceiling; leaks abound. Said a disgusted minister from Ohio last week: "it would be better to let the church collapse. Then all that masonry could be carted away, and a simple impressive monument could be erected to mark Golgotha and the tomb. That's what I came here to see."[46]

Almost a year had passed since King Hussein's visit, and the communities still teetered on the water's edge. Someone had to push them in. On July 14, 1960, representatives of the communities were invited to the governor's office. Hassan Bey informed them of the king's profound interest in the restoration and enquired into the reasons for the delay, given that the scaffolding had been up for almost two years. The unstated threat, already leaked to the press, was that the king would set up a technical commission of three local Arabs, one from each major denomination. If Greeks and Latins continued to be obstructive, the commission itself would be entrusted with the work on behalf of the government.[47]

Two days later, the communities held an emergency meeting at the Greek Patriarchate. At Benedictos's insistence, they all signed a document agreeing to invite their experts to convene in Jerusalem at the end of the month and to stay for as long as it took to overcome the differences between Mallios and Coüasnon and approve the plans. The document was to be presented to the governor in order to avert Jordanian intervention. A disgusted Coüasnon thought the scheme nothing less than a Greek "ultimatum."[48]

A difficult but decisive round of negotiations now followed. The experts got off to a good start by agreeing to a light metal outer covering for the Katholikon dome. They also agreed to install an interlocking system of reinforcement in the vaults, arches, and piers of the Katholikon to neutralize thrust from the cupola.[49]

Before any restoration proper could begin, preliminary agreement had to be reached on the examination and repair of the foundations. In addition, the system of drains and cisterns underneath the basilica, dating back to the earliest times, would have to be cleaned out and investigated. In fact, the entire underlying geology of the Holy Sepulchre required study.

The main bone of contention continued to be payment for this work. Church leaders agreed that the costs associated with foundations under common areas would be borne equally. But whereas the Latins contended that all the foundations were common, the Greeks maintained that they should pay for the repair of the foundations under their property. Otherwise, their property rights under the Status Quo would be brought into question.[50] Once they insisted on this principle, not a shovelful of earth could be dug before possession of contested columns was definitively settled.

On August 5, 1960, high-level delegations, including principal architects and church leaders, were invited to meet the governor to overcome the impasse. They brought with them the sheaf of plans, protocols, and drawings for the first stage of the restoration that had been ready since the year before. This was to be the ecclesiastical equivalent of the 1815 Congress of Vienna, which ended the Napoleonic Wars. When the Latins maintained their claim to share the cost of the foundations, Benedictos forbade Orlandos to sign the plans. Hassan Bey informed the Greek patriarch that although Orlandos was not a resident of Jordan, neither he nor his colleagues would be allowed to leave the country until he signed on the dotted line. He pointed out that the drawings were only a technical issue.

Benedictos did not cave in to what was, after all, an improbable threat. Capitulation on the foundations would, he thought, be the thin end of the wedge. A scandal was only averted by the inclusion above the architects' signatures of the following sentence: "The execution of these plans will not be carried out until the foundations have been examined and consolidated." This proviso made possible the signing of the drawings but not the actual work, since examination of the foundations, which was the trigger for the entire project, could not begin until there was agreement on who would pay for what.[51]

With both Benedictos and Polidori immovable, Hassan Bey, the former judge, now intervened to decide the issue, acting as uninvited arbiter. On September 13, he inspected the site of the dispute in person. On November 10, he decided on the ownership of the columns, mostly in favor of the

Greeks. Out of fourteen columns, he ruled that only three were common to all three communities, six were common to Greeks and Latins, one was common to Greeks and Armenians, and four were the sole possession of the Greeks.[52]

This was his last major decision as mohafez of Jerusalem. On November 19, 1960, at the age of sixty-seven, he was appointed minister of court in recognition of his devotion to the throne and service to his country. It was the fitting apogee of his career. Certainly, this imposing figure, the last official in the grand Ottoman style, had played a central role in the negotiations over the restoration of the Holy Sepulchre, steadily supporting the project throughout, intervening decisively when necessary, refusing to be diverted by diplomatic pressure, remaining immune to corrupt influence. His honest and upright character was universally acknowledged.[53]

While it is difficult to say whether his contribution was indispensable, over the next three years four successive Jordanian officials were unable to survive long as Jerusalem governor because of intrigue, misjudgment, or incompetence. Had this kind of discontinuity marked the previous eight years, it is hard to see how the communities could have made much progress on their own.

Hassan Bey's ruling put the communities in considerable difficulty. None accepted the principle of official arbitration at the holy places. Moreover, Armenians and Latins were aggrieved by the decision. But if they rejected it out of hand, they risked the Jordanian government arrogating to itself Christendom's most sacred site. They were left with no choice, therefore, but to enter into a protracted exchange to persuade Hassan Bey's successor, Ihsan Hashem, to change the verdict.[54]

He declined to do so and was in a strong position. The communities had been divided. The Greeks may not have liked the procedure but had won a notable victory on substance. They now had the government on their side, with Latins and Armenians isolated as obstacles to progress. By the mere fact of their correspondence with the governor, they had tacitly acknowledged his authority.

Summit conferences were in vogue at that time. On June 4, 1961, President John F. Kennedy met with the first secretary of the Soviet Communist Party, Nikita Khrushchev, in Vienna. The next day, leaders of the three major Christian communities in Jerusalem met at the invitation of Ihsan Hashem at the governorate. Neither in Vienna nor in Jerusalem did the parties change their minds. The difference between the two cases was that in Jerusalem, the mohafez had the power to impose his will.

On June 7, 1961, he wrote to church leaders confirming Hassan Bey's original ruling, with one modification to allow Latins and Armenians to save face: The Jordanian government would examine and repair, at its own expense, the base of pillar 2 on the drawings, hitherto considered exclusively Greek. There were ample precedents for the authorities carrying out repairs for reasons of safety or security. He added the traditional proviso from the Mandate period: The decision was "without prejudice to the rights or claims of the interested parties."[55]

Father Polidori, the custos, now realized that he had no choice but to give his consent or risk full-scale Jordanian intervention. For the record, he notified Ihsan Hashem that he did not accept the decision as final and reserved the right to question it in the future. But he accepted it as a basis from which to implement the architects' plans. Patriarch Derderian, who had at long last beaten off Archbishop Tiran Nersoyan in the contest for the patriarchate, agreed. A detailed work schedule was drawn up and signed by community representatives.[56]

On July 3, 1961, monks, the Jerusalem engineer, and a number of day laborers gathered in the Parvis. Without ceremony, a workman opened a manhole into the great cistern that ran under the southern front, and the work of restoration finally began.

| Kiss of Peace

I N A C O R N E R of the Latin galleries is a marble column installed in 1966 during the high summer of restoration. Instead of adopting the Romanesque style used elsewhere, its capital depicts two stylized figures, recognizable as Greek Orthodox and Roman Catholic bishops, embracing against the background of an olive branch. This modern sculpture commemorates the meeting between Pope Paul VI and Ecumenical Patriarch Athenagoras on the Mount of Olives on January 6, 1964. Located a few meters from Calvary and Christ's tomb, it also symbolizes the convergence of two sets of talks: the ecumenical exchange between the Holy See and Phanar (the seat of the Istanbul patriarchate) and the local negotiations between Latins and Greeks over the restoration of the Church of the Resurrection.

When Pope Paul VI announced his intention to visit the Holy Land, Patriarch Athenagoras quickly responded with his declared desire to meet the pope in Jerusalem, where pope and patriarch could meet as pilgrims and equals on holy ground. What had been envisaged as a mainly religious pilgrimage acquired a far-reaching ecumenical dimension.

With the eyes of the world soon to be on Jerusalem, interchurch relations at the holy places and the restoration of the mother church moved to center stage. Reconstruction and reconciliation were inextricably linked. It was inconceivable that the pope would visit the Holy Sepulchre or exchange the kiss of peace with the ecumenical patriarch, after more than five hundred years of schism, while stones fell at the crossing and monks continued to bicker over who was to repair what.

For the two leaders to meet, dramatizing the search for the reunion of their great estranged churches, Greek Orthodox Patriarchate and Franciscan Custody would have to make notable progress at the Church of the Resurrection.

———

The landmark agreements concluded between 1958 and 1960 laid the contractual basis for the restoration. Beginning with the March 1958 accord, local church leaders solemnly committed themselves to working together to save their common sanctuary. But these accords would remain pious aspirations if the communities were unable to work together.

Confidence had to be built and habits of cooperation acquired. A series of developments during July 1961–June 1962 helped shape the new working relationship.

An able and pragmatic cleric now represented the Greek patriarchate on the forum of the Status Quo—the committee of church representatives managing the restoration. Archimandrite Germanos Mamaladis, the new superior of the Holy Sepulchre, a native of Chios, had arrived in Jerusalem in 1934 at the age of fourteen. A close colleague of Patriarch Benedictos, he had headed the patriarchate's finance department and continued to play an important role in fund raising.

His Latin counterpart was Father Albert Rock, who had represented the Custody of the Holy Land in talks since the early 1950s under a number of custroses. With his unrivaled knowledge and experience, he had acquired considerable influence. He and Germanos were able to establish an easy rapport and businesslike relationship. Both enjoyed the full confidence of their principals and were interested in solving practical problems rather than scoring theological points.

There was also a new atmosphere at the common technical bureau. Antellos Mallios had been replaced over the summer as local Greek architect by Leonidas J. Collas, a French speaker who had studied architecture in Paris. He soon established a close friendship with Father Coüasnon, with whom he shared an enthusiasm for archaeology. Collas's conciliatory manner and philosophy of conservation were not at all to the liking of extremists in the patriarchate, who would have preferred Mallios to continue.

The survey of the foundations, which proceeded quickly throughout the summer of 1961, provided an excellent opportunity for these men to bond as a team. Eleven soundings altogether, carried out at the base of the pillars in and around the Katholikon and Calvary, were reassuring about the state of the foundations. They also provided substantial evidence about the early history of the site.[1] Those working on the project were moved by this insight into Christian beginnings, which gave meaning to their labors.

It was found that not all of the church rested on bedrock. To create a level building site, Constantine's builders had hewn away the high ground to the west of Christ's tomb and built a massive wall to contain the hillside. East of the tomb they filled in a large area for the courtyard of the rotunda and a basilica, the Martyrion.

The site had once been part of a vast quarry, covered with earth by the first century. Chisel marks in the living rock are clearly visible in the roof of the underground Chapel of the Invention of the Cross. Excavations showed that the Rock of Golgotha was originally a hillock cut away from the surrounding rock, jutting up like a stone iceberg 10 meters (33 feet) above bedrock.[2]

The quality of the medieval foundations varied, but this was not judged to have affected the soundness of the superstructure. Trouvelot was of the opinion that it was best on the whole not to touch them. Only a few sections needed to be strengthened.[3] In addition, a Constantinian cistern under the Parvis had to be cleaned out and investigated, and the roof of a cave under the southern façade reinforced.

Encouraged by the work on the foundations, Edouard Utudjian, the principal Armenian architect, was convinced that "the long-awaited miracle [had] occurred." The communities' experts and resident architects were collaborating for the sake of the holy places "in a spirit of perfect understanding and mutual comprehension."[4]

Meeting in Athens on October 18, 1961, the experts agreed that having found the foundations in good condition, they could make an immediate start on the consolidation of the edifice. They recommended that work begin at the south façade. This necessitated the early arrival of master foreman Deschamps and the hiring of staff for the CTB.[5]

Cooperation between the communities in the Holy Sepulchre crossed a significant threshold at this time. With the move from below to above ground, disagreements inevitably arose on points of detail. Greeks and Latins disputed ownership of a drain and argued over the replacement of a stone bench. "Deep down, you see," Coüasnon remarked gloomily on November 6, "times haven't changed much."[6]

An eternal pessimist, he was quite wrong. Both sides were establishing the bounds of permissible behavior, not to forestall cooperation but to facilitate it. In the rotunda, the Greeks began to build, without notice, small bedrooms over their storerooms. Coüasnon and Trouvelot hated this, since they should have been informed, and the construction precluded future restoration of the original Anastasis.[7] But this was precisely the point. The Greeks would allow no change in the existing layout of the church, however desirable it might be from the point of view of conservation.

Father Rock, having negotiated the 1958 agreement, understood that strict adherence to the Status Quo was the basic ground rule for the entire operation. In conformity with this principle, he and Archimandrite Germanos concluded, at the turn of the year, written understandings on a number of joint projects. Their content was ostensibly trivial—cooperating to rebuild a partition here, install a glass door there—but they were indicative of the new relationship.[8]

One final crisis remained to be overcome. This was a last stand of reactionaries in the Greek Orthodox Confraternity of the Holy Sepulchre who were opposed to the improvement in Latin–Greek relations and to what they saw as unacceptable concessions in the basilica.

At the beginning of December 1961, there were clashes between Greek and Latin monks at Gethsemane and Bethlehem. On Christmas Eve, a further serious incident took place during the solemn entry of the Latin patriarch into the Church of the Nativity, when a number of Greek monks began throwing bottles. Foreign press and television journalists witnessed the episode, which was extensively reported abroad, causing something of a scandal.

Faced by this blatant act of insubordination, Benedictos acted forcefully to make an example of the culprits and impose discipline on the unruly brotherhood. Eleven monks were banished to the isolated desert monastery of Mar Saba, and on December 29 the holy synod found them guilty of sedition, disobedience, rebellion, disrespect, and desertion. They were defrocked and cut off from the brotherhood "like gangrenous limbs."[9]

Benedictos's tough action sent a clear signal that he was not prepared to let dissident monks disrupt détente between Greeks and Latins. He had staked his reputation on implementation of the restoration and was determined to see it through. His suppression of the Christmas Eve revolt must be considered the point of no return in the rehabilitation of the mother church.

With this, the project took off. In January 1962, the CTB began to remove the plastering and mortar in the upper section of the south transept in order to determine the condition of the masonry. Equipment and materials started to arrive at Jordan's port of Aqaba on the Red Sea. Work on the communities' private areas gathered momentum. Funding issues moved to the fore.

Millions of dollars had to be raised. About $3 million would be needed for the common areas of the church, in addition to large sums for private areas, depending on their size and the individual community's plans. All took it as axiomatic that each of them would seek funds independently.

At the outset, France had appropriated 300,000 new francs as seed money for the preparatory phase of the restoration, the only Catholic country to do so. But Father Vincenzo Cappiello, the new custos, opposed French involvement and declined to draw on these funds during his entire period in office. He preferred to raise money through the worldwide network of Franciscan Commissariats of the Holy Land.[10]

Patriarch Benedictos, too, was eager to tap independent sources of funding. In October 1961, he traveled to the United States, raising the specter of Russian funding in order to loosen American purse strings. Received by President John F. Kennedy at the White House, Benedictos praised the first Catholic president as a great Christian leader and awarded him the Grand Cross of the Order of the Holy Sepulchre.[11] But the trip was unproductive, and he returned across the Atlantic with pledges of only $100,000.

———

Slowly but surely, restoration projects began to sprout and spread throughout the edifice over the course of 1962. What began in odd corners as disjointed repair work gradually took over central spaces of the Crusader basilica. A dark, petrified forest of dilapidation—ancient pillars propped up by buttresses of wood and steel—was transformed into a busy construction site.

The Franciscans began with the restoration of their convent in the northwest corner of the Holy Sepulchre complex and the building of new accommodation for the resident friars. In the spring of 1962, Coüasnon labored on the renovation and refitting of the Latin sacristy. He was pleasantly surprised to discover a fine eleventh-century arch hidden under the plaster, which he put to secondary use as a window in a cell on the floor above.

Under pressure to complete the assignment by Easter week, and single-handedly bearing the added burden of the south transept, Coüasnon begged the custos to complete arrangements for the long-delayed arrival of Henri Deschamps.[12] While impatiently waiting for his contract to come through, Deschamps had attended lectures in Paris on the holy places and read everything he could find on the church. At long last, on June 1, 1962, he arrived on site as specialist foreman for the CTB, Latin foreman, and consultant master mason for the other two communities.

His arrival converted Coüasnon's one-man operation into a sustainable, collective enterprise. Deschamps's initial task was to train stonecutters and masons and to obtain a reliable supply of stone. His men had to be taught the techniques of Crusader masonry, using the tool of choice of the twelfth century, the toothed hammer, handmade so as to reproduce the original dressing. To prepare and lay a single dressed stone took one worker roughly one week. And thousands of stones were needed. The incessant tap and clink of stones being shaped would greet visitors to the edifice for years to come.

The stone chosen was the local Malaki stone Crusader masons had used following a tradition that was supposed to go back to King Solomon. Deschamps located a quarry at Tell al-Nasbe, 7 miles north of Jerusalem. Crude blocks were brought to the building site and cut to shape on the spot. This was easier said than done: the stone was transported by truck to the Zion or Jaffa Gates and then transferred to handcarts for conveyance through the narrow, shop-lined souks of the Old City. Stonecutting took place under a shelter of corrugated iron roofing set up along the eastern side of the Parvis.

The principal architects were favorably impressed on a tour of inspection in August 1962. They found a functioning construction site well supplied with cut stone and other building materials. Workers were being thoroughly trained. But there was no effective system for releasing imported items and equipment from customs, and the communities were eagerly awaiting machinery to lift materials from the Parvis to the roof.[13]

In the Franciscan section, work moved on to the old refectory, then to the Chapels of the Apparition and St. Mary Magdalene, following an agreement between Latins and Greeks. Work began in the Latin galleries in November 1962, removing the overlay of centuries. Sixteenth-century masonry was found to be splintered by iron wedges that had rusted and subsequently expanded. After cleaning, stones that were no longer load bearing were replaced one by one, and then grout was injected under low pressure to provide cohesion to the wall. In the long eastern arm of the galleries, which forms a beautiful hall with light streaming in from high windows, ancient central columns carrying the springing of the arches were found to be so cracked by fire that they would have to be completely replaced.[14]

The Greeks started out modestly, repairing their property around Calvary. Benedictos also ordered work to begin on the monastery of St. Abraham in the Parvis and on the Greek treasury over Calvary.[15] His flagship project was the rehabilitation of the Katholikon. It had been appallingly damaged in 1808 and needed to be reconstructed from top to bottom. The stones on the underside of the eastern arch of the choir were found to be burnt to a depth of 15 centimeters (6 inches). Some had fallen out, and others were in imminent danger of doing so. Demolition of the supporting walls at the crossing revealed the well-proportioned, spacious interior of the Crusader edifice as it had been before the great fire.

Collas faced a major challenge in organizing the Greek construction site. His work was complicated by lack of support from the monks and the insubordination of the Greek foreman, who refused to take orders from Deschamps.[16] On a trip to Athens in October 1962, Collas had the government recall the foreman and impose order. He also settled other internal issues that had delayed the project, including the lack of provision of adequate scaffolding.[17] With the solution of these problems, the erection of the giant piers supporting the Katholikon dome could proceed without hindrance.

Restoration by the CTB began at the same time in the adjacent south transept and Armenian long gallery, or tribune, behind the façade. Removal of plaster and mortar had brought to light a great quantity of badly calcined twelfth-century masonry. The devastated cross vault and supporting columns and walls would have to be totally replaced. In the Armenian long gallery, the central pier and vault had been destroyed in 1808 and would have to be rebuilt. Monks' rooms were marked for demolition to make way for a spacious new long chapel.

On October 16, 1962, the extrados, or exterior of the vaults, over the main entrance at the ground floor level was dismantled. The next day, Deschamps cleared away the plaster and debris from the vault and wall behind the façade in the Armenian long gallery. A little ritual marked the launch of the reconstruction proper. Deschamps placed a bottle of wine from the Trappist monastery of Latrun into the wall before laying the first stone.[18]

Work now proceeded in parallel in the south transept and Katholikon, with competition between the CTB and the Greek technical bureau for skilled masons. Coüasnon deprecated it in strong terms. "This juxtaposition of two independent construction teams competing against each other is painful and stressful. It is odious."[19]

Just before the Greek Orthodox Christmas (January 6, 1963, in Jerusalem) the base of the southwest pier was maneuvered into position, stone by stone. With twenty-five laborers on site—including six stonemasons—tapping, cutting, and laying the great blocks, work proceeded with "frenetic haste." By June 1963, the southwest pier was practically complete, and work on the other piers was proceeding apace. "They are working a bit everywhere," Coüasnon observed. Collas was busy on the southern arcade that leads via the ambulatory to the eastern apse. All the while, the vast task of replacing calcined stones continued without interruption. In a happy discovery, the inner half of one of the great capitals was found preserved intact inside supporting masonry. Rotated 180 degrees, its acanthus-leaf design replaced the exposed outer half that had perished in the flames of 1808.[20]

In August 1963, following the erection in the Parvis of a crane with an electric hoist, installation of a reinforced concrete framework began in the galleries and terraces. Coüasnon and Trouvelot had invested much thought into the planning. Among other things, a 35-degree temperature range on the roof during the summer had to be factored into the equation. A concealed rib cage of beams and pillars would attach the façade to the core of the building and counteract the thrust of vaults and arches, providing a definitive solution to the threat of future earthquakes. Today no visitor suspects that under the flagstones a steel frame is embedded within the structure of the basilica.

Before the historic Paul–Athenagoras meeting of January 6, 1964, the piers of the Katholikon had been largely rebuilt, up to the drum of the dome, the great eastern arch was complete, and the northern arch was under construction. The builders had restored the pillars of Calvary between the Chapel of Adam and the Katholikon, and Collas had repaired the southern arcade. In the Armenian tribune, two half vaults were restored, and an eleventh-century arch repaired. Plans were ready for the central pier behind the façade. Reconstruction of the vault over the south transept was progressing, despite problems with the ribs. On the terraces following the installation of the beams, asphalt was spread and paving laid.[21]

Two political developments complicated the restoration. One was Derderian's lack of legitimacy among his own people, which led to disputes and hindered fund raising. The other was the instability of the Hashemite kingdom, which resulted in a rapid turnover of governors of Jerusalem, making it harder for them to play the role of neutral arbiter.

Escorted by a police contingent, Archbishop Derderian had returned to a sullen Armenian community in March 1960 to reclaim the post of locum tenens. The community, sympathetic toward the expelled Archbishop Nersoyan, assumed that Derderian had secured his return by bribery. Hassan Bey warned that fifty leading Armenians would be held personally accountable for the community's good behavior. Recalcitrant members of the Brotherhood of St. James were expelled, and Derderian was duly elected patriarch by a minimum quorum. King Hussein conveyed his own endorsement of the prelate by conferring on him the Jordan Star, First Class.[22]

On August 21, 1960, Patriarch Derderian was crowned in the Armenian Cathedral of St. James. Rumors that the Armenian community would boycott the ceremony proved ill founded. The king's berat was read out, followed by letters of confirmation and congratulation from the Supreme Catholikos in Etchmiadzin and the Catholikos of Antilias. A reception in the grand audience chamber of the convent "quickly degenerated into chaos, with the Armenian congregation pressing forward, regardless of rank and protocol, to avail themselves of the free eats and champagne."[23]

Nevertheless, Derderian now presided over a divided community. "Derderian is not accepted by the majority of lay Armenians," the British consul general reported, "because of his notoriously immoral private life, his corrupt handling of church funds, his dictatorial behaviour, and his habitual resort to bribery to achieve both unofficial and official ends."[24]

His reputation affected financial support from abroad. He launched an appeal in the spring of 1962, evoking the tragic history of the scattered Armenian people, its spiritual and national heritage in the Holy Land, and the supreme patriotic duty to preserve Armenian Jerusalem in the midst of the Universal Jerusalem.[25] But the Armenian community in the United States, angered at his treatment of Archbishop Nersoyan, was unresponsive. A sum of $300,000 already pledged by the Calouste Gulbenkian foundation of Lisbon was held up because of disagreement over the terms of the donation.

The Greek patriarch, Benedictos, had welcomed Derderian's return from exile, reportedly because he regarded himself as Derderian's intellectual superior and supposedly shared some of his less spiritual proclivities. Benedictos was also confident that Derderian would give him no trouble in the matter of the restoration.[26] He was wrong about this. While Greeks and Latins achieved a businesslike relationship and were eager to press ahead, Deschamps's arrival on site caught the Armenian patriarchate impoverished and unprepared. Concerned by this, Father Rock and Archimandrite Germanos offered the Armenians financial help at a meeting of experts on July 8, 1962, but their Armenian colleague, Father Kapikian, declined.[27]

Derderian chose to play for time and defiantly assert Armenian interests against Greeks and Latins. As the weakest party, he was determined that the restoration should be carried out strictly on the basis of equal rights to possession of the roof and fabric of the edifice.[28] He made his stand over the south transept.

A draft agreement prepared by Rock and Germanos indicated that the terraces to be dismantled were mostly Greek, with some Latin and Muslim waqf rights, and the Armenians completely excluded. Derderian indignantly rejected this, insisting that his community shared possession of the terrace over the south transept and was entitled to join the Greeks in removing the tiles.[29]

The Greeks rebutted this claim, with Latin support, and went ahead. On July 10, 1962, Coüasnon telephoned the secretary of the Armenian patriarchate, Garbis Hintlian, to inform him that work had begun on the vault. "What about the paving?" Hintlian inquired. "There isn't any left," Coüasnon replied. At this, "the circus began."[30]

Derderian immediately protested to the governor, Anwar Nusseibeh, that the Greeks had no right to do this on their own, since the roof was an integral part of the fabric of the church and therefore common property. He cited Cust's section on the roof in his support.[31] Until the question was resolved, work on the terrace should be suspended.

Derderian's motives were both principled and practical. He viewed the roof as jointly owned, just as the foundations under common areas were jointly owned. Moreover, the chapel immediately below the terrace was Armenian and had to be restored as part of the south transept project. What sense did it make, he wondered, for the Greeks to restore the roof by themselves while the Armenians owned the vaults underneath?

On March 7, 1963, the governor issued a decision. He had earlier found that the roof was Greek, since it was reached through their convent. In itself, the lifting of tiles did not constitute an important structural alteration. He therefore ruled that the Greeks could remove the tiles, provided that they replaced them without raising the roof level. He also instructed the Greeks to assist the Armenians in carrying out repairs to their chapel below the terrace.[32]

Derderian now lodged a second complaint about restoration of the well, which is common property but is situated in a yard belonging to the Franciscan convent. Access is via a passage leading off the rotunda. In the past, the Greeks acquired a storeroom in the largely Latin section of the complex, so although the passage is mostly Latin, some of it is in joint Latin–Greek possession. All the communities have right of passage to the well.

On October 4, 1962, church representatives met to discuss the new water, electricity, and sewage systems for the church. This was a key part of the first phase of the restoration, and Derderian was determined to make a further bid for common ownership and equality of status. He would not get a better opportunity, and the eagerness of Greeks and Latins to get started gave him some leverage.

All agreed that the pipeline under the Parvis, south transept, and rotunda was common property. Not so the section that was to run under the passage to the well. Greeks and Latins dismissed Derderian's argument that this, too, was common property. Impatient with what they felt was another spurious claim, Germanos and Rock reached agreement between themselves and set to work.

As in the case of the roof, Derderian immediately sought to have the authorities suspend work, on the ground that he was a coproprietor. His claim was backed by a sheaf of historical documents but rested on two main arguments. One was that a reference in Cust to the "common passage" to the well meant in fact "common ownership of the passage" to the well; the other was that the Armenian community had the right to hang two ladders on the western wall of the passage, indicating possession of the wall and therefore coproprietorship of the passage.

During an investigation on the spot, a Jordanian official found that only the Latins hung their ladders on the wall; the Armenians kept theirs on the ground. Adding that a right of way did not bestow possession, he confirmed the Greek and Latin claims that they, but not the Armenians, were copro-prietors. Anwar Nusseibeh accordingly found against the Armenians.[33]

The failure of Derderian's appeal against this decision should have put an end to the matter. But on January 9, 1963, Anwar Nusseibeh was dismissed after less than a year in office. Months of disarray followed, allowing Derderian to renew his claims to the roof and the well.

Anwar Nusseibeh, Western-educated and head of a venerable Jerusalem family who were the traditional doorkeepers of the Holy Sepulchre, was a highly respected man of impeccable integrity. His dismissal was seen as part of a campaign by Amman to take over key positions on the West Bank. Nusseibeh felt that he was being punished for allowing Jerusalem parliamentarians to speak critically of the government. He also cited a cabinet minister's remark that "they wanted him to do certain things which they were pretty certain he would not agree to"—that is, he could not be counted on to stamp out dissent.[34]

At first, the government feared that Nusseibeh's dismissal might spark hostile demonstrations. On January 12, 1963, the king visited Jerusalem amid a show of military power. The local army commander was quoted as saying that "he had received orders from the King that he was to shoot to kill the leaders of any demonstration."[35]

Nusseibeh was replaced by Fadhl al-Dalqamuni, a civil servant from Irbid on the East Bank. It was an unpopular appointment, and Dalqamuni did not last very long. Rumors began to circulate almost at once of a "shakedown" of local notables by Dalqamuni's officials. He was dismissed at very short notice, and Daoud Abu Ghazaleh, a reliable cabinet minister, was appointed in his stead.[36]

Easter Day, April 14, 1963, was celebrated by all communities in an atmosphere of uncertainty. Arab unity talks were being held in Cairo involving Egypt and two of Jordan's neighbors, Syria and Iraq. The success of the talks would further isolate the Hashemite kingdom, placing Iraq, its eastern neighbor, in the enemy Nasserist camp.

To the Latin patriarch, Alberto Gori, the future for Christians in Jordan had never looked bleaker. "He is a dear old man," a British diplomat reported,

> sorely troubled these days about the erosion of the Christian presence in Jerusalem and district, which he, a Franciscan, has known for many years both as Custos and as Patriarch. His Beatitude remarked that the Christian population of Ramallah, for example, had dropped since 1948 from 12,000 to 2,000. Bethlehem and Beit Jalla were becoming increasingly Islamicised. The Moslem Brotherhood were building

Mosques everywhere in the Old City and were encroaching upon the Christian places wherever they could. The Patriarch thought that the recent news from Cairo would only fortify and increase these tendencies. There would have to be a new Crusade before very long. He was fearful regarding the stability of Jordan and anxious about the future of Jerusalem, which, of course, he could not see as other than an international city.[37]

On April 17, Nasser announced an expanded United Arab Republic. A wave of pan-Arab, Nasserist sentiment swept through Jordan, as did popular demonstrations demanding that Jordan join the union. In Jerusalem, high school students held a demonstration between the Damascus Gate and Herod's Gate. When the unarmed demonstrators marched on the governorate, the army opened fire, causing heavy loss of life.[38] In these circumstances the governor had difficulty giving his undivided attention to abstruse issues of the Status Quo at the Church of the Resurrection.

Lacking funds, Derderian continued to be obstructive. On July 20, 1963, he protested that the Latins had illicitly installed a fixture in the well area and requested yet another suspension of work order. Germanos expressed surprise that they were returning to an issue two previous governors had examined in depth. He begged "our Armenian brothers not to place obstacles in the way, interrupting the renovations in the church of the Holy Sepulchre. The eyes of the world are on you."[39] On September 20, Abu Ghazaleh dismissed Derderian's request.

Derderian might have persisted with his campaign of obstruction but for a change in his fortunes. Despite unpopularity at home, he was on good terms with the two rival prelates of the Armenian world, Catholikos Khoren I of Antilias and Supreme Catholikos Vasken I of Etchmiadzin. On the advice of lay leaders in the United States, Derderian convened a peace parley of the two foes in Jerusalem on October 29, 1963.

The summit was a triumph for Derderian, greatly augmenting his prestige. It was the first visit by a catholikos to Jerusalem in three hundred years and placed Derderian in the role of peacemaker. Insecure and querulous up to this point, he now had a conciliatory reputation to maintain.[40] It also gave a decisive boost to his fund-raising prospects and he was soon on the road seeking donations for his Holy Sepulchre appeal. The stage was set for a second historic act of reconciliation.

The ecumenical movement received a strong boost from Angelo Roncalli, Pope John XXIII, who appealed for peace, church unity, and reconciliation in his first Christmas message after his election in October 1958. On January 25, 1959, he called for an ecumenical council of the universal church, a Second Vatican Council ("Vatican II"). In June 1960, he established the Secretariat for Promoting Church Unity under Augustin Cardinal Bea as the agency for interchurch dialogue.[41]

A career diplomat, Bishop Roncalli had spent twenty years in the Orthodox world, serving as apostolic delegate to Bulgaria (1925–35) and to Greece and Turkey (1935–45). After the war, he was sent as papal nuncio to Paris. On his elevation to the papacy, his wartime efforts on behalf of the starving Greek nation under Italian occupation were recalled with appreciation by Greeks.[42]

The pope was devoted to the Church of the Holy Sepulchre.[43] In 1906, when he was secretary to the bishop of Bergamo, he had come on pilgrimage to Jerusalem, noting in his journal the bishop's description of the "amazement and grief felt by Christians from distant countries when confronted with the disorder, the confusion of people, things, languages, rites and faiths surrounding the holy sepulchre."[44] He had again visited Jerusalem in June 1939 as guest of his old friend Archbishop Gustavo Testa, and he would have witnessed the sorry state of the edifice under scaffolding.

In October 1961, Pope John convened Vatican II as a vehicle for church renewal and ecumenical reconciliation. To encourage the Greek Orthodox Church to send delegates, he began a diplomatic exchange with the Phanar, but the reaction of many of the Greek Orthodox bishops was suspicious and negative. Patriarch Benedictos wrote to Patriarch Athenagoras in July 1962 opposing participation even as observers. "We fear," he wrote, "that the participants will eventually hear and witness anti-orthodox speeches and decisions."[45]

John XXIII died in June 1963. Giovanni Battista Cardinal Montini, who became Pope Paul VI, had spent a career in the Curia, serving from 1937 to 1952 as substitute for ordinary affairs (the equivalent of minister for internal affairs) and would have been conversant with issues surrounding the Holy Sepulchre.

He continued his predecessor's policies. In a speech closing the second session of Vatican II on December 4, 1963, Paul VI stunned the Church by announcing his decision to go on a pilgrimage to the Holy Land after Christmas to pray for the Council, for Christian unity, and for peace. It would be the first visit by a pope to the holy places ever. Publicly, he insisted that his motives were mainly religious.

Two days later, Patriarch Athenagoras, to the equal astonishment of the Orthodox communion, expressed his wish to kneel with Pope Paul at Golgotha and the tomb.

We now know that this dramatic ecumenical initiative was not wholly spontaneous. On September 20, the pope had written a letter in his own hand to Patriarch Athenagoras saying he would do all in his power to reestablish perfect harmony among Christians. The very next day, he wrote a memo for the record about the possibility of making a pilgrimage to the Holy Land and of a fraternal meeting with the various Christian denominations there. Few were privy to this closely kept secret.[46]

Many complicated issues now had to be resolved in a very short time. First was the summit itself. On December 10, the pope sent a special envoy, Father Pierre Duprey, to Patriarch Athenagoras with an astounding message: "I had come to tell him," Father Duprey later recalled, "that the holy father was going as a pilgrim to Jerusalem and that, if he himself were to be in Jerusalem at the same time as a pilgrim, the holy father would be very happy to meet him." Athenagoras responded with delight but wondered about Benedictos's reaction. According to the protocol adopted after the Council of Chalcedon in 451, Constantinople required a prior invitation from Jerusalem to visit the Holy City.[47]

From Istanbul, Father Duprey traveled on to Jerusalem with the delicate assignment of reconciling Patriarch Benedictos to a papal visit and to a meeting of pope and ecumenical patriarch that had already been decided on behind his back. Considering that the 1054 schism had been precipitated by inept diplomacy, it was a daunting task.

Father Duprey, the Vatican expert on the Greek Orthodox Church, was well suited for the mission.[48] A scholar and a linguist, he was a hard worker, an able writer, and a man of action. At age eighteen, he had left Nazi-occupied France for Tunisia to enlist in the French Foreign Legion, afterward joining the African missionary movement the White Fathers. From his time in Tunisia, he had learned to curse like a sailor and sleep on the floor.

Later, with a doctorate from the Oriental Institute in Rome, he went on to study Orthodox theology in Athens and Arabic literature in Beirut. In 1956, he was appointed professor at St. Anne's seminary in Jerusalem and editor of *Proche Orient Chrétien,* a quarterly journal reporting on the Christian communities of the Middle East. He served in the post for five years.

During most of the negotiations on the restoration of the Holy Sepulchre, Father Duprey provided information to the Custody, much of it derived from the Greek press and church publications, giving important insight into both global and local Greek Orthodox concerns. In addition, *Proche Orient Chrétien* published regular reports on the restoration project. Without this intelligence, it would have been hard for the Custody or the Holy See to make much sense of the often-confusing positions of the Greeks in the talks. The journal was particularly enlightening on the embattled worldview of the Greek Orthodox Patriarchate and its internal rivalries.

In 1962 Father Duprey was asked to serve as interpreter-theologian for Greek Orthodox observers at the first session of Vatican II and was then sent on a diplomatic mission to Istanbul to brief Patriarch Athenagoras.

There were mixed signals prior to Duprey's trip to Jerusalem of December 11–12, 1963. At the communal level, Greek–Latin relations had unquestionably taken a turn for the better. That summer, the Franciscan father superior in the Holy Sepulchre had even invited the superiors and monks of the various Orthodox communities to the screening of a movie on the terrace of the Latin convent adjacent to the Anastasis, followed by a meal.[49] The movie, *Marcellino, pan y vino* (Marcellino, Bread and Wine), tells the story of a Spanish boy who, abandoned as a baby by his mother, grows up in a Franciscan friary.

At the personal level, Benedictos was suspicious of the ecumenical movement, was not interested in a Catholic–Orthodox dialogue on theological issues, and regarded Vatican II as an internal affair of the Roman Catholic Church. He was irked that Athenagoras had not consulted him and was cool about Athenagoras coming to Jerusalem. On the other hand, he was known to be interested in an exchange of views with Rome about practical issues such as proselytism, Jordanian policy toward the churches, and the holy places. Moreover, he had established a good working relationship with the Franciscans over repairs at the Holy Sepulchre.[50]

From the airport, Father Duprey checked into St. Anne's, next to St. Stephen's Gate, and then walked up the Via Dolorosa to the Greek Orthodox Patriarchate. Fortunately, he had known Benedictos since his election and remembered the protocol for church visitors to Jerusalem from previous visits by Athenagoras himself and the archbishop of Canterbury, Geoffrey Fisher. In perfect Greek, he presented his request: would his holiness receive the bishop of Rome, the patriarch of the West, in Jerusalem?

Benedictos assured Duprey reluctantly that he would meet the pope, provided that the pope followed the letter of protocol and received Benedictos in turn. If this condition were met, he would cooperate in arranging the program.

Father Duprey then contacted the Armenian Patriarchate and the bishops of other churches in Jerusalem. Derderian was out of the country until the end of December, but his officials showed good will and confirmed that the Armenian patriarch would gladly welcome the pope. Two of them, Karekin Sarkissian and Ardavazt Terterian, had been observers at Vatican II.

Back in Rome, Paul VI approved Benedictos's request, remarking: "Even Jesus visited his own friends, so what is there against his vicar on earth doing the same?"[51]

A complicated series of negotiations now followed. Benedictos had been positive in principle, but the details of this totally unprecedented visit needed to be filled in. He would welcome Paul VI but was sensitive to his own dignity. He would not greet the pope in person at the city gates or at the door of the Holy Sepulchre, since he did not wish the high-level Roman delegation to overwhelm and overshadow him. He preferred to meet the pope privately.[52]

He rejected a request for the pope to make his solemn entry into the Church of the Nativity passing down the main aisle, but agreed to his celebrating mass in front of the Edicule on Saturday afternoon, January 4, which was without precedent under the Status Quo and required delaying the Greek Orthodox after-supper service.[53]

A second set of negotiations, handled by Father Rock and Archimandrite Germanos, concerned Status Quo questions at the Church of the Nativity. Objectively speaking, the issues were trivial, but hardly a Christmas or Easter went by without an incident in the Bethlehem basilica. Clearly, a brawl on the eve of a historic summit would be a disaster.

Compromises were successfully reached on three old disputes: the cleaning of the ten windows of the north clerestory, the route of the Latin procession following the midnight mass on Christmas Eve, and the lighting by the two communities of candles in the Grotto of the Nativity during each other's ceremonies. The significance of the latter compromise was that it implied a modification of the Catholic attitude to acts of schismatic worship in their presence.[54] Rock hoped that the agreements would put an end to unseemly quarrels.[55]

Finally, a breakthrough was made on the outstanding point of contention between Greeks and Latins in the Church of the Resurrection—the ownership of the area known as the Seven Arches of the Virgin between the Katholikon and the northern wall of the church. According to Cust, the Latins held firmans in their favor from the seventeenth and eighteenth centuries, but possession had alternated, and the German scholar Conrad Schick had assigned it to the Greeks on an 1883 map.[56]

Whereas the Greek position was that this section was exclusively in their possession and had been repaired with Latin permission in 1932, the Latin position was that some of the supporting pillars were jointly owned and therefore the vaults should be considered joint property. Moreover, the Latins owned the adjacent Chapel of St. Mary Magdalene and sacristy, and the overhead gallery.

When Rock searched the Custody's archives, he was surprised to discover that the Greek claim was substantially well founded and that in order to overcome Greek opposition to various Latin works of repair in 1932, the

Custody had indeed agreed to the Greeks' replastering and redecorating much of the contested area. In his memorandum on the subject, Father Rock hints that the Custody had been outmaneuvered and that the concessions given away thirty years before had left him with hardly a leg to stand on in the current negotiations.

The Latin Discretorium, the Custody's governing board, considered Rock's findings on September 7, 1963, but instructed him to proceed anyway with a claim that the vault over the north transept be repaired at joint expense. At a meeting of negotiating delegations inside the Holy Sepulchre a few days later, no agreement was reached. The Greeks preferred arbitration by the governor (which they were confident would be in their favor) to Rock's suggestion of a summit between patriarch and custos (which would produce either a compromise or a rupture). Until the affair was concluded, they demanded that the Latins suspend ongoing work on two windows in the eastern wall of the long gallery.

Rock showed his disgust at this condition, which could complicate work in progress in every part of the church, and warned the Greeks that if the Latins were not to be allowed to carry out repairs, neither would they. Specifically, they would not be allowed free passage, needed for building operations, through the Latin galleries to their chapel on Calvary and would have to suspend work there.

By the end of a tough meeting, the Greeks had withdrawn their insistence that the Latins stop work. Collas promised to do his best to dissuade the patriarchate from hardening its position. Otherwise, relations between the communities would suffer, to the detriment of the entire restoration project.[57]

No progress was made for the next three months. The pope's announcement on December 4, 1963, of his impending pilgrimage to the Holy Land effectively broke the impasse. In a letter to the pope the very next day, the custos affirmed the Custody's mission to defend the holy places "in the most humble obedience to the orders of the Holy Father and the Mother Church."[58]

Under the circumstances, Father Rock had no choice but to capitulate. An agreement was quickly concluded between Latins and Greeks, as a consequence of which the entire contested area, including the north transept, the Seven Arches of the Virgin, the Chapel of the Bonds (or Stocks), and the Prison of Christ, passed into Greek possession.

This unprecedented and far-reaching concession was the abandonment of a claim that had been maintained for centuries. It is unclear whether or not the Latins received anything specific in return. However, it is hard to imagine that Father Duprey's mission would have been crowned with success had the problem not been solved.

As a result of this landmark agreement, the way was open to complete the program of restoration of the Church of the Holy Sepulchre. Comprehensive agreement now existed between the Greeks and Latins as to which walls, columns, doors, windows, roofs, and stones were common to two or three communities, and which were separately possessed by one of them. The conditions for the restoration were set.[59]

Intensive last-minute preparations for the pope's visit got under way in Jerusalem. Rarely had such a momentous event been planned at such short notice. In consequence, crowd control arrangements were totally inadequate, while the apostolic delegation mishandled ticket arrangements. In the Holy Sepulchre, a task force of priests of all three major communities had to do their best with brooms, shovels, and feather dusters to tidy up the construction site the church had become.[60]

The papal trip succeeded, in difficult circumstances, as a great act of sacred theater. Against the backdrop of the Christian pilgrimage sites of the Holy Land, the slight figure of the pope, in his white soutane and zucchetto, drew the world's attention to the main themes of Vatican II: renewal and reunion. Among those accompanying the pope were Secretary of State Amleto Cardinal Cicognani, Secretary of the Congregation for the Oriental Churches Gustavo Cardinal Testa (given his red hat by John XXIII), and Father Duprey.

At the Damascus Gate, the Holy Father was greeted by a tumultuous crowd that got completely out of hand. All organization was abandoned, and none of the waiting dignitaries was able to greet him. Instead, soldiers flailing out with whips, canes, and even the palm branches strewn on the ground cleared a path through the throng. Quiet prayer at the Stations of the Cross was ruled out as the pope was borne along to the Church of the Resurrection. During the celebration of the mass, fire broke out among television cables in the scaffolding overhead, but a soldier extinguished it, as the pope, tears on his cheeks, carried on.[61]

On the first evening of his stay, he exchanged reciprocal visits, as agreed, with the Greek and Armenian Orthodox patriarchs of Jerusalem. Both his prepared addresses gave thanks for their cooperation on the restoration. Had it not been for the December 1963 agreement, he could not have come. He told Benedictos:

> It is with joy that we have learned that an atmosphere of frank collaboration now exists between your community, the Catholic community, and the Armenian community, in regard to the work of restoration of the Church of the Holy Sepulchre. For this is the very place where God wishes to reconcile to Himself all things. . . . It is

highly symbolic that despite the burden of history and of numerous difficulties, Christians, though unhappily separated, are working together to restore this temple, which they had first erected when in full unity, and which their divisions have abandoned to dilapidation. . . . We realize the part taken by Your Beatitude in this change of climate, we know the efforts being made on all sides to eliminate points of friction.[62]

The next day, the pope returned to the Holy Sepulchre for an unscheduled second visit as a private pilgrim. Passersby were astonished to see him walking through the Old City to the Holy Sepulchre by himself.[63] There, on his knees before the tomb, he was left alone with his thoughts and prayers.

Finally, on January 6, Paul and Athenagoras met on the Mount of Olives and embraced before the world's media. Athenagoras's wish for the two men to kneel together at Golgotha and the tomb went unfulfilled.

| Three Wise Men

THE POPE AND THE PATRIARCH'S kiss of peace inaugurated a new spirit of cooperation in the Holy Sepulchre. Having embarked on the great task of restoration, the major communities proceeded to tackle problems in a pragmatic manner and steadily maintained the momentum of construction. But they undoubtedly had their ups and downs, and relations were often contentious and sometimes tempestuous.

Visiting Jerusalem in the spring of 1964, the Yale archaeologist Robert Houston Smith acclaimed the restoration as a striking ecumenical symbol for the times.[1] Father Rock explained to him that the communities had discovered "the importance of keeping channels of communication open. Previously the communities had very little contact with one another, even when rubbing shoulders every day inside the church. Now the representatives of the communities regard each other as personal friends. We may have different views, but we stay on friendly terms." His Greek colleague, Archimandrite Germanos, was "a very good and understanding man."

Archimandrite Germanos agreed with Smith that a new spirit had indeed replaced previous discord but preferred to talk of cooperation rather than church unity. "We have our beliefs. We have our differences. We cannot simply forget them." Nor could the third member of the triumvirate, Father Guregh Kapikian, an intense and militant young monk who was serving as director of the Armenian school. Imbued with his people's tragic history, he was devoted to strengthening the Armenian position in the mother church: "The ecumenical spirit may be active elsewhere, but here in this church we're the last to know about it. We fight for our corner as we've always done!"[2]

Born to Armenian holocaust survivors in Jerusalem, Guregh was told by his mother that when she was pregnant with him she dreamt that an angel spoke to her, saying, "when your son is born, a lamp will be lighted for St. James"—the apostle for whom the Armenian cathedral and brotherhood of Armenian monks is named. Roberta Ervine, his assistant in the 1980s, remembers him saying that "the only loyalty that I have in the world is to St. James and that is it."[3] Looking back, he also said, "I did what I had to do as a soldier," and that is how his friends remembered him, as a "soldier of God" and his church.[4]

The key to progress was clerical will at the highest level. After the papal pilgrimage, the Holy See was more dedicated than ever to restoration and interchurch unity. Benedictos and Derderian were also deeply committed to the success of the restoration but would never compromise the identity and independence of their communities. Within the basilica, cooperation had to be anchored in the Status Quo, which embodied the principle of separation, not unity.

Benedictos would ideally have liked to see a unified Anastasis under Greek control, viewing it as the inalienable heritage of his race. Roman Catholics were interlopers, only present because of the historical injustice of the Crusades. Since they could not be evicted, he sought to consolidate the Katholikon as a wholly Greek church, decorated throughout with Greek Orthodox icons and mosaics. Nor would he ever dream of abandoning the neo-Byzantine character of the Edicule.

Derderian, in contrast, made no claim to carry the banner of the universal church. His community's identity had always lain in its national individuality, its fight to survive against non-Christian enemies, from fifth-century Persia to twentieth-century Turkey. The focus of his attention throughout was on the defense of Armenian property rights and the transformation of the Armenian section into a shrine that uniquely reflected his nation's heritage and character.

In 1966, Archimandrite Germanos was elevated to archbishop, and his place as superior and expert on the Status Quo was taken by his experienced deputy, Father Daniel Choriatakis, who had come to Jerusalem from Samos in 1941, at age twenty. Though without formal higher education, he had a phenomenal memory and was called the "walking library."[5]

The three fathers, Daniel, Rock, and Guregh, made up the management forum of the Status Quo, administering the restoration on behalf of their principals until the end. They commissioned work, supervised its implementation, approved expenditures, represented their respective communities in talks, negotiated accommodations, both verbal and written, and protected their Status Quo interests. Their respective church leaders trusted and relied on them, and they had power of attorney to sign minor accords. Only major agreements were signed by their principals. Without formal architectural training, however, they were not always sensitive to the internationally-agreed principles laid down in the 1964 Venice Charter for the conservation and restoration of monuments and sites.

Relations between the experts were realistic rather than euphoric. Negotiations were hard-nosed, and church reunification was never on the agenda. Cooperation was a means to the end of restoration, not a vehicle of reconciliation. The Holy Sepulchre project essentially involved a practical set of arrangements between parties with overlapping interests but without any larger theological dimension.

Nevertheless, the collegial, professional relationship between the three clerics, drawing their authority from church leaders, was crucial to the rescue of the edifice.

All the various shortcomings of the restoration—its neglect of the finer points of conservation, the squabbles on site, the ultimate failure to reconstruct the Edicule—fade into insignificance compared with the achievement of political accommodation.

On his 1964 visit, Robert Houston Smith observed the good atmosphere in the CTB during its honeymoon period. The CTB was conveniently located in rented offices in the Convent of Gethsemane, overlooking the Parvis. Since the communities had decided to dispense with an outside building contractor and do the job themselves, the CTB acted as the project's contractor, employing and paying labor and managing work in common areas of the church. It acted as the liaison with the principal architects abroad, carrying out their instructions and keeping them posted about what was happening on the spot. It also ordered all the materials and equipment needed to keep a building site running.

One morning Smith sat in on a business conversation over cigarettes and coffee between Coüasnon and Collas, the friends whose excellent personal relations facilitated the smooth running of the bureau at this time. Father Rock later joined the group. The discussion ranged over several current topics. How could access to Calvary be improved? The two flights of steps, built by Komnenos in 1809–10 by appropriating a slice of the south transept, were steep and narrow, and had to be perilously ascended in pitch darkness. What could be done about the rock of Calvary itself, which was encased in marble and plaster, and hardly recognizable? Patriarch Benedictos was particularly interested in removing this casing and revealing for all to see the rock on which the cross was believed to have stood.

In Crusader times, Calvary had been entered directly off the Parvis through the Chapel of the Franks, now in Latin possession. But the Greeks would never agree to reopen this door. In 1955, the English architect David Stokes had suggested building a catwalk across the south transept that would be reached by a new stairwell in the Coptic storeroom. This was ruled out, as the Copts would never agree without being recognized as coproprietors.

A related question was whether or not the Jordanian government should pay for repairs in parts of the church belonging to the minor communities, whom the major communities categorically refused to involve in the restoration. This concerned various storerooms and cells belonging to the Copts, as well as their tiny chapel behind the Edicule.

Those present in the CTB wondered how they might continue work in the south transept without disturbing the lamps over the Stone of Unction (the starting point for many processions). The constant problem of the restoration was to build without interrupting the liturgical routine of the Holy Sepulchre.

Smith realized that major issues of principle remained pending and that the architects and communities were feeling their way slowly on all issues, tackling fresh problems on a daily basis. After an hour's conversation, even minor questions remained unresolved because final decisions on most matters required the communities' official approval. Still, the meeting obviously helped to clarify the issues.

Provided the local Greek and Latin architects got on, the CTB was adept at coordinating the communities' separate building activities and finding sensible solutions to practical problems. With sixty workers on site busy on different projects, depending on "each other's good will alone," as Father Coüasnon remarked, "would have been a hazardous undertaking."[6]

If workmen from one of the communities needed to pass through the territory of the other to carry out their work, Collas and Coüasnon dealt with it without fuss. If the Latins privately repaired one wall and the Greeks another, the CTB would restore the corner where the two walls met. In the past, these trivial issues would have required formal negotiations.[7]

Over the period 1964–67, numerous agreements were concluded between the churches, mostly mapping out the territorial dimension of the Status Quo. In the past, the Status Quo had often been hard to determine because of the lack of a single authoritative version to settle the many conflicting claims.

As the restoration progressed, however, thanks to a sustained effort of intercommunal diplomacy, elements of a quasi-legal regime began to appear, consisting increasingly of written agreements the contracting parties freely entered into. This marked the start of a trend away from the customary practice grounded in oral testimony on which the Status Quo had been based.

At the beginning of April 1964, the Armenian patriarchate stretched an electric wire from the Holy Sepulchre to its underground Chapel of St. Helena without waiting for Latin and Greek consent, an infringement of the Status Quo that was intended to create new "facts on the ground." But all they had to do was sit around a table with their Latin and Greek colleagues and explain their needs. On April 6, a simple memorandum of understanding was quickly concluded by which the Greeks agreed to supply electricity from their cable to the Chapel of St. Helena and the Chapel of the Invention of the Cross. The communities also agreed to extend electricity lines to all parts of the church.[8]

A milestone agreement for the repair and restoration of sixteen chapels within the precincts of the Holy Sepulchre and Parvis was signed and sealed on June 17, 1964.[9] The accord laid down certain basic principles of restoration and broadly specified the nature of the work to be carried out. To this day, it constitutes a more or less comprehensive record of chapel ownership.

The ground rules of restoration were as follows. Within their own chapels, the communities could decorate as they saw fit, but any new furniture, movable articles, or altars had to be of the same size as the old ones. They were not allowed to undertake construction that changed the boundaries or the form of any architectural features "facing common places." The Katholikon—the heart of the basilica—was excluded from the accord, and works there of "decoration and embellishment" were deemed to come under the jurisdiction of the Greek Orthodox Patriarchate.

Thus the Status Quo was reaffirmed. "Embellishment," however, was a broad-brush term that might refer to almost anything, from the iconostasis, thrones, and floor mosaics to the design for the interior of the Katholikon dome and the side walls. Structurally, the communities were obliged to conform to the original style. But in other respects they were given broad discretion on their own territories, which make up much of the church.

A wide range of repairs was envisaged; some were minor and some were major modifications involving the removal of nineteenth-century additions. Throughout, plaster was to be stripped away, masonry investigated and replaced where needed, pavement repaired, chapels refurbished and redecorated. Major restorations were envisaged of the Chapel of St. Helena, the Chapel of the Three Marys, the Chapel of St. John (in the Parvis), the Chapel of the Apparition, the Chapel of the Invention of the Cross, and the Chapel of the Franks. In the latter, walls might be removed to restore the chapel to its original state. The arches in the Chapel of Longinus and the Chapel of the Parting of the Raiment in the ambulatory might also be demolished. The altar on Calvary could be shifted eastward to reveal the living rock.

The need for conservation is hardly addressed, and then only in terms of what might not be done, as though these were exceptions to a rule of laissez-faire. In the Latin Chapel of the Franks, the beautiful Romanesque window facing Calvary, once an actual entry, could not be restored to its original function. A stone slab bearing the sign of the cross and Greek lettering in the Latin Grotto of the Invention of the Cross could not be altered. An Armenian oil lamp hanging from the ceiling of the Latin Chapel of St. Mary Magdalene had to be replaced after repair work. Thus the July 1964 agreement is not a mandate for conservation but a politically informed set of guidelines for reconstruction within the confines of the Status Quo.

As with many diplomatic accords, unresolved issues were skirted or obfuscated. For example, the Greeks and Latins had "no objection" to the Armenians restoring the Chapel of Joseph of Arimathea and Nicodemus—subject to the approval of the governor. This was because the Syrian Orthodox community contested Armenian ownership of the area, and the dispute was under active investigation by the Jordanian authorities. It remains unsettled. When not decorated with carpets and altar furniture for a service, the chapel—with its uneven floor, scorched, bare walls, and ramshackle altar—is a study in dereliction.

The governor of Jerusalem continued to play an active and constructive part in helping the communities reach agreement where necessary. Before the January 1965 Orthodox Christmas celebrations, the Greek and Armenian patriarchs settled outstanding differences concerning the Church of the Nativity, following up the Greek–Latin arrangements of a year before.

This paved the way for the signing of an accord at the Holy Sepulchre allowing for the demolition and rebuilding of the separating wall between the Greek treasury and the Armenian chapel known as the Second Golgotha.[10] Once it was agreed that the masonry would be rebuilt on the Greek side and the plastering applied to the Armenian side, it was possible to proceed with the installation of the reinforced concrete frame, a crucial stage in the restoration of the south transept.[11]

Major credit for bringing the parties together in this case was given to the mohafez, Daoud Abu Ghazaleh. Obviously, the favorable climate of interchurch relations had helped, but Abu Ghazaleh was recognized to have worked assiduously to harmonize relations between the Christian communities. He was said to take the practical view that religious peace was essential for promoting tourism to the holy places, which was Jerusalem's major industry.[12] He was also implementing the policy of King Hussein, who took a close personal interest in the Christian community, hoping that this "would increase European support for Jordan in its political and financial difficulties."[13]

The harmonious idyll of cooperation between the communities in the CTB that Robert Smith observed did not survive the replacement of Leonidas Collas by Athanasios Economopoulos in October 1964. A building engineer by training, Economopoulos was the nephew of the Greek prime minister, and Collas claimed he owed his appointment to family connections.[14] He served during a turbulent period of Greek history, and his continuity of tenure, 1964–74, contributed significantly to the impressive progress made on the restoration of Greek areas. He abandoned his predecessor's confiding and liberal approach to the Latins, which the patriarchate had disliked. "This place is too precious for generosity, so we give away nothing," he declared.[15]

Relations on site between Economopoulos and Coüasnon quickly settled into a bad-tempered pattern of disagreement, incomprehension, and mistrust. It would last for the next ten years. The self-confident young Greek's brief was to repair and restore Greek property as expeditiously as possible, while rendering the Anastasis invulnerable to future earthquakes. He gave a high priority to preserving the Status Quo and opposed Coüasnon's tendency to act on his own initiative and extend the scope of the CTB into private areas.

The task of rehabilitating the birthplace of Christian faith was Coüasnon's main mission in life. He saw himself as the guardian of the medieval integrity of the Crusader edifice and found it hard to circumscribe his role. His aim was explicit: "To recover or to safeguard the monument's unity, without harming the special interests of each community." This meant repairing the church in the spirit of the original, with minimal alteration and without incongruous modern embellishments. He never concealed his ecumenical vision. "We do not have three churches," he wrote, "but a single one with several rites, each of which has its place. Is this not a concrete image of the Holy Church?"[16] Single-minded in pursuit of his ideal, he was intolerant of dissent, and sometimes intemperate in word and deed. The French consul general labeled him "violent, impulsive, and stubborn."[17]

Had Economopoulos and Coüasnon shared a common tongue, they might have been better able to sort out their differences. However, Economopoulos, who had only a limited understanding of French, insisted that meetings of the CTB be conducted in English, a language of which Coüasnon at first had an imperfect grasp. The Frenchman grew testy when he missed the nuances of an English presentation. For his part, Economopoulos, who liked papers to be kept in good order, complained—as did others—about Coüasnon's relaxed attitude toward written instructions, failure to keep track of plans, and tendency to leave documents lying around haphazardly.

Their relationship went wrong from the beginning. On December 5, 1964, Economopoulos stopped Coüasnon's workers from pouring the concrete for a reinforced concrete beam that stretched across territorial borders. Claiming that insufficient steelwork had been prepared, Economopoulos had the wooden casing or shuttering peremptorily removed. A professional difference of opinion escalated into an unnecessary confrontation. When Economopoulos criticized him in English before Father Rock, Coüasnon was left feeling humiliated. The inexperienced young Greek had acted discourteously, he thought, displaying a lack of familiarity with the technical problems of the building.[18]

Coüasnon was next angered by Economopoulos's demolition of the facing of the north wall of the Chapel of Melchizedek in May 1965. The chapel is an eleventh-century, late Byzantine structure in the possession of the Greek patriarchate, accessed by stairs leading up from Calvary. A pleasing little octagon, topped by a cupola, it overlooks the northeast corner of the Parvis. In Coüasnon's view, the wall, possibly from the seventh century, was of extreme interest and "should have been conserved at all costs." Its destruction, carried out without his even being consulted, was an act of sheer "vandalism."[19]

By the early summer of 1965, the bad blood between the two men was impeding the smooth functioning of the CTB. Increasingly, they ceased to communicate or cooperate. Coüasnon and Diran Voskertchian, the local Armenian architect representing the Paris-based Utudjian, complained at a meeting of the CTB that Economopoulos had unilaterally diverted scaffolding, owned in common by the communities, from the south façade to the east crossing of the Katholikon. There was only a limited quantity of metal tubing, and it would have been put to better use, the two architects argued, dismantling the supports that still disfigured the front of the basilica. "It is in everyone's interest to work on the façade," Coüasnon pointed out. "We are not in Jerusalem to obstruct each other but to help each other." The Greek attitude created conflict and failed to take "into account the general needs of the construction site."[20]

Economopoulos's view was that completion of the Katholikon, on which he was working flat out, had urgent priority. He claimed that work on the façade was not envisaged in the program the chief architects signed in 1960. In the middle of the session, he went off to look for the document in order to prove his point. He returned with Father Daniel, and an argument ensued between the two Greeks. Coüasnon unwisely intervened, and Father Daniel got up and shook him "like a palm branch." At this point Father Daniel was shown the door, and Economopoulos walked out in protest.[21]

A venomous atmosphere surrounded the meeting of the CTB on June 4, 1965. It started off badly, with an argument about whether English or French was the official language of the bureau. For the rest of the meeting, Economopoulos and Coüasnon could agree on nothing. First, the Greek engineer complained about the work of the new French sculptor, Maurice Tondelier, who was working in the Armenian gallery. According to Economopoulos, Tondelier was carving capitals with acanthus leaves that had four dentils rather than five, as was found elsewhere in the church. Second, he criticized Coüasnon for installing reinforced concrete beams without written instructions from Trouvelot. Third, he forbade Coüasnon's master foreman, Henri Deschamps, from working in Armenian areas, claiming that the principal architects had agreed that he could only work in common areas.

Economopoulos's major allegation was that Coüasnon had falsified the draft minutes of a previous meeting of the CTB. He therefore now insisted on checking Coüasnon's minutes of the last meeting, confirming any erasures and crossings out with his personal stamp. At this Coüasnon exploded, calling Economopoulos a "filthy swine." "Am I a dishonest man," the monk expostulated, "whose words must be questioned at every moment?"[22] After this clash, it became difficult to hold official meetings, if only because Economopoulos now demanded that a stenographer be present at every session, after which twelve copies of the minutes had to be typed up, translated into English, and retyped if there was a typing error.

Christmas 1965 found Coüasnon in a dejected mood. He had again clashed with Economopoulos, this time over the pointing of masonry at the eastern face of the south transept. Arguing that it was Greek property, Economopoulos, backed by Father Daniel, had ordered Deschamps to stop work. The CTB foreman wanted to finish what he had begun, but Father Daniel stood guard to prevent him. The next morning, the pointing was found to have been destroyed during the night. Coüasnon was sure that the work was in a common area but was disabused by Trouvelot, who confirmed that the Greeks were acting within their Status Quo rights. The high interior façades of the south transept were in Greek possession, and this entitled them to face, plaster, and point the outer surfaces. As Trouvelot explained, "Since this right is only oral and traditional, it can only be maintained if they alone undertake surface work in public view. If another community touches it, it would be a public infringement of those rights."[23]

This was followed by a disagreement over the twelfth-century springing stones of the great vault of the bay at the east end of the Katholikon. Economopoulos wanted to replace them with cellular concrete, as part of his plan to strengthen the structure against future earthquakes. Coüasnon maintained that they were in perfect condition and should be left intact, grumbling to Trouvelot: "I can't take any more of it. Latins—Armenians—Greeks—it is too much. I am bent over double."[24]

Matters did not improve after Christmas. Much to Coüasnon's disgust, Economopoulos went ahead and demolished the springing stones. The Dominican father forecast that this would undermine the equilibrium of the entire structure and "bring in its wake the ruin of the edifice."[25] It did not. He was also proven mistaken in insisting, in contradiction to a study by the Greek engineer, on the need for reinforced concrete beams in the south transept. This encouraged Economopoulos to oppose installing them in the north transept—where they really were needed.

The inability of the pair to work together resulted in an expensive two-month delay at the south transept over the summer. While Economopoulos was away in Athens, Coüasnon went ahead and ordered from Jordan a delivery of pumice—a light, sponge-like volcanic stone—as filler for the reconstructed vaults. On his return to Jerusalem on June 22, 1966, the Greek engineer canceled the order on the grounds that the material was not volcanic pumice at all but a metallic oxide of unknown properties that had never been used and should not be tried out on the Holy Sepulchre. "As we know, the History does not speak of volcanoes in Jordan."

Coüasnon was eager to fill the vaults in order to finish waterproofing the terraces over the south transept before the rains. But work had to be suspended as a result of the disagreement. At the beginning of August, Economopoulos traveled to Beirut, where he received what he thought was an excellent offer from a local supplier of superior—if expensive—imported volcanic pumice. Back in Jerusalem, however, laboratory tests confirmed that the Jordanian "metallic oxide" was genuine pumice and that the Lebanese merchant had misled him, criticizing the Jordanian product in order to sell his own. Economopoulos learned that Jordan is famously located in an area of volcanic activity, and that the pumice Coüasnon had originally ordered, at a good price, was indeed suitable for filling vaults. Coüasnon demanded an apology, but never got one.[26]

The two men's relations reached a low point in the fall of 1966, when they were involved in a physical altercation in the CTB, which Coüasnon thought of as his personal domain. On November 8, Economopoulos refused to allow Coüasnon's English assistant, Terry Ball, who was preparing detailed plans of the whole church, to take measurements on Greek property. He suspected Coüasnon of having acquired Greek plans without permission and then passing them off as his own work. The following day, Economopoulos visited the CTB to ask for drawings of the north transept. According to agreed minutes from 1965, studies of common areas were common property, while studies of private areas were private property but had to be placed at the disposal of the other communities.

Coüasnon looked for the drawings but could not find them. However, he refused to open a drawer that he said contained Latin drawings of the north crossing, though not the ones requested. Such an inspection, he later explained, would offensively insinuate that he was to blame for losing the plans. When Economopoulos carelessly picked up a document from Ball's worktable, Coüasnon tried to throw him out, and a scuffle ensued.[27]

As a result of the incident, Coüasnon and Economopoulos stopped talking to each other and began communicating via notes. "He's a sick man stricken with megalomania," Coüasnon fumed. "In these circumstances what relations can I have with Economopoulos? I can only ignore him."[28] Important questions, such as how to waterproof the terrace over the crossing and whether to join the Katholikon to the rotunda with reinforced concrete beams, were referred to the Greek government and the three fathers. This may have delayed decisions but by now did not substantially affect progress.

Internal debates and rivalries exercised the communities almost as much as problems between them. In the Latin section, Coüasnon and Trouvelot's relationship with the Custody of the Holy Land always remained ambiguous. Theoretically, the Custody was the client, Trouvelot the architect, and Coüasnon the architect's local representative. But Trouvelot, since 1962 the French government's inspector general of historical monuments and senior conservationist, did not have a signed contract with the Custody. They had not even paid his travel expenses since 1961. Coüasnon, dividing his time between Latin and common areas, worked on a purely voluntary basis.

In consequence, this was neither a master–servant nor a consultant–patient relationship. Traditional national and ecclesiastical rivalries exacerbated the inherent tension. In June 1964, the Custody turned down Trouvelot's recommendation of a well-qualified French sculptor in favor of an inexperienced Italian, who did not last long. It also deplored the Dominican Coüasnon's independent-mindedness. Trouvelot became increasingly critical of what he considered the Franciscans' penny-pinching, "heartrending" lack of understanding, while Coüasnon was only too aware that his presence on site was "fragile."[29]

In September 1964, the custos complained to Trouvelot that Coüasnon was not spending enough time on the Chapel of the Apparition, also known as the Chapel of the Holy Sacrament, the heart of Franciscan worship in the church. Cappiello insisted that Coüasnon had to choose between his two jobs; the Custody needed a full-time architect who would devote himself exclusively to Latin projects. He also complained that the Dominican was filing Latin documents in the CTB archive. As soon as possible, he intended to place the Latin building program under the supervision of a Franciscan friar.[30]

He chose Father Virgilio Corbo, the Italian archaeologist who had been excavating in the Latin section since 1961 and knew it intimately. Corbo helped out with a number of projects in the Franciscan convent but was not a professional architect, let alone a conservationist, and never enjoyed Trouvelot's confidence. He sorely tried Trouvelot's patience when he excavated the grotto of the Invention of the Cross without informing Coüasnon, causing significant damage.

In the end, Coüasnon continued to work on the Chapel of the Apparition, though he and Cappiello were barely on speaking terms and had incompatible tastes. Coüasnon conceived for the chapel a Romanesque "debauchery of marble and mosaic."[31] Trouvelot agreed that it should have sparkle but suggested greater restraint. In January 1965, a modified design was accepted by a commission of the Custody headed by Rock and another Franciscan who was actively involved in the restoration, Father Ignazio Mancini. Cappiello, who wanted something in the modern idiom, rejected it out of hand, arguing that Coüasnon had failed to capture the mystery of the risen Christ's apparition to his mother. To ensure that Coüasnon did not ignore his instructions, the custos appointed a friar to keep an eye on him in the church. After a short time, the unfortunate friar gave up in embarrassment.[32]

For the Chapel of the Invention of the Cross, Coüasnon designed a traditional marble altar on stone columns. In the niche behind it, the statue of St. Helena holding the discovered cross was to stand on a rough, mound-like plinth, reflecting the hewn, rock walls of the surrounding cave. Here, too, the custos was bluntly critical. "How clumsy," he remarked.[33]

The controversy between the two priests culminated in the Rebaudi affair, a confrontation between two aesthetic philosophies that drew the attention of the highest levels of the Catholic Church. Mario Rebaudi was an Italian sculptor brought in by the Custody in October 1965 to work on the numerous capitals that had to be repaired or replaced in Latin areas. In July 1965, the chief architects had laid down clear guidelines for sculptors. Any replacement carving "had to be a faithful and tasteful adaptation," respecting the style of sculpture in the edifice.

South front, 1956. Courtesy of Elia Photo Service.

Kiss of peace capital, 1966. Photo by Raymond Cohen.

Meeting of experts and architects in common technical bureau, about 1965.
Front row, left to right: Athanasios Economopoulos, unknown man, Edouard
Utudjian, Jean Trouvelot, unknown man, Father Guregh Kapikian, Garbis
Hintlian. Back row, left to right: Father Albert Rock, Diran Voskertchian,
Father Charles Coüasnon, Archimandrite Germanos Mamaladis, Father Daniel
Choriatakis, Bishop Garabet Antriassian. Courtesy of Elia Photo Service.

Father Coüasnon (seated) toasts Athanasios Economopoulos (standing), about 1966. Courtesy of Ibrahim Zarour.

Jordanian governor Anwar al-Khatib, on visit to church, 1967, shakes hands with Father Rock while Father Daniel looks on. Courtesy of Ibrahim Zarour.

Mario Rebaudi sculpts capital. Courtesy of Custody of the Holy Land.

Pilgrims in rotunda under scaffolding, August 1967. Photo by Fritz Cohen. Courtesy of Israel government press office.

Chapel of St. Nicodemus. Photo by Raymond Cohen.

Coptic chapel behind Edicule. Photo by Raymond Cohen.

Fr. Coüasnon in last year, 1976. Courtesy of Custody of the Holy Land.

Work on rotunda dome, 1979. Courtesy of Custody of the Holy Land.

Restored Chapel of Three Marys, 2003. Photo by Raymond Cohen.

Boundary on Calvary between Greeks and Latins. Photo by Raymond Cohen.

Edicule and rotunda, 2006. Photo by Rivka Cohen.

The Latin building team at lunch, 1965. Standing, left to right: two unnamed masons, Mario Rebaudi, Terry Ball, Henri Deschamps, two unnamed masons; sitting, left to right: George Papadopoulos, Charles Coüasnon, Claude Berthézène, Maurice Tondelier. Photo by Tony Saulnier/*Paris Match*.

Coüasnon was therefore surprised in December 1965 when Rebaudi proposed a modern composition for a restored capital. In a "very amicable" conversation, the French monk pointed out that the design was "too alien" to the surrounding Crusader capitals and asked the Italian sculptor to remain close to the original. Rebaudi, however, defended his position, arguing that he must be allowed to work "in complete freedom in conformity with his own taste and professional conscience."[34]

It soon became clear that Rebaudi's contract indeed guaranteed him freedom of expression and that he enjoyed the full backing of the Custody. The sculptor was not subservient to the architect, Trouvelot was informed, and the Custody had the final decision. Trouvelot argued in vain that those working on such "an ancient and very venerable monument" were bound "to conserve scrupulously the character and artistic work of their predecessors." If everyone followed his fantasy, the result would be chaos and disaster.[35] Coüasnon agreed, foreseeing that the Rebaudi precedent would open the floodgates to stylistic license. The Armenians had already asked Maurice Tondelier, the Latin sculptor, to carve a sculpture of the Catholikos of Etchmiadzin among the flowers and a capital bearing the design of an eagle with wings outspread— both completely incongruous in a Romanesque church.[36]

In early February 1966, Rebaudi presented a startling study for the capital, its theme the recent pilgrimage of Pope Paul VI to Jerusalem. Ignoring Coüasnon and Trouvelot's protests, the custos approved the model on February 21, 1966, and Rebaudi began work. An outraged Coüasnon immediately launched an impassioned campaign to have the decision rescinded. "We cannot in all conscience allow the monument to be disfigured under our very noses without raising the alarm," he declared.[37] Scheduled to pass through Rome in mid-March, he considered lobbying the pope in person but had to content himself with a Curia official, a diplomat in the French embassy to the Holy See, and the superior of his order. Trouvelot did his bit in Paris.

On his return to Jerusalem in May, Coüasnon was invited to meet the apostolic delegate, Monsignor Agostino Sepinski, a former minister general of the Franciscan order. Sepinski told him that he had received a letter on Rebaudi's capital from Archbishop Angelo Dell'Acqua, a senior Curia official close to the pope. Sepinski assured Coüasnon that he would have the custos stop the work at once.[38]

After a suspension lasting several months, while the issue was presumably discussed by the apostolic delegation and the Custody of the Holy Land, Rebaudi was finally allowed to go ahead with his cubist-influenced capital depicting pope and patriarch embracing in their historic kiss of peace.

In the Greek section of the church, responsibility for the restoration was, strictly speaking, borne by the Greek government on behalf of the Greek Orthodox Patriarchate. The architects were Greek government functionaries, and the foreman, workers, and materials were paid for with funds coming out of the Greek national budget. This inserted an element of tension into the situation, since the Jerusalem patriarchate was preoccupied with defending its particular conception of the Status Quo, while the government was sensitive to broader international factors. The convent was also less concerned with the principles of the Venice Charter than were internationally recognized conservationists in Athens.

Theoretically, Economopoulos was the representative of the Greek architect-in-chief in Athens. But political developments relieved Economopoulos of close professional supervision, enlarging both his own role and the autonomy of the Greek patriarchate. At first, there was an attempt to reassign responsibility for work at the Holy Sepulchre from the antiquities service of the ministry of education and cults to a special commission of the foreign ministry, with the intention of providing the principal architects, Trouvelot and Utudjian, with a stable and authoritative interlocutor. This failed, but the Greek architect, Eustathios Stikas—a signatory of the Venice Charter and longtime colleague of Orlandos—was relieved of his functions in January 1965.

Over the next two years, at least five different Greek experts were fleetingly involved in the project at the Athens end. Political uncertainty reigned in the Greek capital. In July 1965, George Papandreou resigned as prime minister amid massive demonstrations by his supporters protesting what they described as a "royal coup d'état." Only in September was Stephanos Stephanopoulos able to scrape together a parliamentary majority, which ruled until the military putsch of April 1967.

In August 1966 and again in March 1967, Stikas was restored to his position amid talk of "cabals" and "internal Greek quarrels." At times, Trouvelot simply did not know to whom to address correspondence but was left in no doubt that Economopoulos was becoming increasingly influential.[39] The French consul general in Jerusalem, Christian d'Halloy, later gave his assessment of the consequences of this instability. Frequent changes of experts, he bitterly concluded, had allowed Economopoulos "to sow confusion in the work of restoration and give instructions opposed to decisions reached in common by the three experts."[40]

As for the Armenian patriarchate, work was financed, as already mentioned, by the Gulbenkian Foundation of Lisbon and by a group of Armenian-American bankers. The principal Armenian architect, Utudjian, and his

Jerusalem representative, Voskertchian, served at the pleasure of the local patriarchate. This left Patriarch Derderian and Father Guregh more or less insulated against outside interference.

Their general scheme was to create a more fitting, spacious setting for Armenian worship and communal activity by reconstructing and embellishing their section in accordance with Armenian tastes and traditions. They saw no particular merit in Romanesque architecture and were not interested in conservation. Archbishop Germanos was not far wrong when he observed that this was "not restoration but renovation" and that the Armenians were "trying, by destroying every vestige of the past, to put their signature on the restoration project."[41]

In concrete terms, this meant that Guregh wanted to demolish his community's existing divan, move the stairs ascending from the ground floor to the gallery, remodel the basement, create a new chapel in the tribune over the south transept, extend the Second Golgotha by replacing the eleventh-century wall with an arch, and open up a door into the sacristy. This program bore no resemblance to any known philosophy of conservation and put Guregh on a collision course with the other communities.

Little by little, Guregh, without any professional qualifications, had taken direct control of the Armenian construction site, acting as both contractor and client. No one supervised his building activities. Come rain or shine, he arrived immediately after school to give orders to his foreman and workers. In December 1965, when Voskertchian objected to his program of demolition, he hired his own designer. After the new year, he gave orders to demolish clandestinely the eleventh-century wall in the gallery. This was somewhat hazardous, as the wall buttressed the Arch of Triumph. Emergency supports had to be urgently inserted. An appeal by Coüasnon to Utudjian brought about a temporary suspension of the work.[42]

The matter came to a head at a meeting of the three fathers and their resident architects on February 22, 1966. Germanos and Rock demanded the restoration of the wall to its previous condition, threatening to stop work in common areas. Germanos and Guregh almost came to blows, and Rock walked out. But the Rebaudi affair had eroded the moral authority of Greeks and Latins to temper Armenian aspirations. Trouvelot also lacked an effective ally in Athens.[43]

Over the Easter holiday in April 1966, while everyone else took a break, the Armenians went ahead with the demolition of the Byzantine wall. Against the explicit advice of Utudjian, they also had reliefs sculpted in the Armenian style. This was a turning point in the restoration, when inhibitions against the division of the mother church into three denominational churches disappeared. Enjoying the full confidence of his principal, Guregh was able to create an Armenian enclave within a Byzantine-Crusader monument.

In July 1966, he initiated work on a new divan and further demolitions without a prior study of the problem and no proper plan.[44] Voskertchian lamented his master's instruction to destroy an eleventh-century arch bearing the old stairs: "Yet again a useless and harmful demolition will be carried out without our being able to do anything about it."[45]

———

The evidence of discord in these unfortunate episodes was deeply disillusioning. Following the mid-1966 meeting of principal architects in Jerusalem, Trouvelot lamented: "I was more troubled than usual by the lack of understanding and even the hostility towards us of a certain number of people. Contrary to what one might think, the Holy Sepulchre is not a place of peace and serenity because all passions, even the meanest, are found there."[46]

Yet if human imperfection was everywhere evident, a restored Holy Sepulchre was undeniably emerging from the pain and labor. At the end of 1966, Trouvelot could look back with cautious satisfaction: "In spite of everything, the work has progressed well this year, one sees the results, which is something."[47]

| The Keys

Ahead of Easter 1967, the Parvis was cleared of the stone-masons' hut, along with the crude blocks of Malaki limestone. To the deep satisfaction of the communities, the disfiguring steel shoring was removed from the north and south façades after more than thirty years.

Easter Sunday arrived early that year on March 26. There was a blizzard all day in the Jerusalem area, to the astonishment of the large contingent of pilgrims who had arrived by boat and plane from Europe, expecting Mediterranean sunshine. The traditional procession of consuls and clergy accompanying the Latin patriarch to the Holy Sepulchre took place amid snow squalls. The ceremony unfolded in a full rotunda, while outside a peaceful Jerusalem lay under a gathering blanket of snow.[1]

Twelve days later, on April 7, 1967, Israeli Mirage jets shot down six Syrian MIGs in full view of the Damascus crowds, beginning the slide into the Six Day War.

June 5, 1967, started as a normal working day in the Holy Sepulchre. The stonecutters and dressers set to work in the Parvis. Deschamps, the master mason, supervised the lifting of finished stones onto the roof with the electric hoist. George Papadopoulos, the Greek sculptor, also winched up his carved capitals, thinking that they would be safer inside the church if anything happened. Berthézène and Panaiotis, the Latin and Greek foremen, were busy inside the basilica. Terry Ball arrived at about 8.30 a.m. from his lodgings in the Casa di Santiago and went up to the office that he shared with Coüasnon in the CTB.

Ball worked as best he could on detailed drawings of the façade. From the next office came the distracting blare of martial music and announcements in Arabic.

At about ten o'clock, someone brought the news that war had broken out in the south. Economopoulos was anxious to consult with Coüasnon about what to do with the workers, but Coüasnon was in the École Biblique that day. Ball phoned him, and they decided to send the workers home to be with their families. Deschamps, an imperturbable old soldier, carried on with his work. Ball was walking home with his toolbox along Christian Road when the deafening noise of artillery sent him back to the church. He and Papadopoulos retreated inside, and one of the monks served them lunch of bread, ham, and arak in a room off the rotunda.[2]

With hindsight, the June 1967 war seems almost inevitable. On May 22, after expelling the UN Emergency Force from Egypt's border with Israel, President Nasser closed the Red Sea to Israeli shipping. A week later, King Hussein flew to Cairo to sign a defense treaty with the Egyptian leader. There was growing tension in Jerusalem on both sides of the armistice line, and many foreigners left, but as the days passed and nothing happened, some felt it may have been a false alarm.

While Ball was walking to work on June 5, an Israeli official, Rafi Levi, was making his way from his office just off Jaffa Road to the Mandelbaum Gate. He drove down Tribes of Israel Road, passing army reservists and military vehicles, and crossed the Street of the Prophets, with Lord Plumer's old house on one corner and Antonio Barluzzi's Italian Hospital on the other.

Levi, Hebron-born and fluent in both Hebrew and Arabic, had been in charge of the Mandelbaum Gate checkpoint since 1951, when he completed his military service. Two or three times a week, for years, he had met his Jordanian counterpart to arrange transit permits and alleviate the humanitarian problems of a divided city. As usual, the two men shook hands and exchanged greetings. There was nothing much to do or say, so they parted awkwardly: "We'll meet some time, let's see how things work out, here's hoping for the best."[3]

That afternoon, the Arab Legion took Government House, the UN's Jerusalem headquarters, in an offensive move. Even so, neither Levi Eshkol, Israel's prime minister, nor Moshe Dayan, his defense minister, wanted a war with Jordan, their most moderate neighbor.[4] They already had a war in the Sinai and dreaded a bloody battle for the Old City, fearing heavy casualties and damage to the holy places that would spark a crisis in relations with the Catholic nations of Europe and Latin America. As Dayan put it laconically, "I don't need that Vatican; leave it alone."[5]

But diplomatic efforts to achieve a cease-fire failed, and Israeli forces cut off East Jerusalem in fierce fighting. On June 7, paratroops entered the Old City through St. Stephen's Gate. At this the governor, Anwar al-Khatib, surrendered to the Israeli commander, informing him that Jordan had decided not to defend the city and had withdrawn its troops.[6] This saved lives and minimized destruction. St. Anne's Church, by St. Stephen's Gate, had been hit, as had the Dormition Abbey, next to Zion Gate, and the tower of St. Stephen's Basilica outside the Damascus Gate; elsewhere there was only minor damage. Although Jordanian soldiers had set up a firing position on the roof of St. Savior's, the convent had not been fired on.[7]

The Church of the Holy Sepulchre was also spared any harm. On the morning of June 8, an Israeli major arrived to identify and account for the foreign civilians present. Unshaven, after days sleeping in temporary quarters in the Latin and Greek convents, all were safe. Mario Rebaudi took a group of exhausted young Jewish soldiers from all over the world for a guided tour of the basilica. There was a sense that an era had ended. Terry Ball wrote to a friend that it was no good "lamenting the old life—it has gone, the Arabs threw it away and the Israelis are what [there] is in their area of control."[8]

As a result of the capture of the Old City, a wave of messianic euphoria swept the Jewish world. Before the war, most ministers had assumed that Israel would not be able to hold on to the Old City; afterward, they saw no alternative. Completely unexpectedly, the government of Israel found itself responsible for the Christian holy places of Jerusalem. There were no plans for this contingency, and officials had imperfect knowledge of the issues at stake. Now the Jewish state found itself in an encounter with the Christian world to which both sides brought distinctly mixed feelings.

Most Israelis knew very little about Christianity, except for the suspicion that it did not wish them well because it taught that "the Jews crucified Christ." The Spanish Inquisition, blood libels, Easter pogroms, and the Holocaust loomed large in the national consciousness. After World War II, Israel had taken in much of the remnant of European Jewry. Many survivors brought with them memories of persecution. Only recently, the Israeli historian Saul Friedländer had raised troubling questions about the silence of the Holy See in the face of the Nazi "final solution to the Jewish problem."[9]

At the same time, since the time of its founder, Theodore Herzl, the Zionist movement had been in awe of the pope's influence and never gave up hope of enlisting his support. After the founding of the state of Israel, soundings were made about the possibility of diplomatic recognition on the part of the Holy See. When they realized that this was out of the question, Israeli diplomats continued patiently to cultivate contacts in the Vatican and exchange views, with the aim of removing causes of friction and slowly improving relations.[10]

The Catholic Church also brought its own baggage to the encounter. Most people in the Catholic Church knew very little about Judaism other than that "the Jews crucified Christ." Nevertheless, in October 1965, Pope Paul VI had promulgated the declaration *Nostra Aetate* on the attitude of the Church to non-Christian religions, which reformulated church teaching on the Jews. At its heart was the following reinterpretation of Christian scripture:

> True, the Jewish authorities and those who followed their lead pressed for the death of Christ; still, what happened in His Passion cannot be charged against all the Jews, without distinction, then alive, nor against the Jews of today. Although the Church is the new people of God, the Jews should not be presented as rejected by God or accursed, as if this followed from the Holy Scriptures.[11]

In the long run, this theological reformulation, exculpating the Jews from the eternal stain of deicide, would have far-reaching implications for Catholic–Jewish relations in general, and relations between the Holy See and the state of Israel in particular. But it would take time for this conciliatory message to filter down through the ranks. In the meantime, not everyone in the Catholic Church was yet ready to abandon old attitudes.

At the political level, the Holy See had never endorsed Zionist aspirations for an "ingathering of the exiles." It had weighty theological objections. It was concerned about the disruptive social and economic impact of an influx of Jews on Arab society. Moreover, it suspected the Zionist movement, with its kibbutzim and radical social policies, of being a Trojan horse for bolshevism.

The 1948 war seemed to confirm Catholic fears of the destabilizing impact of a Jewish state on the Middle East. Diplomatic recognition of Israel, they worried, might endanger Christian communities in the Arab world, exposed by the retreat of the colonial powers. Christians in Jordan were considered especially vulnerable during the years of revolutionary and pan-Arab ferment. There was also great sympathy within the Custody of the Holy Land and the Latin patriarchate for the Palestinian refugees.

The outcome of the Six Day War, followed by the growing realization that the Jews intended to retain East Jerusalem, came as a shock to the Catholic world. Muslim control of the holy places was not a cause for rejoicing, but Catholics had gotten used to it. Jewish sovereignty, in contrast, aroused feelings of rivalry going back to the early centuries of Christianity.[12]

As early as June 7, the pope expressed his fervent wish for the safe-guarding of the holy places, proposing that Jerusalem be declared an open city. Speaking in the name of an anxious Christian world, he called for the Holy City to remain a refuge for the defenseless and the wounded. As on his 1964 pilgrimage, he made no reference to Israel.

Within a few days, it became clear that the pope believed that the internationalization of Jerusalem, the policy adopted after the 1948 war, remained the best solution. On June 26, he proposed that the city have its own statute, internationally guaranteed, and on July 1, the Vatican's UN observer explicitly called for an international regime for the protection of Jerusalem and its holy places.[13]

Israel's position was staked out in two declarations also made on June 7. In one, Moshe Dayan proclaimed the reunification of the hitherto divided capital of Israel. "We have returned to the most sacred of our holy places, never to part from it again." Israel had not come, he added, "to possess ourselves of the holy places of others, or to interfere with the members of other faiths, but to safeguard the city's integrity and to live in it with others in unity."

For his part, Levi Eshkol convened a meeting of the heads of religious communities. Quiet had been restored to Jerusalem, he told them. "You can be quite certain that no harm of any kind will be permitted to the holy places." Religious leaders would be contacted, so that they could "continue their spiritual activity undisturbed." Arrangements for the holy places of Judaism, Islam, and Christianity, he proposed, should be made by clergymen of each religion, not the government. In the Christian case, he referred to a "council of Christian dignitaries."[14]

Eshkol did not refer to the Status Quo on June 7. On June 9, at a meeting with church leaders in East Jerusalem's Ambassador Hotel, Rafi Levi, the district commissioner, did so explicitly.[15] There was no concealing, however, that his government had reservations on the subject. Under the terms of the Status Quo in force during the British Mandate, Jewish worship at the Wailing Wall and at the Tomb of the Patriarchs in Hebron had been tightly restricted. Israel had no intention of perpetuating what it saw as "degrading and discriminatory regulations."[16] But the government for some time did not fully grasp Israeli obligations under the Status Quo and indeed its advantages.

On June 27, Israel's parliament, the Knesset, passed a law providing for the protection of the holy places. In an address to an audience that included the Greek, Latin, and Armenian patriarchs, the prime minister declared his government's commitment "to preserve the holy places, to ensure their religious and universal character, and to guarantee free access."

Israel was determined to extend its sovereignty over a unified Jerusalem and resolved to deflect anticipated Christian pressure to withdraw by proposing a form of functional autonomy to the churches under which they themselves would run the holy places. Since the main threat to the extension of Israeli sovereignty came from internationalization, vigorously backed by France and the Vatican, it became essential to offer an attractive and credible alternative.

Over the next weeks and months, Israel seized the initiative and proposed to the Holy See an agreement on the Christian holy places. This would include various elements: guarantees of freedom of access and worship; an extraterritorial special status for the holy places analogous to that of a diplomatic mission; and the administration of the holy places by the religious communities concerned "in accordance with existing rights and practices."

Most important, Israel would acknowledge the Vatican as the "sending state" of Christian clerics, coordinating all Christian interests in Jerusalem—first among equals.[17] This seemed to mean that Israel and the Holy See would have a relationship functionally equivalent to diplomatic relations, that the Holy See would be thought of as appointing clerics, irrespective of denomination, and that those clerics would enjoy immunities usually accruing to representatives under the Vienna Conventions on Diplomatic and Consular Relations. But the concept was unclear and raised more questions than it answered.

The idea was first put to the Vatican by Israel's ambassador to Italy, Ehud Avriel, in June 1967 and explored by a Vatican emissary, Monsignor Angelo Felici, on a mission to Jerusalem a few weeks later. According to Israeli sources, the pope reported on it on July 26 at a meeting with Ecumenical Patriarch Athenagoras, who rejected it. Patriarch Benedictos was invited but declined to attend. In its reply to Israel, the Holy See ruled out a formal agreement in the absence of peace between Israel and the Arab states.[18]

Rabbi Yaacov Herzog, director general of the prime minister's office, and Agostino Cardinal Casaroli, the Vatican's secretary for extraordinary ecclesiastical affairs, discussed a variant over the course of 1968. Herzog proposed a de facto arrangement that Israel would put into effect with the Vatican's secret consent. During the talks, Herzog made clear that Israel "would continue to honor the Status Quo as long as there was not full agreement between the Christian communities and sects to change it."[19]

Israel's initiative was a long shot that would require a turnabout by the Holy See. Besides, it would be very difficult for the various Christian communities to put aside their differences in a governing council for the holy places. The Greek Orthodox Church would never accept papal primacy. Equally, the Latins could not accept their existing subordinate status under the Status Quo. Rumors of secret diplomatic contacts agitated Greeks and Armenians. The talks ended inconclusively.

But Israel made some gains. Talks between Israel and the Vatican— which soon became widely known—undermined the call for internationalization of the city and the attempt by the Soviet Union and the Arab states to diplomatically isolate the Jewish state. The Vatican was reassured that Israel was committed to protecting the holy places. Other churches were given an incentive to make their own separate accommodations with Israel. Finally, valuable time was gained, including the 1967 and 1968 fall sessions of the UN General Assembly, which passed without resolutions on the internationalization of Jerusalem.

With the defeat of Jordan, it was essential that Israel establish contact with officials and church leaders in the Old City. As guardians of the holy places for hundreds of millions of Christians, they held the key to legitimizing Israel's position there. Dayan appointed Rafi Levi as his adviser for Jerusalem and the occupied territories. It was an imaginative appointment. Thanks to his long involvement at the Mandelbaum Gate, Levi may not have known much about theology, but he did know many of the characters in the drama and treated them with courtesy and consideration.

Culturally, he was totally at home in his new role. When Levi met the deeply hurt former governor, Anwar al-Khatib, at a private dinner in the Old City, Levi could appease him in flowery Arabic with the words "Ya basha, in fact there has been no change. You are a Hebronite and I am a Hebronite. It is an inheritance. You were a Hebronite mutassarif. It is not a stranger who has taken over but another Hebronite. Do not be angry. We have come to the meal to enjoy ourselves."[20] Of course, this was quite fantastic, simply a soothing turn of phrase. But it was effective.

After East Jerusalem was incorporated into the municipality of Jerusalem under Israeli law on June 28, 1967 (within greatly extended boundaries), Levi was appointed mutassarif. This suited his interlocutors, as it suggested continuity with the British and Jordanian periods. The office was less important than it sounded, however, because in the Israeli system of government, the district commissioner was a middle-ranking official who lacked the authority of a Jordanian mutassarif.

For the crucial first months, Rafi Levi had special responsibility for the Christian communities.[21] On the evening of June 7, a few hours after Israeli forces entered the Old City, Levi visited the Greek Orthodox Patriarchate to pay his respects to Patriarch Benedictos. "You used to visit me all the time," he said. "You used to come over to West Jerusalem. Now it's my turn to visit you." From the Christian Quarter he went across to the Armenian Quarter to pay a courtesy call on Patriarch Derderian.

Entering these dialogues, Israel's interests were clear. In the first instance, it wanted Greeks and Armenians to recognize the unification of Jerusalem and work together with Israel. As the official who issued travel permits and visas to their clergy, and who could help in many ways with the bureaucracy, Levi successfully obtained letters from them in which they agreed to cooperate with the Israeli administration, provided it maintained the Status Quo at the holy places. Levi assured them: "What, the Ottomans gave you the Status Quo, the British protected it, the Jordanians protected it, we will not infringe it."

The Latins, supported by the Anglicans, sent petitions and memoranda to the United Nations protesting the Israeli presence. Levi dissuaded Benedictos and Derderian from signing.

For the future, Israel wanted to establish mutually beneficial long-term relationships with the Greeks and Armenians. Much of West Jerusalem had been built on land bought or leased from the two churches during the Mandate period. They would, it was hoped, now provide the land on which to build the new, unified Jerusalem.

It soon emerged that the two patriarchs, with a preponderance of rights and influence in Jerusalem, had no interest in following the Latins' lead and were indeed eager to "collaborate" with Israel, as the disgusted French consul general, Christian d'Halloy, put it.[22] Benedictos had two supreme interests to defend. One was his community's preeminent position at the holy places under the Status Quo, in the face of suspected Latin ambitions. The other was Greek domination of the Confraternity of the Holy Sepulchre, in the face of Arab Orthodox encroachment. Israel's arrival in the Old City saved him from the latter fate, and he would never forget it.

The diplomatic maneuvering that followed the war gravely perturbed Patriarch Benedictos. He would have no truck with internationalization, which brought the risk of giving Catholic powers a major say in running Jerusalem. He sent a vehement telegram to Prime Minister Eshkol protesting the Israeli talks with the Vatican on the holy places, which in his view were nobody's affair but that of the local Christian communities. On the same grounds, he dissociated himself from Ecumenical Patriarch Athenagoras's talks with the pope.[23]

Quickly, the Greeks proved receptive to Israeli feelers. At the June 27 gathering of religious dignitaries, Benedictos made a short speech, after the prime minister's address, expressing his appreciation for Eshkol's promise to protect the holy places and for the good behavior of the Israeli army.[24] At the end of November 1967, he sent a memorandum to the government proposing a formal agreement reaffirming the Status Quo and regulating questions of jurisdiction, property rights, taxes, and permanent residence visas for monks with foreign citizenship. This was a reasonable basis for an agreement, though for tactical reasons the government preferred to leave open the option of an accord with the Vatican.

Patriarch Derderian was no less eager to establish a working relationship with Israel. He had no reason to regret the departure of Jordanian authority, which had instituted oppressive regulations for Christian schools and prohibited the churches from acquiring real estate. Israelis and Armenians found a source of mutual sympathy in their common history of persecution.

In August 1967, Derderian submitted a memorandum to the Israeli government endorsing many of its ideas, such as extraterritorial status for the holy places, while stressing the importance of maintaining the Status Quo.[25]

———

The very first official communication from the major Christian communities to Rafi Levi concerned the restoration of the Church of the Holy Sepulchre, which hostilities had interrupted. The communication arrived by telegram on June 22, 1967, pointedly addressed to him as "representative of the foreign ministry," not of the ministry of the interior, since the communities wished to emphasize that East Jerusalem was occupied territory and not part of Israel. Now that life was returning to normal, they asked that the CTB resume work on the restoration.[26] They felt that completion of the first stage of the project was within their grasp.

Several practical difficulties had to be dealt with. First, the communities had a short-term cash problem. Before the war, the communities had kept their accounts in the East Jerusalem branches of Amman banks, and deposits were transferred to the Jordanian capital daily. After the war, all accounts were frozen indefinitely. The financial status of the churches needed to be urgently clarified and new arrangements set up.

The supply of stone had to be renewed. Only a limited quantity could ever be kept in the Parvis of the basilica. The rest was brought in straight from the quarry and stored until needed in a nearby yard. A few days after the arrival of the Israelis, the area next to the Wailing Wall was bulldozed to make way for a large plaza, and the quarried stone was buried under mounds of rubble, where it remained for months.

Finally, there was a labor shortage. Stone workers and other skilled craftsmen from the West Bank, which was under military occupation, were not allowed to travel to Jerusalem, which had been effectively annexed to Israel. Could work permits be arranged for them?[27]

Until all these problems could be sorted out, there were inevitable delays, and the restoration progressed unevenly. Deschamps, who before the war had been a candidate for retirement as work in common areas wound down, now found himself busier than ever, with Economopoulos eager to call on his services in Greek areas. Even after being hospitalized with jaundice at the beginning of 1968, he continued to come to work for several hours a day. Sadly, it was the onset of terminal illness. Sent back to his native Burgundy to recuperate, he hoped until almost the end to be able to return to his beloved Jerusalem. He was awarded the French National Order of Merit before he died in January 1969. A mass in his honor was concelebrated in the Holy Sepulchre in the presence of his friends and coworkers.

Rivalries continued between the major communities. These were "the true cause of the difficulties met with in the restoration of the Holy Sepulchre," Christian d'Halloy, the French consul general, argued in August 1968—"a restoration that for over a year has been conducted with a lack of harmony liable to compromise the final result."[28]

An important question was what part the Israeli administration would play in facilitating work on the Holy Sepulchre. The answer, it emerged, was a limited one that fell well short of the active, arbitral role Hassan Bey had carved out.

The major reason for the change was the reticence of the major communities, who made a rule of excluding the Israeli authorities from the settlement of disputes. Their longstanding view had always been that only they had possessory rights and that the role of government should be restricted. They had never welcomed the intervention of either Britain or Jordan in the repair of the church. When the sovereign was Israel, additional political complications appeared that had not existed before.

Given the ongoing Arab–Israeli conflict and Arab hostility to Israel, flagrant ecclesiastical cooperation with the Jewish state might have led to anti-Christian reprisals in the Arab world. "It was no longer possible," Canon Edward Every observed, "for the Orthodox and the Armenians to ask for the arbitration of the government in matters connected with the restoration, without putting themselves in an extremely embarrassing situation with their laity and with the Christians in the Arab countries. I don't say that it was never done, but there was a great reluctance." Since they could no longer appeal to the government, they were obliged to make "agreements between themselves, slowly, sometimes extremely slowly."[29]

Israel rarely got involved, and always at the communities' invitation. Unlike either the Mandate authorities or the Hashemite kingdom, Israel had no important stake or interest in the restoration of the Holy Sepulchre. Besides, the danger of the building's collapse had been removed. Of course, Israel did have a vital interest in demonstrating that it could be relied on to safeguard the holy places, as a failure to do so would undermine the legitimacy of its rule.

When the religious affairs ministry took over responsibility for the Christian holy places in 1968, it was instinctively reluctant to get drawn into restoration issues. Israel Lippel, the deputy director general at the time, took an unambiguously hands-off view: "We are not interested in the Christians accusing the Jews once again of murdering Jesus and I do not think that we should interfere in these matters. They should deal with it by themselves."[30] The ministry would provide assistance within the limits of law and custom if asked or if a complaint was lodged, but they would not do much more.

The broad outlines of Israel's role emerged in the early years after Israel's arrival in the Old City as the result of certain formative experiences. One informal encounter typified the overall reserve of the relationship.

At the outbreak of the Six Day War, the Armenian architect Voskertchian returned to his home in Amman. After the cease-fire, he was unable to travel back across the Jordan to Jerusalem, and not until August 1968 did he manage to return to work. In the meantime, the Armenians needed an architect. Their choice fell on a local Israeli. He was unacceptable to either Coüasnon or Economopoulos, who refused to work with him.

Consul general d'Halloy hinted that the Jewish architect would be an agent of Israeli interests in the church, part of a scheme to take over the holy places. "By this appointment," he claimed, "the Israeli government will be in a position to be kept fully informed of the relationships, disagreements, and rivalries between the three communities responsible for safeguarding the Holy Sepulchre."[31]

Under the circumstances, the Israel antiquities authority, under its director, Avraham Biran, preferred to keep out of the restoration altogether. He could certainly have been of assistance. Deterred by the potential for confrontation and unpleasantness at the holy places, he maintained that they were none of his business.[32]

Serious disputes between the major communities that would in the past have received the Jordanian governor's attention were now no longer referred to the Israeli authorities, unless violence was involved. For instance, a dispute between Greeks and Armenians over rights to the window frames and parapet of the south façade went unresolved. The communities were also reluctant for some years to involve the Israelis in a dispute with the sheikh of the al-Khanka mosque over access to its terraces, which was essential to the completion of repairs to the vaults of the Latin convent.

A legal test of the boundaries of government authority took place in the summer of 1968. In the course of rebuilding their sacristy, the Armenians decided to demolish and rebuild the wall dividing it from the Coptic sacristy. Under the Status Quo, they were not obliged to ask permission of the Copts, whose right to hold property in the Holy Sepulchre is not officially recognized.

When the work started, the Copts turned to Inspector David Chen, a police officer who headed the department of aliens and had worked as a liaison with the Christian communities since the 1967 war. He managed to obtain their confidence and, indeed, affection. More diplomat than policeman, he rarely wore a uniform but dressed smartly in civilian clothes. Besides Hebrew and English, he was fluent in Arabic and French. A man of great tact and courtesy, he had the ability to leave his listeners with a sense that he listened to their problems and wanted to alleviate them.[33]

Chen, playing the traditional Israeli police role of community mediator, asked the Armenians to stop work, but they rejected his intervention. The Coptic bishop, Basilios, then protested to the ministry of religious affairs, which prevaricated.

Working at night, the Armenians broke through the wall on July 22, 1968. The Copts hired an Israeli lawyer, who successfully applied to the local magistrate's court for an injunction to stop the work, and a date was set to try the case. At this, all hell broke loose, as the local courts had no jurisdiction over Status Quo issues. It was for the authorities, the major communities pointed out, to make an administrative ruling on such matters. If the Status Quo could be changed by court action, they opined, nothing was safe. On July 26, they submitted a stiff joint letter of protest to the government.

At this point, the magistrate recognized that he had made a mistake. He apologized, acknowledging the jurisdiction of the government, and the injunction was withdrawn. By August 1, the work was finished, and Saul Colbi, director of the ministry of religious affairs' department for Christian communities, the new authority on Status Quo issues, took no further action.[34]

Even so, a difference had been revealed between Anglo–Jordanian and Israeli administration of the Status Quo. Before 1967, the authorities had no difficulty in making administrative rulings about the Status Quo. This changed with the Six Day War. Under the Israeli system, dispute settlement is primarily the role of the courts, and arbitration of the kind the Jordanian governors adopted is mostly the prerogative of judges and rabbis. Excluding the courts (under the 1924 order-in-council) therefore created a vacuum that officials were never able to fill.

By 1970, Israel had weathered the storm over Jerusalem. It treated the churches correctly and compensated them for war damage. The Status Quo had been scrupulously maintained, and all in all, the churches had no complaints.[35] Relations between the government and the Greek and Armenian patriarchates were excellent. Relations with the Latins were proper. A new promenade from the municipality to the Jaffa Gate was being laid on Greek land, thanks to the benevolence of Benedictos. In October 1969, the pope received Abba Eban, Israel's foreign minister.

Meanwhile, Israel faced continuing challenges to its security. In March 1969, President Nasser of Egypt renounced the United Nations cease-fire of June 10, 1967, and launched a full-scale military offensive that aimed to dislodge the Israeli army from the banks of the Suez Canal. The outbreak of a war of attrition with Egypt, with heavy casualties from artillery bombardments of Israeli positions, totally shifted Israel's priorities. Until an American-sponsored cease-fire came into effect on August 7, 1970, Israel was overwhelmingly preoccupied with the conflict with Egypt.

This was the context for a crisis in the Church of the Resurrection that resulted from a property dispute between the Coptic and Ethiopian churches. The bone of contention was two small chapels, the Chapel of the Angels (also known as the Four Living Creatures) and the Chapel of St. Michael, and the passage leading to them from the courtyard of the Deir al-Sultan (the "Sultan's monastery") on the terrace over the Chapel of St. Helena. This passage provided the Copts with convenient access from St. Anthony's monastery to the Parvis and their chapel in the rotunda. The affair had international political and ecclesiastical ramifications.

The background to the dispute lay in the ancient relationship between the Coptic (Egyptian) and Ethiopian churches. The Coptic Church, which has been present in the Church of the Holy Sepulchre since earliest times, traces its origins back to St. Mark, the author of the second Gospel. St. Anthony is credited with setting up the first monastery in Egypt in 305.

When the Ethiopian royal dynasty adopted Christianity in the fourth century, the new church became a bishopric of Alexandria, its *abuna,* or bishop, appointed by the Coptic Church. The two churches have been in spiritual and dogmatic communion ever since. It was only in 1951, after a long campaign for greater autonomy, that an Ethiopian was appointed abuna for the first time. As a result of a severe deterioration in relations between the revolutionary Egypt of President Gamal Abdel Nasser and the empire of Haile Selassie, the two churches moved to a final break. In 1959, the Ethiopian Church became autocephalous, that is, headed by its own primate.[36]

The property dispute between Copts and Ethiopians in Jerusalem closely tracked the deteriorating political relations between the two countries. For centuries, the Ethiopians had their own chapels in the Holy Sepulchre but grew steadily poorer under Ottoman rule. In the seventeenth century, they lost their rights to the Greeks and became yamaklik or subordinates of the Armenians.[37] The quarrel over the Deir al-Sultan, the passage, and the two chapels goes back to a plague in 1838 that wiped out the local Ethiopian monastic community. When fresh monks were eventually sent out from Addis Ababa, they were allowed to reoccupy the Deir al-Sultan and pray in the Chapel of the Angels but the Coptic patriarchate treated them as guests, not residents. Their archive was said to have been burnt during the plague.[38]

In the 1950s, the Jordanian government set up a committee to examine the two communities' contending claims. Its findings, confirmed by the governor, Ihsan Hashem, on February 22, 1961, in a "historical decision," declared Abyssinian "ownership" of the Deir al-Sultan, the two chapels, and the passage, and transferred the keys of the passage to the Ethiopians. However, as a result of Egyptian government intervention, the decision was suspended on April 1 (but not annulled) and the previous situation restored.[39]

Before and after the Six Day War, there was tension between the two communities, with quarrels over issues such as the lighting of the courtyard of the Deir al-Sultan at Easter and repairs to the Ethiopian monks' dwellings. The Copts regularly threw stones at Ethiopian processions from the high windows of their monastery in protest of alleged violations of the Status Quo. For reasons that were not clear at the time, the underlying property dispute burst into the open at Easter 1970.[40]

Just after midnight on Easter Sunday, Anba Basilios, the Coptic Orthodox archbishop of Jerusalem and the Near East, was at prayer with his monks at their chapel in the Holy Sepulchre. In the middle of the service, he was told that the Ethiopians had changed the locks on the doors at both ends of the disputed passage.

Archbishop Basilios immediately sent a monk to verify the information, but when the monk arrived at the door to the passage in the corner of the Parvis, a policeman barred his way. The police prevented other monks, who went the long way around to the Deir al-Sultan, from approaching the door at the upper end of the passage. It proved impossible that night to get in touch with either the police minister or his commanders. All subsequent attempts to regain the keys and use of the passage—by the archbishop and his lawyer, by appeals to the police and the government—proved equally fruitless. On April 27, Abuna Joseph, the Ethiopian Orthodox archbishop of Jerusalem, openly declared that the Ethiopians had regained their historical rights.

The next day, the Coptic bishop petitioned the high court to have the new locks removed and the previous ones restored. In March 1971, the court sat in judgment. It began by pointing out that under the 1924 order-in-council, it had no authority to decide on the merits of the dispute between the Copts and the Ethiopians over possession of the passage and the two chapels. This was the government's responsibility. Rather, its decision was directed to the petitioner's request to restore the situation on the eve of the incident.

In its decision, the court criticized the passive behavior of the police throughout and commented that they had done nothing at all to come to the aid of the Copts. There was not the slightest proof that the Ethiopians had been in previous possession of the disputed site. The court went on to find in favor of the Copts' request.

But at the very end of the judgment, in a puzzling twist, the court decided that implementation of the order should be delayed for twenty-one days, to give the government the opportunity to deal with the substantive dispute. In justification of this decision, the court sketched out very briefly three arguments: that the substantive dispute should not be separated from the immediate dispute over possession; that equity demanded that relief not now be given; and that the government had not had sufficient time to decide between the opposing claims.[41]

Following this surprising judgment, the government set up a cabinet committee to deal with the substantive dispute, at the same time issuing an interim order leaving the site in possession of the Ethiopians. This order effectively annulled the decision of the high court, which now declined to get involved in an area that came under government jurisdiction. Over the next few years, various compromise proposals for a settlement were explored, but proved unacceptable to the parties concerned. The committee was re-appointed in diverse forms, most recently in February 1993. The keys remain in Ethiopian hands.

It is now possible to reconstruct the collusion between the government of Israel and the Ethiopian Church that led to the events of the night of April 25–26, 1970. The story begins just after the Six Day War, when Abuna Joseph, through his lawyer, asked the prime minister to restore the passage and the chapels to the Ethiopian Church.[42] In the fall of 1967, Levi Eshkol delegated the request to the cabinet committee on the holy places, and in

Addis Ababa the Israeli ambassador unwisely promised the head of the Ethiopian Church, Abuna Basilios, that the matter would be settled in twenty days.[43] As time went by, the Israeli embassy came under pressure from the ecclesiastical authorities of the Ethiopian Church to deliver on its promise.

Since the 1950s, Israel had cultivated good relations with Ethiopia, a Christian country in a largely Muslim and often hostile neighborhood. Both had a common enemy—Egypt's President Nasser, who was supporting the struggle of the Eritrean Liberation Movement for independence from Ethiopia. Ethiopia's location just north of the Bab al Mandeb Straits—the choke point between the Red Sea and the Indian Ocean—gave it great geostrategic importance for Israel, which wished to secure its freedom of navigation from its southern port of Eilat to East Africa, India, and the Far East. Ethiopia was the only country along the Red Sea that was willing to allow Israeli ships to use its ports. Its importance only increased after the Six Day War—whose catalyst had been the closing of the more northerly Straits of Tiran to Israeli shipping.

In mid-1968, Israel sent as ambassador to Ethiopia its foremost diplomatic entrepreneur and fixer, Uri Lubrani. Born into a wealthy Haifa family, Lubrani had been a wireless operator on an immigrant ship running survivors of the Nazi death camps through the Royal Navy blockade of Palestine. He went on to study at the London School of Economics, later becoming David Ben Gurion's personal secretary. A fat, jolly man with a loud laugh, he had charm, resourcefulness, and an extensive network of connections.

Lubrani's instructions as ambassador were to work toward a security alliance and close political cooperation between Israel and Ethiopia.[44] This involved coordinating a substantial program of Israeli military and economic aid, and training the Ethiopian army, security services, and Eritrean emergency police.[45] At about this time, a top-secret survey described Israel as having "a most vital interest in the existence of a strong Ethiopia."[46]

With the outbreak of the War of Attrition along the Suez Canal in March 1969, Lubrani's mission took on an urgent, clandestine dimension, code-named "coffee": the imperative to secure for Israel base facilities, now essential for intelligence gathering and naval operations in the Red Sea.

It is not surprising, therefore, that the Israeli ministry of foreign affairs was throughout highly sympathetic to the Ethiopian request and sought a formula that would enable the keys to be handed over. It was deeply impressed by the Ethiopian Church's influence on public opinion and its power in state affairs. Its status seemed to be demonstrated when the Israeli chargé d'affaires observed the emperor mounting the steps of the abuna's palace while bowing from time to time to the abuna, who awaited him impassively at the top.[47] In fact, the emperor used the church as an instrument of state, not the reverse.

Before the renewal of hostilities with Egypt, Jochanan Bein, the head of the Africa department at the foreign ministry, favored Israel giving the keys to the Ethiopians in exchange for their upgrading their consulate general in Jerusalem to an embassy. The puzzle to be solved was "the tactical question of implementing the transfer while avoiding giving the impression that the Israeli government was violating the Status Quo at the holy places, an issue to which the Christian world was highly sensitive."[48]

Bein's idea suffered from a drawback. It was the church and not the Ethiopian government that had raised the matter, and the government carefully avoided getting involved. Besides, the abuna himself rejected any linkage between the two issues, arguing that he was only asking for what he was entitled to by a decision of the Jordanian court. He would advocate for the opening of a Jerusalem embassy, but the question was out of his hands.[49]

The Israeli government's deliberations on the question of the keys required an in-depth legal study of the Status Quo in general and the 1924 order-in-council in particular. The two key questions were whether the Status Quo could be changed and, if so, by whom.

Yechiel Elissar, the lawyer who directed the foreign minister's office, had no doubt that under the Mandate, the high commissioner had had the exclusive authority to rule on Status Quo issues. He cited Edward Keith-Roach's opinion of October 31, 1939, that the Copts could not take the government to court on a Status Quo issue and that the high commissioner's decisions were final and binding until a commission on the holy places was established.

However, in Elissar's view the Jordanian government decision of 1961 to transfer *ownership* of the Deir al-Sultan and the two chapels to the Ethiopians was unprecedented and legally unsound. This was borne out not only by the sultan's firmans, which granted rights of usage and not ownership, but also by the fact that the sultan transferred *possession* from time to time from one community to another. (One may possess or hold something without owning it. It also followed from this reasoning that the major communities were not the owners as they claimed.) Elissar therefore argued that both Jordanian decisions, to transfer the keys and to claw them back, were violations of the Status Quo, though the major communities had made no protest at the time.

He also observed that the 1924 order-in-council was not set in stone, because under article 4 it could be revoked, altered, or amended. Nor was it the case that the Roman Catholic Church was wedded to the Status Quo of

1852. "They have never accepted it because it curtailed the rights granted them by previous firmans." His impression was that none of the major communities saw the situation of the Deir al-Sultan as satisfactory. He ignored the 1878 Treaty of Berlin.

His conclusion was threefold. First, the sovereign could alter the Status Quo. Second, implementation of the 1961 decision could not be the grounds for transferring the keys. Third, the cabinet committee on the holy places was authorized to settle the dispute.[50]

Moshe Ben-Zeev, the legal adviser to the government—whose opinion, in the Israeli system, is considered binding on the government—disagreed with this analysis. In his view, in a democracy, disputes should normally be settled by the courts. It was true that the 1924 order-in-council had ruled this out, envisaging a special commission on the holy places. Had they so wished, he was convinced, the mandatory authorities in their lawmaking capacity could have set up such a body by another order-in-council. The conclusion he drew was that only the Knesset, Israel's legislature, and not the executive branch, was entitled to establish a legal tribunal to settle disputes concerning the holy places.[51]

Theodor Meron, the legal adviser to the foreign ministry, agreed with this. He also warned about the diplomatic consequences of a decision to transfer the keys. It was of "the utmost importance to avoid Israel being accused of a wish to harm the Status Quo at the holy places."[52]

For Israel to introduce legislation to set up a commission on the holy places was out of the question. The international outcry would be deafening. It had been hard enough to resist the pressure to internationalize Jerusalem; to challenge the Christian world at the holy places would be futile. Moreover, Israel had unquestionably committed itself, albeit informally, to maintaining the Status Quo.

Israel therefore found itself caught in a dilemma. On the one hand its strategic security interests apparently required transferring the keys to the Ethiopians; on the other hand it was locked into the Status Quo. Only the religious affairs ministry was sensitive to the complexities and indeed benefits of the Status Quo, but its views tended to be disregarded.

The ostensible drawback of the Status Quo was its very advantage. It tied the hands of the sovereign, thereby releasing it from the onerous burden of making unwelcome decisions calculated to please only the beneficiary and certain to displease everyone else. Wisely administered, it allowed the parties to "live and let live" at the holy places. And in its Jordanian version, drawing on the Muslim tradition of arbitration, it actually gave the sovereign some room to maneuver.

For a year, Israel did nothing while the Ethiopian Church seethed with resentment at being misled. On May 1, 1969, Uri Lubrani was invited to the abuna's palace, where he was confronted by the synod of the church. In a tense atmosphere, the abuna angrily described his church's disappointment at Israel's unfulfilled assurances and procrastination. They failed to understand why Israel hesitated to carry out King Hussein's decision to transfer the keys to them. "They saw the present situation as intolerable and a grave insult to their feelings," Lubrani wrote. Something had to be done.[53]

Lubrani's report, in the second month of the War of Attrition, compelled action. Jochanan Bein admitted that the "deed must be done," and transfer of the keys had to be decoupled from the opening of an Ethiopian embassy in Jerusalem. Within days, the foreign ministry recommended transferring the keys without conditions. Foreign Minister Abba Eban was scheduled to visit Ethiopia in July. This would be a good time to inform the Ethiopians of Israel's decision.[54]

On May 26, the cabinet committee on the holy places made the decision to transfer the keys by interim order, an act of government that could later be renewed. This was an attempt to square the circle. There would be no determination of the ownership of the site, and the principled disagreement between the two communities could continue in the future. There would be no change in the formal Status Quo—as Israel interpreted it—but, in the meantime, the Ethiopians rather than the Copts would hold the keys.[55]

This cleared the way for Eban's suitably portentous declaration, read out to the abuna at a private ceremony in his palace in Addis Ababa on July 3, 1969:

> I have the honour and pleasure to inform Your Excellency that the Government of Israel has decided to recognise the historical rights of the Ethiopian Church upon Dir-es-Sultan, without prejudice and detriment to the historical status and rights of other Christian communities.
>
> The Government of Israel will therefore and as a token of friendship to the Imperial Government and people of Ethiopia assist the Ethiopian Church in the restoration of their rights, including the possession of the key to the South Gate and the key of the Church of the Angel Michael.
>
> Taking into consideration the manifold complexities of this problem, it is proposed that the modalities for this change will be worked out between the Ethiopian Church authorities and the Israel Government authorities concerned.[56]

Needless to say, this declaration by the Israeli government casts new light on the events of the night of Easter 1970 and the purpose of the cabinet committees that were subsequently set up to find a solution to the Deir al-Sultan dispute. It reinforces the Coptic claim that Israeli policemen and not Ethiopian monks changed the locks.

The carefully choreographed charade was the solution to the problem of how to divert attention from a change in the Status Quo. The answer was first conceived in the fertile mind of Uri Lubrani, who suggested that Israel might have "to stage a show before announcing the positive decision." Some "ruse" or other might be required.[57]

It did not take long for Israel to regret its action: The War of Attrition ended within a few months, and Ethiopia displayed scant gratitude for the keys. A Jerusalem embassy was never opened, despite explicit promises Haile Selassie and his prime minister made in 1971.[58] Worse, in December 1971 Ethiopia cosponsored a UN resolution hostile to Israel. This was considered particularly unhelpful, since at this time the Coptic community had launched an international campaign for the return of the keys, including appeals to the U.S. president, Richard Nixon, and the United Nations.

Leah Sidis, an official in the Africa department of the foreign ministry, wondered whether Israel might consider returning the keys to the Copts.[59]

As a result of the 1973 October war, Israel's relations with Ethiopia and Egypt underwent a reversal. Ethiopia broke off diplomatic relations with Israel, and in 1974 the emperor was deposed. In 1979, Israel signed a peace treaty with Egypt, which then began to exert pressure in favor of the Copts. Nevertheless, Israel refrained from restoring the keys to the Copts for fear of endangering El Al Israel airlines flights through Ethiopian airspace and later of hampering the emigration of Ethiopian Jews to Israel.

In response to the 1971 interim order and the formation of the cabinet committee, the churches expressed grave concern at the intervention of the government in a matter that should come under an "independent higher authority."[60] In a joint protest to Prime Minister Golda Meir, the leaders of the three major communities pointed out the serious nature of questions concerning the holy places. They reminded Meir that the Israeli government had an obligation to safeguard the Status Quo and that any change should only be by "common agreement of the religious communities concerned."[61]

The churches suspected that the police had turned a blind eye to the violation of the Status Quo because Israel was at war with Egypt and its political interests demanded a gesture toward Haile Selassie. In their view, it was totally unacceptable for the Israeli government to exploit its authority at the holy places for narrow political gain. Moreover, the episode cast serious doubt on Israel's willingness and ability to objectively administer the Status Quo.

Looking back, Israel Lippel, who was deputy director general of the ministry of religious affairs at the time, completely agreed with this assessment of the events of Easter 1970. In his opinion, "the Government of Israel committed a serious error. It mixed up foreign policy and politics with the most sensitive religious questions in the Christian world. When you favor political considerations over the maintenance of the Status Quo you invite pressures and complications."[62]

Israel's blunder had the practical effect of largely removing it as a conciliatory force in the difficult and protracted deliberations that were soon to get under way for the second stage of the restoration. The affair reinforced the initial inhibitions of many Israelis about getting entangled with Christian issues.

Moreover, the body charged with dealing with the churches in Israel, the religious affairs ministry, had been shown to be a weak player within the government. At the first major challenge to the Status Quo, more powerful ministries had shrugged off its warnings. Even if it wanted to play a constructive role, its influence was nothing like that of its British and Jordanian predecessors.

On the whole, the churches themselves were even less inclined than before to seek the help of the government with the restoration. If the Israelis could not be relied on to preserve the Status Quo, and were likely to be unduly influenced by "political considerations," it was thought best to keep them out of it.

CHAPTER THIRTEEN

To the Rotunda

THE PRINCIPAL ARCHITECTS did not meet for almost two years after the June 1967 war. When they convened on May 28, 1969, the main item on the agenda was the restoration of the rotunda. They faced a problem that would have challenged the greatest architectural minds in history. They had somehow to re-create a setting that would convey the mystery of the Resurrection, where people could reflect, worship, and seek inspiration. At the same time, they had to remain true to the original, an amalgam of styles from four different periods, while remaining within the iron grip of the Status Quo.

Not much of the Emperor Constantine's original structure was left above ground after the destruction of the Martyrion by the Fatimid Caliph Hakim in 1009. Only the bases of the circular colonnade of eighteen pillars surrounding the tomb, and the polygonal outer wall, to a height of 11 meters above bedrock, were preserved. These remains provided the ground plan and foundations for a reconstituted late Byzantine church completed about 1040.[1] Like its predecessor, this was a round church, with pillars, ambulatory, and gallery encircling the rebuilt Edicule. Courses of thin red bricks from this period are visible throughout the galleries and at ground level next to the Triumphal Arch, which the Crusaders built to link the rotunda to their own new basilica, consecrated in 1149.[2]

The 1808 conflagration wrought havoc on the monument. To save it, Komnenos of Mytilene sheathed damaged columns in rectangular piers of masonry and plaster, rebuilt the arcades and galleries, walled up the ambulatory as an additional reinforcement, and constructed a neo-Byzantine

Edicule, modeled on the nearby tomb of Absalom. He also restored the cone roof over the rotunda, but this was damaged in 1834 and eventually replaced with the present dome in 1869.

On the eve of the modern restoration, the interior of the—by now dilapidated—rotunda was strutted with emergency scaffolding. It looked like a great birdcage. Far overhead all that remained of the decoration on the ceiling were "indistinct patches of peeling fresco."[3] The little light in the cavernous space came from a glazed lantern on top of the dome.

Before the communities could come up with a plan, a substantial amount of technical and political preparatory work was required. At first, the experts tended to favor consolidating the original pillars. Each community would be responsible for its own pillars.[4] Some questions of possession were not finally settled until 1976.

Soundings indicated that the interior façade of the Anastasis was exactly as drawn in seventeenth- and eighteenth-century engravings. Under Komnenos's plaster, the broken and burned remnants of half the original pillars were found in various stages of decay. Some were Byzantine, some Crusader. As became evident, it would be totally impractical to restore them.[5]

Another debate focused on the dimensions of the pillars. Trouvelot and Utudjian favored slender columns like the originals. They pointed out that such pillars had supported the Anastasis for seven hundred years before the fire destroyed their resistance.[6] But the Greek view, that thicker pillars would be better able to withstand future earthquakes, prevailed.

At their August 1970 meeting, the experts discussed two major options for the rotunda. One was to consolidate the building, leaving it in the architectural form established in 1810. The other was to recreate the eleventh-century structure. In the end, the Greeks preferred the first option for compelling Status Quo reasons.[7]

By 1971, the rotunda was a hive of activity. Deschamps's replacement as foreman was René Morel, a calm, methodical twenty-seven-year-old from Lyons who spoke good English. Despite initial Greek objections, the Latins began on the base of the double columns on their side of the Triumphal Arch, while the Armenians set to work on the other.

One by one, new stone pillars were erected in place of Komnenos's emergency piers over the course of 1972–73. Several broke during installation. Morel and his men became adept at taking down columns complete with their bases and capitals without causing harm. An observer described the operation of dismantling the old and raising the new—requiring pinpoint precision in the positioning of an object weighing 22 tons—as "tense and breathtaking."[8]

The new columns were made from the finest Mizzi Ahmar marble and were modeled on pillars found near Lake Tiberias. Polished to a high pink sheen, they match the rosy marble that sheathes the Edicule. They vary in commemoration of the originals. Pillars 1 and 18 preserve their double form, sit on round pedestals, and have superimposed capitals that recall an improvisation of the Crusader masons. Square piers retain their shape throughout. Pillars 2 and 3 have square pedestals of differing height and shape, and the position of the fillets, the circular bands around the columns, also varies. Most pedestals bear a cross pattée—a cross with slightly concave arms.

The question of the capitals proved contentious and protracted, reviving the old controversy over the Byzantine versus Crusader identity of the edifice. In the fall of 1971, Coüasnon installed rough-cut trapezoidal blocks on the new Latin columns. Economopoulos vigorously complained at this, arguing that a trapezoid-shaped capital had not existed in Byzantine architecture before the eleventh century. It was, he claimed, an attempt "to present a real Byzantine monument, which had not been touched by the Crusaders, as a Gothic monument of the thirteenth or fourteenth century."[9]

At a meeting of experts and delegates on October 7, 1972, two completely different designs were presented. On the basis of his findings in the rotunda, Coüasnon had prepared a model of a Corinthian capital, displaying two rows of acanthus leaves. Economopoulos had prepared a Byzantine basket-style capital inspired by an existing capital in the Chapel of St. Helena.[10]

Having rejected both these alternatives, the communities studied a number of variations over the next two years. At a meeting in September 1974, the experts chose in principle a fifth-century design found in the ruins of Corozain (Korazim) in the vicinity of the Sea of Galilee. Associated with neither late Byzantium nor the Crusader kingdom of Jerusalem, it evoked a primordial period of church harmony.[11]

It took Coüasnon eighteen months to translate this design into an acceptable blueprint. The Corinthian capital, in cross-section, resembled a four-pointed star. In contrast with the pink Mizzi Ahmar of the columns, it was decided to use creamy royal Malaki stone for the capitals. It was easier to work and blended in with the surrounding masonry of the arcades, balustrade, and galleries. Stonemasons sculpted the capitals on the spot from blocks already in place, working from a full-size model.

The Israeli contribution to the restoration of the rotunda was negligible. During the early 1970s, a dispute over the waterproofing of the terraces, a confrontation between mosque and church, raised serious difficulties and served to map out the limits on the Israeli role.

The affair had its origins in the anomalous situation in the northwest corner of the Holy Sepulchre complex, where Saladin expropriated what had been the Latin patriarchate under the Crusader kings and converted it into a mosque. Ever since, the terrace above the present Latin convent can only be reached from the roof of the al-Khanka Mosque or by climbing down a ladder from the upper terraces. In order to repair the convent's ancient vaulting, supporting walls, and rooftop paving, workers for the Custody needed free access to the al-Khanka terrace. Restoration of the drum and dome of the Anastasis would also require such unimpeded access.

The problem first arose in January 1967, as a result of an altercation between the sheikh and imam of the al-Khanka Mosque, Abd al-Mouati al-Alami, and CTB workers who had begun work on the terrace. Living in a home on the roof, the sheikh was involved in a longstanding dispute with the Islamic Council of Jerusalem over his rights as trustee of the Salah al-Din al-Ayyoubi Waqf, the body responsible for the mosque in Muslim law. He claimed that he had the historical right to use the dwelling and that it was up to him as trustee and no one else to carry out repairs to the terrace.[12]

Work had to be stopped, and the Jordanian governor came to examine the problem for himself. Following a three-way negotiation in which the governor performed ably as an arbiter, the Custody concluded an agreement with the Jordanian government acknowledging that the mosque had the right to use the outer surface of the terrace but also affirming the Latin right to repair the underlying structure. In order to enable the Custody to carry out essential repairs to the vaults and walls of the convent, the Jordanian DPW would first strip away the tiles. Workmen would then be allowed free access to the terraces.

After the 1967 war, with the Jordanian government no longer there to enforce the agreement, Sheikh al-Alami forcibly blocked entrance to the terrace and caused damage to the church. Imperfect drainage arrangements and the decayed state of the roof meant that water collecting on the terrace tended to trickle down into the convent and Anastasis. The sheikh dumped gravel and earth on the roof, which impeded runoff into drains. Water leaking from rabbit hutches and chicken coops he kept up there did not help matters. In the winter of 1970–71, water dripped all the way down to ground level, damaging convent property and seeping into the walls and vaults of the tribune and Anastasis. Since the upper part of the rotunda, dating from the eleventh century, and the fourth-century lower part are bound with earth mortar containing practically no lime, this threatened to further undermine the structure, with a danger of partial collapse.[13]

A cat-and-mouse game now began between the Custody and the sheikh. Workmen would climb down to the terrace to remove the obstructions, and the sheikh would replace them shortly afterward. This happened on several occasions. The Custody asked the Waqf for permission to carry out the necessary repairs and to install a temporary corrugated iron roof over the terrace to keep out the rain. In return for his consent, Sheikh al-Alami demanded a large sum of money. The Custody rejected him out of hand.

Heavy autumn rains brought the issue to a head. In Paris, Trouvelot sought a diplomatic solution to the problem and held a long meeting with the United Nations Educational, Scientific and Cultural Organization (UNESCO). But this international body, he was told, was legally powerless to intervene in what was considered a private dispute. He was advised to approach the Holy See, which could use its connections in the Muslim world to intervene in a friendly way.[14]

On December 15, 1971, Morel climbed down to the terrace at seven o'clock in the morning to clear away obstructions. This time the night-shirted sheikh called the police and submitted a complaint. Morel was taken into custody and released after two hours. Sheikh al-Alami now took him to court—the first skirmish in a long legal wrangle.

Until this episode, Father Rock had declined to involve the Israeli authorities, arguing that he wished to avoid political complications and accusations of benefiting from the Israeli occupation. As an Arab from Ain Karim, whose family had fled in 1948, he also, in Trouvelot's words, had "very understandable reactions towards the Jews."[15] Rock argued that the Custody should patiently await the outcome of the Jerusalem Islamic Council's case against the sheikh. In his view, the Status Quo was a set of arrangements involving corporate entities, not individuals, and it would be a breach of precedent to deal directly with the sheikh.

Father Coüasnon was dismayed by what he saw as Rock's passivity in the face of a danger to the very stability of the monument. On December 23, he broke ranks and on his own initiative submitted a detailed memorandum to Saul Colbi, the expert for the Israeli ministry of religious affairs. Writing both in his capacity "as the architect responsible for the works of the Custody of the Holy Land" and out of a sense of overall responsibility for the endangered edifice, he asked Colbi to "force the Custody to carry out its obligations" by ordering it to put in place a temporary roof over the terrace.[16]

Nothing came of this initiative. Colbi was in no position to force either Father Rock or Sheikh al-Alami to do anything. Neither he nor anyone else in the Israeli system could rule administratively on issues of the Status Quo. No Israeli official had the power of a British district commissioner or Jordanian governor, and, after the debacle of the keys, the political authorities were loath to interfere in the Church of the Holy Sepulchre.

Normally in Israel, a disputed question of competencies or rights comes before the courts, where it is settled judicially. But this was ruled out in the case of the Status Quo by the 1924 order-in-council. On February 10, 1972, the local magistrates' court turned down the sheikh's suit for trespass on the ground that it was not competent to deal with matters coming under the Status Quo. If neither the local courts nor the government could make a ruling, and the Custody declined either to negotiate with the sheikh or call on the good offices of the Israelis to act in some kind of intermediary role, it was unclear how the matter could be resolved.

Father Rock's view at first was that the Israeli authorities should restrict themselves to maintaining public order. On March 14, 1972, the three major communities wrote to Prime Minister Golda Meir, informing her that work on the terrace would soon recommence and holding her responsible for its being carried out without impediment. An agreement was then concluded with the Jerusalem Waqf by which it waived any objection to the Christian communities removing the tiles from the terrace. The affair seemed settled. The problem was that it was not the Jerusalem Waqf but Sheikh al-Alami, as trustee of the Salah al-Din al-Ayyoubi Waqf, who was in effective charge of the al-Khanka Mosque.

On July 10, 1972, work finally began. From now until the end of November, it was repeatedly interrupted by the sheikh's complaints to the police and to the courts. He alleged invasion of his privacy, trespass, and damage to his property caused by work on the terrace.

On July 27, Morel crossed a notional boundary and mistakenly began to raise tiles on the sheikh's property. The sheikh immediately called the police and had the work stopped. At first, Father Rock appealed for help to the Jerusalem Waqf. When this proved ineffective, he finally agreed with Father Daniel to bring in the Israeli officials David Chen and Rafi Levi to try and sort out the problem. This was a considerable retreat.

Meeting with community experts, Levi suggested that the common-sense solution was for them to arrive at a compromise directly with the sheikh. Rock replied that since the time of the Turks, the communities had only dealt with corporate bodies like the Waqf. His own preference was for the

Israelis to bypass the sheikh by enforcing the authority of the Jerusalem Waqf, if necessary by bringing in the police. This would have quickly solved the problem. But since the 1967 war, the Waqf and the Israeli government had refused to recognize each other.

Father Rock came up with the suggestion that the DPW carry out the job, just as had been agreed with the Jordanians in 1967. Indeed this was the solution Cust, in his 1929 report, had long ago described in a situation where repairs had to be carried out to contested property, such as the terraces.

Levi and Chen liked the idea. The next day they brought along the DPW engineer and the deputy president of the magistrates' court to see the problem for themselves. All agreed that the work in question should be carried out first thing the next morning, before the magistrates' court opened and the sheikh could apply for another injunction. By nine o'clock the following morning, August 4, the tiles in the disputed area had been raised.

Temporarily outwitted, Sheikh al-Alami returned to his cat-and-mouse game, successfully blocking, through legal means, the work of waterproofing and retiling at the intersection of the terrace and the wall of his dwelling. On October 25, 1972, another meeting was held between church representatives and Israeli officials. Levi had invited Sheikh al-Alami along, hoping to thrash out a compromise. Daniel had no objection to this, but Rock did. As a result, while Jews and Christians discussed the matter in Levi's office, the Muslim cleric waited outside.

Levi opened the session by proposing two technical solutions. Rock was ready to accept whatever would put a stop to the seepage of water into the church but wanted, as before, the work to be carried out by the DPW. Levi's condition for this was that the communities give the sheikh a guarantee that they would repair any damage caused to his property. Rock was opposed: Alami could not be trusted and was capable of again blocking the free runoff of water from the terrace. It was the sheikh who should give the guarantee.

A week later, Levi made one last effort to mediate a compromise between the parties. At his suggestion, the communities agreed to write a letter to the government containing the requested guarantee. Levi then gave a copy to the sheikh. But the moment for conciliation had passed. On November 19, al-Alami returned to court to seek yet another injunction for the communities to stop work on the wall of his home. It belonged to him and the Salah al-Din al-Ayyoubi Waqf, and the communities had no rights there.[17]

Until this date, Father Rock had consistently refused to appear in an Israeli court. However, the communities' Israeli lawyer pointed out that failure to do so at this point could have serious consequences. If a decision went against the Custody, it would simply not be able to carry out the work.

The custos, Father Erminio Roncari, accordingly agreed to hire a firm of Israeli lawyers to represent the Custody in the case.

On November 27, the court threw out the suit on the grounds that it was not competent to treat Status Quo issues. Besides, it observed, the proprietor of the al-Khanka Mosque had an obligation to avoid damaging his neighbors' property. This cleared the way to the repair and waterproofing of the convent roof.[18]

As construction of the colonnade progressed, preliminary work began on the restoration of the great dome. The cupola over the rotunda had been reconstructed in 1869 at the joint expense of Russia, France, and the Ottoman Empire. Superficial examination through binoculars, carried out without benefit of scaffolding, suggested that it was in poor shape. Its metal framework seemed to be badly rusted and in a state of decomposition. There was fear that it could easily cave in and fall on someone's head.[19]

At an August 1970 meeting, the principal architects had discussed two possible configurations of the great dome.[20] One possibility was to recreate the eleventh-century cone. Ferdinando Forlati, Marangoni's successor as proto of St. Mark's Basilica, Venice, had suggested this idea in a 1954 essay.[21] But the more realistic option was to retain the familiar and pleasing hemispherical dome of 1869. In any case, everything would depend on the actual state of the iron frame, which had not been examined closely for a century.

In March 1973, Utudjian conducted an external examination of the dome on behalf of the principal architects. He removed a couple of panels to examine the metallic mounts, the insulation, and the covering. Over several days of investigation, helped by Morel, he concluded that the frame was "in a relatively good condition and very probably did not need to be totally replaced." Corroded metal could be repaired on the spot; replacing the entire frame would require a helicopter. The protective masonry had been ineffective, but the corrosion did not go deep. The insulation panels had crumbled away and could be restored using a light insulating material. To safeguard the dome's external appearance, its external cover should be lead, as before. Altogether, he concluded, the restoration should be relatively easy and not take more than a year.[22]

Utudjian reported back to his colleagues, and it was agreed that a more detailed survey of the cupola, which consisted of inner and outer shells supported by wrought-iron trusses, was needed. This would require removal of the inner plaster coating and the exterior render, which had been applied to the damaged outer surface of the dome in the early 1950s to keep out the rain. Bids for scaffolding should be solicited.[23]

The winning bid, submitted by Entrepose of Paris, called for a tubular assembly resting on the recently reconstructed balustrade of the galleries, leaving the paving around the Edicule uncluttered. In May 1975, M. Crosnier, the French firm's representative, arrived in Jerusalem in order to supervise the construction of the scaffolding.

After only a week, the work was halted because of an unresolved dispute between the communities. Before agreeing to proceed, the Greeks demanded acknowledgment of their ownership of the upper gallery that runs around the inside of the drum, the door and staircase giving access to it from the upper terraces, and the items it contains. Who had the right to dust the interior of the dome itself? For the scaffolding to be completed, the Greeks had to remove the grilles and lamps from the gallery, and they wanted an agreement protecting their rights before they did so.

Crosnier waited for two weeks to see if a solution could be found. Realizing that a happy outcome was unlikely in the near future, he returned to France with the scaffolding half completed.[24] Trouvelot was at a loss to understand why the Greeks had decided to mix the question of ownership of the gallery with the common work of repair and consolidation.[25] Since only they had access to the gallery from their convent, its seizure by another community would require an improbable commando operation.

A long and difficult negotiation now followed. Church experts argued their cases in traditional legal terms, citing precedents and documents in support of their contending claims, as if there were a judge present to weigh the evidence and settle the matter. There had always been an adjudicator before 1967, first the Mamluk and Ottoman shari'a courts, then the district commissioner or governor under the British and Jordanians. By 1975, such a mechanism no longer existed, yet the communities continued to go through the legal motions.

On March 3, 1976, the leaders of the three major communities signed agreements that settled key issues under contention at the time and paved the way for the final stage of the restoration of the rotunda.[26] Following the signing, Crosnier was able to return to Jerusalem and complete the erection of the scaffolding on May 21.

The first agreement said in its preamble that the three churches would carry out the restoration of the great dome at their shared expense, thereby removing any lingering doubts about the equal status of the Armenians as co-owners of the church. In substance, ownership of the upper gallery was settled by a clause acknowledging the Greeks' right to dust the cupola "as far as one can reach." Pillars 10 and 11 were allocated to the Armenians; pillar 12 to the Greeks. A separate accord signed the same day settled the location and shape of two bells in the Armenian Chapel of the Three Marys. Altogether, these agreements constituted a package of mutual accommodations involving a balanced exchange of benefits between Greeks and Armenians.

The negotiating styles of the Greek and Armenian experts were very different. Archimandrite Daniel vigorously defended the interests of the Greek Patriarchate, but his manner was soft-spoken, and he was inclined to try and work out a solution with his interlocutor in a conciliatory way. He liked to pore over color charts, going into intricate detail, breaking down a problem into numerous elements.

In contrast, Bishop Guregh Kapikian was filled with single-minded passion for his cause. Daniel Rossing, the new Israeli director of the Christian communities department of the ministry of religious affairs, described him as "how can I put it diplomatically, a fighter. In which case, he could also at times become very angry and you saw it on his face, you heard it in his voice, in his words."[27]

This episode effectively marked a major shift in the way disputes concerning the Status Quo were handled. They were now negotiated directly and not settled by an umpire. If in appearance the contest was about lawful rights, in reality it was a straightforward negotiation in which the parties got what they negotiated, not what they deserved. Legal arguments were just one means of rhetorical persuasion, albeit an important one. The most common tactics were trade-offs and package deals.

It was the culmination of a trend that had begun in the 1950s when the communities had begun to negotiate among themselves. In the past, though, the Jordanian governor was there to help in the event of a deadlock in the talks. Now, there was no governor to fall back on. The main beneficiaries of this new system were the Armenians, who made up for the loopholes in their legal documentation with hard bargaining. In a three-cornered negotiation, where decision-making is by consensus, the weakest party has enhanced leverage. It can hold out for concessions by withholding consent until its demands are met. Guregh's skilful use of this tactic helped the Armenians gain acceptance as full-fledged coowners of the church.

Throughout this period, the Israeli authorities made no rulings on the Status Quo but continued to carry out the sort of law-and-order functions they had performed in the al-Khanka terrace affair. Invariably, they only intervened in the event of a dispute between a major community and a minor community, not between major communities.

Despite controversy over its status in Jerusalem, according to international law, Israel was incontestably responsible for keeping the peace. There were several incidents at this time for the authorities to deal with. One was particularly difficult. On the morning of Easter Sunday, 1975, a fight between Copts and Armenians broke out at the back of the rotunda.

Historically, there have been numerous scuffles at this spot. According to the major communities, the Copts have rights of usage, but not ownership, of the chapel behind the Edicule and rooms opposite in the walled-off ambulatory. The Copts claim ownership—they have been there since 1573—and would like to expand into the narrow corridor separating the two areas. As the Coptic chapel is about the size of a broom closet, worshipers have to stand outside. But the corridor is common property, and under the Status Quo the Copts are not allowed to wash the floor, put rugs out, or block the passage of other communities, who have right of way at all times, even during Coptic services.

Two other factors added to Coptic resentment. One was the Deir al-Sultan affair, which left them deeply hurt. The other was their failure to be accepted as a major community in their own right. Ever since the subject of restoration of the Holy Sepulchre first came up in the 1930s, the Coptic Patriarchate had written numerous letters to the authorities demanding to participate in the project as co-owners. The big three, who considered the Copts, as in the Ottoman period, still to be the subordinates of the Armenians, rejected this pretension out of hand.

Brother Fabian Adkins, a Franciscan friar from Australia, provided a graphic eyewitness account of the brawl:

> It was my first Easter Sunday. I'd only been there about a month. I was the sacristan so I had to set up the tomb. It was four in the morning, the Armenians had finished their liturgy and were just going in the back of the tomb. Something happened, I wasn't sure what it was. But the screaming and the yelling, and I thought, "God what's going on here?" So I went and called our superior to come down. I said, "There's some big fight going on." The Coptics had put their lectionary two inches into the rotunda, and the Armenian bishop as he walked through, he kicked it. Of course, the Bible went flying one way and the lectionary went another way. And this started the fight. Anyhow, this superior of the Armenians who had kicked this lectionary, he raced up to the gallery and the Coptics were after him, they had pickaxes and they were screaming. It happened about 4:30 in the morning. At that time we had to call Father Rock, then they had to call Bishop Guregh, and the Greeks. They wouldn't let the door be opened at all. It was eight o'clock. David Chen had to come and Daniel Rossing came.

They were sorting this argument out. Well, the argument went on and they all had to go into the Armenian *diwana*. They all had coffee, then they all had a little cognac, and that was as good as gold.[28]

Israel was ready, if invited, to mediate—though not adjudicate—conflict. There is a crucial distinction between the two. In the case of adjudication or arbitration, the third party makes binding decisions. In the case of mediation, the third party provides advice that the disputants can accept or reject. Community mediation is a regular feature of policing in Israel, whether between quarrelsome neighbors or rival clans. Acting as mediator, the third party facilitates or assists adversaries in reconciling their differences. It tries to get them to understand each other's point of view, to communicate better, and to think through the consequences of their actions. It may also make constructive suggestions and bridging proposals.

There is a single instance of successful Israeli mediation in the Holy Sepulchre at this time. Possession of pillars 10, 11, and 12 was settled in an agreement that also stipulated that the wall behind the pillars was to be restored by the three major communities acting in common. Indeed, there was no way to replace the pillars without demolishing the wall. The Copts, however, claimed ownership of the wall. Since the Coptic Patriarchate had no role in the restoration and even its rooms were to be restored by others, complications were in store.

On July 11, 1977, the CTB began work on the columns. It had not gotten very far when the Coptic monks began throwing stones at the workers. If the Copts were not to be allowed to restore their own property, no one else would. At this point, the communities had no choice but to call in the Israeli police. Work could not continue in these circumstances, and the restoration of the dome was held up.[29]

The CTB had just completed its extensive survey of the wrought-iron skeleton of the rotunda dome. It discovered that the original structure had been manufactured to a remarkably high standard of accuracy a century earlier in St. Petersburg, and, contrary to initial impressions, was sufficiently well preserved to be retained, with modifications. Despite impurities, the iron was weldable, and the arches and trusses could safely bear the existing loadings. The communities were now eager to solicit bids on the project.[30]

Daniel Rossing and David Chen represented the government in the dispute between the Copts and the big three. They decided to shuttle back and forth between the parties, who would not meet directly, in order to find a solution. The point of departure was that the wall had to come down, and precedent indicated that the authorities should carry this out. There were three problems. First, how would the Copts save face? They insisted that since it was their wall, they pay for the repair. Second, how would they overcome the lack of enthusiasm of the Israeli DPW, which had no expertise in dealing with ancient buildings? Third, was the floor space that was released when the bulky old wall was replaced to be treated as part of the storeroom behind it, and therefore private, or part of the rotunda, and therefore common?

From the start, the Coptic archbishop, Dr. Anba Basilios, realized that there would have to be a compromise. He understood, though the threat was never made explicit, that the government could just go ahead and demolish the wall. Community experts were prepared to be flexible but would never admit Coptic claims to co-ownership. After several months of patient diplomacy, a consensus was eventually negotiated that would allow work on the pillars and wall to go ahead.

According to the terms of the understanding, the masonry wall would indeed be torn down. In its place would be a temporary partition of wooden boards, while scaffolding would support the arches under the galleries. The question of the new floor space was skirted. The DPW would carry out the job using the CTB's own skilled workers, to be paid for by the government.[31]

The success of this agreement lay in the fact that it gave the major communities what they needed without denying the claims of the Copts or causing them to lose face. Crucially, it specified the operation in detail but was unwritten, making it easier for both sides to swallow concessions. Since only a temporary wall was to be constructed, issues of principle could be settled later. In 1999, when everyone had forgotten about the original episode, the Israeli authorities, represented by Daniel Rossing's successor, Uri Mor, finally built the new wall.

The third function performed by the Israeli government to assist the restoration was the preservation of public safety. Following the precedent Britain had set during the Mandate, the authorities thought that they had the right and duty to intervene in the event of a potential danger to the public.

This might entail bringing in the DPW to make emergency repairs, installing firefighting equipment, or introducing measures of crowd control on a special occasion. It usually required, however, the communities' explicit or implicit consent. They might dislike government interference, and certainly would insist that nothing be done to jeopardize their rights, but they recognized that they had to be practical and that sometimes the government had to do what was necessary to prevent death or injury.

The public safety issue came to the fore in 1985 in connection with the Chapel of Joseph of Arimathea or St. Nicodemus. This chapel is located in the western apse of the rotunda, added to Constantine's round church by Patriarch Modestos in the seventh century. To the left of the chapel, a low entrance leads down steps into a cave containing ancient Jewish rock-cut tombs from the Second Temple period, traditionally associated with Joseph and Nicodemus.

Since at least the mid-nineteenth century, this chapel has been contested by the Armenian and Syrian Orthodox communities. While the Syrians claimed that it was wholly theirs, the Armenian position, accepted by the Greeks and Latins, was that it was their property, with the Syrians enjoying rights of usage only. After a number of violent quarrels over repairs, the Turkish government ruled that neither party could act without the consent of the other. In the event of disagreement, essential work would be carried out by the government at public expense. All subsequent rulers have accepted this arrangement.[32] Unfortunately, since the communities cannot agree, the chapel has been almost totally neglected, apart from minimal repairs, for the last 130 years.

Despite this, the Syrian Orthodox community conducts services here every Sunday. It is its last foothold in the church. Because of its historical associations, it is of interest to visitors. Apart from candles, the burial cave is unlit. In the 1930s there was a minor crisis when the Armenians unilaterally installed electricity.

In 1985, Daniel Rossing received a series of complaints from individuals who had fallen into a hole in the burial cave, not visible in the darkness. It was not particularly deep, but people were breaking arms and legs. Brother Adkins recalls that "one cardinal slipped in there and did his back in." Clearly, something had to be done about it.

After months of negotiations, the Armenian and Syrian communities grudgingly agreed just before Christmas to have the hole roped off, using posts on heavy bases. Because the posts were not permanently fixed in place, this was not considered a change in the Status Quo. However, it was not a satisfactory solution. In the dark, confined space, people kept stumbling into the hole.[33]

Rossing continued to shuttle between the parties. If the parties could not agree to fill in the hole, surely they would accept his installing a grate at government expense? His argument was "this cannot go on, people are breaking legs, you've got to reach an agreement." To which each community replied, "Yes, it really shouldn't happen, but this is ours and I'm not willing, I can't allow anybody else to go ahead and make repairs."[34] While this illustrated the intransigence of the disputants, it also reflected the extreme caution of the Israeli authorities.

The hole still exists and will remain there until the Armenians and Syrians agree on an overall solution to the chapel. But one day, with Easter and the ceremony of the Holy Fire looming, a DPW grate suddenly appeared over the hole. Neither Armenians nor Syrians made any protest.

———————

Besides his work in common areas and on the terraces, Father Coüasnon's contribution to the restoration of Latin areas during these years was as eventful as it was indispensable. Among other things, after 1967 he worked on the Chapel of Mary Magdalene, invested much time and effort in the decor of the Chapel of the Apparition, for which he designed the paving, and designed and executed the enlarged door and grilles for the Chapel of the Franks in 1972–73. He designed and installed the imperial door of the Latin gallery in 1975, and much else.

Yet he continued to be a thorn in the side of the Custody and refused to accept its right to decide by itself on the decoration of shrines that he considered the common property of all Christianity. The custos's insistence on lifting the sixteenth-century paving of the Chapel of Mary Magdalene distressed him deeply. Nor could he refrain from bitterly criticizing Rebaudi's latest sculptures. In May 1968, at the age of sixty-four, he scuffled with the Italian sculptor on the Parvis, grazing his arm and tearing his shirt.[35] After this, the volatile priest was excluded from the gallery where Rebaudi was working.

The Custody had no time for Father Coüasnon's aesthetic views, though Trouvelot and d'Halloy, the French consul general, shared them. Father Rock maintained that "an architect was an engineer, not an artist." Coüasnon, Rock insisted, had no business trying "to impose his point of view" when it came to matters of decoration. In Rock's defense, he was the only one of the three Status Quo experts to work closely with an architect. By 1969, Daniel and Guregh were more or less doing what they liked.[36]

In the spring of 1969, the Custody threatened to dismiss Coüasnon, though it is unclear where they expected to find another architect and conservationist of his stature who was prepared to work long hours without pay. To keep his job, he had to promise Trouvelot, who pleaded on his behalf and warned that he would work with no one else, to accept the instructions of the Custody without argument.[37] In August 1969, he was hospitalized for three weeks following a minor heart attack.

The French government awarded the Legion of Honor to Coüasnon in 1973. To the end, he defended uncompromisingly his vision of beauty and authenticity. His last project in the Latin section was supposed to be the repaving of the Franciscan galleries overlooking the rotunda. In February

1976, he and Trouvelot pressed the custos, Father Maurilio Sacchi, to conserve in situ the remains of ancient mosaics, paving the rest with white tesserae. These tiny stone cubes would be more beautiful, he argued, than the marble tiling proposed by the Custody, and only slightly more expensive.

But the Discretorium decided to go ahead with its original plan. "Sometimes," the custos explained, "the 'beautiful' and the 'practical' do not concur. What interests us most is the practical side, especially when the 'beautiful' is not absolutely necessary." While the restoration of the walls was the unique province of the CTB, everything concerning ornamentation and decoration was the exclusive affair of the Custody.[38]

In his reply, Coüasnon effectively bowed out. Someone else, he wrote the custos, would have to supervise the work in the gallery, while he focused on the common work of the cupola and the capitals in the rotunda. He rejected the division between restoration and decoration. "The mission of the architect," he wrote, "is an architectural mission where technical problems are not dissociated from strictly architectural problems that you deem to be those of ornamentation and decoration." How could one draw such a distinction in the case of the rotunda capitals or the imperial door into the tribune? Were these not questions of "architecture in its decorative role?" he asked.[39]

This was his last written pronouncement on the subject. On November 12, 1976, Father Charles Coüasnon died of a heart attack, aged seventy-two. Among his notes are the words of a French woman he had overheard outside the Holy Sepulchre: "It is the most beautiful church that I know."[40] Coüasnon's life's work was to help preserve that heritage.

| At Last, Light

ENGINEERS PLANNING TO RECONSTRUCT the great dome over the rotunda were surprised to learn that one of the expectations of the Latin architect, Yves-Marie Froideveaux, Jean Trouvelot's successor, was that it be able to withstand the impact of a mortar shell.[1] In fact, the envisaged $2 million dome would be pierced but not destroyed by a direct hit and would be strongly resistant to earthquake and fire. It would carefully retain the handcrafted texture of the 1869 dome, to avoid the sharp contours of a machine-made structure, thereby fitting in with the natural stone surroundings of the Old City.

In the face of competition from American, French, Italian, and Greek firms, the British structural engineers Campbell, Reith, & Partners had won a 1978 tender to carry out the project. The notice called for "an internal and external shell, as light as possible, over the existing steel dome trusses" and "external roofing of lead, copper, aluminum or other light material of timeless and aesthetic value."[2]

Technically, these were straightforward requirements. What fascinated senior partner Ian Reith and Stuart Goodchild, the associate in charge, was the knowledge that they had been given the unique task of restoring the dome over the best known shrine in the Christian world. They were to preserve a cherished feature of the skyline of the Old City of Jerusalem.

The cupola they were asked to reconstruct on the existing iron semiarches, they learned, was the third configuration of dome to cover the Anastasis. From 335 to 614, when a Persian army burned the church, there had been a low, Pantheon-type dome; from 638 until 1863, a timber cone open to the sky; and from 1869 the current hemisphere, rebuilt in wrought iron in 1863–69 by Charles Mauss. It was this structure that was to be repaired and strengthened.[3]

This time, a fail-safe design would ensure its long-term resilience, combining lightness with rigidity. Steel connections would link the thin concrete outer shell to the repaired wrought-iron arches. Both shell and arches would be capable of supporting the total loading independently of each other. Even if future corrosion weakened the iron frame, the overall structure would not be seriously affected. With a light plaster inner shell, the restored dome would be 100 tons lighter than the Russian original but still able to take whatever form of decoration the communities decided on—mosaic, fresco, or painting.

Because of the difficulty of finding local craftsmen of sufficient skill and experience, almost all those who worked on the project—steelworkers, concrete sprayers, plasterers, welders, and lead workers— came from Britain. It was to be an unforgettable experience for all concerned—religious, cultural, culinary, and professional.

The project from beginning to end took about eighteen months, while in the church worship continued as usual. Preliminary demolition of the rotten outer shell in July 1979 provoked a fresh protest from Sheikh al-Alami of the adjacent al-Khanka Mosque. Fearing fresh litigation and delays, with possible heavy financial losses, the Greek and Latin communities agreed to pay him 40,000 Israeli pounds altogether (about $4,000 at today's values). They also agreed that an engineer would conduct an investigation to determine exactly what damages had already been caused to his dwelling.[4]

There were surprises for visitors to the church before Christmas 1979, when debris fell off the edge of the scaffold work deck. Otherwise, the project proceeded uneventfully on schedule. Repair and consolidation of the iron frame took place in the chill of winter. This involved grit blasting to remove corrosion, with associated dust and noise, replacement of buckled plates and trusses, and painting with three coats of protective red lead. There was delight and astonishment for the team when snow fell in February but less pleasure in the oppressively hot late spring as the *hamsin* wind blew in from the eastern deserts.

During the long summer months without rain, with the surrounding hills visible from the terraces parched and brown, the outer concrete shell was constructed—concrete of crushed local limestone and Ashkelon sand sprayed in two layers on a metal mesh framework. The final shape was achieved using hand trowel and a good eye, and the sheet lead finally applied. With the fall, and the hoped-for relief of approaching rain, came the installation of the light plaster ceiling.

By December 1980, all work was done on the contract, and the beautiful gray dome regained its ancient place at the heart of the Old City. The scaffolding was left in place for the decoration of the ceiling, but it could not be long before the massive platform, which totally obscured the dome, came down. The feeling was, as Father Sacchi noted with satisfaction, that after more than twenty years the project was about to be completed. Just a few tasks remained.[5]

On August 21, 1981, the forum of the Status Quo met to consider the final stages of the restoration of the mother church. The debate was wide ranging. Different views were expressed on whether or not to open the windows in the drum. The tomb was discussed at length. The old bone of contention, repair versus restoration, came up. Should the rock be uncovered? Should the bulbous cupola atop the Edicule be removed? They wondered how access to the tomb could be improved. Should the door of the Edicule be enlarged? Might an exit be constructed? Expert studies were commissioned on various issues: lighting in the church, the repair of the paving, the Edicule.

The expert architects had first broached the question of the decoration of the ceiling of the great dome in February 1981, with three options mentioned: plain plaster, a mosaic, or a fresco. There were already sharply different views on what design would be most fitting for the vast space over the very centerpiece of the edifice, the place of the Resurrection. At the August meeting, the parties agreed to avoid inscriptions or emblems peculiar to a particular tradition so as not to offend each other's sensitivities. Otherwise, nothing positive was concluded.

Now, with the end in sight, work on the Anastasis ground to a halt. The communities deadlocked on the question of decoration. In the meantime, nothing was done about the lighting, the Edicule, or the paving, while the scaffolding loomed oppressively overhead. This meant that though the surrounding pillars and masonry had been reconstructed and the dome repaired, the rotunda remained shrouded in gloom, and the corseted Edicule, with its dilapidated surrounding court, was left untouched. After two decades of cooperation and achievement, the relationship between the communities reverted to the wary rivalry that had existed in the bad old days. What had gone wrong?

Clearly, the subject of decoration was inherently difficult, touching on acutely felt issues of religious symbolism and raising the ultimate question of the identity and ownership of the edifice, whether Greek or Latin. Father Coüasnon had not been replaced after his death, so there was no longer anyone on the spot to work for the common good. Nor was there a Hassan Bey figure, able to shepherd the parties toward agreement, if necessary imposing a decision. Israel's role, by choice and circumstances, was limited.

But the main problem was that the project had lost its motor. The leading individual in the entire project, the "patriarch open to reason," His Beatitude Kyr Benedictos I, had departed the scene. On December 10, 1980, at the very moment that the great dome was completed, this formidable ecclesiastic had died at the age of eighty-eight, after standing at the helm of his church for almost twenty-four years. He had ruled his monks firmly, exercised full control over the finances of the patriarchate, and dedicated himself to the repair of the Church of the Resurrection.[6]

His successor was Damianos Karivalis, crowned Patriarch Diodoros I in February 1981. From 1962 Diodoros had served as patriarchal vicar in Amman, Jordan, where he built and invested extensively. After his enthronement, his reign was marked by controversy. First he was suspected by the Israelis of being pro-Arab; then he was accused by the Arabs of land sales to Israel. He fiercely defended Greek control of the patriarchate in the face of the longstanding Arab claim for a greater say in the running of the church. He clashed with other Orthodox leaders over an attempt to extend Jerusalem's jurisdiction to local churches in Australia and North America. Throughout, he resisted overtures to engage in an ecumenical dialogue with Roman Catholics, arguing that it would simply encourage proselytization.[7]

He was seriously embarrassed in 1987 when Israeli criminal investigation department officers searched the limousine bringing him back to Israel from Jordan, following an intelligence tipoff. Four and a half kilograms of heroin and nearly three kilograms of gold bars were reportedly found concealed throughout his vehicle. His driver was taken in for questioning. After a six-week news blackout, the authorities publicly cleared the patriarch of any involvement in the smuggling.[8] No further news on the episode was subsequently released.

Diodoros was obese and diabetic, and his health steadily declined. He suffered acutely from pain in his legs and needed to live in comfort, enjoying a spacious home on the Greek coast where he could recuperate. He came to rely increasingly on the secretary to the patriarchate, Archbishop Timotheos, an accomplished administrator and linguist. Bishop Daniel, whom Benedictos had made superior of the Holy Sepulchre, lost influence.

Patriarch Diodoros continued work on Greek areas of the church, including the Katholikon, though an expensive new marble iconostasis was abandoned in the face of domestic criticism.

For most of his reign, he also lacked the determination or flexibility to hammer out the sort of timely and pragmatic agreements with Latins and Armenians that had marked Benedictos's rule.

<hr>

During the long years of contention, the communities had been able to give free rein to their very different tastes and preferences in the embellishment of private areas. These differences were the immediate reason for the dispute over the ceiling. Striking aesthetic variety was indicative of broad theological and philosophical diversity.

Church art creates the space for religious experience. It provides an apt setting for worship, instills awe, and evokes faith—to help believers partake in the mystery of the life, death, and resurrection of Jesus Christ. To do this, it must succeed in depicting the central motifs of Christianity, including, importantly, scenes from Jesus' life, in a moving way that taps deep-seated emotion. Ideas that are hard to convey in words can be portrayed through art with extraordinary economy and effect.

Over centuries, certain images and themes have acquired profound significance and resonance for individual churches. People of faith are naturally deeply attached to their own particular traditions of representation. An attack on a cherished symbol is like an attack on the faith itself.

Even flags and banners have significance. Much Greek Orthodox property in Jerusalem, including the bell tower in the Parvis of the Holy Sepulchre, the patriarchate, the Monastery of the Cross, and so on, flies both the blue and white Greek national flag and the church's own red cross of St. George. Only the Notre Dame pontifical hospice, owned by the Vatican, flies the yellow papal banner bearing St. Peter's crossed keys.

Given the division of the Church of the Resurrection that is enshrined in the Status Quo, the only practical rule of decoration is that each community is to have total stylistic freedom in its own section. One might object to the aesthetic diversity this entails, but it reflects a realistic live-and-let-live ethic. But whose design should prevail in common areas?

Permission for structural innovations in private areas during the restoration had to be specially requested and tended to be granted on the basis of reciprocity. In the Chapel of the Three Marys, for instance, the Armenians wanted to replace the old iron frame shrine commemorating the fainting of Mary with a higher marble baldequin. In return, the Greeks requested and received a new marble plaque with a Greek Gospel text next to the main entrance to the Chapel of Adam.[9]

All three communities invested great care and attention in their private sections. Each possessed its own unique character. Arguably, each reflected a particular agenda and response to the challenges of modernity.

The prevailing tone chosen for Greek Orthodox areas was neo-Byzantine, a highly ornamental style harking back to the characteristic forms of Byzantine art. It delights in glowing icons and mosaics portraying scenes from the life of Christ in figurative style. Brightness and luminosity are of the essence, so gold, silver, and vivid colors are featured. "If we were free to conduct the repairs ourselves," Patriarch Diodoros told a journalist in 1983, "we would build these shrines with gold."[10]

Intricate designs decorate floors, stone, and ironwork. The pavement of the Katholikon features a copy of the excavated twelfth-century floor, its geometrical pattern of circles within herringbone and checkered borders recreated in white, red, and black marble imported from Greece. Woodwork, including doors, picture frames, and furniture, is embellished with fine carving, sometimes inlaid with precious stones and metals. Plush lamps and candelabra, brass and silver, brilliantly ornament marble altars that stand on miniature neoclassical columns.

Ideas central to Orthodox belief underpin this art. Icons and images of saints reflect the celestial glory, exemplify the doctrine of the Incarnation, and manifest humankind's spiritual power to redeem creation. They are an aid to devotion and help inculcate church teaching. The luminosity of this art expresses the mystic presence in the world of the divine light that heralded the transfiguration of the risen Christ.[11] For the Greeks, the church is a joyful place. It is no accident that they call it the Anastasis, or Resurrection, and not the Holy Sepulchre.

Greek Orthodox taste is conservative, reflecting an unchanging liturgy, a lack of interest in theological innovation, and a sense of continuity with an illustrious past. At the same time, antique features of the Katholikon were disposed of unsentimentally. For instance, Patriarch Benedictos tore down the well-preserved seventeenth-century iconostasis, beautifully carved and gilded, and inlaid with exquisite icons (one remarkable surviving icon can be viewed in the entry hall of the new Greek patriarchal palace) and ordered a massive new stone and marble structure from Greece. A suggestion by the experts that a lower construction would better preserve the spatial harmony of the Katholikon was brushed aside.[12] When Diodoros was elected patriarch in February 1981, he declared that he was going to stop the work as unworthy of the Anastasis.[13] He then, despite some criticism, ordered yet another rococo white marble structure.

In emphatic contrast, a sober, functional décor, avoiding bright colors, in the modern idiom, was chosen for the refurbished Latin chapels. The Chapel of Mary Magdalene is paved in marble with black and white concentric circles and squares. The altar, the work of the French sculptor Philippe Kaeppelin, is fronted with crossed arms, symbol of the Franciscans, in embossed copper. Trouvelot was "a bit perplexed" by the altar and thought the arms "arid and angular."[14] Over the altar hangs another angular, embossed representation of the "noli me tangere" (touch me not) encounter between the risen Christ and Mary Magdalene.

The adjacent Chapel of the Apparition also aims for a simple, modern decor, though the floor is a warmer, interlocking mosaic carpet in shades of gray, ochre, red, and black. Kaeppelin's altar is unadorned white marble on a cross-shaped pedestal. It is backed by an apse faced with royal blue glass tesserae speckled with gold bearing a cross-shaped tabernacle of uneven gunmetal strips. On the wall hangs another embossed abstract of the apparition of Jesus to his mother, and on the lateral wall a line of austere statuettes of the Stations of the Cross. On the celebrant's left, the Column of the Flagellation is displayed in a wall niche. Designed by Trouvelot to achieve a medieval effect, it has a bronze base resting on four small spheres. Weathered, basin-like copper lamps surround the upper walls.

The decor reflects the more contemporary style of church decoration that appeared following Vatican II and Pope Paul VI's December 1963 call for churches to be adorned with "the art of our own days." Modern art was a backdrop for liturgical innovation, reflecting a wish to open up the Catholic Church and make the Gospels more relevant. The juxtaposition of Latin and Greek styles within a few yards of each other strikingly illustrates the two churches' diametrically opposing sensibilities and responses to modernity.

The Armenian restoration was more explicitly didactic. "One of our specific aims," Bishop Guregh explained in 1975, "has been to Armenize our section of the Basilica. The Armenian Church has a strong sense of national identity as well as religious—the same dual awareness that the Jews have."[15] Bishop Guregh was the only one of the three fathers to possess a very clear conception of what he wanted to achieve in his church's section, which was to educate Armenian visitors about their heritage. He would do this by illustrating through the medium of art the history of the Armenians as a Christian nation from the adoption of Christianity as the state religion in 301 to the present day.

Replicas of great works of Armenian art, original items, and artifacts brought from Armenia are exhibited in a celebration of Armenian civilization through the ages. It all evokes the beginnings of Armenian Christianity, the splendor and tragedy of Armenian history, past kingdoms, periods of independence and then subjugation, lands lost to Turkey or Russia, churches destroyed, communities annihilated.

Two plaques in the Armenian galleries inform the visitor that renovation of the Armenian section began in 1962 and ended in 1973, and was consecrated at an opening ceremony attended by Patriarch Derderian and Patriarch Shnork of Istanbul in 1975. Areas renovated included the rectory office, the dining room, the Second Golgotha, and the Chapel of the Three Marys. Six canopied altars were constructed. Embellishment continued through 1981.

The visitor to the Chapel of the Three Marys, which is also the vestibule of the Armenian section, is greeted by a wall-length mosaic of the Crucifixion in red, blue, and gold, inspired by an illumination in a thirteenth-century Armenian manuscript. A marble baldequin in the shape of the *veghar*, the priestly hood that evokes the peak of Mount Ararat, commemorates the spot where Mary, the mother of Jesus, fainted. It replaces a metal structure previously on the spot and generated some controversy at the time. Armenian processions start out from here, and the Gospel recalling the Crucifixion is read aloud.

Historical references are ubiquitous. In the Chapel of St. Helena, a new floor mosaic, dedicated to the martyrs of the Armenian holocaust, shows the major churches built in Armenia in the fourth and fifth centuries. Behind the patriarchal chair in the rectory office (also used as a divan or reception room and chapel) is a striking wall mosaic. Its lower section depicts the great historical monuments and architectural masterpieces associated with the major sites of ancient Armenia—Etchmiadzin, Ani, Akhtamar, Hripsime, Zvartnots. Its upper section pictures the cityscape of the new Armenia—skyscrapers, public monuments and buildings, parks.

Stained-glass windows in the office portray great Armenian theologians and men of letters—St. Sahag, Naregatzi, and Datevatzi. The mosaic before the altar is a copy of a sixth-century original found on the Mount of Olives and depicts in finely observed detail an abundance of living creatures and produce. A Madonna and Child is a copy of a tenth-century sculpture from a church on an island in Lake Van.

Bold colors are used wherever possible. "The Armenians are essentially a rural people," Bishop Guregh explained, "with a natural affinity for the countryside and for sharp primary colors."[16] There is meticulous attention to detail: wrought-iron grilles forming the balustrade of the stairway feature the peacock, an ancient symbol of eternal life. Pilgrim crosses dated 1721 are preserved at the top of the stairs.

The gallery known as the Second Golgotha, mostly Crusader but with elements from the period of Constantine Monomachus, now contains scenes from Armenian history, including the Battle of St. Vartan against Persia in 451. An inset shows King Thridates, the pagan king who first slaughtered Christians but then released St. Gregory from prison and converted his people to Christianity. Eighteenth-century *khatchkar* stone crosses are set into the walls. The canopied main altar is in the shape of a traditional Armenian church. Nearby panels immortalize Patriarch Derderian and the Catholicos of Etchmiadzin, Vasken I, seated on patriarchal thrones like medieval monarchs. Plaques throughout commemorate donors.

Much of the sculpture is the work of the local craftsman Hrair Boyajian. Besides copies of Armenian sculpture of powerful simplicity, he also carved lace-like designs in wood and stone, skillfully interweaving natural and geometric forms. Among his other work are delicately worked oak doors and paneling, and carved monastic stone seats.

———

Somehow, amid this aesthetic and cultural diversity, the three communities had to find common ground if they were to decorate the great dome, dismantle the scaffolding in the rotunda, and finish the restoration. As with all work in common areas, no community could impose its preference on the others. Any design would have to reflect a consensus arrived at by discussion.

From the outset of the talks in 1981, the Greeks effectively set the agenda, demanding a golden mosaic. They had an overall plan for the basilica, envisaging great neo-Byzantine mosaics embellishing its public spaces—the ceilings of both domes, the wall behind the Stone of Unction facing the entrance, and the Triumphal Arch. "We wanted to revive the old magnificence of the church," Metropolitan Daniel later explained; "mosaics are traditional here."[17]

He was referring to the golden age of Byzantium in the Holy Land, from the fourth to the seventh centuries, not to the period of the Crusader kingdoms. But he was ready to be flexible about the details. At a meeting on February 18, 1983, he presented four possible designs in the neo-Byzantine style worked in gold on a dark blue background with decorative gold elements: a Christ Pantocrator surrounded by four winged creatures; a paschal lamb; and two variants of a cross.[18]

The new principal Latin architect (following Froideveaux's death), Yves Boiret, strongly opposed a mosaic, agreeing with the custos's view that the ceiling should be left plain. In his opinion, a mosaic would be too heavy for the light inner dome to bear.[19] Father Rock agreed, adding that a mosaic might be dislodged by a sonic boom. Father Prodormo, a Franciscan and a trained architect, joining them, added that neo-Byzantine decor would disrupt the aesthetic harmony of the Crusader church.[20]

Behind the technical and aesthetic arguments lay a political objection to a Greek design. Not all Franciscans opposed the idea of a mosaic. After all, there were mosaics throughout the original Crusader edifice, one of which—a powerful Christ Pantocrator—survives on the ceiling of the Latin chapel on Calvary. Ravenna Cathedral has fine Byzantine mosaics. But in Father Rock's view, choice of a golden mosaic would unacceptably imply that the Anastasis was a Byzantine church.

Bishop Guregh also opposed a mosaic, favoring a fresco. His own chief architect, Diran Voskertchian, who had succeeded Utudjian in 1975, concurred that a mosaic was structurally impossible and artistically inappropriate. "A golden skull-cap," he argued, would be out of place in an essentially "plain and simple" building.[21]

It was decided to consult two laboratories separately to determine if a mosaic was technically feasible. The results were contradictory. The Paris laboratory of France's historical monuments section advised that there would be a problem with a mosaic; the Greek laboratory in Thessalonika drew the opposite conclusion. Boiret ruled out a mosaic under any circumstances and threatened to resign if the proposal was approved—effectively killing off the mosaic once and for all.

A protracted suspension of talks followed the rejection of the Greek proposals. John Barnes, writing for *U.S. News and World Report* at Easter 1985, deplored the "air of shabby decay" the church wore. He concluded that the communities were probably never going to agree on a decoration for the rotunda ceiling.[22]

Regular meetings on the dome resumed after Easter but without any decision being made. Discussion also continued inconclusively of other items on the agenda, such as lighting, sewage, and the flooring. In November 1985, the suggestion was made of restoring the sculpted panels to the lintels over the entrance, but nothing came of that either. Once momentum had been lost, it became difficult to make progress on anything.

By now the Greeks had commissioned a mosaic for the Katholikon dome, and the feeling in the Armenian community was that they were deliberately "treading water" in the rotunda, ultimately determined to install matching mosaics in the two domes. Meanwhile, they were in no hurry.[23]

In April 1987, the forum of the Status Quo decided that each community would commission an artist to prepare a neutral design "drawn from no one tradition." The three experts would make their recommendations, but the final choice would be up to their leaders.[24]

Asked if it was true that the Greek patriarchate had given up on a mosaic and agreed to a painting, Bishop Daniel replied: "Well yes, but we still believe we should have a mosaic. We've got time to wait. Fifty years, that's nothing. We'll put the mosaic up eventually, we have the patience."[25]

In February 1988, the three wise men and their architects reported the results of their search but failed to concur on a single design. The Latin artist had drawn a celestial vision of angels, the Greek a cross with vines on an interlace background, and the Armenian an abstract pattern of a sunburst in gold, ochre, turquoise, and white. The architects were then asked to choose a specialist in sacred art to prepare a design incorporating elements present in all three drawings.

When they met in Athens in March 1989, the architects had not located such an artist but had the bright idea of extracting the common features of the drawings already commissioned to build up a composite design. They soon came up with a sketch that looked acceptable to all sides, featuring gold rays and stars against a turquoise background edged with angels or cherubs.[26]

Boiret realized that the compromise was artistically banal, art by committee, but saw it as possessing a great virtue: it set aside the differences dividing the communities and focused on what united them. In this sense it created a link, a witness to their common Christian heritage. At the time he viewed it as a "joyful and comforting consummation."

The communities accepted the compromise, a breakthrough after ten years. However, it proved extraordinarily difficult to find an artist able to work up the rough sketch into a detailed blueprint that would be generally acceptable. No artist of the first rank would execute a design that others had already conceived. Nor did an artist of completely neutral nationality and religion, other than a Japanese Buddhist, come to mind. Perhaps a team of three should be chosen? In the end it was decided to approach design consultants, first from Germany, then France, but neither firm was able to produce a design that met with general approval.[27]

There was always something wrong—the pattern of the rays, the amount of gold, the shape of the angels. On September 17, 1991, the three fathers, the chief architects, and their artists went up into the dome to look at the latest drawings. On this occasion, Greeks and Armenians disagreed on the appearance of the angels, now six-winged seraphim, represented differently in the two traditions. A few days later the seraphim were eliminated altogether. As Bishop Guregh put it, they "would look either like Orthodox, Armenian or Latin."[28]

In May 1992, Latins and Armenians agreed on a design of rays on an ochre background, but the Greeks objected to the veins within the rays. They proposed instead golden rays without veining. The others retorted that in that case, the dome should simply be left as it was, without decoration. Before Christmas, the communities were on the verge of abandoning the negotiation. It might be best just to clean the dome and leave the decoration for a better time.[29]

At a final meeting in May 1993, Father Rock proposed plain ochre without any pattern, which Bishop Daniel and Bishop Guregh rejected as not a "decoration." Having given up more than they had ever intended, first a mosaic, then a figurative decoration, the Greeks were not about to concede a touch of color, especially gold. Deadlock descended again.

There is no way of knowing how long these sterile debates might have continued. But with growing interest from the international press and disappointment that "the rusting web of poles"[30] was still in place, the outside world now intruded in the form of UNESCO.

Despite the 1989 compromise, Boiret had become increasingly concerned about what he considered unacceptable and unilateral Greek activities in the edifice. In September 1989, he had flown in from Paris to discover to his dismay that the Greeks were, without notice, replacing the southern wall at the crossing behind the Stone of Unction. They had already demolished the temporary partition and had pickaxed deep grooves into the twelfth-century walls and flooring, and they were pouring cement for an antiseismic wall in reinforced concrete. At a stormy meeting, Boiret disputed the Greek claim that they were simply acting within their Status Quo rights. The protests of both Boiret and Voskertchian were ignored, and the wall was hurriedly completed and would become the surface for a controversial mosaic greeting visitors on their entry into the mother church.

In September 1991, Boiret was upset by what he perceived as another unilateral act by the Greeks—the erection of scaffolding under the Katholikon dome in preparation for the installation of a new mosaic. He was appalled by the prospect of the Crusader walls disappearing under a covering of garish neo-Byzantine mosaics, alien to the Romanesque original and irremediably compromising the authenticity of the Holy Sepulchre.[31]

Boiret and Voskertchian concluded that the situation had become totally unacceptable. Boiret therefore decided to ask UNESCO to intervene in the matter. Since 1974, Professor Raymond Lemaire, an eminent Belgian architect and one of the original signatories of the Venice Charter, had been coming to Jerusalem each year on behalf of UNESCO to report on Israel's activities in and around Arab East Jerusalem. A devout Catholic, he had followed, with mounting distress, deviations from sound conservation practice in the restoration of the Holy Sepulchre.

In August 1992, the director general of UNESCO, Federico Mayor, sent out a delegation of international experts with Professor Lemaire to study the question. In his appearance before the team, Boiret suggested that instead of thinking in terms of "decoration," architects should consider how best to create the right conditions for the outpouring of emotion and veneration felt by the thousands of pilgrims who visited the site each year. This required solving such problems as the difficulty of access to the church, the mediocre organization of space, and the drawbacks of the present Edicule.[32]

The UNESCO report, which the director general personally presented to church leaders in March 1993, was a devastating critique, charging that the restoration presented "exceptionally serious problems." Mildly critical of the Latins and Armenians, it castigated the south transept wall. One meter (39 inches) thick and 10 meters (39 feet) high, it was said to "destroy the spatial configuration of the monument and misrepresent its historical character," completely blocking off the crossing. Members of the team doubted the aesthetic value of the large neo-Byzantine mosaic of the entombment of Christ decorating the wall—and confronting visitors as they approached the Stone of Unction.

Indeed, the UNESCO team was generally unhappy about the mosaic decor envisaged for the basilica and expressed concern about the mosaic planned for the Katholikon dome. They warned that the wellsprings of neo-Byzantine art had dried up and deplored "the poverty, not to say the shallowness, of the artistic inspiration and talent that characterize the works" in the Holy Sepulchre. With clear reference to the dome of the rotunda, they recommended a provisional halt to any further work.[33]

During his March 1993 visit to Jerusalem, Federico Mayor cautioned church leaders that if they failed to act, they risked the removal of the Old City of Jerusalem from the list of World Heritage sites, a penalty with moral but without material consequences. However, this threat had been used effectively to dissuade the Egyptian government from building a highway near the pyramids.

Mayor proposed that UNESCO conduct a comprehensive archaeological survey, but the communities told him, in so many words, to mind his own business. As "the sole and exclusive competent authorities," they resolved not to allow any international body to intervene in their affairs.[34] And UNESCO now discovered that it was impossible, in the face of Jordanian objections, to impose the sanction of declassification.

This disregard for international opinion was too much for Boiret and Voskertchian to swallow. At a meeting of the three communities on October 13, 1993, they fully endorsed UNESCO's criticisms and joined its call to suspend decoration of the great dome, awaiting proper archeological research. Meanwhile, they proposed that priority should be given to three urgent projects in common areas: repaving, overhaul of the "rotten and dangerous" electrical installations, and repair of the Edicule.

No consensus could be reached on the adoption of any of these recommendations, which were jointly proposed by the Latin and Armenian communities but vetoed by the Greeks. After the meeting, Boiret and Voskertchian wrote a scathing critique in which they condemned the Greeks' "illicit" actions and lamented the "incontestable threat" to one of the holiest sites in the world.[35]

―――――

Many observers followed these disturbing events with growing dismay. However, the straitjacket the Status Quo imposed was nothing new, and the Greeks would not be swayed by criticism of what they chose to do in their own areas, particularly when it came from avowed Catholics such as Raymond Lemaire, Federico Mayor, and Yves Boiret.

Of particular concern, though, was the fact that the restoration was in limbo with the millennium approaching, and with it a planned pilgrimage to the Holy Land by Pope John Paul II. The pilgrimage was to be one of the crowning events of an illustrious pontificate. It was inconceivable that thirty-six years after Pope Paul VI's own historic visit to Jerusalem his successor would encounter the sight of rusty scaffolding obscuring the dome over Christ's tomb, a graphic demonstration of the disappointing progress of ecumenism.

If the unsightly construction was to come down, the parties had to reach an agreement on the decoration of the dome. The question was how, given that negotiations were deadlocked. Though the three experts had signed an agreement in July 1991 on the parameters of a design, they were as far away as ever from translating them into a definitive blueprint. After so long on the job, there was a suspicion that the old warriors had lost their touch.

The solution to the conundrum came through Monsignor Robert Stern, the head of the Catholic Near East Welfare Association, a New York–based organization that works in tandem with the Pontifical Mission for Palestine (a body set up in 1949 to assist the Palestine refugees) from an office around the corner from the New Gate; it funds humanitarian activities among local Palestinian Catholics.

On one of Stern's regular visits to Jerusalem, George Doty, a prominent Catholic philanthropist from Rye, New York, accompanied him. A retired partner of the investment banking firm Goldman Sachs, Doty had funded many worthy causes, including a contribution in 1990 of $1.5 million toward the restoration of the dome of the church at Fordham University, the Jesuit University of New York.[36]

Doty was a longtime knight of the Equestrian Order of the Holy Sepulchre and had visited the edifice as a pilgrim with his wife, Marie, many times over the years. He was the ideal private donor to fund the decoration of the rotunda dome and rid it of its thicket of iron and wood. "We saw the need," his wife later said. "It's the birthplace of Christianity. It's more fitting that it not be under scaffolding."[37] Doty offered to give whatever help was needed.

It is unclear whether the initiative originated with Doty, Stern, or the Vatican. What is clear is that Doty's offer held out the prospect of solving everyone's problem. In normal circumstances, it would have been unthinkable for a Catholic institution to fund a common project in the Holy Sepulchre single-handedly, given the basic rule of the Status Quo: he who pays owns. But these were not normal circumstances, as the UNESCO report had deeply embarrassed the Greek Orthodox Patriarchate. Dismissive of the report in public, the ailing Patriarch Diodoros and Archbishop Timotheos, the vigorous and pragmatic secretary of the patriarchate, were eager for a way out of this public relations disaster.

On October 15, 1993, at the height of the UNESCO row, Stern, armed with Doty's pledge, met with the two Greek ecclesiastics to present his proposal. A benefactor who wished to assist the completion of the interior decoration of the rotunda dome was prepared to make a substantial donation to the custodians of the Basilica to fund a jointly agreed plan.

This donor, he explained, had chosen the Pontifical Mission because he trusted it "to see to it, quietly and effectively, that the means are placed in your hands and in those of the two other custodians of the Basilica. While observing all of the proper protocols and obligations imposed by tradition and the Status Quo, he clearly intends to help you enhance this mother church of Christendom." Discretion was of the essence, and his identity would be kept confidential to avoid opposition from the Confraternity of the Holy Sepulchre.[38] (This proved a vain hope.)

Patriarch Diodoros grasped at Stern's proposal as a heaven-sent way out of his difficulties. He immediately expressed his complete support for the project. Patriarch Manoogian proved equally supportive, while pointing out that the greatest challenge would be to arrive at an artistic consensus satisfactory to everyone. He suggested that perhaps the time was ripe for a meeting of the three principals in person in order to establish appropriate guidelines for the architects and artists.

With a meeting of minds at the highest level, Stern's local representative, Brother Donald Mansir, now took over. Bypassing the three fathers, the big three agreed that the Pontifical Mission would look for a neutral artist and assume responsibility for implementing the project.[39] They knew it would be difficult to find a design that did not favor any one church but at least concurred on the broad outlines, rays of the sun and stars.[40]

For his choice of artist, Brother Donald turned to an acquaintance from Fresno, California. Ara "Corky" Normart was a spare-time abstract artist who headed an advertising firm. Baptized into the Armenian Orthodox Church, he was a practicing Episcopalian. His appeal lay in his business background, which would help him handle predictably tough talks with church leaders.

"He's very creative, he's imaginative and he can market things well," Mansir said later. "It was very important that we be able to sell something to three different cultures. He's humble in the very best sense; he wouldn't let ego get in the way of the project." He added, "Artistically this was going to be fairly limited."[41]

Astounded by his commission, Normart prepared forty computer-generated drawings over a five-week period.

On August 17, 1994, the advertising man from California together with Catholic officials from New York made a presentation to church leaders in Jerusalem assisted by a plastic scale model consisting of an illuminated, upturned bowl sitting on a framework 6 feet high. Each leader in turn sat under it and looked up, as if he were actually in the rotunda.

Normart's proposed design consisted of a wreath of golden "tongues" encircling the dome's lantern, meant to represent an explosion of light, a metaphor for the Resurrection. Twelve rays would represent the apostles, each tipped with three points to suggest the Trinity, against a background of mother-of-pearl, symbolizing the luminous cloud that led the Israelites in the desert. The decorations would be in three dimensions and artificially illuminated.

One by one, the prelates approved the design and agreed that an engineering firm should be hired to prepare a plan for its implementation.[42]

Reaction to the scheme was mixed. Bishop Guregh was distraught, and wrote a long missive to Patriarch Manoogian claiming that the irregular decision-making procedure violated the Status Quo. Neither the three fathers nor their architects had been consulted, and Boiret submitted his resignation to the

Custody. He thought the design "completely ridiculous, senseless, not beautiful, overdone."[43] It was a slap in the face for UNESCO. George Hintlian complained that the design would inspire nobody. Bishop Daniel, along with other members of the Greek brotherhood, was gravely disappointed that there was to be no mosaic.[44] There were murmurings, too, of a capitulation to the Latins.

"It is not the best that we could have done," Archbishop Timotheos admitted. "Church leaders have bypassed traditional procedures and given up some of their authority to accomplish a task that would otherwise have taken forever. It was a way out of the deadlock."[45]

The design is not beautiful but it is inoffensive, a compromise that served its purpose, the dismantling of the scaffolding in time for the millennium. After all, the alternative was not a work of art to compete with Michelangelo's Sistine Chapel ceiling, but continuing stalemate.

The British engineering firm of Campbell Reith Hill, which had constructed the dome in 1980, submitted a proposal for installing the decoration. Presenting the plan on November 9, 1995, Stuart Goodchild, the supervising partner—who had worked on the original project—was able to lay to rest concerns about the ability of the inner dome to carry the weight of decorations. The thin plaster shell, he explained, was simply a false ceiling suspended from the trusses. An additional supporting structure attached to the iron frame had always been intended. Thus one of the main Latin and Armenian objections to a mosaic had been based on a misunderstanding.[46]

The signing of the contract paved the way for planning the millennium celebrations. Church leaders, in a meeting just before Christmas 1995, agreed to set up an interdenominational committee. Such diplomacy at the summit had again become possible in the revived atmosphere of ecumenism. "We shall not spare any effort," their published statement read, "to make the celebration of this great event in the history of salvation a means for ushering in the light of peace."[47]

Construction of the decorations went ahead, despite last-minute nerves on the part of the Greek patriarchate, which was under pressure to back out. This time, the overall project manager was Father Dennis Madden, the new director of the Pontifical Mission, and not the CTB, which had been moribund since the installation of the rotunda dome in 1980. He paid the bills and coordinated the range of specialists to be involved in a project that drew on technology that had never been seen before in the sixteen centuries of the edifice.[48] Corky Normart had designed an ultramodern construction for the new millennium.

An air filtration system was installed between the dome's inner and outer shells to handle the soot and smoke at the Holy Fire ceremony from thousands of candles. Sanded lime plaster, able to cope with Jerusalem's temperature changes, was applied to the vast dome.

The rays were made from glass-reinforced plaster mounted on hidden stainless steel supports attached to the wrought-iron trusses. Once in place, they were gilded with sheets of twenty-three-and-a-half-carat gold. They were lit up from behind and below, while additional fiber optic light rods illuminated the inner decorative ring. The ceiling was finished in an opalescent yellow to draw the light down from the lantern, with its special low-transmission, high-reflection glass.[49]

And so the scaffolding under the rotunda that had kept the Anastasis in gloom for twenty years could finally come down.

On January 2, 1997, in the presence of Jerusalem's great and good, the Greek and Armenian patriarchs and the custos ceremonially inaugurated the newly decorated rotunda dome. Never before in history had the edifice witnessed a ceremony in which the leaders of all three major churches shared the pulpit.

For Fathers Daniel, Rock, and Guregh, seated in the audience before the Tomb of Christ, it was the culmination of a lifelong mission. They had achieved what had once seemed inconceivable—making common cause to save the mother church. To the sound of church bells and applause, the canvas drapes were pulled back, revealing the renovated dome.[50]

And there was light.

| Trouvelot's Choice

S O   H O W   D I D   H I S T O R I C A L   antagonists manage to overcome their profound differences in order to restore the Church of the Resurrection? Obstacles to the restoration were formidable indeed: contested possession, deep-seated mistrust, differences of theology, language, and culture.

Any attempt to make sense of these events must begin with the logic of relations between the resident churches. This is a holy place in the possession of a most unusual gathering—a society of churches. A solution to the problem of the decayed fabric of the building had to be grounded in this reality. Ordinary societies are able to achieve their goals because of what they have in common. Apart from the fundamentals of Christian belief, bonds between the communities were notably scarce in a shrine known for its disharmony.

Yet, although the Church of the Resurrection may seem like a peculiar society, divided and contentious, in some respects it resembles a kind of collectivity very familiar to political scientists—the international system. Hedley Bull famously called this an "anarchical society," a society without a ruler.

In the Holy Sepulchre, a set of autonomous communities pursues particular rather than general interests. Each community has a strong sense of history and identity separating it from the others, and jealously defends its individuality. Yet all interact on a daily basis on a broad range of issues in the absence of an authority that can definitively settle disputes. They inhabit a defined space that has territories and boundaries secured by guards. There are frontier incidents and the possibility of violence. Leaders pursue agendas and have constituencies that they must satisfy.

In an anarchical society, relations between the members are guided by mixed motives, that is, at one and the same time the propensity to conflict and the unavoidability of cooperation. Given opposing interests and claims, disagreements are to be expected. There is no single generally accepted version of truth and justice. In theory, each community would like all the resources for itself and if it had the opportunity would go ahead and seize them. However, since it lacks the power, it is obliged to coexist with the others to preserve the system. Chaos would benefit no one.

A complete breakdown of order is unlikely in the Holy Sepulchre because of the presence of the state, which performs a "peacekeeping" or policing function. The Status Quo prevents the final settlement of disputes, and therefore removal of the underlying causes of conflict, by ruling out access to the courts. This is not very different from the international system, where states are not obliged to submit their disputes to international adjudication or arbitration.

However, the Status Quo does provide the indispensable basis for order in the church, in the form of an archaic body of customary law. It, too, is unusual but not unique, resembling the rules of behavior found in traditional societies, handed down from an illiterate age when oral witness and customary practice, visible for all to see, were essential to preserving rights.[1]

Conflict in the edifice is often blamed on the Status Quo. It is true that before the restoration, it fell short in two respects: there were disparities between the communities' versions of it, and it failed to provide guidance for the repair of common areas. These problems had to be solved for the restoration to go ahead.

Otherwise, the Status Quo has acted as a set of living arrangements, permitting coexistence among churches locked in an antagonistic relationship. Without the Status Quo, their cooperation would be altogether precluded. Fearing chaos and the loss of rights, the communities have a strong interest in preserving the Status Quo. Disorder would merely distract them from their vocation of worship.

The Latins have never concealed their preference for the pre-1757 status quo, but in the absence of a mutually agreed alternative are as meticulous in observance of the current version as are its main territorial beneficiaries, the Greeks.

Reliance on the Status Quo generates a way of thinking frequently observed in international relations. We can call it "the logic of the thin end of the wedge." According to this mental rule of thumb, membership in society commits the parties to keeping the rules intact; they may not pick and choose. Selective maintenance, it is believed, simply undermines the integrity of the whole by letting in the thin end of the wedge. Any unopposed breach would invite a cascade of violations—"give them an inch and they'll take a mile." Awareness of this precept disposes the parties to extreme vigilance. The archbishop of Canterbury, Geoffrey Fisher, was right when he observed on a pilgrimage to the mother church in 1960 that the denominations "watch like cats lest anyone gain an inch not his."[2]

Without the reassurance that the restoration would fully protect its rights, no party would have agreed to it. Formal Latin acceptance of this from 1958 onward paved the way for the restoration. Thus, the Status Quo was not an obstacle to progress. On the contrary, its clarification and elaboration were the necessary conditions for saving the church.

Jean Trouvelot provided a very succinct explanation of the master mechanism that made it all possible in a letter to his friend and colleague Charles Coüasnon, someone to whom compromise in matters of principle did not come easily. In order to subsist from one generation to the next under a succession of governments, he argued, the communities had learned to guard their relative independence jealously, and it would be difficult, if not impossible, to change that. In such circumstances, two ways of acting to promote the restoration presented themselves, he said:

> One is to use strong measures, the imposition of directives. That has to have the backing of a powerful administration, disposing of vigorous means of persuasion. But this is not the case here and if we employed this method on our own, without external support, we should turn the other communities against us without obtaining a positive result. Diplomacy, negotiation, and above all persuasion, remain the only methods—this is not timidity—to gradually alter habits and prejudices.[3]

Just as in any dispute among states, diplomacy was the only way to achieve progress in the Holy Sepulchre. It was slow and frustrating, but the alternatives were worse. In the 1930s, the Mandate government refused to negotiate with the communities as equals, thereby wasting an opportunity for restoration by consent. Since the authorities could not impose their will, this wrongheaded approach condemned the edifice to a generation of continuing neglect.

Similarly, Monsignor Testa's plan aimed to rebuild the basilica and bring peace to the communities by imposing Latin preeminence and reducing the other churches to subordinate status. But this could only happen if the Axis powers won the war. The scheme of an imposed solution simply impeded the restoration by fostering illusions on the Latin side and fears on the Greek side.

Once the major communities woke up to the gravity of the situation and the realization that they were faced by what I will call Trouvelot's Choice—between "strong measures" and the way of "diplomacy, negotiation, and above all persuasion"—they chose the latter. For some readers, the thought that the Church of the Resurrection was "bargained over" may be distasteful. But if agreement and compliance are the necessary ends, then negotiation is the necessary means.

Over the period 1951–61, the balance of conflict and cooperation in relations between the communities gradually shifted in favor of cooperation. The society of churches had always been a conflict system in which disagreement was rife and communication sporadic. It evolved into something more closely approximating a diplomatic system, in which discussion of problems, conducted by church representatives according to accepted procedures, became a regular occurrence.

Discussion of problems enabled many to be settled, some to be obfuscated, and yet others to be postponed indefinitely. The fundamental anomaly of a basilica that is the abode of rival churches, each of which believes that it is the exclusive repository of truth, could not of course be finally resolved. Diplomacy, however, allowed conflict to be transcended so that the mission could be accomplished. The Holy Sepulchre restoration is therefore a paradigm of conflict management, not of conflict resolution.

A set of necessary circumstances that had not previously existed facilitated the success of diplomacy. First and foremost was the sobering realization, as a result of the 1949 fire, that the edifice was threatened and that if the communities did not work together on a solution, then the Jordanian authorities would do the job themselves. The communities feared that if the state repaired the building they would lose their rights of possession and the autonomy they had struggled for centuries to preserve.

To take the next step, there had to be a meeting of minds at the highest level in Jerusalem. With the compliance of the Custody of the Holy Land ensured, cooperation was facilitated by the elections of the Greek Orthodox patriarch Benedictos in 1957 and the Armenian Orthodox patriarch Derderian in 1960. Wholly committed to the project, these were powerful, practical prelates who were able to assert their authority over sometimes unruly monks and deliver agreement.

A tough but fair Jordanian governor, the former judge Hassan Bey al-Katib, intervened at critical moments to break deadlocks. Backed by King Hussein, he acted as arbitrator in the Arab tradition. His skillful use of deadlines and warnings provided the churches with strong incentives to comply. Fear of Jordanian involvement in the project encouraged them to close ranks among themselves.

Jordan's successful rejection of outside interference was also vital. In the past, the communities had been able to evade hard choices by appealing to outside patrons to exert influence on their behalf. Moreover, the great powers had not always been able to distinguish between their own prestige and the local needs of their ecclesiastical clients.

There was a businesslike relationship between the experts who were responsible for managing the Status Quo on behalf of their communities. Together they formed the diplomatic corps of the society of churches. Enjoying the full confidence of their principals, these men—the Greek bishops Germanos and Daniel, the Franciscan Father Rock, and the Armenian Bishop Guregh—sought to achieve denominational advantage, but were also ready to accommodate each other's vital needs. These clerical diplomats handled disagreement without sentimentality, according to the rule of negotiation that applies in all situations of mixed motives: "It's not love that is at work here; it's a question of common interests."[4]

Finally, a common technical bureau brought together a team of architects representing the communities. It functioned at two levels: distinguished international architects bore overall responsibility for the project, and resolved many issues, thanks to their diplomatic skills and common professional language. Their local representatives did not always get on well together at a personal level but invariably solved outstanding technical problems in the end.

Since the 1997 inauguration of the rotunda dome, the third and final stage of the restoration, the reconstruction of the Edicule and surrounding courtyard, awaits implementation. Given the political will, this project is certainly feasible at the technical level. During the 1990s, Martin Biddle used traditional methods of architectural archaeology and the modern survey method of photogrammetry to make a record of the Edicule and the floor of the rotunda.[5]

Besides the Edicule, the electrical system in the church has to be completely overhauled, the air filtration system in the dome repaired, and new public facilities installed. Coptic rooms and the Chapel of Nicodemus must also be restored.

Thanks to the work of the experts, most of the Status Quo has been set down in the form of written agreements. Father Athanasius Macora, the Latins' expert on the holy places for the past decade, who has collated these documents, argues that "we are aware of each other's rights 95 percent of the way." He would like to see the communities "go the full distance."[6]

The major communities have not achieved perfect harmony and continue to have their differences of opinion. But violence is becoming increasingly infrequent.[7] The norm is now discussion—demonstrated during the restoration to be the most appropriate method of handling disagreement. An eventual accord to cooperate on restoring the Edicule should not be beyond the bounds of human ingenuity, though no reader of this book can have any illusions about the obstacles to be overcome.

Whatever the future holds, the mother church is in better shape today than it has been for five hundred years. Here and there the odd calcined stone is left to remind us of the dereliction from which the edifice was saved. Light and space have returned to its ancient halls, and its walls and pillars stand sound and true. For the host of pilgrims who visit it every year, it is a uniquely precious memorial and inspiration to faith. Because of—and not despite—its flaws, it is a place of enormous character and humanity.

Ambulatory A processional corridor around the sides of a church.

Apse A semicircular, vaulted space recessed into the outer wall of a church.

Arcade The structure formed by a series of arches supported on columns.

Atrium A high enclosed space at the entrance to a church.

Baldaquin A decorative canopy, supported on pillars, over an altar.

Balustrade A range of small pillars, topped by a rail.

Beam A horizontal support, incorporated into a structure, bearing weight.

Capital The broad top of a pillar, often decorated.

Chancel The eastern section of a church, separated from the congregation, used by the celebrant at a service.

Chapel Part of a church, sometimes quite small, containing an altar used for communion.

Choir The central hall of the church where services are celebrated. It is used by the congregation in the Church of the Holy Sepulchre, which lacks a separate nave.

Colonnade A row of columns.

Cornice A horizontal projecting band running along the top of a wall.

Crossing The towering space formed in a cruciform church at the intersection of the transepts and the central hall.

Crypt An underground vault beneath a church that may contain tombs or an altar.

Drum A cylindrical wall supporting a dome.

Edicule The "little house" or self-standing structure containing the Tomb of Christ.

Extrados The curved, external surface of an arch or vault.

Frieze A band of decorative sculpture over a door or window.

Gallery An elongated overhead chamber, supported by pillars, open on one side to an interior space.

Iconostasis In Orthodox churches, the screen, often decorated with icons, separating the main body of the church from the area containing the altar.

Loggia An arcaded gallery open on one side to the street.

Mausoleum A building containing one or more tombs.

Nave The western section of a church where the congregation assembles. It is lacking in the Church of the Holy Sepulchre.

Parvis The enclosed courtyard before a building.

Pendentive A triangular, concave segment between a dome and a pair of supporting arches.

Pier A high, solid mass supporting a structure.

Pilaster A rectangular, upright shaft, often attached to a wall.

Plinth The section at the bottom of a wall or column that projects outward.

Portal The impressive doorway of an important building.

Portico A high covered area formed by a line of pillars at the front of a building.

Rib An elongated projection on the underside of a vault or ceiling.

Romanesque An architectural style used in the Middle Ages, characterized by semicircular arches over doors and windows, vaulted ceilings, sturdy rounded pillars, and bold decorative features.

Rotunda A round, high building surmounted by a dome.

Sacristy The room where the sacred vessels and vestments are kept and where the priest changes for Communion.

Springing The point on an arch at which it begins to curve upward and inward.

Telltale A strip of glass or chalk fixed over a crack that breaks if there is continuing movement of the structure.

Transepts The north-south lateral arms of a church that project at right angles from the central hall.

Tribune The French term for gallery.

Tympanum The space above a doorway framed by an arch, often decorated with a carving.

Vault The arched space forming the ceiling in buildings not using reinforced concrete.

Voussoirs The wedge-shaped stones of an arch, vault, or dome.

Abu Ghazaleh, Daoud Jordanian governor of Jerusalem, 1964–65.

Altounian, Mardiros Principal architect of the Armenian Orthodox Patriarchate, 1954–58.

Ball, Terry Assistant to Charles Coüasnon, 1964–67.

Barlassina, Archbishop Luigi Latin patriarch of Jerusalem, 1920–47.

Barluzzi, Antonio Architect of the Custody of the Holy Land, 1919–55.

Benedictos, Archbishop Greek Orthodox patriarch of Jerusalem, 1957–1980.

Berthézène, Claude Building foreman in Latin areas, 1964–70.

Boiret, Yves Principal architect of the Custody of the Holy Land, 1983–94.

Cappiello, Father Vincenzo Custos of the Holy Land, 1962–68.

Collas, Leonidas J. Resident architect of the Greek Orthodox Patriarchate, 1961–64.

Coüasnon, Father Charles Resident architect of the Custody of the Holy Land, 1954–76.

Coupel, Pierre Principal architect of the Custody of the Holy Land, 1954–55.

Cust, Lionel George Arthur District officer, Jerusalem, 1923–31; author of *The Status Quo in the Holy Places*.

Dalqamuni, Fadhl Jordanian governor of Jerusalem, 1963.

Damianos, Archbishop Greek Orthodox patriarch of Jerusalem, 1897–1931.

Daniel (Choriatakis), Bishop Greek Orthodox superior of the Holy Sepulchre and expert on the Status Quo, 1966–2001.

Derderian, Archbishop Yeghishe Armenian Orthodox patriarch of Jerusalem, 1960–90.

Deschamps, Henri Master foreman of common technical bureau, 1962–68.

Diodoros, Archbishop Greek Orthodox patriarch, 1981–2000.

Diotallevi, Father Ferdinando Custos of the Holy Land, 1919–24.

Economopoulos, Athanasios Resident building engineer of the Greek Orthodox Patriarchate, 1964–74.

Faccio, Father Giacinto Custos of the Holy Land, 1950–55.

Froideveaux, Yves-Marie Principal architect of the Custody of the Holy Land, 1977–83.

Germanos (Mamaladis), Archimandrite Greek Orthodox superior of the Holy Sepulchre and expert on the Status Quo, 1960–66.

Gori, Archbishop Alberto Custos of the Holy Land, 1937–49; Latin patriarch of Jerusalem, 1950–70.

Guregh (Kapikian), Bishop Armenian Orthodox expert on the Status Quo, 1954–2003.

Harrison, Austen St. Barbe Chief architect, Palestine department of public works, 1923–38.

Harvey, William Consultant architect of the Palestine government, 1930–38.

Hashem, Ihsan Jordanian governor of Jerusalem, 1949–51, 1960–61.

Hoade, Father Eugene Franciscan writer on the holy places; member of the Discretorium.

Holliday, Clifford Architect and town planner; civic adviser to the city of Jerusalem, 1922–26; adviser to Palestine government, 1927–34.

Husayni, Adnan Jordanian governor of Jerusalem, 1956–57.

Katib, Hassan Jordanian governor of Jerusalem, 1951–56, 1957–60.

Keith-Roach, Edward Deputy district commissioner of Jerusalem, 1927–31; district commissioner of Jerusalem, 1937–43.

Khalidi, Hussein Jordanian high custodian of the holy places, 1951–52.

Khatib, Anwar Jordanian governor of Jerusalem, 1965–67.

Komnenos, Nikolaos Greek architect from Mytilene who restored the Holy Sepulchre, 1809–10.

Kyriakos (Spyridonides), Archimandrite Greek Orthodox superior of the Holy Sepulchre and expert on the Status Quo, 1927–60.

Lazzeri, Father Angelico Custos of the Holy Land, 1955–57.

Levi, Rafi District commissioner of Jerusalem, 1967–86.

Luke, Harry Charles Assistant governor of Jerusalem, 1920–24; chief secretary to the Palestine government, 1928–30.

Mallios, Antellos Resident building engineer of the Greek Orthodox Patriarchate, 1958–61.

Manoogian, Archbishop Torkom Armenian Orthodox patriarch of Jerusalem, 1990–.

Marangoni, Luigi Custodian of the Basilica of San Marco, Venice; consultant architect of the Custody of the Holy Land, 1934, 1938–41.

Morel, René Building foreman in Latin areas, 1970–73.

Nashashibi, Ragheb Pasha Mayor of Jerusalem, 1921–35; Jordanian high custodian of the holy places, 1951.

Neuville, René French consul general, Jerusalem, 1946–52.

Nusseibeh, Anwar Jordanian governor of Jerusalem, 1962–63.

Orlandos, Anastasios K. Principal architect of the Greek Orthodox Patriarchate, 1954–61.

Panaiotis, George Building foreman in Greek areas, 1965–67.

Papadopoulos, George Sculptor in Greek areas, 1964–67.

Paraskévopoulos, Periclis Consultant building engineer to Greek Orthodox Patriarchate, 1950s.

Polidori, Father Alfredo Custos of the Holy Land, 1957–62.

Rebaudi, Mario Sculptor in Latin areas, 1965–68.

Richmond, Ernest Director of antiquities, Palestine government, 1927–37.

Rock, Father Albert Franciscan expert on the Status Quo, 1954–1998.

Roncari, Father Erminio Custos of the Holy Land, 1969–74.

Sacchi, Father Maurilio Custos of the Holy Land, 1974–80.

Storrs, Sir Ronald British governor of Jerusalem, 1917–26.

Testa, Archbishop Gustavo Apostolic delegate to Palestine, 1934–42, 1948–53.

Timotheos, Archbishop Greek Orthodox patriarch of Jerusalem, 1939–55.

Tondelier, Maurice Sculptor in Latin and Armenian areas, 1965–66.

Trouvelot, Jean Principal architect of the Custody of the Holy Land, 1955–77.

Utudjian, Edouard Principal architect of the Armenian Orthodox Patriarchate, 1960–1975.

Vincent, Louis Hugues (1884–1960) Dominican archaeologist and historian of Jerusalem.

Voskertchian, Diran Resident architect of the Armenian Orthodox Patriarchate, 1960–75; principal architect, 1975–97.

Wauchope, General Sir Arthur High commissioner to Palestine, 1931–38.

Wolley, C. T. Civil engineer; consultant on the Holy Sepulchre, 1947, 1955.

Abbreviations

ACTS	*Acta Custodiae Terrae Sanctae*	
AMAEI	Archivio del Ministero degli Affari Esteri Italiano, Rome	
	AP	Affari Politici (1951–56)
CADN	Centre des Archives Diplomatiques, Nantes	
	JC	Jerusalem Consulate, general dossiers
	R S-S	Rome St.-Siège, embassy dossiers
CTB	Common technical bureau	
CTSA	Custodia di Terra Santa Archives, Jerusalem	
	BP	Barluzzi Papers
EB	École Biblique, Jerusalem	
	CP	Coüasnon Papers
IAA	Israel Antiquities Authority Archives, Jerusalem	
	ATQ	British Mandate, record files
	Jm	Israel Government, inspection files, Jerusalem
ISA	Israel State Archives, Jerusalem	
	CS	British Mandate, chief secretary's files
	DPW	British Mandate, Department of Public Works files
	FM	Israel Foreign Ministry files
	JG	Jordanian Governor's dossiers
LP	Lambeth Palace Archives, London	
	G23	Jerusalem Holy Places 1938–81
MECA	Middle East Centre Archives, St. Antony's College, Oxford	
	J & EM	Jerusalem and East Mission files
POC	*Proche Orient Chrétien*	

PRO　Public Records Office (now National Archives), London
　　　　FO　Foreign Office files
　　　　CO　Colonial Office files
USNA　United States National Archives, College Park, Maryland
　　　　SD　State Department, decimal files

Preface

1. Te Radar, "Maddened Monks Show Mayoral Wannabes the Way," *New Zealand Herald*, Oct. 1, 2004.

Chapter 1　The Earthquake

1. *Doar Hayom*, July 12, 1927, quoted in Ron Avni, "The 1927 Jericho Earthquake" (Ph. D. diss., Ben Gurion University, 1999), 2:35.
2. Quoted in M. Blanckenhorn, "Das Erdbeben im Juli 1927 in Palästina," *Zeitschrift des Deutschen Palästina-Vereins* 50 (Oct. 1927): 292.
3. "Le tremblement de terre du 11 Juillet," *Jérusalem: Revue Mensuelle Illustrée* 138 (July–Aug. 1927): 97.
4. Avni, "Jericho Earthquake," 2:35.
5. Archbishop Aristarchos, telephone interview with author, July 16, 2003.
6. Quoted by Pope John Paul II in homily in Holy Sepulchre, Mar. 26, 2000; www.vatican.va/.
7. Michael Sabbah, Latin patriarch of Jerusalem, speech, June 15, 2001; available at the website of the Holy Land Christian Ecumenical Foundation: www.hcef.org/hcef/index.cfm/ID/90.
8. H. A. Drake, "The Return of the Holy Sepulchre," *Catholic Historical Review* 70 (Apr. 1984): 263–67.
9. *Apologia of St. John of Damascus against Those Who Decry Holy Images*; available at the website of Fordham University Center for Medieval Studies: www.ccel.org/ccel/damascus/icons.pdf.
10. Averil Cameron and Stuart G. Hall, trans., *Eusebius, Life of Constantine* (Oxford: Clarendon Press, 1999), bk. 3, pp. 25–47, 132–37.
11. Credit for it usually goes to Emperor Constantine IX Monomachos (1042–55), but Martin Biddle, on the basis of documentary evidence, convincingly attributes it to Constantine's predecessor, Michael IV Paphlagon (1036–41). See Martin Biddle, *The Tomb of Christ* (Stroud, England: Sutton, 1999), 77–78.
12. Ibid., 92–98.
13. Sabino de Sandoli, *The Church of Holy Sepulchre: Keys, Doors, Doorkeepers* (Jerusalem: Franciscan Printing Press, 1986).
14. Since 1968, the friars have elected a short list of three candidates, but the final selection is still made by the Holy See.
15. George A. Gingas, trans., *Egeria: Diary of a Pilgrimage* (New York: Newman Press, 1970), 125–26.

16. On the schism see Steven Runciman, *The Eastern Schism* (Oxford: Clarendon Press, 1955), and Philip Sherrard, *The Greek East and the Latin West* (London: Oxford University Press, 1959).

17. Bernardin Collin, *Les lieux saints* (Paris: Presses Universitaires de France, 1962), 48.

18. Bernardin Collin, *Receuil de documents concernant Jérusalem et les lieux saints* (Jérusalem: Imprimerie des Franciscains, 1982), 96.

19. Edward Every, "The Cust Memorandum and the Status Quo in the Holy Places," *Christian News from Israel* 23 (spring 1973): 230.

20. Frédéric Jansoone de Ghyvelde, "Règlement du Saint-Sépulcre," in Collin, *Recueil de documents*, 97–118.

21. James Finn, *Stirring Times, or Records from Jerusalem Consular Chronicles of 1853 to 1856* (London: C. Kegan Paul, 1878), 2:458.

22. Edward Keith-Roach, *Pasha of Jerusalem* (London: Radcliffe Press, 1994), 171.

23. Jansoone de Ghyvelde, "Règlement," 117.

24. Ibid., 118.

25. George Everett Jeffrey, *The Holy Sepulchre* (Cambridge: Cambridge University Press, 1919), 68.

26. "Population Is Helpless," *New York Times*, July 15, 1927.

27. A Pilgrim, "Anglo-Catholic Pilgrimage," *Church Times*, Aug. 26, 1927.

28. Symes to Colonial Office, July 22, 1927, PRO CO 733/142/13.

29. 202 H.C. Deb. 5 s. 1244–5, 27 July 1927.

Chapter 2   Mr. Cust's Immobile Machine

1. John Presland, *Deedes Bey* (London: Macmillan, 1942), 277–79.

2. Joseph F. Broadhurst, *From Vine Street to Jerusalem* (London: Stanley Paul, 1936), 130–35.

3. T. E. Lawrence, *Seven Pillars of Wisdom* (New York: Doubleday, 1935), 453.

4. Ronald Storrs, *Orientations* (London: Ivor Nicholson & Watson, 1937), 326.

5. C. R. Ashbee, *A Palestine Notebook 1918–1923* (New York: Doubleday, 1923), 181.

6. Norman and Helen Bentwich, *Mandate Memories* (New York: Schocken Books, 1965), 41; Storrs, *Orientations*, 337–45.

7. Sir Anton Bertram and Harry Charles Luke, *Report of the Commission Appointed by the Government to Inquire into the Affairs of the Orthodox Patriarchate of Jerusalem* (London: Oxford University Press, 1921), app. F, 292–305.

8. Waggett memorandum, Dec. 1918, in Jane Priestland, ed., *Records of Jerusalem 1917–1971* (Oxford: Archive Editions, 2002), 1:244, 251.

9. Storrs, *Orientations*, 483.

10. Harry Charles Luke, *Cities and Men: An Autobiography* (London: Geoffrey Bles, 1953), 2:220.

11. Daphne Tsimhoni, "The Greek Orthodox Patriarchate of Jerusalem during the Formative Years of the British Mandate in Palestine," *Asian and African Studies* 12 (Mar. 1978): 85–88; see also LP, Davidson Papers, vols. 398, 399.

12. *Les lieux saints de la Palestine* (Jérusalem: Imprimerie des PP. Franciscains, 1922), 7, 8.

13. Walter Zander, *Israel and the Holy Places of Christendom* (London: Weidenfeld & Nicolson, 1971), 192.

14. John Mandaville, "Give to the Waqf of Your Choice," *Saudi Aramco World* 24 (Nov.–Dec. 1973): 2–5.

15. For the sake of consistency, the Greeks should have also dispensed with the Ottoman firmans on which they based many of their rights of possession and usage, but they did not do so in practice.

16. Bliss memorandum, June 4, 1919, IAA ATQ, Holy Sepulchre, vol. 1.

17. Barlassina to Storrs, May 30, 1925, PRO CO 733/97; Barlassina to Keith-Roach, Nov. 18, 1927, PRO CO 733/144/13.

18. Sophie Irene Loeb, *Palestine Awake* (New York: Century, 1926), 44–45.

19. Storrs, *Orientations*, 461.

20. MacInnes to Davidson, Mar. 12, 1924, LP, Davidson Papers, vol. 399.

21. Storrs, *Orientations*, 474.

22. Bertram and Luke, *Report*, 8, 24, 36.

23. Luke to Bell, Oct. 9, 1923, LP, Davidson Papers, vol. 399.

24. Sir Anton Bertram and J. W. A. Young, *Report of the Commission Appointed by the Government of Palestine to Inquire and Report upon Certain Controversies between the Orthodox Patriarchate of Jerusalem and the Arab Orthodox Community* (London: Oxford University Press, 1926), 91–93.

25. "Moral Abuses of the Confraternity," June 26, 1926, LP, Davidson Papers, vol. 399.

26. Buxton to Douglas, Jan. 26, 1927, LP, Douglas Papers, vol. 35.

27. Great Britain, Colonial Office, No. 33, Palestine Royal Commission, *Memorandum Prepared by the Government of Palestine* (London: His Majesty's Stationery Office, 1937), 39.

28. Douglas V. Duff, *Bailing with a Teaspoon* (London: John Long, 1954), 117.

29. D. Mpatistatou, *Proceedings and Decisions of the Pan-Orthodox Council in Constantinople* (Athens, 1982), 69; available at the website of the Orthodox Christian Information Center: www.orthodoxinfo.com.

30. L. G. A. Cust, *The Status Quo in the Holy Places*, facs. ed. (Jerusalem: Ariel, 1980), 15.

31. Ferdinando Diotallevi, *Diario di Terrasanta* (Milan: Edizioni Biblioteca Francescana, 2002), 123–25, 185–86, 215, 402–3.

32. Luke, *Cities and Men*, 2:206; Cust, *Status Quo*, 29.

33. Walter Zander, "On the Settlement of Disputes about the Christian Holy Places," *Israel Law Review* 8 (July 1973): 346–50; Sergio I. Minerbi, *The*

Vatican and Zionism: Conflict in the Holy Land, 1895–1925 (New York: Oxford University Press, 1990), 69–82.

34. Symes to Plumer, December 29, 1926, PRO CO 733/132/2.

35. Quoted in Zander, "On the Settlement of Disputes," 351–54.

36. Diotallevi, *Diario*, 15.

37. Zander, "On the Settlement of Disputes," 353–61, 363.

38. Lionel Cust, *King Edward VII and His Court* (London: John Murray, 1930), vii, xviii, 208–9, 242–43; "Sir Archer Cust," *Times* (London), May 23, 29, 1962.

39. Luke to Amery, Oct. 30, 1928, PRO CO 733/152/5.

40. Cust, *Status Quo*, 12, 22; Every, "Cust Memorandum," 232–33.

41. Archbishop Timotheos, interview with author, Jerusalem, May 26, 2002.

42. Storrs, *Orientations*, 514–15; Loeb, *Palestine Awake*, 42–54.

43. Storrs, *Orientations*, 351–53; Ashbee, *Palestine Notebook*, 14–17; Diotallevi, *Diario*, 67.

44. Themelis to Douglas, Jan. 15, 1938, LP, Douglas Papers, vol. 35.

45. Barnabas Meistermann, *Guide to the Holy Land* (London: Burns Oates & Washbourne, 1923), 120.

46. Storrs, *Orientations*, 473.

47. Cust, *Status Quo*, 16.

48. Storrs, *Orientations*, 473.

49. Diotallevi, *Diario*, 30 31, 223, 394.

50. Storrs, *Orientations*, 351.

51. Diotallevi, *Diario*, 78, 86, 128–29, 187.

52. Ashbee, *Palestine Notebook*, 149.

53. Storrs to patriarchs, May 23, 1925, PRO CO 733/97.

54. Barlassina to Storrs, May 25 and 27, 1925, PRO CO 733/97.

55. Minerbi, *The Vatican and Zionism*, 57–59, 67–69; Storrs, *Orientations*, 472; minute, author unknown, Nov. 25, 1925, PRO CO 733/104.

56. Barlassina to Storrs, June 2, 1925, PRO CO 733/97.

57. Amery to Plumer, Nov. 27, 1925, PRO CO 733/104.

58. *White Paper on the Wailing Wall Dispute*, Cmd. 3229 (London: His Majesty's Stationery Office, 1928), 5–6.

59. Holliday report, "Preliminary Examination of the Holy Sepulchre," June 9, 1926; Lees to chief secretary, June 10, 1926, both in PRO CO 733/128/8.

60. Cust, *Status Quo*, 22.

61. Ibid., 13.

62. Marangoni to Jacopozzi, "Report," Mar. 19, 1934, CTSA BP.

Chapter 3 Ready to Fall

1. A Pilgrim, "The Diary of the Pilgrimage," *Church Times*, Aug. 26, 1927.

2. Consul general of France to minister of foreign affairs, Dec. 7, 1927, CADN JC, series B, box 154.

3. René Neuville, *Heurs et malheurs des consuls de France a Jérusalem* (Jerusalem: Ronald Press, 1947), 1:45.

4. "Technical Report upon the Condition of the Dome over the Catholicum of the Church of the Holy Sepulchre, Jerusalem," September 1927, IAA ATQ, Holy Sepulchre, vol. 1.

5. Minutes of the 31st ordinary meeting of the archaeological advisory board, Oct. 24, 1927, ISA CS 4145/907.

6. Amery to Plumer, Aug. 8, 1928, IAA ATQ/199, box 49.

7. Consul general of France to minister of foreign affairs, Dec. 7, 1927, CADN JC, series B, box 154.

8. Keith-Roach to Symes, Nov. 2, 1927, PRO CO 733/144/13.

9. Barlassina to Keith-Roach, Nov. 18, 1927, ISA CS 23/10.

10. Symes to Chancellor, Nov. 19, 1927; Symes to Keith-Roach, Nov. 23, 1927, both in ISA CS 23/10.

11. Steven Erlanger, "A Grande Dame of a Bygone Jerusalem," *New York Times*, Oct. 29, 2005.

12. Quotations in Daniel Bertrand Monk, *An Aesthetic Occupation* (Durham, N.C.: Duke University Press, 2002), 68, 151.

13. E. T. Richmond, Introduction to William Harvey, *Church of the Holy Sepulchre Jerusalem: Structural Survey Final Report* (London: Oxford University Press, 1935), vii, xi.

14. Keith-Roach to Symes, June 7, 1927; Richmond to Symes, Sept. 23, 1927, both in IAA ATQ 113.

15. Father Louis Hugues Vincent, "Note sur le St. Sépulcre," May 6, 1952, CADN JC, series B, box 154.

16. Richmond to Keith-Roach, Mar. 13, 1928, IAA ATQ 113.

17. Richmond to Keith-Roach, Nov. 3, 1932, IAA ATQ/2/113.

18. Harry Charles Luke, "The Christian Communities in the Holy Sepulchre," in C. R. Ashbee, ed., *Jerusalem 1920–1922* (London: John Murray, 1921), 46–56; Luke, *Prophets, Priests and Patriarchs* (London: Faith Press, 1927).

19. Luke to Amery, Nov. 15, 1928, ISA CS 23/10.

20. Amery to Chancellor, Mar. 4, 1929, ISA CS 23/4.

21. Minutes of the 35th ordinary meeting of the archaeological advisory board, Oct. 8, 1928, IAA ATQ/1/113.

22. Lambert to Luke, July 22, 1929, ISA CS 23/10.

23. Minutes of meeting with regard to repairs to the Holy Sepulchre, July 30, 1929, IAA ATQ/2/113.

24. William Harvey, *The Preservation of St. Paul's Cathedral and Other Famous Buildings* (London: Architectural Press, 1925).

25. William Harvey, "A Particular Description of the Church," in R. Weir-Schultz, ed., *The Church of the Nativity at Bethlehem* (London: B. T. Batsford, 1910), 1–12.

26. William Harvey, "Rebuilding of the Dome over the Katholikon," Mar. 1931, PRO CO 733/210/9.

27. Nicholas Halaby, "Ashlar Masonry Dome Construction: Case Study of Reconstruction of the Dome of the Katholikon, Church of the Holy Sepulchre, Jerusalem," Jan. 1973, PRO CO 10/142, summarized as "Twentieth-Century Stone Dome Builders Learn from the Ancients," *New Civil Engineer*, July 12, 1973, 34–35.

28. Harrison memorandum, "Repairs to Ancient Buildings," Aug. 13, 1932, ISA CS 4145/902.

29. Rowlands to chief secretary, Aug. 25, 1932, ISA CS 4145/902.

30. Edward Keith-Roach, *Pasha of Jerusalem* (London: Radcliffe Press, 1994), 131–32.

31. Waddington, "Damage Report on State of Church," Aug. 1932, IAA ATQ, Holy Sepulchre, vol. 1.

32. E. T. Richmond, "Note on the Condition of the Church of the Holy Sepulchre," Aug. 25, 1932, PRO CO 733/226/17.

33. Vincent to Richmond, Sept. 24, 1932, ISA DPW 4956/13.

34. Rowlands to chief secretary, Oct. 31, 1932, ISA CS 24/11.

35. E. T. Richmond, memorandum, Feb. 6, 1936, ISA CS 23/10; consul general of France to minister of foreign affairs, Mar. 4, 1934, CADN JC, series B, box 154.

36. Cunliffe-Lister to Wauchope, Jan. 7, 1933, PRO CO 733/226/17.

37. Williams to Harvey, July 27, 1933, PRO CO 733/247/14.

38. "Historical Note on the Repairs to the Dome of the Church of the Holy Sepulchre," n.d. [c. Mar. 1934], PRO CO 733/247/14.

39. Campbell to chief secretary, May 24, 1933; Trusted to Cunliffe-Lister, June 1, 1933; Campbell to chief secretary, Oct. 26, 1933, all in ISA CS 23/10.

40. Memorandum, June 1933, PRO CO 733/247/14; Williams to secretary of Treasury, June 22, 1933; Williams to Harvey, July 27, 1933, both in ISA CS 23/4.

41. 288 H.C. Deb. 5s., 1698–99, 25 Apr. 1934; 289 H.C. Deb. 5s., 298–99, 2 May 1934; ibid., 289 H.C. Deb. 5s., 298–99, 734–35, 7 May, 1934; 307 H.C. Deb. 5s., 891, 11 Dec. 1935.

42. Sir Anton Bertram and Harry Charles Luke, *Report of the Commission Appointed by the Government to Inquire into the Affairs of the Orthodox Patriarchate of Jerusalem* (London: Oxford University Press, 1921), 36; Sir Anton Bertram and J. W. A. Young, *Report of the Commission Appointed by the Government of Palestine to Inquire and Report upon Certain Controversies between the Orthodox Patriarchate of Jerusalem and the Arab Orthodox Community* (London: Oxford University Press, 1926), 81–82, 91–93.

43. William Harvey, Preliminary Report, Sept. 26, 1933, IAA ATQ/4/113.

44. Max Nurock, acting chief secretary, memorandum, Sept. 27, 1933, ISA CS 23/10.

45. William Harvey, Second Report, October 28, 1933, IAA ATQ/4/113.

46. Wauchope to Cunliffe-Lister, December 1, 1933, PRO CO 733/247/14.

47. Harvey, *Church of the Holy Sepulchre*, 21–27.

48. Hathorn Hall to Cunliffe-Lister, Oct. 10, 1933, ISA CS 23/10.

Chapter 4 *William Harvey's Temporary Repairs*

1. An. Orlandos and Per. Paraskévopoulos, "Exposé de vues sur les rapports préliminaires de Mr. W. Harvey concernant l'état du St. Sépulcre et mesures proposées pour sa consolidation," Feb. 18, 1934, ISA CS 25/34.

2. Angelo de Benvenuti, "Luigi Marangoni e la 'Scala Nuova' del Palazzo di Venezia," *Rivista Dalmatica* 33 (Mar.–June 1962), 59–66; minister, Cairo to Reynaud, Mar. 14, 1940, CADN JC, series B, box 154.

3. Luigi Marangoni, *La Chiesa Del Santo Sepolcro In Gerusalemme* (Jerusalem: Custodia di Terra Santa, 1937), 83–86.

4. Marangoni to Jacopozzi, "Relazione," Mar. 19, 1934, CTSA BP.

5. Chief secretary to church leaders, draft only preserved, Mar. 1934, ISA CS 25/24.

6. Aumale to foreign minister, Mar. 4, 1934, CADN JC, series B, box 154.

7. Acting district commissioner to chief secretary, Feb. 10, 1934, ISA CS 25/34.

8. Harvey appendices to final report, Apr. 14, 16, 17, 1934, IAA ATQ/4/113.

9. Hugues Vincent, "Note sur le mémoire de M. l'architecte W. Harvey concernant la restauration du Saint-Sépulcre," May 21, 1936, EB CP.

10. Hugues Vincent, "L'Église du Saint-Sépulcre en péril," *Comptes rendus des séances de l'année 1938 de l'Académie des Inscriptions et Belles-Lettres* (October 1938): 426–33.

11. Harvey, note, Mar. 15, 1935, IAA ATQ/3/113.

12. William and John H. Harvey, "The Structural Decay of the Church of the Holy Sepulchre," *Palestine Exploration Quarterly* 70 (July 1938): 156–61.

13. Richmond to chief secretary, Sept. 21, 1934, IAA ATQ/199(a).

14. Amery to Chancellor, Mar. 4, 1929, ISA CS 23/4.

15. 288 H.C. Deb. 5s. col. 1698.

16. 289 H.C. Deb. 5s. cols. 299, 734–35.

17. Campbell to chief secretary, May 24, 1933; Trusted to Cunliffe-Lister, June 1, 1933, both in ISA CS 23/10.

18. Downie, memorandum, June 1933, PRO CO 733/247/14.

19. Minutes of archaeological advisory board, Mar. 1, 1933, ISA CS 4145/907; Jacopozzi to Richmond, Apr. 25, 1933, IAA ATQ/2/113; MacLaren to Jacopozzi, June 12, 1933, ISA CS 23/10.

20. Horace B. Samuel, *Unholy Memories of the Holy Land* (London: Hogarth Press, 1930), 106–7, 148–50.

21. Richmond to chief secretary, Oct. 30, 1933, IAA ATQ/199.

22. Cunliffe-Lister to Wauchope, Nov. 16, 1934, IAA ATQ/5/113.

23. Wauchope to Thomas, Jan. 18, 1936, PRO CO 733/300/1.

24. Thomas to Wauchope, Feb. 27, 1936, PRO CO 733/300/1.

25. Hathorn Hall to church leaders, May 2, 1936, PRO CO 733/300/1.

26. Marangoni to Barluzzi, May 28, 1936, CTSA BP.

27. Since 1929, at the request of London, a representative of the Holy See without formal diplomatic accreditation had replaced Barlassina, the querulous Latin patriarch, as the government's interlocutor. The custos retained direct local responsibility for the holy places on behalf of the Roman Catholic Church.

28. Testa to Hathorn Hall, December 5, 1936, PRO CO 733/336/7.

29. Hathorn Hall to Testa, July 3, 1937, ISA CS 28/10.

30. Counselor to embassy to foreign minister, May 3, 1938, CADN JC, series B, box 154.

31. Waddy to Bell, Sept. 5, 1923, LP, Davidson Papers, vol. 399.

32. Canon Bridgeman's report, Apr. 29, 1938, MECA, J & EM XIX/3.

33. Keladion to colonial secretary, Jan. 15, 1938, LP, G23.

34. Harvey to undersecretary, colonial office, November 18, 1937, PRO CO 733/336/7.

35. Keith-Roach to church leaders, Dec. 1937, PRO CO 733/336/7.

36. Kouchoukian to Keith-Roach, Feb. 3, 1938, PRO CO 733/374/10.

37. Keladion to colonial secretary, Jan. 15, 1938, LP, G23.

38. Translation of Testa letter, Jan. 22, 1938, PRO CO 733/374/10.

39. MacMichael to Ormsby-Gore, May 16, 1938, PRO CO 733/374/10.

40. Graves to Harvey, November 18, 1937, PRO CO 733/336/7.

41. William Harvey, "Two Great Shrines in Danger," *Times* (London), February 16, 1938.

42. William Harvey, "Church of the Holy Sepulchre, Jerusalem," Mar. 31, 1938, CADN JC, series B, box 154. See also William Harvey, "Inspection of the Church of the Holy Sepulchre from 23rd to 29th March, 1938," *Palestine Exploration Quarterly* 70 (July 1938): 160–61.

43. "Church of the Holy Sepulchre," *Times* (London), Apr. 8, 1938.

44. Note, Feb. 1947, PRO CO 371/98503.

45. British legation Athens to Dept., May 14, 1938, PRO CO 733/374/10.

46. Downie note, May 10, 1938, PRO CO 733/374/10.

47. MacMichael to MacDonald, June 25, 1938, PRO CO 733/374/10.

48. Keith-Roach to Thompson, October 5, 1938, in Robert L. Jarman, ed., *Political Diaries of the Arab World: Palestine and Jordan* (London: Archive Editions, 2001), 3:363–70.

Chapter 5   Monsignor Testa's Temple

1. JC to Eastern Dept., Jan. 30, 1950, PRO FO 371/82232.

2. Hathorn Hall to Williams, Oct. 20, 1934, PRO CO 737/259/8.

3. Barluzzi to Testa, June 3, 1936, CTSA BP.

4. Jacopozzi to Barluzzi, July 17, 1936, CTSA BP.

5. Testa to Hathorn Hall, Dec. 5, 1936, PRO CO 733/336/7.

6. Hathorn Hall to Ormsby-Gore, Mar. 18, 1937, PRO CO 733/336/7.

7. Keith-Roach to chief secretary, Jan. 25, 1940, ISA CS 28/10.

8. Luigi Marangoni, *La Chiesa del Santo Sepolcro in Gerusalemme* (Jerusalem: Custodia di Terra Santa, 1937), 16.

9. Hugues Vincent, "L'Église du Saint-Sépulcre en Péril," *Comptes rendus des séances de l'année 1938 de l'Académie des Inscriptions et Belles-Lettres* (October 1938): 433.

10. Downie note, May 5, 1938, PRO CO 733/374/10.

11. Counsellor, consulate general Jerusalem to foreign minister, May 3, 1938, CADN JC, series B, box 154.

12. The story of his life is told in Daniel M. Madden, *Monuments to Glory: The Story of Antonio Barluzzi* (New York: Hawthorn Books, 1964).

13. Pacifique Gori, "Un grand architecte, Antoine Barluzzi, 1884–1960," *La Terre Sainte* (Feb. 1961): 36–39.

14. Antonio Barluzzi, diary no. 3, 1935, 6, CTSA BP.

15. Marangoni to Barluzzi, Dec. 19, 1935, CTSA BP.

16. Marangoni to Barluzzi, Feb. 22, 1936, CTSA BP.

17. Marangoni to Barluzzi, Sept. 14, 1935, CTSA BP.

18. Marangoni to Barluzzi, July 12, 1938, CTSA BP.

19. Testa to Barluzzi, Nov. 19, 1938, CTSA BP.

20. Diana Rice, "Random Notes for Travelers," *New York Times*, Aug. 14, 1938.

21. Barluzzi to Testa, Nov. 28, 1938, CTSA BP.

22. Barluzzi to Testa, Dec. 6, 1938, CTSA BP.

23. Testa to Barluzzi, Dec. 1, 1938; Barluzzi to Marangoni, Dec. 5, 1938, both in CTSA BP.

24. Barluzzi to Marangoni, Dec. 6, 1938, CTSA BP.

25. Marangoni to Testa, Apr. 26, 1939, CTSA BP.

26. F. Charles-Roux, *Huit ans au Vatican, 1932–1940* (Paris: Flammarion, 1947), 299.

27. "Pope Pius May Visit Rome," *New York Times*, Apr. 1, 1939.

28. Owen Chadwick, *Britain and the Vatican during the Second World War* (Cambridge: Cambridge University Press, 1986), 20, 24.

29. Camille M. Cianfara, "Psychosis of War Fomented in Rome," *New York Times*, Mar. 21, 1939.

30. Chadwick, *Britain and the Vatican*, 48, 57–58.

31. "Fascist Newspaper Sees Pope's Support," *New York Times*, June 25, 1939.

32. Pedrazzi to Mussolini, May 19, 1927, in Ministero degli Affari Esteri, *I Documenti Diplomatici Italiani*, seventh series (Rome: Istituto Poligrafico dello Stato, 1967), 5:217.

33. Paolo Pieracini, "Il Patriarcato Latino di Gerusalemme (1918–1940)," pt. 1, *Il Politico* 63 (Apr.–June 1998): 225–26; pt. 2, *Il Politico* 63 (Oct.–Dec. 1998): 635.

34. Quoted in Anthony Rhodes, *The Vatican in the Age of the Dictators, 1922–1945* (London: Hodder and Stoughton, 1973), 67.

35. *Times* (London), Mar. 14, 1929.
36. De Salis, report, Feb.12, 1942, PRO FO 371/33414.
37. Marangoni to Barluzzi, Dec. 1, 1939, CTSA BP.
38. Marangoni to Barluzzi, Dec. 20, 1939, CTSA BP.
39. Bellorini to Keith-Roach, Jan. 25, 1940, ISA CS 28/10.
40. Ibid.
41. Bennet, minute, Mar. 21, 1940, PRO CO 733/421/18.
42. "Official Communiqué," n.d., ISA DPW 4956/14.
43. Testa to Barluzzi, Mar. 9, 1940, CTSA BP.
44. Marangoni to Barluzzi, Sept. 11, 1940, CTSA BP.
45. "Progetto della Santa Sede per i restauri al Santo Sepolcro," *Giornale d'Oriente,* Mar. 6, 1940.
46. Marangoni to Barluzzi, Apr. 7, 1940, CTSA BP.
47. Elio Zorzi, "L'E. 42 e il Santo Sepolcro," *Corriere della sera,* Mar. 15, 1940.
48. Marangoni to Barluzzi, Apr. 7, 1940, CTSA BP.
49. Custodia di Terra Santa, *Il Santo Sepolcro di Gerusalemme: Splendori, miserie, speranze* (Bergamo: Istituto Italiano D'Arti Grafiche, 1949), 133–34. Actual publication of the volume was delayed until 1950.
50. "Telegrams in Brief," *Times* (London), June 20, 1940; Odo Russell, "Italy and Palestine," *Times* (London), Aug. 2, 1940; De Salis report, Feb. 12, 1942, PRO FO 371/33414.
51. Chadwick, *Britain and the Vatican,* 119, 131, 137.
52. Ciano report, July 7, 1940, in Malcolm Muggeridge, ed., *Ciano's Diplomatic Papers* (London: Odhams Press, 1948), 377.
53. Von Mackensen to foreign ministry, July 17, 1940, in *Documents on German Foreign Policy,* series D (London: Her Majesty's Stationery Office, 1957), 10:252.
54. "46 Killed in Palestine Raid," *New York Times,* July 25, 1940.
55. "50 Civilians Killed at Tel-Aviv," *Times* (London), Sept. 11, 1940; "Italians Resort to Air Murder," *Times* (London), Sept. 12, 1940; "The Bombing of Tel-Aviv," *Times* (London), Sept. 17, 1940.
56. Custodia di Terra Santa, *Il Santo Sepolcro,* 11–18, 133–45; Testa to Marangoni, Aug. 16, 1940, CTSA BP.
57. Marangoni to Barluzzi, Sept. 11, 1940, CTSA BP.
58. Marangoni to Barluzzi, Sept. 12, 1940, CTSA BP.
59. Marangoni to Barluzzi, Oct. 30, 1940, CTSA BP.
60. Osborne to Maglione, Feb. 12, 1942, in *Actes et documents du Saint-Siège relatifs à la Seconde Guerre Mondiale* (Rome: Libreria Editrice Vaticana, 1969), 5:428–29.
61. Rhodes, *The Vatican in the Age of the Dictators,* 279.
62. Newton report, Jan. 27, 1942, PRO FO 371/33414.
63. Testa to Marangoni, Dec. 24, 1942; Marangoni to Barluzzi, Jan. 20, 1943, both in CTSA BP.

64. Testa memorandum, Apr. 19, 1947; cover letter, Testa to Maglione, Apr. 24, 1947, both in CTSA BP.

Chapter 6 The Fire

1. The following account is based on "Summary of Events in Arab Palestine during the Month of November, 1949," British Consulate General, Jerusalem, December 5, 1949, PRO FO 371/75329; P. Stefano Sesnic, "Mentre brucia la cupola del S. Sepolcro," *La Terra Santa* 25 (Jan. 1950): 3–6; R. P. Hugues Vincent, letter of November 24, 1949, in *Comptes rendus des séances de l'année 1949 de l'Académie des Inscriptions et Belles Lettres* (Oct.–Dec. 1949): 417–19; Sir Alec Kirkbride, *From the Wings: Amman Memoirs 1947–1951* (London: Frank Cass, 1976), 114–15; "Fire Threatens Dome of the Holy Sepulchre," *New York Times*, November 25, 1949; " £10,000 Damage to Holy Sepulchre," *Church Times*, Dec. 9, 1949.
2. Father Athanasius Macora, interview with author, Jerusalem, Mar. 19, 2002.
3. Kirkbride, *From the Wings*, 115.
4. Father Louis Hugues Vincent, "Note sur le St.-Sépulcre," Mar. 6, 1952, CADN R S-S, box 1480.
5. Sesnic, "Mentre brucia la cupola," 5–6.
6. See Kimberly Katz, "Building Jordanian Legitimacy: Renovating Jerusalem's Holy Places," *Muslim World* 93 (Apr. 2003): 211–32.
7. See Bernard Wasserstein, *Divided Jerusalem* (London: Profile, 2001), 149–50, 155–58.
8. Ibid., 155–56; Sir John Bagot Glubb, *A Soldier with the Arabs* (London: Hodder and Stoughton, 1957), 127.
9. Joseph Nevo, *King Abdallah and Palestine: A Territorial Ambition* (London: Macmillan, 1996), 166.
10. Quoted in Walter Zander, *Israel and the Holy Places of Christendom* (London: Weidenfeld & Nicolson, 1971), 77.
11. Ibid., 76.
12. Tawfik Al-Khalil, "Jerusalem from 1947 to 1967: A Political Survey" (M.A. diss., American University of Beirut, 1969).
13. Clark to Oliver, Sept. 17, 1951, PRO FO 371/91397. Martin Biddle, emeritus professor of history at Oxford University, reports that Crown Agent records show that two cases of files reached London in August 1948 and were transferred to the colonial office, but there the trail goes cold (telephone conversation with author, July 24, 2004).
14. Monypenny to Furlonge, Aug. 18, 1951, PRO FO 371/91397.
15. Ibid.
16. Thompson to Newton, Nov. 17, 1944, PRO FO 371/91397; Pollock to Sheringham, Feb. 23, 1950, PRO FO 371/82233.
17. Amman legation to foreign ministry, Sept. 19, 1951, AMAEI AP, folder 811.

18. Ibid.

19. "Al S. Sepolcro," *La Terra Santa* 24 (Mar.–Apr. 1949): 61.

20. Consulate general, Jerusalem to Eastern Dept., Mar. 11, 1950, PRO FO 371/82233.

21. Zander, *Israel and the Holy Places*, 78–79.

22. Gene Currivan, "New Plan for Holy Sepulcher," *New York Times*, Dec. 28, 1949; Gene Currivan, "Plans for Restoration of Holy Sepulcher," *New York Times*, Dec. 30, 1949.

23. Zander, *Israel and the Holy Places*, 82.

24. "Plans for the Protection of the Holy Places," *Church Times*, Feb. 24, 1950.

25. "Abdullah Defies Ouster by League," *New York Times*, Apr. 23, 1950.

26. British legation Amman to Eastern Dept., Aug. 10, 1950, PRO FO 371/82232.

27. Terza to foreign ministry Rome, Aug. 6, 1950, AMAEI AP, folder 811.

28. Consulate general Jerusalem to Foreign Office, Jan. 20, 1950, PRO FO 371/82232; la Sablière to minister, May 6, 1953, CADN R S-S, box 1480.

29. Macartney to Fisher, Feb. 10, 1950, LP, G23.

30. Perowne to Furlonge, Oct. 2, 1950, PRO FO 371/82232.

31. Royal berat, MECA, J & EM XVII/5.

32. Zander, *Israel and the Holy Places*, 87–88; Walker to Furlonge, June 25, 1951, PRO FO 371/91397.

33. Jerusalem engineer to governor of Jerusalem, Apr. 20, 1952, ISA JG 17/20; Albert Rock, *The Status Quo in the Holy Places* (Jerusalem: Franciscan Printing Press, 1989), 50.

34. Terza to foreign ministry, Sept. 25, 1951, AMAEI AP, folder 811.

35. Legation to Holy See to Foreign Office, Apr. 5, 1951; Walker to Furlonge, June 25, 1951, PRO FO 371/91397; "Les lieux saints," *POC* 1 (1951): 139.

36. Dow to Bevin, Jan. 15, 1951, PRO FO 371/91397.

37. British legation to the Holy See to Foreign Office, Apr. 5, 1951, PRO FO 371/91397.

38. Walmsley to Eastern Dept., June 11, 1952, PRO FO 371/98503; Amman legation to foreign ministry Rome, Sept. 19, 1951, AMAEI AP, folder 811.

39. Monypenny to Furlonge, Aug. 18, 1951, PRO FO 371/91397.

40. Interior minister to governor of Jerusalem, May 28, 1952, ISA JG 17/20.

41. Walmsley to Eastern Dept., June 11, 1952, PRO FO 371/98503.

42. Walmsley to Eastern Dept., Aug. 20, 1952, PRO FO 371/98503.

Chapter 7 Hassan Bey Takes Charge

1. See e.g. Edward Every, "The Church of the Holy Sepulchre, Past, Present and Future," *Ecumenical Review* 4 (Jan. 1952): 190.

2. "The Church of the Holy Sepulchre," *Times* (London), Sept. 30, 1955.

3. Albert Rock, *The Status Quo in the Holy Places* (Jerusalem: Franciscan Printing Press, 1989), 50.

4. La Sablière to minister, Mar. 14, 1954, CADN R S-S, box 1480.

5. Kirkbride, *From the Wings*, 124–25.

6. Terza to foreign ministry Rome, Feb. 27, 1952, AMAEI AP, folder 811.

7. Terza to foreign ministry Rome, Sept. 25, 1951, AMAEI AP, folder 811.

8. Jerusalem district engineer to Jerusalem governor, Apr. 20, 1952, report attached to ISA JG 17/20.

9. Laforge to Beauchamp, Jan. 17, 1956, CADN JC, D/suppl., box 388.

10. Letter on the seventh centennial of the Custody, Aug. 20, 1950, in Bernardin Collin, *Receuil de documents concernant Jérusalem et les lieux saints* (Jérusalem: Imprimerie des Franciscains, 1982), 64–75.

11. Terza to foreign ministry, Rome, Mar. 4, 1952, AMAEI AP, folder 811.

12. Father Louis Hugues Vincent, "Note Sur Le St.-Sépulcre," May 6, 1952, CADN R S-S, box 1480.

13. Soragna to foreign ministry, Mar. 12, 23, 27, 1952, AMAEI AP, folder 811.

14. Neuville memorandum, Apr. 16, 1952; Neuville memorandum, May 1, 1952; Neuville to governor, May 29, 1952, all in ISA JG 17/20.

15. Neuville memorandum, May 1, 1952, ISA JG 17/20.

16. Katib to Neuville, Apr. 30, 1952, ISA JG 17/20.

17. Khalidi to prime minister of Jordan, June 11, 1952, ISA JG 17/20.

18. Walmsley to Foreign Office, June 11, 1952, PRO FO 371/98503.

19. Joseph Coy Green diary, entry for Feb. 16, 1953, MECA GB 165–0317.

20. George Hintlian, interview with author, Jerusalem, May 14, 2003.

21. Ibid.

22. Al-Khalidi to al-Josi, n.d.; al-Josi to prime minister, Apr. 15, 1952, both in ISA JG 17/20.

23. Walmsley to Foreign Office, June 23, 1952, Sept. 2, 1952; Walker to Wardrop, Nov. 28, 1952, all in PRO FO 371/98503; Faccio to Katib, Oct. 6, 1952; Derderian to governor, Nov. 5, 1952, both in ISA JG.

24. Walmsley to Foreign Office, Sept. 2, 1952, PRO FO 371/98503.

25. Wikeley to Brewis, Feb. 23, 1954, PRO FO 371/110853.

26. Summary of Tyler dispatch to State Dept., Feb. 23, 1954, PRO FO 371/110853. See also LP, G23, May–July 1954.

27. Victor Azarya, *The Armenian Quarter of Jerusalem* (Berkeley: University of California Press, 1984), 115.

28. *Custody of the Holy Land Newsletter*, Feb. 1, 1979, 2.

29. A. Arce, "The Custody of the Holy Land," *Christian News from Israel* 19 (May 1968): 37–38.

30. Green diary, entry for Aug. 31, 1952.

31. Ibid., Jan. 8, 1953.

32. La Sablière to minister, May 6, 1953, CADN R S-S, box 1480.

33. Church of the Holy Sepulchre report by Freeman, Fox Partners, May 1947, IAA ATQ, Holy Sepulchre, vol. 1. Also see interim statements and correspondence in ISA DPW 4956/16.

34. Wolley to chief secretary, Feb. 24, 1947, PRO CO 733/478/5.

35. Walmsley to Foreign Office, Sept. 2, 1952, PRO FO 371/98503.

36. Custodie de Terre-Sainte, *Le Saint-Sépulcre: Études et projets de restauration* (Jerusalem: Franciscan Printing Press, 1956); memorandum, Feb. 1954, CADN R S-S, box 1480.

37. Memorandum, Feb. 1954, CADN R S-S, box 1480.

38. La Sablière to foreign minister, Feb. 8, 1954, CADN R S-S, box 1480.

39. Wikeley to Brewis, Feb. 22, 1954, PRO FO 371/110853.

40. "Experts to Try to Save Holiest Christian Shrine," *New York Times*, May 27, 1954.

41. Custodie de Terre-Sainte, *Le Saint-Sépulcre,* 77–80.

42. Every to Stewart, July 30, 1954, LP, G23.

Chapter 8 Terrors in the Way

1. La Sablière to minister, July 17, 1954, CADN R S-S, box 1480.

2. La Sablière to Hassan Bey al-Katib, Aug. 4, 1954, ibid.

3. "La restauration du Saint-Sépulcre," *POC* 4 (1954): 260–61, 363.

4. "La restauration de la basilique du Saint-Sépulcre," *Le Moniteur Diocésain* 20 (Jan. 1955): 22–23; Every to Waddams, Nov. 29, 1954, LP, G23.

5. Terry Ball, interview with author, Wulberswick, Feb. 17, 2007.

6. Coüasnon to Coupel, Nov. 20, 1954, EB CP; Coüasnon to custos, Nov. 20, 1954, EB CP; Every to Waddams, Nov. 29, 1954, LP, G23; Cole to State Dept., Apr. 1, 1955, USNA SD 884.413/4-155.

7. "La restauration de la basilique du Saint-Sépulcre," *Le Moniteur Diocésain* 20 (Jan. 1955): 23.

8. Cole to State Dept., Feb. 28, 1955, USNA SD 884.413/2-2855.

9. Wikeley to Rose, May 18, 1955, PRO FO 371/115663.

10. Beauvais to foreign minister, Feb. 4, 1955, CADN R S-S, box 1480; Beauvais to Coüasnon, Feb. 7, 1955, EB CP.

11. Following account based on Custodie de Terre-Sainte, *Le Saint-Sépulcre: Études et projets de restauration* (Jerusalem: Franciscan Printing Press, 1956), 60–62.

12. Ibid., 61.

13. Quoted in "La restauration du Saint-Sépulcre," *POC* 7 (1957): 168.

14. Custodie de Terre-Sainte, *Le Saint-Sépulcre,* 39–56.

15. Miller minute, Apr. 18, 1955, PRO FO 371/115615; Rose to Wikeley, Nov. 10, 1955, PRO FO 371/115617.

16. Wikeley to Rose, Apr. 7, 1955; Wikeley to Rose, May 19, 1955; ambassador, Amman to Rose, June 24, 1955; Rose minute, June 4, 1955, all in PRO FO 371/115663.

17. De Beauvais to foreign minister, Feb. 14, 1955, CADN R S-S, box 1480.

18. Arthur minute, Apr. 13, 1955, PRO FO 371/115663.

19. Chancery, Tel Aviv to Levant dept., May 3, 1955; Hadow minute, May 10, 1955; chancery, Amman to Levant dept., May 18, 1955; Rose minute, June 4, 1955; Wikeley to Rose, July 12, 1955, all in PRO FO 371/115663.

20. Aide-mémoire, Jerusalem, Mar. 16, 1955, PRO FO 371/115615.

21. Hassan al-Katib memorandum, Mar. 25, 1955, PRO FO 371/115615.

22. Pro-mémoire, June 8, 1955, PRO FO 371/115615.

23. Rose memorandum, June 27, 1955, PRO FO 371/115616.

24. Bergus memorandum, Aug. 25, 1955, USNA SD 884.413/8-2555.

25. Chancery, Athens to Levant dept., July 26, 1955, PRO FO 371/115616.

26. Bailey to Rose, June 30, 1955, PRO FO 371/115616.

27. Brouillet to Pinay, Nov. 25, 1955, CADN R S-S, box 1480.

28. Waddams note to file, June 14, 1955, LP, G23.

29. Rose memorandum, June 24, 1955, PRO FO 371/115615.

30. Hadow to British legation to Holy See, July 12, 1955; Athens embassy to Levant dept., July 26, 1955, both in PRO FO 371/115615.

31. French memorandum, Sept. 20, 1955; Bergus to Wilkins, October 7, 1955, both in USNA SD 884.413/10-755.

32. Husseini to Laforge, Sept. 24, 1955, PRO FO 371/115617.

33. Aide mémoire, n.d., PRO FO 371/115617.

34. Consul general to foreign minister, June 13, 1955, CADN R S-S, box 1480.

35. David Stokes, "The Basilica of the Holy Sepulchre," *Architect and Building News* 207 (Oct. 27, 1955): 522.

36. "La restauration de la Basilique du Saint-Sépulcre," *La Terre Sainte* (autumn 1955): 74–75.

37. "Rapport," Aug. 24, 1955, in Custodie de Terre-Sainte, *Le Saint-Sépulcre,* 1–11.

38. "Travaux Urgents," Aug. 24, 1955, in Custodie de Terre-Sainte, *Le Saint-Sépulcre,* 2.

39. "Observations," Aug. 26, 1955, in Custodie de Terre-Sainte, *Le Saint-Sépulcre,* 29–34.

40. *Aigyptos*, Oct. 24, 1955, quoted in "Le Saint-Sépulcre.—Existe-il réellement un danger d'écroulement de l'église de la Résurrection?" *POC* 5 (Sept. 1955): 360–61.

41. Consul general to foreign minister, Oct. 10, 1955, CADN R S-S, box 1480.

42. Duke to Rose, Sept. 15, 1955, PRO FO 371/115617.

43. Laforge to foreign minister, Jan. 5, 6, 1956, CADN R S-S, box 1488; Laforge to Beauchamp, Jan. 17, 1956, CADN JC, D/suppl., box 388.

44. Consul general to foreign minister, Oct. 31, 1955, CADN R S-S, box 1480.

45. Consul general to foreign minister, Nov. 14, 1955, CADN R S-S, box 1480.

46. Consul general to foreign minister, Oct. 31, 1955, CADN R S-S, box 1480.

47. Shuckburgh to Wikeley, Sept. 21, 1955, PRO FO 371/115617.

48. Trouvelot to Faccio, Nov. 24, 1955, CADN JC, D/suppl., box 388.

49. "Le nouveau Custode de Terre Sainte," *La Terre Sainte* (Jan.–Feb. 1956): 9–12.

50. Consul general to foreign minister, Oct. 31, 1955; Brouillet to Pinay, Nov. 25, 1955, both in CADN R S-S, box 1480.

51. Lazzeri to Laforge, Apr. 3, 1956, EB CP.

52. Daphne Tsimhoni, *Christian Communities in Jerusalem and the West Bank since 1948* (Westport, Conn.: Praeger, 1993), 37–40.

53. Geren to State Dept., Aug. 15, 1955, USNA SD 884.413/8-1555; Elting to State Dept., Feb. 9, 1956, USNA SD 884.413/2-956.

54. Victor Azarya, *The Armenian Quarter of Jerusalem* (Berkeley: University of California Press, 1984), 115–17; Ara Sanjian, "The Armenian Church and Community of Jerusalem," in Anthony O'Mahony, ed., *The Christian Communities of Jerusalem and the Holy Land* (Cardiff: University of Wales Press, 2003), 71–84.

55. Laforge to foreign minister, Mar. 27, 1956, CADN JC, D/suppl., box 388.

56. Trouvelot to Laforge, Apr. 29, 1956, CADN JC, D/suppl., box 388.

57. Maillard to ambassador to Holy See, Apr. 23, 1956; Laforge to foreign minister, May 16, 1956, both in CADN R S-S, box 1480.

58. Laforge to foreign minster, June 12, 1956, CADN R S-S, box 1480; Custodie de Terre-Sainte, *Le Saint-Sépulcre*, 143.

59. Laforge to foreign minister, July 25, 1956, CADN R S-S, box 1480.

60. Ron Fuchs and G. Herbert, "Representing Mandatory Palestine, Austen St. Barbe Harrison and the Representational Buildings of the British Mandate in Palestine 1922–37," *Journal of the Society of Architectural Historians of Great Britain* 43 (2000): 281–333.

61. Custodie de Terre-Sainte, *Le Saint-Sépulcre*, 146, 148.

62. Laforge to foreign minister, July 25, 1956, CADN R S-S, box 1480.

63. "P. Eugene Hoade," *ACTS* 1 (Oct.–Dec. 1956): 196.

Chapter 9 A Patriarch Open to Reason

1. "Au patriarcat grec orthodoxe," *POC* 7 (1957): 90–91; "His Beatitude Benedictos I," *Christian News from Israel* 20 (autumn 1970): 39.

2. Panos to State Dept., Feb. 9, 1956, USNA SD 884.413/2-2156.

3. "Au patriarcat grec orthodoxe," *POC* 7 (1957): 163.

4. Ibid, 92–93.

5. *Ekklisia*, Oct. 20, 1959, quoted in "Au patriarcat grec orthodoxe," *POC* 9 (1959): 365.

6. "Demonstration in Istanbul," *Times* (London), Sept. 7, 1955; "Survey of Istanbul Riot Damage," *Times* (London), Nov. 14, 1955.

7. "Tension Keeps Pilgrims Away from Holy Places," *Times* (London), Dec. 24, 1956.

8. "Talks in Jerusalem on Church Union," *Times* (London), Nov. 30, 1959; "Visite de S.S. Mgr. Athénagoras, patriarche oecuménique," *POC* 9 (1959): 365–66.

9. Laforge to foreign minister, May 15, 1957, CADN R S-S, box 1480.

10. Laforge to foreign minister, July 31, 1957, CADN R S-S, box 1480.

11. Wendelin to State Dept., June 14, 1960, USNA SD 884.413/6-1460; Laforge to foreign minister, Mar. 12, 1957, CADN R S-S, box 1480.

12. "La restauration du Saint-Sépulcre," *POC* 7 (1957): 167.

13. Laforge to Trouvelot, Oct. 22, 1957, CADN JC, D/suppl., box 388.

14. "Lettori, scriveteci . . . ,"*La Terra Santa* 34 (Mar. 1958): 92; Trouvelot to Laforge, July 27, 1957, CADN JC, D/suppl., box 388.

15. Trouvelot to Laforge, July 27, 1957, CADN JC, D/suppl., box 388.

16. Mallios letter of Mar. 14, 1958, in Ignazio Mancini, "È stato raggiunto l'accordo sui restauri al SS. Sepolcro," *La Terra Santa* 34 (June 1958): 167–68.

17. Mancini, "È stato raggiunto l'accordo," 168; "La restauration de la basilique du S.-Sépulcre," *Le Moniteur Diocésain* 24 (May–June 1958): 97.

18. Laforge to foreign minister, July 2, 1957, CADN R S-S, box 1480.

19. Laforge to Trouvelot, Sept. 30, 1957, CADN JC, D/suppl., box 388.

20. Laforge to foreign minister, Oct. 23, 1957, CADN R S-S, box 1480; Trouvelot to Laforge, Oct. 8, 1957, CADN JC, D/suppl., box 388.

21. Cole to State Dept., May 17, 1957, USNA SD 884.413/5-1757.

22. Bird memorandum, Dec. 2, 1957, USNA SD 884.413/12-1157.

23. Franklin to State Dept., Feb. 20, 1958, USNA SD 884.413/2-2058.

24. Charles Johnston, *The Brink of Jordan* (London: Hamish Hamilton, 1972), 54–61.

25. Laforge to Trouvelot, Oct. 22, 1957, CADN JC, D/suppl., box 388.

26. *Le Moniteur Diocésain* 24 (May–June 1958): 97; Favereau to foreign ministry, Apr. 4, 1958, CADN R S-S, box 1480.

27. Attachment to Wendelin to State Dept., June 14, 1960, USNA SD 884.413/6-1460. Original French text in Favereau to foreign minister, Apr. 16, 1958, CADN R S-S, box 1480.

28. Mancini, "È stato raggiunto l'accordo," 165.

29. Merrien to foreign minister, Sept. 17, 1958, CADN R S-S, box 1480.

30. Coüasnon to Trouvelot, Feb. 23, 1959, EB CP.

31. Trouvelot to Coüasnon, Oct. 30, 1959, EB CP.

32. Quoted in "La restauration du Saint-Sépulcre," *POC* 9 (1959): 166.

33. Trouvelot to Coüasnon, Feb. 26, 1959, EB CP; Coüasnon to Favereau, Mar. 16, 1959, CADN R S-S, box 1487; Trouvelot to Coüasnon, Apr. 12, 1959, EB CP.

34. Agreement, May 27, 1959, EB CP.

35. Consul general to Lloyd, Aug. 22, 1959, PRO FO 371/142201.

36. Quoted in "La restauration du Saint-Sépulcre," *POC* 9 (1959): 267–68.

37. Wendelin to State Dept., June 16, 1960, USNA SD 884.413/6-1460.

38. Coüasnon to Trouvelot, Aug. 1, 1959, EB CP.

39. Coüasnon to St.-Marie, Mar. 7, 1960, CADN JC, D/suppl., box 388.

40. Coüasnon to Trouvelot, Mar. 14, 1960, EB CP.

41. Trouvelot to Orlandos, Mar. 14, 1960, EB CP.

42. Trouvelot to Coüasnon, June 12, 1959, EB CP.

43. Coüasnon to St.-Marie, May 25, 1960, CADN R S-S, box 1487.

44. Trouvelot to Coüasnon, July 9, 1960, EB CP; Service du Levant note, Apr. 5, 1960, CADN R S-S, box 1487.

45. St.-Marie to Couve de Murville, Mar. 16, 1960, CADN JC, D/suppl., box 388; St.-Marie to Couve de Murville, Mar. 26, 1960, CADN R S-S, box 1487; Trouvelot to Polidori, July 9, 1960, EB CP.

46. "Tottering Sepulchre," *Time*, June 13, 1960, 60.

47. St.-Marie to Couve de Murville, July 11, Aug. 13, 1960, CADN R S-S, box 1487.

48. Coüasnon to Trouvelot, July 16, 1960; Coüasnon to St.-Marie, July 25, 1960, both in EB CP.

49. "Rapport technique sur les travaux à exécuter au Catholicon du St. Sépulcre," July 31, 1960, EB CP.

50. Wendelin to State Dept., Sept. 29, 1960, USNA SD 884.413/8-2660.

51. Ibid.; consul general to Levant dept., Aug. 28, 1960, LP, G23.

52. "Inizio dei lavori di restauro al SS.mo Sepolcro," *ACTS* 6 (May–Aug. 1961): 105.

53. Consulate general to Levant dept., Nov. 24, 1960, PRO FO 371/151053.

54. St.-Marie to Couve de Murville, Nov. 11, Dec. 12, 1960, CADN R S-S, box 1487.

55. "Dai Santuari: Bollettino informativo n. 8," *ACTS* 6 (May–Aug. 1961): 105.

56. St-Marie to Couve de Murville, July 20, 1961, CADN R S-S 1487.

Chapter 10 Kiss of Peace

1. The definitive report is Virgilio C. Corbo, *Il Santo Sepolcro di Gerusalemme*, 3 vols. (Jerusalem: Franciscan Printing Press, 1982). Also see Charles Coüasnon, *The Church of the Holy Sepulchre Jerusalem* (London: Oxford University Press, 1974).

2. St.-Marie to Couve de Murville, Aug. 9, 1961, Aug. 31, 1961, Oct. 2, 1961, CADN R S-S, box 1487.

3. Trouvelot to Coüasnon, Aug. 16, 1961, EB CP.

4. Utudjian to Coüasnon, Sept. 15, 1961, EB CP.

5. Untitled report, Oct. 18, 1961, EB CP.

6. Coüasnon to Trouvelot, Nov. 6, 1961, EB CP.

7. Trouvelot to Coüasnon, Dec. 17, 1961, EB CP.

8. "Agreement," December 24, 1961, "Statement," Apr. 9, 1962, unpublished documents, courtesy of Father Athanasius Macora.

9. Spectator, "Fantasia . . . più che realtà," *La Terra Santa* 38 (Feb. 1962): 53–54; "Incident à Bethléem," *POC* 12 (1962): 66.

10. "Note sur le don fait par la France pour les travaux de restauration du Saint-Sépulcre," Nov. 18, 1967, CADN JC, D/suppl., box 249.

11. "Greek Orthodox Head Calls President Dedicated Leader," *Washington Post,* Oct. 7, 1961.

12. Coüasnon to custos, Feb. 25, 1962, EB CP.

13. St.-Marie to Couve de Murville, Aug. 21, Sept. 18, 1962, CADN R S-S, box 1487.

14. Charles Coüasnon, "Restauration de la Basilique du St.-Sépulcre," *La Terre Sainte* (1964): 315.

15. Archimandrite Sebastias Germanos, "The Restoration of the Most Holy Church of the Anastasis," pt. 1, *Nea Sion* 60 (1965): 69–78.

16. Coüasnon to Trouvelot, Oct. 22, 1962, EB CP.

17. Coüasnon to Trouvelot, Nov. 5, 1962, EB CP.

18. Coüasnon workbook, entry for Oct. 17, 1962, EB CP.

19. Coüasnon to Trouvelot, Dec. 23, 1962, EB CP.

20. Coüasnon to Trouvelot, Jan. 4, 1963, Jan. 8, 1963, June 2, 1963, EB CP.

21. Coüasnon to Trouvelot, Dec. 1, 1963, EB CP.

22. Walsh to Levant dept., Mar. 28, 29, 1960, in Jane Priestland, ed., *Records of Jerusalem 1917–1971* (Oxford: Archive Editions, 2002), 7:146, 150; Brash to Rothnie, Aug. 12, 1960, 7:158.

23. Brash to Rothnie, Aug. 26, 1960, in Priestland, *Records of Jerusalem,* 7:161.

24. Maitland to Morris, Oct. 30, 1963, in Priestland, *Records of Jerusalem,* 7:329.

25. Edouard Utudjian, "The Restoration of the Basilica of the Holy Sepulchre in Jerusalem," *Le Monde Souterrain* 135 (July-Sept. 1963): 297.

26. Walsh to Beith, Apr. 8, 1960, in Priestland, *Records of Jerusalem,* 7:154–55.

27. Father Vitaly Gambin, sacristan's logbook, 1959–62, entry for July 8, 1962, unpublished manuscript, courtesy of Father Athanasius Macora.

28. Derderian to Nusseibeh, Nov. 21, 1962, ISA JG 2704/68.

29. Gambin logbook, entry for June 3, 1962.

30. Coüasnon to Trouvelot, July 14, 1962, EB CP.

31. "As being part of the main fabric of the Church the provisions of the Status Quo apply as regards any important structural alterations." Derderian to Nusseibeh, Aug. 9, 1962, ISA JG 2704/68.

32. Cited in Marad to Nusseibeh, July 12, 1963, ISA JG 2704/68.

33. Abu Ghazaleh to Nusseibeh, Oct. 10, 1962; Cappiello to Nusseibeh, Oct. 28, 1962; Marad to Abu Ghazaleh, Dec. 12, 1962, all in ISA JG 2704/68.

34. Maitland to Foreign Office, Jan. 11, 1963, in Priestland, *Records of Jerusalem,* 7:262–63; Maitland to Miller, Jan. 31, 1963, 7:267–68.

35. Maitland to Foreign Office, Jan. 12, 1963, in Priestland, *Records of Jerusalem,* 7:262.

36. Maitland to Morris, Jan. 18, 1963, in Priestland, *Records of Jerusalem,* 7:265.

37. Maitland to Parkes, Apr. 19, 1963, in Priestland, *Records of Jerusalem,* 7:273–74.

38. Maitland to Hiller, Apr. 24, 1963, in Priestland, *Records of Jerusalem,* 7:275–79; Maitland to Hiller, May 29, 1963, ibid., 7:287–90; "Jerusalem Rioting Quelled," *New York Times,* Apr. 21, 1963.

39. Protocol of meeting with governor, July 30, 1963, ISA JG 2704/68.

40. Every to Satterthwaite, Dec. 21, 1963, LP, G23.

41. Documents on the ecumenical movement, in E. J. Stormon, ed., *Towards the Healing of Schism* (New York: Paulist Press, 1987).

42. P. Duprey, "Réactions orthodoxes au pontificat de Jean XXIII et à ses premiers actes," *POC* 9 (1959): 56–57.

43. Loris F. Capovilla, *Giovanni XXIII* (Milan: San Paolo, 1994), 144; Mario Benigni and Goffredo Zanchi, *Giovanni XXIII* (Milan: San Paolo, 2000), 87–88.

44. John XXIII, *Journal of a Soul* (New York: McGraw-Hill, 1965), 167.

45. "Au patriarcat grec orthodoxe," *POC* 12 (1962): 282.

46. Thomas F. Stransky, "Paul VI's Religious Pilgrimage in the Holy Land," in Rodolfo Rossi, ed., *I viaggi apostolici di Paolo VI* (Brescia: Istituto Paolo VI, 2004), 341–73.

47. Ibid., 366–68.

48. Tom Stransky, "Pierre Duprey," *Ecumenical Dictionary* online (Oct. 2003); Father Thomas Stransky, interview with author, Jerusalem, Dec. 29, 2005.

49. Guillaume Rossi, "Les Grecs Orthodoxes," *La Terre Sainte* (1964): 207.

50. Extract from Every letter, Nov. 5, 1963, PRO FO 371/172266.

51. Stransky, "Paul VI's Religious Pilgrimage," 368–69.

52. Every to Satterthwaite, Dec. 21, 1963, LP, G23.

53. "Trattative con i Greci e gli Armeni Ortodossi," *ACTS* 9 (Jan.–June 1964): 31–33.

54. Every to Satterthwaite, Dec. 31, 1963, LP, G23.

55. Henderson to Stirling, Dec. 18, 1963, LP, G23.

56. L. G. A. Cust, *The Status Quo in the Holy Places*, facs. ed. (Jerusalem: Ariel, 1980), 27–28.

57. P. Rock, "Pro Memoria: Transetto Nord," September 1963, unpublished document, courtesy of Father Athanasius Macora.

58. Cappiello to Pope Paul VI, Dec. 5, 1963, *ACTS* 9 (Jan.–June 1964): 5–6.

59. Every to Satterthwaite, Dec. 31, 1963, LP, G23.

60. Alan McGregor, "A Welcome Truce in Holy Places," *New York Times*, Dec. 30, 1963.

61. MacInnes to Ramsey, Jan. 6, 1964, LP, Ramsey Papers, vol. 65; Maitland to Butler, Jan. 16, 1964, PRO FO 371/178051; "Pope in Tears, Offers Prayers at Jesus' Tomb," *New York Times*, Jan. 5, 1964.

62. "Texts of Pope's Discourses to Patriarchs," *New York Times*, Jan. 5, 1964.

63. Stransky, interview.

Chapter 11 Three Wise Men

1. Robert Houston Smith, "The Church of the Holy Sepulcher: Toward an Ecumenical Symbol," *Yale Review* 55 (Oct. 1965): 34–56.

2. David Holden, "The Unholy Row over the Tomb of Christ," *Saturday Evening Post*, Apr. 9, 1966, 86.

3. Professor Roberta Ervine, interview with author, Kingston, New York, June 9, 2004.

4. "50th Anniversary of Bishop Guregh Kapikian's Ordination Celebrated in Grand Style," *Armenian Reporter*, July 7, 2001.

5. Information provided by Father Dimitrios and Metropolitan Isichios of the Greek patriarchate, telephone interviews with author, Nov. 24, 2006.

6. Charles Coüasnon, "Les travaux de restauration du Saint-Sépulcre," *Comptes rendus des séances de l'année 1966 de l'Académie des Inscriptions et Belles-Lettres* (Apr. 1966): 212.

7. *Newsweek*, July 27, 1964, 42.

8. "Agreement on Electricity to Chapel of St. Helena," Apr. 6, 1964, ISA JG 2704/68.

9. Unpublished document, June 17, 1964, courtesy of Father Athanasius Macora.

10. So named because the Armenians acquired it when they lost their foothold on Golgotha opposite in 1439.

11. Minutes of meeting of CTB, Jan. 15, 1965, EB CP.

12. Wilson to State Dept., Mar. 1, 1965, USNA RG 59.

13. Canon Edward Every, interview with author, Lingfield, Surrey, Jan. 26, 2003.

14. Collas to Trouvelot, Dec. 1, 1964, EB CP.

15. Holden, "The Unholy Row," 80.

16. Coüasnon, "Les travaux de restauration," 212–13; Père Coüasnon, "Note sur les travaux de restauration de la Basilique du Saint Sépulcre," Mar. 10, 1966, CADN R S-S, box 1487.

17. D'Halloy to minister of foreign affairs, Sept. 22, 1966, CADN R S-S, box 1487.

18. Coüasnon to Trouvelot, Dec. 5, 1964, EB CP.

19. Coüasnon to Trouvelot, May 18, 1965, EB CP.

20. Coüasnon to Trouvelot, May 26, 1965; minutes of meeting of common technical bureau, May 28, 1965, both in EB CP.

21. Coüasnon to Trouvelot, June 4, 1965, EB CP.

22. Coüasnon to Trouvelot, June 4, 1965, EB CP.

23. Coüasnon to Trouvelot, Oct. 22, 1965; Trouvelot to Coüasnon, Nov. 21, 1965, both in EB CP.

24. Coüasnon to Trouvelot, Dec. 16, 1965, EB CP.

25. Coüasnon to Trouvelot, May 5, 1966, EB CP.

26. Economopoulos to Coüasnon, Aug. 8, 1966; Coüasnon memorandum, n.d., both in EB CP.

27. Economopoulos to Coüasnon, Nov. 9, 1966; Coüasnon to Chatzidakis, Nov. 13, 1966, both in EB CP.

28. Coüasnon to Trouvelot, Jan. 7, 1966, EB CP.

29. Coüasnon to Trouvelot, Jan. 7, Sept. 1, 1964; Trouvelot to Coüasnon, June 8, 1964, both in EB CP.

30. Cappiello to Trouvelot, Sept. 9, 1964, CADN JC, D/suppl., box 249.

31. Coüasnon to Trouvelot, Aug. 6, 1964, EB CP.

32. Coüasnon to Trouvelot, Apr. 9, 1965, EB CP.

33. Coüasnon to Trouvelot, Jan. 1, 1966, EB CP.

34. Coüasnon to Trouvelot, Dec. 8, 1965, EB CP.

35. Guerra to Trouvelot, Dec. 12, 1965; Trouvelot to Guerra, Dec. 27, 1965, both in EB CP.

36. Coüasnon to Trouvelot, Jan. 1, 14, 1966, EB CP.

37. Coüasnon, "Note sur les travaux de restauration de la Basilique du Saint Sépulcre," Mar. 10, 1966, CADN R S-S, box 1487.

38. Coüasnon to Trouvelot, May 5, 1966, EB CP.

39. Trouvelot to Coüasnon, Aug. 24, Nov. 1, 1966, EB CP.

40. D'Halloy to minister of foreign affairs, Sept. 9, 1970, CADN JC, D/supp., box 249.

41. Archbishop Sebastias Germanos, "The Restoration of the Most Holy Church of the Anastasis," pt. 2, *Nea Sion* 64 (1969): 15.

42. Coüasnon to Utudjian, Jan. 14, 1966; Utudjian to Voskertchian, Jan. 18, 1966, both in EB CP.

43. Coüasnon to Trouvelot, Feb. 22, 1966, EB CP.

44. Coüasnon to Utudjian, July 12, 1966, EB CP.

45. Coüasnon to Trouvelot, Nov. 23, 1966, EB CP.

46. Trouvelot to Coüasnon, June 1, 1966, EB CP.

47. Trouvelot to Coüasnon, Dec. 18, 1966, EB CP.

Chapter 12 The Keys

1. "Les fêtes de Pâques," *Le Moniteur Diocésain* 33 (Mar.–Apr. 1967): 47–49.

2. Terry Ball, interview with author, Walberswick, Feb. 16–17, 2007, and Terry Ball private papers, courtesy of Terry Ball.

3. Rafi Levi, interview with author, Jerusalem, Mar. 13, 2003.

4. Avi Shlaim, *The Iron Wall* (New York: Norton, 2000), 243–44.

5. Arye Baron, *Personal Stamp: Moshe Dayan during and after the Six Day War* (Tel Aviv: Yediot Ahronot, 1997), 64.

6. Bernard Wasserstein, *Divided Jerusalem* (London: Profile, 2001), 207.

7. "La Guerra Arabo-Israeliana (5–7/6/1967)," *ACTS* 12 (May–Dec. 1967): 118.

8. Terry Ball, draft of private letter, July 4, 1967, courtesy of Terry Ball.

9. Saul Friedländer, *Pius XII and the Third Reich* (London: Chatto & Windus, 1966).

10. Uri Bialer, *Cross on the Star of David: The Christian World in Israel's Foreign Policy 1948–1967* (Bloomington: Indiana University Press, 2005).

11. Website of the Holy See, "Documents of the II Vatican Council."

12. "Le problème des lieux saints chrétiens," *POC* 17 (1967): 337–38.

13. Walter Zander, *Israel and the Holy Places of Christendom* (London: Weidenfeld & Nicolson, 1971), 111–12.

14. Ibid., 98, 101.
15. Rafi Levi, interview with author, Jerusalem, June 7, 2007.
16. Meron Benvenisti, *Jerusalem: The Torn City* (Jerusalem: Isratypeset, 1976), 266.
17. Ibid.; draft agreement, n.d., ISA FM 4191/5.
18. Yehiel Elissar, "The Christian World and the Holy Places," n.d., ISA FM 4024/8.
19. Herzog to Eban, July 11, 1968, ISA FM 4191/5.
20. Levi interview, Mar. 13, 2003.
21. After a bureaucratic turf war, the religious affairs ministry formally took over, though Levi remained engaged for many years. The municipality, the police, the interior ministry, and the foreign ministry were also involved.
22. D'Halloy to foreign minister, July 28, 1967, CADN R S-S, box 1481.
23. Ibid.
24. Benedictos's oral statement, July 27, 1967, ISA FM 4191/5.
25. Derderian to Government of Israel, Aug. 14, 1967, CADN R S-S, box 1481.
26. Representatives of three communities to Levi, June 22, 1967, ISA FM 1390/5.
27. Evan M. Wilson, *Jerusalem, Key to Peace* (Washington, D.C.: Middle East Institute, 1970), 108, 116.
28. D'Halloy to foreign minister, Aug. 6, 1968, CADN R S-S, box 1482.
29. Canon Edward Every, interview with author, Lingfield, Surrey, Jan. 26, 2003.
30. Israel Lippel, interview with author, Jerusalem, May 1, 2002.
31. D'Halloy to foreign minister, July 28, 1967, CADN R S-S, box 1481.
32. Magen Broshi, interview with author, Jerusalem, June 24, 2003.
33. Daniel Rossing, telephone interview with author, Sept. 11, 2005.
34. Benvenisti, *Jerusalem*, 274–75; Marlen Eordegian, "British and Israeli Maintenance of the Status Quo in the Holy Places of Christendom," *International Journal of Middle East Studies* 35 (May 2003): 327, citing Bishop Guregh Kapikian's diary of the holy places.
35. Lewen to Moberly, June 5, 1968, PRO FCO 17/659.
36. Haggai Erlich, *The Cross and the River: Ethiopia, Egypt, and the Nile* (London: Lynne Rienner, 2001), 15–17, 123–24.
37. Anthony O'Mahony, "Pilgrims, Politics and Holy Places: The Ethiopian Community in Jerusalem until ca. 1650," in Lee I. Levine, ed., *Jerusalem: Its Sanctity and Centrality to Judaism, Christianity, and Islam* (New York: Continuum, 1999), 467–81.
38. Finn to Palmerston, Nov. 30, 1850, in Enrico Cerulli, *Etiopi in Palestina Storia della communità etiopica di Gerusalemme*, 2 vols. (Rome: Liveria dello Stato, 1947), 2:277.
39. Ihsan Hashem to Coptic and Abyssinian archbishops, Feb. 22, 1961, Apr. 1, 1961, ISA FM 4175/5.
40. Following account largely based on *Coptic Patriarchate v. Minister of Police* (1970) (I) 25 *P.D.* 225.

41. Walter Zander, "Jurisdiction and Holiness: Reflections on the Coptic-Ethiopian Case," *Israel Law Review* 17 (July 1982): 263.

42. Krongold to Warhaftig, July 12, 1967; Krongold to Eshkol, Sept. 3, 1967, both in ISA FM 4175/6.

43. Lubrani to foreign ministry, May 1, 1969, ISA FM 4175/5.

44. Lubrani to Sidis, Nov. 11, 1970, ISA FM 4564/6.

45. Zach Levey, "Israel's Strategy in Africa, 1961–67," *International Journal of Middle East Studies* 36 (Feb. 2004): 77.

46. "Israel-Ethiopia cooperation," May 19, 1971, ISA FM 4564/6.

47. Efrati to Bein, Jan. 8, 1968, ISA FM 4175/5.

48. Bein to Eban, Jan. 19, 1968, ISA FM 4175/6.

49. Efrati to Bein, Apr. 26, 1968, ISA FM 4175/5.

50. Elissar to Eban, Feb. 21, 1968, ISA FM 4175/5.

51. Ben-Zeev to minister of justice, Mar. 13, 1968, ISA FM 4175/5.

52. Meron to Ben-Zeev, n.d., ISA FM 4175/5.

53. Lubrani to foreign ministry, May 1, 1969, ISA FM 4175/5.

54. Bein to Addis, May 11, 1969, Bein to Elissar, May 18, 1969, both in ISA FM 4175/5.

55. Africa dept. to Addis, May 27, 1969, ISA FM 4175/6.

56. Eban declaration, July 3, 1969, ISA FM 4175/6.

57. Lubrani to Bein, May 20, 1969, ISA FM 4175/5.

58. Foreign ministry to embassy Addis, July 11, 1971, ISA FM 4564/6.

59. Sidis to embassy Addis, Dec. 12, 1971, ISA FM 4564/6.

60. "Conflit entre Coptes et Éthiopiens au sujet d'un passage donnant accès au Saint-Sépulcre," *POC* 21 (1971): 186.

61. Campbell to State Dept., Apr. 8, 1971, USNA RG 59, box 3072.

62. Interview, *Kol Ha'ir*, Mar. 11, 1986, 11.

Chapter 13 To the Rotunda

1. Martin Biddle, *The Tomb of Christ* (Stroud, England: Sutton, 1999), 77–78.

2. Joseph Patrich, "The Early Church of the Holy Sepulchre in the Light of Excavations and Restoration," in Yoram Tsafrir, ed., *Ancient Churches Revealed* (Jerusalem: Israel Exploration Society, 1993), 101–17.

3. Shalom Cohen, "Renovations at the Holy Sepulchre," *Jerusalem Post*, Dec. 24, 1970.

4. CTB, "Report of the Meeting of the Three Communities and Two Experts Present on May 28, 1969," unpublished document, courtesy of Father Athansius Macora; Archbishop Sebastias Germanos, "The Restoration of the Most Holy Church of the Anastasis," pt. 2, *Nea Sion* 64 (1969): 12–15.

5. Charles Coüasnon, "La restauration du Saint-Sépulcre," *Bible et Terre Sainte* 140 (Apr. 1972): 8–17.

6. Trouvelot to Coüasnon, Aug. 5, 1970, EB CP. The original of column 2 excavated by Coüasnon was 52 cm in diameter. Its replacement is 110.5 cm in diameter (courtesy of Father Athanasius Macora).

7. Minutes of meeting of experts, Aug. 29, 1970, EB CP.

8. Gabriella Rosenthal, "Restoration at the Church of the Holy Sepulchre," *Jerusalem Post*, Mar. 31, 1972.

9. Economopoulos to Coüasnon, Mar. 13, 1972, EB CP.

10. Minutes of meeting of experts, Oct. 7, 1972, EB CP.

11. "Reunion of experts of Sept. 27, 1974," unpublished document, courtesy of Father Athanasius Macora.

12. Coüasnon to Trouvelot, Jan. 25, 1967, EB CP.

13. Coüasnon report, Mar. 24, 1971, EB CP.

14. Trouvelot to Coüasnon, Nov. 24, 1971, EB CP.

15. Trouvelot to Coüasnon, Oct. 9, 1969, EB CP.

16. Ch. Coüasnon, "Basilica of the Holy Sepulchre," Dec. 1971, IAA Jm/1/6/5/h.

17. Jerusalem magistrate's court, civil file 5992/72, Nov. 23, 1972.

18. Father Alberto Rock, "Pro-Memoria: Terrazzo Del SS. Sepolcro," Nov. 1972, unpublished document, courtesy of Father Athanasius Macora.

19. Report of convocation, Nov. 19, 1971, unpublished document, courtesy of Father Athanasius Macora.

20. *Bolletino informativo della Custodia di Terra Santa sui Restauri Della Basilica del S. Sepolcro* 9 (1991): 8.

21. Ferdinando Forlati, *Il Santo Sepolcro di Gerusalemme* (Venice: n.p., 1954), 10.

22. Report of Utudjian visit, Mar. 26–Apr. 1, 1973, EB CP.

23. "Restauration de la Basilique du St.-Sépulcre," *La Terre Sainte* (1973): 263–66.

24. For a discussion of the question see Albert Rock, *The Status Quo in the Holy Places* (Jerusalem: Franciscan Printing Press, 1989), 37–52.

25. Trouvelot to Coüasnon, June 27, 1975, EB CP.

26. "Agreement," Mar. 3, 1976, unpublished document, courtesy of Father Athanasius Macora.

27. Daniel Rossing, interview with author, Jerusalem, Mar. 5, 2003.

28. Brother Fabian Adkins, interview with author, Washington, D.C., Oct. 30, 2003.

29. Daniel, Rock, and Guregh to Ben Eliahu, July 18, 1977; Daniel, Rock, and Guregh, memorandum, Aug. 12, 1977, unpublished documents, courtesy of Father Athanasius Macora.

30. I. H. Reith, "A Dome in Jerusalem," *Structural Engineer* 60A (Jan. 1982), 23–28.

31. Uri Sahm, "Israel Serving Its Christian Communities," *Christian News from Israel* 27 (winter 1979): 3–7; Daniel Rossing interview.

32. L. G. A. Cust, *The Status Quo in the Holy Places*, facs. ed. (Jerusalem: Ariel, 1980), 23–26.

33. Aviva Bar-Am, "Churches for All Faiths," *Jerusalem Post*, Dec. 24, 1985.

34. Daniel Rossing, interview with author, Jerusalem, Apr. 23, 2002.

35. Coüasnon to Rebaudi, May 17, 1968, EB CP.
36. Trouvelot to Coüasnon, Jan. 4, 1969, EB CP.
37. Trouvelot to d'Halloy, May 31, 1969, CADN JC, D/suppl., box 249.
38. Sacchi to Coüasnon, Feb. 17, 1976, EB CP.
39. Coüasnon to Sacchi, June 2, 1976, EB CP.
40. Coüasnon, draft for a lecture, May 16, 1972, EB CP.

Chapter 14 At Last, Light

1. Stuart Goodchild, telephone interview with author, Sept. 22, 2005.
2. Common technical bureau, Feb. 10, 1978, unpublished document, courtesy of Father Athanasius Macora.
3. The following account draws on I. H. Reith, "A Dome in Jerusalem," *Structural Engineer* 60A (Jan. 1982): 23–28; I. H. Reith, "Discussion: A Dome in Jerusalem," *Structural Engineer* 61A (Apr. 1983): 126–27. Also reported in "Jerusalem Dome," *Concrete Quarterly* 130 (July-Sept. 1981): 10–11.
4. *Bolletino informativo della Custodia di Terra Santa sui restauri della Basilica del S. Sepolcro* 9 (1991): 16.
5. Ibid., 17, 18.
6. "A New Greek Orthodox Patriarch in Jerusalem," *Christian News from Israel* 27 (1982): 187–88.
7. Felix Corley, "Obituary: Patriarch Diodoros I," *Independent*, Dec. 27, 2000; William A. Orme, "Diodoros I, 77, Top Patriarch of Greek Faith in Holy Land," *New York Times*, Dec. 21, 2000.
8. Bernard Josephs, Haim Shapiro, and Murad Al-Imari, "Greek Patriarch Fears for His Life," *Jerusalem Post*, Mar. 27, 1987.
9. George Hintlian, interview with author, Jerusalem, June 23, 2003.
10. Haim Shapiro, "Battle for the Belfry," *Jerusalem Post*, June 28, 1983.
11. Timothy Ware, *The Orthodox Church* (London: Penguin, 1997), 30–33, 119.
12. Minutes of meetings of experts and communities, Oct. 7, 1972, EB CP.
13. Shapiro, "Battle for the Belfry."
14. Trouvelot to Coüasnon, Aug. 26, 1973, EB CP.
15. Aroushan, "Armenian Restoration in the Basilica of the Holy Sepulchre," *Christian News from Israel* 26 (winter 1976), 18.
16. Ibid.
17. Barry Parker, "Major Renovation Starts at Christianity's Holiest Shrine," *Agence France Presse,* Jan. 31, 1995.
18. Archbishop Timotheos, telephone interview with author, Sept. 14, 2005; Brother Fabian Adkins kindly supplied photos of the mosaics.
19. Yves Boiret, interview with author, Paris, Nov. 30, 2005.
20. Brother Fabian Adkins,, interview with author, Nazareth, Nov. 17, 2005.
21. Voskertchian to Manoogian, Feb. 27, 1990, unpublished document, courtesy of Professor Roberta Ervine.

22. John Barnes, "A Modern Tower of Babel in Holy Land," *U.S. News & World Report,* Apr. 8, 1985, 44.

23. George Hintlian, interview with author, Jerusalem, May 8, 2003.

24. *Bolletino informativo della Custodia di Terra Santa sui restauri della Basilica del S. Sepolcro* 10 (1991): 24.

25. Adkins interview, Washington, 2003.

26. *Bolletino informativo della Custodia di Terra Santa sui restauri della Basilica del S. Sepolcro* 10 (1991): 25, 26.

27. Yves Boiret, "L'expérience d'un architecte dans la Basilique du Saint Sépulcre de Jérusalem et la Basilique Saint-Sernin de Toulouse," paper delivered to the Académie des Sciences et Lettres de Montpellier," June 2–3, 2005; *Bolletino informativo della Custodia di Terra Santa sui restauri della Basilica del S. Sepolcro* 11 (1991): 28–30.

28. Bishop Guregh's notes of meetings, Sept. 17, 23, 1991, unpublished documents, courtesy of Professor Roberta Ervine; Karin Laub, "Congregations Take Major Step in Holy Sepulchre Restorations," Associated Press, Apr. 14, 1992.

29. Bishop Guregh's notes of meetings, May 5, Dec. 14, 1992, unpublished documents, courtesy of Professor Roberta Ervine.

30. Barry Parker, "Rival Churches Near Accord to Restore Dome of Holy Sepulchre," *Agence France Presse,* Apr. 15, 1992.

31. Yves Boiret, "La Basilique du Saint-Sépulcre de Jérusalem: Histoire et situation actuelle," unpublished document, courtesy of Yves Boiret.

32. Yves Boiret, "Le Saint-Sépulcre de Jérusalem," *Chroniques* (1993): 78–81.

33. UNESCO, *Jerusalem and the Implementation of 26 C/Resolution 3.12,* report no. 142 EX/14, Paris, Oct. 1, 1993.

34. "Minutes of the Meeting of the Representatives of the Three Communities," May 12, 1993, unpublished document, courtesy of Professor Roberta Ervine.

35. "Report on the Church of the Holy Sepulchre," attached to Boiret to Prodomo, October 15, 1993, unpublished document, courtesy of Father Athanasius Macora.

36. "Over the Years," available at the website of Fordham University.

37. Hilary Appelman, "New Rotunda Unveiled at Traditional Site of Jesus' Tomb," Associated Press, Jan. 2, 1997.

38. Stern to Nazzaro, Oct. 26, 1993, unpublished document, courtesy of Father Athanasius Macora.

39. Dennis J. Madden, "A Church Transformed," *Catholic Near East* 23 (Apr. 1997), available at Pontifical Mission website, www.pontificalmission.org.

40. Michael Krikorian, "A Simple Cross Ends Decades of Divisions," *Los Angeles Times,* Dec. 30, 1995.

41. Ibid.; David Hale, "Fairy Tale Comes True," *Fresno Bee,* Mar. 2, 1997.

42. Ibid.; "Agreement for the Decoration of the Great Dome of the Church of the Holy Sepulchre," Aug. 17, 1994, unpublished document, courtesy of Father Athanasius Macora.

43. Boiret interview.

44. Mary Curtius, "Holy Sepulcher Paint Job an Act of Faith," *Los Angeles Times*, Apr. 15, 1995.

45. Haim Shapiro, "Holy Sepulcher Cupola Unveiled after 68 Years under Wraps," *Jerusalem Post*, Jan. 3, 1997.

46. Goodchild interview.

47. Donald Mansir, "A Turning Point for Christendom," *Catholic Near East* 22 (Apr. 1996), available at Pontifical Mission website, www.pontificalmission .org.

48. Goodchild interview.

49. Elaine Knutt, "Let There Be Light," *Building*, Mar. 27, 1997, 49.

50. Appelman, "New Rotunda."

Chapter 15 *Trouvelot's Choice*

1. Trouvelot to Coüasnon, Nov. 21, 1965, EB CP.

2. Fisher tour diaries, Nov. 24, 1960, LP, Fisher Papers, vol. 291.

3. Trouvelot to Coüasnon, Oct. 23, 1960, EB CP.

4. Fr. Athanasius Macora, interview with author, Jerusalem, Oct. 24, 2002.

5. Martin Biddle, *The Tomb of Christ* (Stroud, England: Sutton, 1999), 120–37.

6. Father Athanasius Macora, telephone interview with author, Dec. 23, 2005.

7. For a recent treatment of this question see Victoria Clark, *Holy Fire: The Battle for Christ's Tomb* (London: Macmillan, 2005).

BIBLIOGRAPHY

Archives

Archivio Storico del Ministero degli Affari Esteri, Rome (AMAEI)
Centre des Archives Diplomatiques, Nantes (CADN)
Custodia di Terra Santa Archives, Jerusalem (CTSA)
École Biblique Archives, Jerusalem (EB)
Israel Antiquities Authority Archives, Jerusalem (IAA)
Israel State Archives, Jerusalem (ISA)
Lambeth Palace Archives, London (LP)
Middle East Centre Archives, St. Antony's College, Oxford (MECA)
Public Records Office, London (now National Archives) (PRO)
United States National Archives, College Park, Maryland (USNA)

Interviews

Brother Fabian Adkins, Oct. 30, 2003, Nov. 17, 2005
Archbishop Aristarchos, Oct. 17, 2002, July 16, 2003
Terry Ball, Feb. 16–17, 2007
Ambassador Avi Binyamin, May 5, 2002
Yves Boiret, Nov. 30, 2005
Dr. Magen Broshi, June 24, 2003
Archbishop Christodoulos, May 28, 2003
Father Dimitrios, Nov. 24, 2006
Professor Roberta Ervine, June 9, 2004
Canon Edward Every, Jan. 26, 2003
Shmuel Evyatar, June 3, 2003
Stuart Goodchild, Sept. 22, 2005
Yossi Hershler, July 3, 2003

George Hintlian, Oct. 8, 2002, May 8, 2003, June 23, 2003

Metropolitan Isichios, Nov. 24, 2006

Father David Jaeger, June 3, 2002

Father Norayr Kazazian, Jan. 30, 2006

Rafi Levi, Mar. 13, 2003, June 7, 2007

Israel Lippel, May 1, 2002

Father Athanasius Macora, Mar. 19, 2002, May 29, 2002, Oct. 24, 2002, Jan. 16, 2003, July 6, 2003, Sept. 7, 2005, Dec. 23, 2005.

Dr. Theodossios Mitropoulos, Jan. 3, 2002, Feb. 27, 2003, May 2, 2003, July 7, 2003, Feb. 1, 2006

Uri Mor, Jan. 22, 2001

Daniel Rossing, Apr. 23, 2002, Mar. 5, 2003, Sept. 11, 2005

John Seligman, June 20, 2003

Haim Shapiro, May 6, 2003

Ambassador Yitzhak Shelef, Dec. 26, 2005

Archbishop Shirvanian, July 21, 2003

Father Thomas Stransky, Dec. 29, 2005

Archbishop Timotheos, May 26, 2002, Sept. 14, 2005

Dr. John Tleel, Jan. 30, 2006

Ambassador Yael Vered, Mar. 20, 2003

Newspapers and Other News Sources

Agence France Presse

Associated Press

Bolletino informativo della Custodia di Terra Santa sui Restauri Della Basilica del S. Sepolcro

Church Times

Custody of the Holy Land Newsletter

Economist

La Terra Santa

La Terre Sainte

Le Moniteur Diocésain

New York Times

Newsweek

Palestine Post/Jerusalem Post

Palestine Weekly

Proche Orient Chrétien

Time

Times (London)

Washington Post

Official and Semiofficial Publications

Actes et documents du Saint-Siège relatifs à la Seconde Guerre Mondiale. Vol. 5. Rome: Libreria Editrice Vaticana, 1969.

Bertram, Sir Anton, and Harry Charles Luke. *Report of the Commission Appointed by the Government to Inquire into the Affairs of the Orthodox Patriarchate of Jerusalem.* London: Oxford University Press, 1921.

Bertram, Sir Anton, and J. W. A. Young. *Report of the Commission Appointed by the Government of Palestine to Inquire and Report upon Certain Controversies between the Orthodox Patriarchate of Jerusalem and the Arab Orthodox Community.* London: Oxford University Press, 1926.

Documents of the II Vatican Council. Website of the Holy See, available at www .vatican.va/archive.

Documents on German Foreign Policy. Series D. Vol. 10. London: Her Majesty's Stationery Office, 1957.

Great Britain. Colonial Office No. 33. Palestine Royal Commission. *Memorandum Prepared by the Government of Palestine.* London: His Majesty's Stationery Office, 1937.

Ministero degli Affari Esteri. *I Documenti Diplomatici Italiani.* Seventh series. Vol. 5. Rome: Istituto Poligrafico dello Stato, 1967.

Parliamentary Debates. Commons. Fifth series. Vols. 202, 288, 289, 307.

United Nations Educational, Scientific and Cultural Organization. *Jerusalem and the Implementation of 26 C/Resolution 3.12.* Report no. 142 EX/14. Paris, Oct. 1, 1993.

United Nations. Special Committee on Palestine. "Oral Evidence Presented at Private Meetings." In *Report of the General Assembly,* vol. 4, annex B, A/364/ Add. 3. New York, July 15, 1947.

White Paper on the Wailing Wall Dispute, Cmd. 3229. London: His Majesty's Stationery Office, 1928.

Books and Periodical Articles

Abel, Félix-Marie. "Le récent tremblement de terre en Palestine." *Revue Biblique* 36 (Oct. 1927): 571–78.

Abel, Félix-Marie, and Louis Hugues Vincent. *Jérusalem, recherches de topographie, d'archéologie et d'histoire,* 2 vols. Paris: J. Gabalda, 1914, 1926.

"À la Basilique du Saint-Sépulcre." *Le Moniteur Diocésain* 33 (Nov.–Dec. 1967): 173–74.

Al-Khalil, Tawfik. "Jerusalem from 1947 to 1967: A Political Survey." M.A. diss., American University of Beirut, 1969.

Arce, A. "The Custody of the Holy Land." *Christian News from Israel* 19 (May 1968): 31–42.

Aroushan. "Armenian Restoration in the Basilica of the Holy Sepulchre." *Christian News from Israel* 26 (winter 1976): 16–19.

Ashbee, C. R. *A Palestine Notebook 1918–1923.* New York: Doubleday, 1923.

Avni, Ron. "The 1927 Jericho Earthquake." Ph.D. diss., Ben Gurion University, 1999.

Azarya, Victor. *The Armenian Quarter of Jerusalem.* Berkeley: University of California Press, 1984.

Bahat, Dan. "Does the Holy Sepulchre Church Mark the Burial of Jesus?" *Biblical Archaeology Review* 12 (May–June 1986): 26–45.

Baron, Arye. *Personal Stamp: Moshe Dayan during and after the Six Day War.* Tel Aviv: Yediot Ahronot, 1997.

Benigni, Mario, and Goffredo Zanchi. *Giovanni XXIII.* Milan: San Paolo, 2000.

Bentwich, Norman and Helen. *Mandate Memories.* New York: Schocken Books, 1965.

Benvenisti, Meron. *Jerusalem: The Torn City.* Jerusalem: Isratypeset, 1976.

Bialer, Uri. *Cross on the Star of David: The Christian World in Israel's Foreign Policy 1948–1967.* Bloomington: Indiana University Press, 2005.

Biddle, Martin. *The Tomb of Christ.* Stroud, England: Sutton, 1999.

Blanckenhorn, M. "Das Erdbeben im Juli 1927 in Palästina." *Zeitschrift des Deutschen Palästina-Vereins* 50 (Oct.1927): 288–96.

Boiret, Yves. "Le Saint-Sépulcre de Jérusalem." *Chroniques* (1993): 78–81.

Broadhurst, Joseph F. *From Vine Street to Jerusalem.* London: Stanley Paul, 1936.

Broshi, Magen. "Excavations in the Holy Sepulchre in the Chapel of St. Vartan and the Armenian Martyrs." In *Ancient Churches Revealed*, ed. Yoram Tsafrir, 118–22. Jerusalem: Israel Exploration Society, 1993.

Cameron, Averil, and Stuart G. Hall, trans. *Eusebius, Life of Constantine.* Oxford: Clarendon Press, 1999.

Capovilla, Loris F. *Giovanni XXIII.* Milan: San Paolo, 1994.

Cerulli, Enrico. *Etiopi in Palestina: Storia della communità etiopica di Gerusalemme.* 2 vols. Rome: Liveria dello Stato, 1947.

Chadwick, Owen. *Britain and the Vatican during the Second World War.* Cambridge: Cambridge University Press, 1986.

Charles-Roux, F. *Huit ans au Vatican, 1932–1940.* Paris: Flammarion, 1947.

Chevignard, Jean. "In Memoriam: Le Père Coüasnon o.p. 1904–1976." *La Terre Sainte* (1977): 70–71.

————. "Le Père Charles Coüasnon—In Memoriam." *Christian News from Israel* 26 (spring 1977): 107–8.

Clark, Victoria. *Holy Fire: The Battle for Christ's Tomb.* London: Macmillan, 2005.

Collas, L., Ch. Coüasnon, and D. Voskertchian. "Communication du Bureau Technique des travaux du Saint-Sépulcre." *Revue Biblique* 69 (1962): 100–107.

Collin, Bernardin. *Les lieux saints.* Paris: Presses Universitaires de France, 1962.

————. *Receuil de documents concernant Jérusalem et les lieux saints.* Jérusalem: Imprimerie des Franciscains, 1982.

Corbo, Virgilio C. *Il Santo Sepolcro di Gerusalemme.* 3 vols. Jerusalem: Franciscan Printing Press, 1982.

Coüasnon, Charles. "Restauration de la Basilique du St.-Sépulcre." *La Terre Sainte* (1964): 308–15.

———. "Les travaux de restauration du Saint-Sépulcre." *Comptes rendus des séances de l'année 1966 de l'Académie des Inscriptions et Belles-Lettres* (Apr. 1966): 209–25.

———. "Les travaux de restauration au Saint-Sépulcre." *POC* 19 (1969): 244–48.

———. "La restauration du Saint-Sépulcre." *Bible et Terre Sainte* 140 (Apr. 1972): 8–17.

———. *The Church of the Holy Sepulchre Jerusalem.* London: Oxford University Press, 1974.

Curzon, Robert. *Visits to Monasteries in the Levant.* London: John Murray, 1849.

Cust, L. G. A. *The Status Quo in the Holy Places.* facs. ed. Jerusalem: Ariel, 1980.

Cust, Lionel. *King Edward VII and His Court.* London: John Murray, 1930.

Custodia di Terra Santa. *Il Santo Sepolcro di Gerusalemme: Splendori, miserie, speranze.* Bergamo: Istituto Italiano D'Arti Grafiche, 1949.

Custodie de Terre-Sainte. *Le Saint-Sépulcre: Études et projets de restauration.* Jerusalem: Franciscan Printing Press, 1956.

De Benvenuti, Angelo. "Luigi Marangoni e la 'Scala Nuova' del Palazzo di Venezia." *Rivista Dalmatica* 33 (Mar.–June 1962): 59–66.

De Sandoli, Sabino. *The Church of Holy Sepulchre: Keys, Doors, Doorkeepers.* Jerusalem: Franciscan Printing Press, 1986.

Diotallevi, Ferdinando. *Diario di Terrasanta.* Milan: Edizioni Biblioteca Francescana, 2002.

Dorgelès, Roland. *La caravane sans chameaux.* Paris: Albin Michel, 1928.

Drake, H. A. "The Return of the Holy Sepulchre." *Catholic Historical Review* 70 (Apr. 1984): 263–67.

Duckworth, H. T. F. *The Church of the Holy Sepulchre.* London: Hodder and Stoughton, 1922.

Duff, Douglas V. *Sword for Hire.* London: John Murray, 1934.

———. *Bailing with a Teaspoon.* London: John Long, 1954.

Duprey, Pierre. "Réactions orthodoxes au pontificat de Jean XXIII et à ses premiers actes." *POC* 9 (1959): 56–63.

Eordegian, Marlen. "British and Israeli Maintenance of the Status Quo in the Holy Places of Christendom." *International Journal of Middle East Studies* 35 (May 2003): 307–28.

Erlich, Haggai. *The Cross and the River: Ethiopia, Egypt, and the Nile.* London: Lynne Rienner, 2001.

Every, Edward. "The Church of the Holy Sepulchre, Past, Present and Future." *Ecumenical Review* 4 (Jan. 1952): 184–90.

———. "The Cust Memorandum and the Status Quo in the Holy Places." *Christian News from Israel* 23 (spring 1973): 229–34.

Finn, James. *Stirring Times, or Records from Jerusalem Consular Chronicles of 1853 to 1856.* London: C. Kegan Paul, 1878.

Forlati, Ferdinando. *Il Santo Sepolcro di Gerusalemme.* Venice: self-published, 1954.

Friedländer, Saul. *Pius XII and the Third Reich.* London: Chatto & Windus, 1966.

Fuchs, Ron, and G. Herbert. "Representing Mandatory Palestine, Austen St. Barbe Harrison and the Representational Buildings of the British Mandate in Palestine 1922–37." *Journal of the Society of Architectural Historians of Great Britain* 43 (2000): 281–333.

Germanos, Sebastias. "The Restoration of the Most Holy Church of the Anastasis." Pt. 1. *Nea Sion* 60 (1965): 69–78.

———. "The Restoration of the Most Holy Church of the Anastasis." Pt. 2. *Nea Sion* 64 (1969): 12–15.

Gingas, George A., trans. *Egeria: Diary of a Pilgrimage.* New York: Newman Press, 1970.

Glubb, Sir John Bagot. *A Soldier with the Arabs.* London: Hodder and Stoughton, 1957.

Golubovich, Giolamo. *Biblioteca Bio-Bibliografica della Terra Santa e dell'Oriente Francescano.* New series, vol. 2. Florence: Collegio di S. Bonaventura, 1922.

Gori, Pacifique. "Un grand architecte, Antoine Barluzzi, 1884–1960." *La Terre Sainte* (Feb. 1961): 36–39.

Halaby, Nicholas. "Twentieth-Century Stone Dome Builders Learn from the Ancients," *New Civil Engineer,* July 12, 1973, 34–35.

Harvey, William. "A Particular Description of the Church." In *The Church of the Nativity at Bethlehem,* ed. R. Weir-Schultz, 1–12. London: B. T. Batsford, 1910.

———. *The Preservation of St. Paul's Cathedral and Other Famous Buildings.* London: Architectural Press, 1925.

———. *Church of the Holy Sepulchre Jerusalem: Structural Survey Final Report.* London: Oxford University Press, 1935.

———. "Inspection of the Church of the Holy Sepulchre from 23rd to 29th March, 1938." *Palestine Exploration Quarterly* 70 (July 1938): 160–61.

Harvey, William, and John H. Harvey. "The Structural Decay of the Church of the Holy Sepulchre." *Palestine Exploration Quarterly* 70 (July 1938): 156–61.

Holden, David. "The Unholy Row over the Tomb of Christ." *Saturday Evening Post,* Apr. 9, 1966, 80–85.

Holliday, Eunice. *Letters from Jerusalem during the Palestine Mandate.* London: Radcliffe Press, 2002.

Jansoone de Ghyvelde, Frédéric. "Règlement du Saint-Sépulcre." In *Receuil de documents concernant Jérusalem et les lieux saints,* ed. Bernardin Collin, 97–118. Jérusalem: Imprimerie des Franciscains, 1982.

Jarman, Robert L., ed. *Political Diaries of the Arab World: Palestine and Jordan.* Vol. 3. *1937–1938.* London: Archive Editions, 2001.

Jeffrey, George Everett. *The Holy Sepulchre.* Cambridge: Cambridge University Press, 1919.

"Jerusalem Dome." *Concrete Quarterly* 130 (July–Sept. 1981): 10–11.

John XXIII. *Journal of a Soul.* New York: McGraw-Hill, 1965.

Johnston, Charles. *The Brink of Jordan*. London: Hamish Hamilton, 1972.

Katz, Kimberly. "Building Jordanian Legitimacy: Renovating Jerusalem's Holy Places." *Muslim World* 93 (Apr. 2003): 211–32.

Keith-Roach, Edward. "Pageant of Jerusalem." *National Geographic Magazine* 52 (Dec. 1927): 635–707.

———. *Pasha of Jerusalem*. London: Radcliffe Press, 1994.

Kirkbride, Sir Alec. *From the Wings: Amman Memoirs 1947–1951*. London: Frank Cass, 1976.

Krüger, Jürgen. *Die Grabeskirche zu Jerusalem*. Regensburg: Schnell & Steiner, 2000.

Lawrence, T. E. *Seven Pillars of Wisdom*. New York: Doubleday, 1935.

"Les fêtes de Pâques." *Le Moniteur Diocésain* 33 (Mar.–Apr. 1967): 47–49.

Les lieux saints de la Palestine. Jérusalem: Imprimerie des PP. Franciscains, 1922.

"Le tremblement de terre du 11 Juillet." *Jérusalem: Revue Mensuelle Illustrée* 138 (July–August 1927): 97.

Levey, Zach. "Israel's Strategy in Africa, 1961–67." *International Journal of Middle East Studies* 36 (Feb. 2004): 71–87.

Loeb, Sophie Irene. *Palestine Awake*. New York: Century, 1926.

Luke, Harry Charles. "The Christian Communities in the Holy Sepulchre." In *Jerusalem 1920–1922*, ed. C. R. Ashbee, 46–56. London: John Murray, 1921.

———. *Prophets, Priests and Patriarchs*. London: Faith Press, 1927.

———. *Cities and Men: An Autobiography*. Vol. 2. London: Geoffrey Bles, 1953.

Madden, Daniel M. *Monuments to Glory: The Story of Antonio Barluzzi*. New York: Hawthorn Books, 1964.

Madden, Dennis J. "A Church Transformed." *Catholic Near East* 23 (Apr. 1997).

Mancini, Ignazio. "È stato raggiunto l'accordo sui restauri al SS. Sepolcro." *La Terra Santa* 34 (June 1958): 164–68.

Mandaville, John. "Give to the Waqf of Your Choice." *Saudi Aramco World* 24 (Nov.–Dec. 1973): 2–5.

Mansir, Donald. "A Turning Point for Christendom." *Catholic Near East* 22 (Apr. 1996).

Marangoni, Luigi. *La Chiesa del Santo Sepolcro in Gerusalemme*. Jerusalem: Custodia di Terra Santa, 1937.

Medebielle, Pierre. "Vers la restauration du Saint-Sépulcre." *La Terre Sainte* (Nov. 1962): 213–21.

———. "La restauration du Saint-Sépulcre a commencé." *Le Moniteur Diocésain* 29 (Mar.–Apr. 1963): 34–39.

———. "La restauration en cours de la Basilique du Saint-Sépulcre." *Le Moniteur Diocésain* 30 (May–June 1964): 187–94.

Meistermann, Barnabas. *Guide to the Holy Land*. London: Burns Oates & Washbourne, 1923.

Minerbi, Sergio I. *The Vatican and Zionism: Conflict in the Holy Land, 1895–1925*. New York: Oxford University Press, 1990.

Monk, Daniel Bertrand. *An Aesthetic Occupation*. Durham, N.C.: Duke University Press, 2002.

Moschopoulos, Nicephore. *La Terre Sainte*. Athens: n.p., 1957.

Muggeridge, Malcolm, ed. *Ciano's Diplomatic Papers*. London: Odhams Press, 1948.

Neale, John Mason. *A History of the Holy Eastern Church*. London: John Masters, 1850.

Neuville, René. *Heurs et malheurs des consuls de France à Jérusalem*, vol. 1. Jerusalem: Ronald Press, 1947.

Nevo, Joseph. *King Abdallah and Palestine: A Territorial Ambition*. London: Macmillan, 1996.

"A New Greek Orthodox Patriarch in Jerusalem." *Christian News from Israel* 27 (1982): 187–88.

"Nuovo conventino al Ss.mo Sepolcro." *La Terra Santa* 44 (Feb. 1968): 41–47.

O'Mahony, Anthony. "Pilgrims, Politics and Holy Places: The Ethiopian Community in Jerusalem until ca. 1650." In *Jerusalem: Its Sanctity and Centrality to Judaism, Christianity, and Islam*, ed. Lee I. Levine, 467–81. New York: Continuum, 1999.

Patrich, Joseph. "The Early Church of the Holy Sepulchre in the Light of Excavations and Restoration." In *Ancient Churches Revealed*, ed. Yoram Tsafrir, 101–17. Jerusalem: Israel Exploration Society, 1993.

Pieracini, Paolo. "Il Patriarcato Latino di Gerusalemme (1918–1940)." Pt. 1 *Il Politico* 63 (Apr.–June 1998): 207–56; Pt. 2 *Il Politico* 63 (Oct.–Dec. 1998): 591–639.

Presland, John. *Deedes Bey*. London: Macmillan, 1942.

Priestland, Jane, ed. *Records of Jerusalem 1917–1971*. Vols. 1 and 7. Oxford: Archive Editions, 2002.

Reith, I. H. "A Dome in Jerusalem." *Structural Engineer* 60A (Jan. 1982): 23–28.

———. "Discussion: A Dome in Jerusalem." *Structural Engineer* 61A (Apr. 1983): 126–27.

"Restauration de la Basilique du St.-Sépulcre." *La Terre Sainte* (1973): 263–66.

Rhodes, Anthony. *The Vatican in the Age of the Dictators, 1922–1945*. London: Hodder and Stoughton, 1973.

Rock, Albert. *The Status Quo in the Holy Places*. Jerusalem: Franciscan Printing Press, 1989.

Rossi, Guillaume. "Les Grecs Orthodoxes." *La Terre Sainte* (1964): 202–8.

Runciman, Steven. *The Eastern Schism*. Oxford: Clarendon Press, 1955.

Sahm, Uri. "Israel Serving Its Christian Communities." *Christian News from Israel* 27 (winter 1979): 3–7.

Samuel, Horace B. *Unholy Memories of the Holy Land*. London: Hogarth Press, 1930.

Sanjian, Ara. "The Armenian Church and Community of Jerusalem." In *The Christian Communities of Jerusalem and the Holy Land*, ed. Anthony O'Mahony, 71–84. Cardiff: University of Wales Press, 2003.

Sesnic, Stefano. "Mentre brucia la cupola del S. Sepolcro." *La Terra Santa* 25 (Jan. 1950): 3–6.

Shapira, Avi, Ron Avni, and Amos Nur. "A New Estimate for the Epicenter of the Jericho Earthquake of 11 July 1927." *Israel Journal of Earth Sciences* 42 (1993): 93–96.

Sherrard, Philip. *The Greek East and the Latin West.* London: Oxford University Press, 1959.

Shlaim, Avi. *The Iron Wall.* New York: Norton, 2000.

Smith, Robert Houston. "The Church of the Holy Sepulcher: Toward an Ecumenical Symbol." *Yale Review* 55 (Oct. 1965): 34–56.

Spectator. "Fantasia . . . più che realtà." *La Terra Santa* 38 (Feb. 1962): 53–54.

Stokes, David. "The Basilica of the Holy Sepulchre." *Architect and Building News* 207 (Oct. 27, 1955): 515–22.

Storrs, Ronald. *Orientations.* London: Ivor Nicholson & Watson, 1937.

Stormon, E. J., ed. *Towards the Healing of Schism.* New York: Paulist Press, 1987.

Stransky, Thomas F. "Paul VI's Religious Pilgrimage in the Holy Land." In *I viaggi apostolici di Paolo VI,* ed. Rodolfo Rossi, 341–73. Brescia: Istituto Paolo VI, 2004.

Tsimhoni, Daphne. "The Greek Orthodox Patriarchate of Jerusalem during the Formative Years of the British Mandate in Palestine." *Asian and African Studies* 12 (Mar. 1978): 77–121.

———. *Christian Communities in Jerusalem and the West Bank since 1948: An Historical, Social, and Political Study.* Westport, Conn.: Praeger, 1993.

Utudjian, Edouard. "La restauration de la Basilique du Saint-Sépulcre à Jérusalem." *Le Monde Souterrain* 134 (Apr.–May–June 1963): 261–69.

———. "The Restoration of the Basilica of the Holy Sepulchre in Jerusalem." *Le Monde Souterrain* 135 (July–Aug.–Sept. 1963): 291–96.

———. "Où en sont les travaux de restauration de la basilique du Saint-Sépulcre à Jérusalem?" *Le Monde Souterrain* 142 (Apr.–May–June 1965): 328.

Vincent, Louis Hugues. "L'Église du Saint-Sépulcre en péril." *Comptes rendus des séances de l'année 1938 de l'Académie des Inscriptions et Belles-Lettres* (Oct. 1938): 426–33.

———. Letter of November 24, 1949. In *Comptes rendus des séances de l'année 1949 de l'Académie des Inscriptions et Belles Lettres* (Oct.–Dec. 1949): 417–19.

Ware, Timothy. *The Orthodox Church.* London: Penguin, 1997.

Wasserstein, Bernard. *Divided Jerusalem.* London: Profile, 2001.

Weir-Schultz, R., ed. *The Church of the Nativity at Bethlehem.* London: B. T. Batsford, 1910.

Wilson, Evan M. *Jerusalem, Key to Peace.* Washington, D.C.: Middle East Institute, 1970.

Zander, Walter. *Israel and the Holy Places of Christendom.* London: Weidenfeld & Nicolson, 1971.

———. "On the Settlement of Disputes about the Christian Holy Places." *Israel Law Review* 8 (July 1973): 331–66.

———. "Jurisdiction and Holiness: Reflections on the Coptic-Ethiopian Case." *Israel Law Review* 17 (July 1982): 245–71.

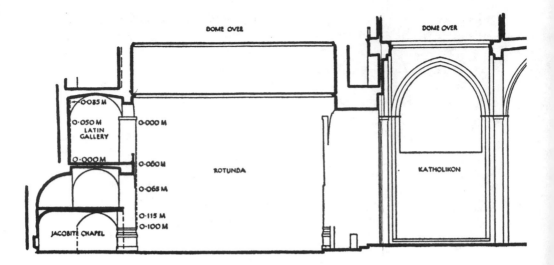

DOME OVER

DOME OVER

0.085 M

0.050 M
LATIN
GALLERY

0.000 M

0.000 M

0.060 M

ROTUNDA

KATHOLIKON

0.065 M

0.115 M
0.100 M

JACOBITE CHAPEL

WILLIAM HARVEY, ARCHITECT

PLAN OF CALVARY

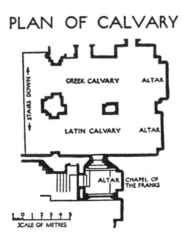

STAIRS DOWN

GREEK CALVARY

ALTAR

LATIN CALVARY

ALTAR

ALTAR

CHAPEL OF
THE FRANKS

SCALE OF METRES

LONG SECTION LOOKING NORTH

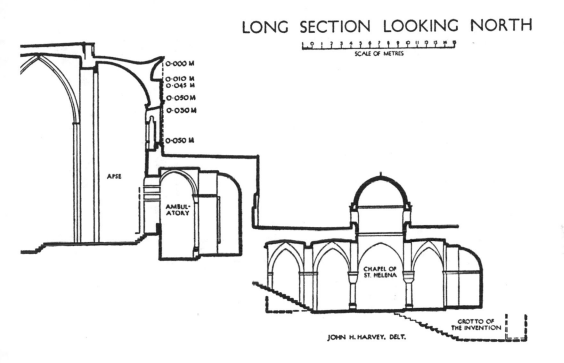

SCALE OF METRES

0·000 M
0·010 M
0·045 M
0·050 M
0·030 M

0·050 M

APSE

AMBUL-
ATORY

CHAPEL OF
ST. HELENA

GROTTO OF
THE INVENTION

JOHN H. HARVEY. DELT.

PLAN OF CHAPEL OF ST. HELENA

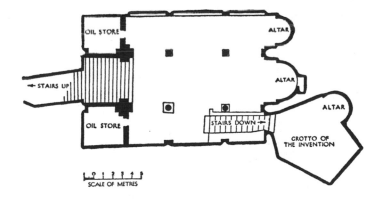

OIL STORE

ALTAR

ALTAR

STAIRS UP

ALTAR

OIL STORE

STAIRS DOWN

GROTTO OF
THE INVENTION

SCALE OF METRES

CROSS SECTION LOOKING EAST

SCALE OF METRES

REBUILT

PENDENTIVE -

0·000 M

0·025 M

LATIN GALLERY.

0·165 M
0·035 M

0·140 M

BYZANTINE ARCADE

NORTH AISLE

WILLIAM HARVEY, ARCHITECT.

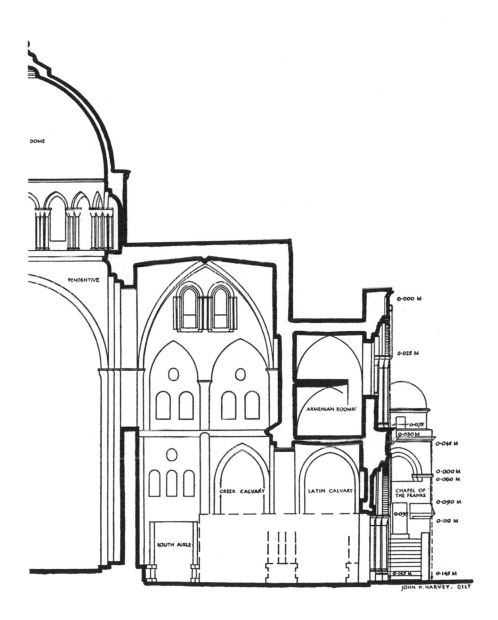

DOME

PENDENTIVE

0·000 M

0·025 M

ARMENIAN ROOMS

0·075

0·030 M

0·045 M

GREEK CALVARY

LATIN CALVARY

0·000 M
0·060 M

CHAPEL OF
THE FRANKS

0·090 M

0·095

0·110 M

SOUTH AISLE

0·145 M

0·145 M

JOHN H. HARVEY. DELT

MAIN SOUTH FRONT

SCALE OF METRES

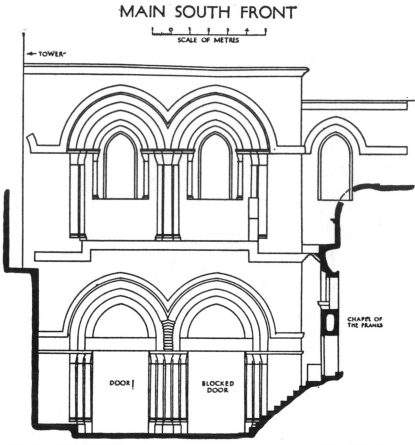

← TOWER

CHAPEL OF
THE FRANKS

DOOR I

BLOCKED
DOOR

WILLIAM HARVEY, ARCHITECT.   JOHN H. HARVEY, DELT.

NORTH WALL

SCALE OF METRES

MODERN PARAPET

LATIN SACRISTY

DOOR

WILLIAM HARVEY, ARCHITECT.   JOHN H. HARVEY, DELT.

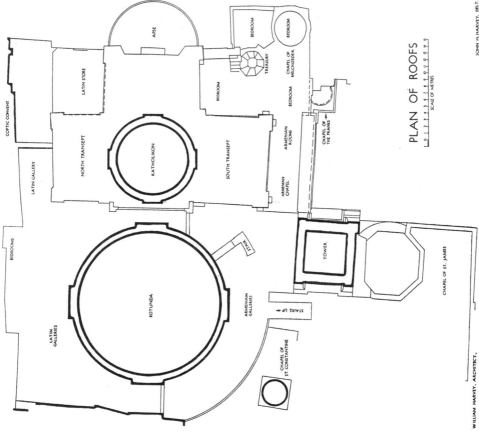

PLAN OF ROOFS

SCALE OF METRES

WILLIAM HARVEY, ARCHITECT.

JOHN H. HARVEY, DELT.

COPTIC CONVENT

LATIN GALLERY

BEDROOMS

LATIN GALLERIES

NORTH TRANSEPT

LATIN STORE

APSE

KATHOLIKON

ROTUNDA

SOUTH TRANSEPT

BEDROOM

BEDROOM

TREASURY

BEDROOM

CHAPEL OF MELCHIZEDEK

BEDROOM

ARMENIAN CHAPEL

ARMENIAN ROOMS

CHAPEL OF THE FRANKS

STAIR

ARMENIAN GALLERIES

STAIRS UP

TOWER

CHAPEL OF ST. JAMES

CHAPEL OF ST. CONSTANTINE

Coptic Orthodox community: Chapel behind Edicule, 168; and church councils, 6; disputes involving, 191–201, 212–14; and outbreaks of violence, 10, 88, 212–13; patriarchate, 78, 100, 194, 212, 213; and restoration, 100, 106, 168, 213–14, 240; and Status Quo, 5, 56, 100, 112, 192, 212, 213–14

Corbo, Virgilio, 176

Coüasnon, Charles: and CTB, 116, 137, 139, 152, 168, 179, 182, 183, 217; and Custody of the Holy Land, 150, 175–77, 216–17; and Greeks, 140, 141, 142, 147, 148, 152, 167, 171–75; life story, 112–13, 171, 216–17, 220; and restoration, 112–13, 123, 124, 133, 134, 137, 150, 152, 168–69, 204, 216–17; and Rock, 123, 136, 206; and Israel, 191

Council of Nicaea, 3

Council of the League of Nations, 21, 22

Coupel, Pierre, 108, 112

Crosnier, M., 210

crossing, 4, 39, 41, 42, 43, 44, 48, 50, 123, 134, 146, 151, 172, 175, 229, 230

Crusader architecture, 3, 4, 7, 33, 41, 44, 70, 108, 121, 138, 140, 150, 151, 168, 171, 177, 180, 202, 203, 204, 226, 227, 229

Crusaders, 3, 5, 25, 201, 204, 205, 226

Cunliffe-Lister, Sir Philip, 52, 54

Cunningham, Sir Alan, 85

cupola over Katholikon. See Katholikon, dome

Cust, Lionel George Archer, 22–23, 28

Cust memorandum, 22–23, 87, 155, 161, 208

Custody of the Holy Land: and al-Khanka terrace affair, 205–8; and conservation in 1930s, 48, 50, 53, 62, 67; historical role, 5, 16, 26, 99; and Israeli government, 184, 206, 207, 208–9; and lawsuits, 21, 208–9; leadership of, 125, 135; and restoration, 47–50, 56, 57, 59, 105, 108, 112, 113, 120, 121, 126, 140–41, 147, 154–55, 159, 162, 175–77, 216–17, 234, 239; and Testa plan, 73, 91, 109

Custos, role of, 5, 105, 125, 135, 147, 150, 162, 176, 177, 209, 216–17, 235

Dalqamuni, Fadhl al-, 156

Damascus Gate, 2, 157, 163, 183

Damianos, Patriarch, 14–16, 18–19, 20, 25, 32, 57, 130

Daniel (Choriatakis), Bishop, 166–67, 173, 207–8, 211, 216, 221, 226, 228–29, 234, 235, 240

D'Aubigny, Philip, 25

Dayan, Moshe, 182, 185, 187

Deir al-Sultan dispute, 191–201, 212

Dell'Acqua, Angelo, 177

Department of Public Works (DPW): British Mandate, 30, 31, 34, 35, 36, 37, 38, 39–40, 58, 62, 63; Israeli, 208, 214, 216; Jordanian, 80, 92, 97, 98, 103, 205

Derderian, Patriarch Yeghishe: and financial issues, 104, 119, 126, 153, 157; and Israeli government, 188, 189; life story, 99; as locum tenens, 99, 104, 119, 120; and patriarchal elections, 126, 127, 136, 137, 145, 153, 239; and pope's Holy Land visit, 160, 188; and restoration, 154–57, 166, 179, 188, 225, 226

Israel, 187, 193; and Jordan, 96,
100, 115, 132; and Latins, 6, 16,
113, 115–16, 131, 145–46, 158,
159–61, 186–87; leadership of, 5,
125; and pope, 158, 187; property
of, 18, 30, 53, 78, 90, 104, 222;
and repairs during Mandate, 29,
30, 31, 36, 37, 39, 47, 62, 120;
and proposed replacement of
edifice, 78, 85, 91; and
restoration, 57, 108, 113, 115–16,
120, 121, 122, 127, 132, 151,
154–55, 177; and restoration
proposals, 50, 56, 59, 115, 121,
134, 141–42; and Status Quo, 7,
8, 10, 16, 17, 27, 90, 115, 122,
132, 144, 161–62, 169, 232, 237;
and World War I, 14–15. See also
specific individuals
Greeks. *See* Greek Orthodox
Patriarchate
Green, Joseph C., 105, 106
Gulbenkian Foundation of Lisbon, 105,
154, 178

Hadi, Ruhi Pasha Abd al-, 106
Hagia Sophia in Constantinople, 4, 48
Hall, John Hathorn, 55–56, 65
Hamid, Abdul, 24
Harrison, Austen St. Barbe, 36, 39–40,
127–28, 134
Harvey, William: reports, 37–39,
42–48, 50, 51, 53, 54, 55, 58, 59,
60, 61; temporary shoring of
church, 44–45, 48, 49, 51, 58–59,
61, 66, 96; textbook of, 37, 41, 49
Hashem, Ihsan, 92, 93, 144, 145, 194
Hashem, Sayed Ibrahim, 137
Herzl, Theodore, 183
Herzog, Yaacov, 186
Hintlian, George, 234
Hitler, Adolf, 74–75
Hoade, Eugene, 62, 67, 128

Holliday, Cliff, 27, 28, 50
Holy Fire ceremony, 9–10, 59, 216,
234
Holy See. *See* Vatican
Husayni, Adnan al-, 128, 132, 133
Hussein, King, 102, 105, 106, 136,
137, 140, 142, 153, 171, 182,
199, 239

internationalization of Jerusalem. *See*
Jerusalem, internationalization of
Islam and Muslims, 3, 5, 6–7, 10, 85,
96, 156, 184, 185, 205, 206
Islamic Council of Jerusalem, 205, 206
Israel: and Greek Orthodox
Patriarchate, 104, 187, 188–89,
221; and Holy See, 186–87, 188,
190, 193; and Holy Sepulchre,
190–92, 195–201, 204, 206–9,
211–16, 221; and Jordan, 105,
125; and 1948 war, 85, 104, 123;
and 1956 war, 128; and 1967 war,
181–83, 205; and War of
Attrition, 193, 200
Israelian, Kevork, 99
Italy: and British Mandate, 31; and
Catholic church, 16, 65, 71, 72,
75, 79; and Jordan, 89, 93, 100,
101, 118; and proposed
replacement of edifice, 64–65, 80;
and restoration, 125, 135, 175;
rivalry with France, 21, 51, 68,
101, 103, 119, 126, 135; and
World War II, 64, 68, 71–72, 75,
78, 79, 80

Jacopozzi, Nazzareno, 53, 65, 70
Jaffa Gate, 13, 24, 193
Jerusalem: internationalization of,
85–86, 89–91, 92, 93, 117,
185, 186, 187, 188; under
British Mandate, 13–17, 23–28;
under Israeli administration,

Roman Catholic patriarchate. *See* Latin patriarchate

of, 20, 24, 26, 93, 100, 169;
working of, 8–11, 20, 22, 24–28,
90, 107, 169, 192, 197–98, 200,
207, 209, 211, 215, 222, 233,
237–38